PRODUCTIVITY, TECHNOLOGY AND
ECONOMIC GROWTH

Productivity, Technology and Economic Growth

Edited by

Bart van Ark

Simon K. Kuipers

and

Gerard H. Kuper

University of Groningen, The Netherlands

KLUWER ACADEMIC PUBLISHERS
BOSTON / DORDRECHT / LONDON

A C.I.P. Catalogue record for this book is available from the Library of Congress.

ISBN 0-7923-7960-8

Published by Kluwer Academic Publishers,
P.O. Box 17, 3300 AA Dordrecht, The Netherlands.

Sold and distributed in North, Central and South America
by Kluwer Academic Publishers,
101 Philip Drive, Norwell, MA 02061, U.S.A.

In all other countries, sold and distributed
by Kluwer Academic Publishers,
P.O. Box 322, 3300 AH Dordrecht, The Netherlands.

Printed on acid-free paper

Printed in the Netherlands.

Preface

This volume includes most papers presented at a conference on "Productivity and Living Standards" that was organised at the University of Groningen in September 1998. It was the third conference since 1993 organised jointly by the Centre for Economic Growth (CCSO), the CPB Netherlands Bureau for Economic Policy Analysis and the Dutch Ministry of Economic Affairs.[1] For the occasion of this conference, the N.W. Posthumus Institute, the interuniversity research school on economic and social history in the Netherlands, also acted as co-organiser.

Apart from the impressive contributions by the authors of the papers in this volume, we could not have completed this volume without the help of many persons and institutions. First we are grateful to various sponsoring bodies that helped to finance the conference at which these papers were presented and extensively discussed. Apart from financial contribution by the main organisers, financial support was also granted by NWO Humanities, research institute SOM, Stichting Groninger Universiteitsfonds, De Nederlandsche Bank NV and the Department of Economics of the University of Groningen.

We are grateful to a number of anonymous referees, who at the request of the publishers, provided useful comments on some of the papers in this volume. We particularly would like to thank the discussants of the papers at the conference for their comments which have been used by most authors in

---

[1] Schoonbeek, L., E. Sterken and S.K. Kuipers (eds.) (1995), *Methods and Applications of Economic Dynamics*, Contributions to Economic Analysis, Vol. 228, North-Holland, Amsterdam.
Brakman, S., H. van Ees and S.K. Kuipers (eds.) (1998), *Market Behaviour and Macroeconomic Modelling*, MacMillan/St. Martin's Press.

revising their paper. We are also grateful to Theo van de Klundert, who provided a very useful summary of the discussions and the papers at the end of the conference. We made thankfully use of his remarks in making suggestions to the authors and in writing the introduction to this book.

Our greatest thanks go to Saskia van Bergen, who set herself with this huge task to edit the papers, harmonise formats, process comments on the proofs, *etc.*.

Groningen, June 2000

Bart van Ark
Simon K. Kuipers
Gerard H. Kuper

Contributors

Bart van Ark, University of Groningen and N.W. Posthumus Institute, The Netherlands
h.h.van.ark@eco.rug.nl

Eric Bartelsman, Ministry of Economic Affairs and Free University (Amsterdam), The Netherlands
ebartelsman@alum.mit.edu

Barry Eichengreen, University of California (Berkeley) and Research Department, International Monetary Fund, USA
eicheng@econ.berkeley.edu

Jan Fagerberg, University of Oslo and Norwegian Institute of International Affairs, Norway
jan.fagerberg@esst.uio.no

Robert J. Gordon, Northwestern University (Evanston), USA
rjg@nortwestern.edu

Jakob de Haan, University of Groningen, The Netherlands
j.de.haan@eco.rug.nl

Bas Jacobs, University of Amsterdam, The Netherlands
jacobs@fee.uva.nl

Simon K. Kuipers, University of Groningen, The Netherlands
s.k.kuipers@eco.rug.nl

Gerard H. Kuper, University of Groningen, The Netherlands
g.h.kuper@eco.rug.nl

Frank R. Lichtenberg, Columbia University (New York), USA
frank.lichtenberg@columbia.edu

Jim Malley, University of Glasgow, UK
j.malley@socsci.gla.ac.uk

Joel Mokyr, Northwestern University (Evanston), USA
j-mokyr@nwu.edu

Anton Muscatelli, University of Glasgow, UK
v.muscatelli@udcf.gla.ac.uk

Richard Nahuis, Catholic University of Brabant (Tilburg), presently at CPB,
Netherlands Bureau for Economic Policy Analysis, The Netherlands
r.nahuis@cpb.nl

Marieke Rensman, CCSO and Department of Economics, University of
Groningen, presently at CPB, Netherlands Bureau for Economic Policy
Analysis, The Netherlands
m.rensman@cpb.rug.nl

Paul Tang, CPB, Netherlands Bureau for Economic Policy Analysis, The
Netherlands
p.j.g.tang@cpb.nl

Bart Verspagen, University of Eindhoven and MERIT, University of
Maastricht, The Netherlands
bart.verspagen@merit.unimaas.nl

Henry van der Wiel, CPB, Netherlands Bureau for Economic Policy
Analysis, The Netherlands
h.p.van.der.wiel@cpb.nl

Jan Luiten van Zanden, University of Utrecht, The Netherlands
janluiten.vanzanden@let.uu.nl

Contents

Figures

Tables

Chapter 13

Chapter 1

Introduction

Bart van Ark, Simon K. Kuipers and Gerard H. Kuper
Department of Economics, University of Groningen

1. INTRODUCTION

During the past two centuries the world economy has experienced unprecedented growth. Between 1820 and 1997, the world's Gross Domestic Product in constant prices has increased by about 2.2 per cent per year on average, which is between six and seven times more than the world growth rate during the preceding period, 1500 to 1820 (Maddison, 1995). However, the fortunes of growth have been distributed unequally over time as well over space. In most regions of the world economy growth rates of GDP accelerated since 1870 and once again since 1950. However, in terms of living standards countries have benefitted to different degrees given the large differences in population growth rates. As a consequence income per head of the population in Northwest Europe, North America and Japan has increased much faster than in the rest of the world, although some countries and regions in other parts of the world have shown remarkable capability to catch up for at least some periods of time. Since the mid 1970s growth of the world economy has slowed down, even though the overall growth rate is still considerably higher than before 1950. Most recently, signs of a new phase of growth acceleration in the United States have been related to the success of information and communication technologies as a source of growth (Oliner and Sichel, 2000; Jorgenson and Stiroh, 2000).

A major issue of research on long-term economic growth is to understand what explains the diversity in performance between regions and countries. What has caused the acceleration of growth since 1870, the extraordinary rapid growth between 1950 and 1973, and the slowdown since 1973? Why

1

has the population in Europe, Japan and North America benefitted most strongly from the "golden era" between 1950 to 1973? Why have all regions except East Asia faced a substantial slowdown in growth since 1973? To what extent has the acceleration of output growth arisen from putting more resources into the production process, from a more efficient use of those resources, or from more and better technologies? Do we have the theoretical tools and empirical understanding to unambiguously distinguish between these sources of growth? And how important is the broader historical, institutional and political context in which the sources of growth are analysed?

The papers in this volume deal with these questions for the subgroup of advanced economies in Europe and the United States. In a nutshell it may be stated that all papers argue that the key factor behind long-run economic growth has been productivity, and that the latter has been primarily driven by technological change. Moreover, most papers show implicitly or explicitly that technological change holds an endogenous component which makes it at least partly dependent on growth itself. Finally, technology appears to have interacted strongly with investment in physical and human capital as well as with changes in historical, political and institutional settings. These messages may not sound all that new or original. Of course, they aren't. The really remarkable point in our view is that, with the developments in theoretical and empirical work on productivity and growth over the past three quarters of a century, these main observations still hold.

This volume of papers will make it possible to assess what has been gained following the earlier work on growth, and which ideas and concepts we believe will stay with us in future work. The contributions to this volume (and to the conference that preceded this publication) come from different fields in economics, including economic history, macroeconomic modelling, microeconomic research on longitudinal data and the economics of technological change and innovation. Most papers have a strong empirical flavour and take a long-term perspective of at least a few decades, and in some cases up to one century (Gordon) or even two centuries (van Zanden and Mokyr). The papers also have a wide geographical coverage. Some papers (for example, those by Gordon, Malley *et al.*, and Lichtenberg) provide evidence on the US economy, others deal primarily with European countries, in some cases in comparison to other OECD countries (for example, Eichengreen and Vazquez, Mokyr, Fagerberg and Verspagen, and Rensman and Kuper). Finally, some papers are specifically focussed on the Netherlands (such as van Zanden, van Ark and de Haan, van der Wiel, Bartelsman and Jacobs *et al.*).

In this introductory chapter we will first briefly review the various theoretical and conceptual approaches which may be employed to disentangle the sources of growth. We use the distinction between accumulation, productivity and technology as a device to structure the debate. The first two tend to emphasise the importance of investment and increased efficiency in use of resources, whereas the latter puts the contribution of invention and innovation to productivity into the spotlight. Taking the papers in this volume together, it appears to us that the most powerful explanations of economic growth are those which combine these various perspectives on growth, in particular when these provide an explicit focus on historical, institutional and political factors in the growth process. We will then continue to discuss the key messages from the papers in this volume, which we have organized as follows. Chapters 2 to 4 deal with the long-run aspects of economic growth. Chapters 5 to 8 discuss the determinants of productivity. Finally, Chapters 9 to 13 focus on the role of technology and innovation as the key determinants of growth.

2. ANALYTICAL APPROACHES TO ACCUMULATION, PRODUCTIVITY AND TECHNOLOGY

To disentangle the sources of economic growth one requires an analytical framework to assess the contribution of various factors to growth. This involves the formulation of theories, models and hypotheses on the role of accumulation, productivity and technology. Over the past decades these areas have been partly the domain of economists and partly of economic historians. However, as yet there is no consensus on what emphasis should be given to the key factors behind growth and how these are linked.

Accumulation concentrates on the role of investment and the effect of investment on the stock of physical, human and natural resources. The work of Harrod (1946) and Domar (1947) set the scene for macroeconomic growth theory and measurement. This was pursued by Kaldor (1957, 1966) and others who explained productivity growth from the demand-side, stressing that the interaction between savings and demand for investment was the key to the accumulation of capital and technology. The traditional neoclassical approach also starts from the accumulist perspective by relying on a production function framework (Solow, 1956; Swan, 1956). It concentrated on the supply side arguing that capital accumulation itself would bring the economy to a steady state. In their view only exogenous technological and organisational change could bring the economy to a higher rate of economic growth.

In the empirical work on the sources of growth the contribution of productivity became more directly visible. Following the pioneering work of

Clark (1940) and Kuznets (1956-1967) to the construction of national accounts of GDP and other macroeconomic variables, growth accounting developed as a critical tool to measure the contribution of various determinants to output and productivity growth.[1] Tinbergen (1942), Abramovitz (1956) and Solow (1957) defined output as a function of labour and capital, weighted at their respective factor shares in value added. They then identified a "residual" which accounts for the difference in the growth of output and the contribution of the inputs. This residual has been named "total factor productivity growth" (or the "Solow residual") and has often, in particular by economists, been equated with technical progress. According to these early growth accounting studies, total factor productivity growth contributed very substantially to economic growth. Kendrick (1961, 1976) contributed to the growth accounting tradition by augmenting factor inputs with the quality of labour (distinguished by levels of education, and age- and sex-composition) and capital (distinguished by vintage effects). Another strand in the growth accounting tradition focussed in more detail on the opening up of the "black box," *i.e.* the residual, that remains after allowing for the contribution of the quantity and quality of labour, capital and land to growth. The work by Denison (1962, 1974, 1979, 1985) has been of fundamental importance in understanding the role of economies of scale, allocation of resources, advances in knowledge, and the effects of irregularities in demand.

In the growth literature of the 1960s a discussion emerged on the extent to which technical progress was, at least partly, embodied in the factor inputs (Solow, 1960). Salter (1960), who introduced the vintage approach to capital accumulation, argues that capital accumulation is the main vehicle of technical progress. However, he emphasized that a clear distinction between technical progress and economies of scale was needed and that the latter contributed significantly more to growth than the former. Jorgenson separated investment from productivity by applying a rigorous criterion, namely that investments concern commitment of current resources in the expectation of future returns, which implies that the returns can be internalised by the investor.[2] In contrast, productivity relates to incomes that are generated externally to the economic activities undertaken by the investor. Hence productivity is associated with spillovers and externalities that cannot be appropriated. The effects of substitution between labour and capital or between different types of capital is therefore part of the investment process, leaving less room for productivity growth as a

---

[1] See van Ark (1997), in particular Volume II, part 3 on "Growth Accounting and Productivity."

[2] See Jorgenson (1995) for an overview of papers by himself and his associates on productivity.

contributing factor to growth than in the more aggregate growth accounting approaches.[3] In his paper to this volume, Gordon (Chapter 2) provides an extensive update of the American work on growth accounting and an original interpretation of U.S. growth spanning the whole period from 1870 to 1996. Growth accounting techniques are also applied in other papers in this volume, including the papers by Eichengreen and Vazquez (Chapter 3) and van Ark and de Haan (Chapter 6).

Maddison (1972, 1982, 1991, 1996) extended growth accounting to international comparisons. Apart from comparing the growth contributions of augmented inputs between countries, he also quantified foreign trade effects, catch-up effects, structural effects and economies of scale on output growth. Maddison identified these factors as typical "proximate" sources of growth as they directly contribute to changes in output growth. In addition, Maddison also emphasized the importance of "ultimate" sources of growth which are related to the political-institutional environment, and he stressed the importance of historical events. Hence this growth accounting strand can be linked to the historical approaches towards economic growth, which will be discussed later.

During the 1970s it almost seemed as if a deadlock in growth studies had been reached. It became increasingly clear that the traditional approaches in growth theory and measurement could not fully explain the divergent economic performance in the world economy. Nor was it clear why the productivity slowdown since 1973 continued for such a long time. Dissatisfied with this failure of traditional growth economics to shed light on actual growth performance, the pioneers in new growth theory, in particular Romer (1986, 1990) and Lucas (1988) who built upon the neoclassical tradition, and Scott (1989) who expanded his work along Kaldorian lines of thinking, aimed to uncover the determinants of permanent growth. In particular they stressed the role of increasing returns to capital employed and externalities. Whereas this earlier work in new growth theory looked for a more prominent role for physical and human capital in growth models, now that the dust has somewhat settled, the main message from new growth theory appears to be that technology and, more broadly, knowledge, need to be modelled as the main endogenous variables in explaining differences in growth performance across countries. Many of these ideas were not really new as these were identified and measured by the earlier generations of

---

[3] Harberger (1998) represents yet another approach to growth accounting. He interprets the TFP residual as "real cost reductions" which, when expressed in money terms, can be made additive. Harberger also stresses the importance of the multiplicity of sources from which real cost reductions can arise, and emphasizes the need to look at TFP performance at firm level to understand these sources. See also Hulten (2000) for an overview of approaches to TFP measurement.

growth theorists and growth accountants. The novelty, however, lies in the attempts to model and test these ideas on the basis of econometric specifications and by giving a greater role to the firm which creates new knowledge in an environment of imperfect competition.

Empirical studies have more or less rejected the possibility of increasing returns on physical capital (Barro and Sala-i-Martin, 1992). In the case of human capital, Mankiw, Romer and Weil (1992) argued that a Solow model characterised by constant returns to scale but augmented with human capital as a separate input greatly strengthens the explanatory power of the model. The most convincing approach to increasing returns comes from models on ideas and knowledge. In these models the spillovers from returns on R&D, or from inventions and innovations, are seen as the main engines of growth. Recently, this approach has been refined by Aghion and Howitt (1992, 1998). The papers in this volume by Malley *et al.* (Chapter 5), Jacobs *et al.* (Chapter 10), Lichtenberg (Chapter 11), Fagerberg and Verspagen (Chapter 12), and Rensman and Kuper (Chapter 13) extensively use regression techniques. All these papers also give an explicit role to technology variables. Lichtenberg's paper draws specifically on data on new products in the pharmaceutical industry that affect hospitalization and mortality rates. The other papers extensively use data on research and development and patents at macroeconomic and sectoral level.

The "new growth" approaches have opened up new avenues to model the role of technological change in economic growth by making the Schumpeterian concept of "creative destruction" at firm level an essential part of knowledge models. This greater role for knowledge matches remarkably well with older approaches that put technological change more explicitly in the spotlight. These approaches take investment in human and physical capital as a necessary but not sufficient factor to achieve growth. They emphasise that countries require entrepreneurship, innovation and learning before they can employ new technologies to achieve growth. The technology approaches to growth are of a more hybrid nature than the accumulation and productivity approaches, and most studies have strong "Schumpeterian" characteristics as they give an explicit role to firms, to organisational change, management, marketing and finance and to the discontinuous nature of technological change (Schumpeter, 1943).

One range of studies recognised that the assumptions of rational optimisation and perfect foresight, which are characteristic of the neoclassical approach, are not adequate in explaining the process of technological change. The evolutionary approach to economic growth therefore analyses strategies to optimise (not maximise) profits under assumptions of bounded rationality. These theories put much emphasis on the uncertainties of the search process and the importance of "routines" in these searches (Nelson and Winter, 1982). A major problem of these microeconomic evolutionary models is that they cannot be solved analytically, but require computer simulations. A calibration of the Nelson and Winter model with the time series on U.S. sources of growth from 1909 to 1949 suggests results which are broadly in line with Solow's growth accounting results for 1957.[4]

A second group of studies in the Schumpeterian tradition has a more historical flavour to it, and these are strongly represented in this volume. Crafts (1997) emphasises that much of the research by economic historians on technological change has largely gone unnoticed by growth economists. Much of this historical work focuses on factors which determine the role of institutions in the process of technological change. For example, von Tunzelmann (1995) shows how the organisation of science and technology, together with that of finance, production, *etc.*, form a national system of production and innovation, which differs over time and across space. This institutional approach helps to explain the economic supremacy of certain nations and regions at different points in time. The paper by Mokyr (Chapter 9) in this volume provides a first step towards a theory of knowledge in which institutions, markets, geography and culture determine the creation of a pool of knowledge and the new techniques that emerge from it. Mokyr discusses his model in the light of the case Industrial Revolution in Britain at the end of the 18th century.

The other question which has been addressed by economic historians is why countries catch up or fall behind the technology leader. In this respect the concepts of "path-dependency," "technological lock ins" and "absorptive capacity" are quite important. The work by David (1975, 1985) has shown how the initial choice of techniques has led to differential rates of technological progress in the United States and the United Kingdom, and why the former eventually managed to take over leadership from the latter. Gordon (Chapter 2) uncovers some of the reasons for U.S. leadership during the twentieth century, as the U.S. accounted for the bulk of major inventions since the second half of the 19th century. In general, early 20th century Europe suffered from a lack of absorptive capacity due to technological incongruence relative to the U.S., which was due to different resource and factor endowments and smaller market size.[5] However, as Gerschenkron (1962) states, this situation can be overcome by benefitting from the advantages of backwardness. The catch-up track, however, is not without cost. According to Abramovitz, the social capability to catch up, which includes "the state of a country's political, commercial and financial

---

[4] Silverberg and Verspagen (1995) describe a number of macroeconomic evolutionary models that can be solved analytically.

[5] See also Broadberry (1997).

institutions, its levels of general and technical education, and the experience of its entrepreneurs and managers with large-scale organisation and practice" crucially determines the potential for catch-up (Abramovitz, 1991, p.20). Hence catching up partly requires investment in physical capacity, like infrastructure and industrial complexes, and in human capital, but equally important is the building of new institutions. Clearly this determines a role for governments in formulating policies on organisation of labour and financial markets and on creation and adaptation of new technology through R&D, education and training, *etc.*. The papers by Eichengreen and Vazquez (Chapter 2), van Zanden (Chapter 3), van Ark and de Haan (Chapter 6), van der Wiel (Chapter 7), Bartelsman (Chapter 8), and Fagerberg and Verspagen (Chapter 12) address elements of institution building which are important for growth acceleration or catch-up growth.

3.   IDENTIFYING GROWTH REGIMES

Productivity is a concept that typically requires a long-run perspective. Indeed only in the long run productivity growth will have a decisive effect on sustainable growth and improvement in living standards. Significant breaks in long-run productivity trends mainly occur because of changes in technological regimes and the evolution of new institutions, sometimes following system shocks which the western world has experienced more than once during the 20th century.[6]

The long-run perspective makes it possible to identify growth regimes which, due to some of the reasons described above, can remain locked in for quite some time. Chapters 2 to 4 typically deal with such growth regimes. The paper by Gordon (Chapter 2) provides a detailed growth accounting analysis of U.S. economic growth since 1870. Building upon the previous work of Denison, Jorgenson and others, Gordon makes careful adjustments for changes in the composition of labour and capital. His main finding is that there is much less variation in multifactor productivity growth over time than observed before. Essentially the whole period 1870 to present represents, in Gordon view's, one big wave that is determined by the timing of inventions.

The paper by van Zanden (Chapter 3) fits remarkably well to the Gordon paper, even though the analytical framework differs. Van Zanden analyses macroeconomic data for the Netherlands from 1807 onwards, and tries to identify differences between "equilibrium" and "disequilibrium" growth paths. The latter is seen as fundamentally different from steady state growth, as it emphasises the transitional dynamics of the movements of one steady-

---

[6]   See, for example, Baumol, Blackman and Wolff (1989).

state regime to another. Van Zanden finds that much of the slower growth in the Netherlands compared to Belgium during the 19th century is due to the fact that the former did not show the classic features of a Gerschenkronian growth spurt of industrialisation. The post World War II period was typically one of rapid changes in trend growth, investment and distribution of income. Like Gordon, van Zanden points at the crucial impact of the second industrial revolution, *i.e.* the introduction and spread of electricity, on 20th century growth of the Dutch economy.

Van Zanden's paper also points at the role of institutional rearrangements after World War II, which is the main theme of the third paper in this section by Eichengreen and Vazquez (Chapter 4). This paper widens the view towards Europe as a whole, and extends on the first author's earlier work on the critical role of institutions in postwar European growth (Eichengreen, 1996). In this paper they argue that not only output, investment and exports were greatly enhanced by corporatist labour relations and the creation of European international institutions, but that these relations and institutions were also crucial in exploiting the technological backlog that existed after the war period, and supported in particular technology transfers and incremental innovations.

4. THE DETERMINANTS OF PRODUCTIVITY GROWTH

The study of the sources of economic growth and the measurement of multifactor productivity have a long tradition as described above. Before discussing the papers, a brief review on what has been learned from empirical evidence obtained so far may be useful. The typical growth accounting work has tended to show fairly large (TFP) residuals which could not be fully explained, and were in one case identified by Abramovitz as a "measure of our ignorance." The more econometric version of growth accounting, as developed by Jorgenson, tended to give a greater role to investment and substitutions between different types of inputs, but still left a large chunk of growth unexplained. The large battery of papers based on growth regression on the whole tend to find a positive relation between GDP per capita growth and investment and, to a lesser extent, education variables, and a negative relationship with the share of government consumption in GDP and with initial income per capita. The latter effect represents a catch-up effect, which has become exhausted and featured as a strong reason for the growth slowdown since 1973. Indeed traditional growth accounting studies have tended to ascribe a much bigger part of the slowdown since 1973 to the actual decline in productivity rather than to the exhaustion of the catch-up effect *per se*.[7] Another important development, represented in many of the papers in this volume, is the inclusion of institutional and political variables in the models. However, the regression results must be regarded at best as illustrative with regard to the sources of growth because this accounting method can be quite sensitive to the specification of the variables and the countries included in the regression.

The first paper in this section by Malley, Muscatelli and Woitek (Chapter 5) provides a useful link between short-term and long-term productivity analysis by linking changes within the business cycle to their impact on long-term economic growth. The authors employ panel data to adjust total factor productivity measures for the United States for factor utilisation. They find that such adjustments weaken the impact of technology shocks on employment growth. In some cases such shocks even have negative effects because of sticky prices and "creative destruction" effects.

The papers by van Ark and de Haan (Chapter 6), van der Wiel (Chapter 7), and Bartelsman (Chapter 8) all deal with the Dutch economy. Since the late 1980s the Dutch economy has shown an above average growth performance and a rapid increase in employment. The paper by van Ark and de Haan (Chapter 6) draws the attention to the divergent trends of rapid growth in income per capita and slow labour productivity growth in the Netherlands since the 1980s. They argue that transitory forces such as a rise in service activities and creation of low-wage employment do not explain much of the growth slowdown. They also do not find much evidence of a slow diffusion of technology to service industries. They conclude that a further monitoring of the effects of product market regulation and deregulation is a fruitful avenue for further research.

Using a micro-data set for firms, the paper by van der Wiel (Chapter 7) provides further substance on the productivity slowdown in one of the fastest growing sectors of the past decade, *i.e.* business services. In this sector productivity growth has been more or less zero according to the measures presented here. These data show, however, a huge heterogeneity in performance across firms even within the same industry. The paper finds that between 1987 and 1995 entering firms were less productive than incumbents in the sector, which seriously impacted the aggregate given the high entry rate. Van der Wiel suggests that lack of competition in new market segments in combination with a shift towards demand for these new products is the most promising explanation of these phenomena.

Both the papers by van der Wiel and Bartelsman use longitudinal micro-data on firms. Bartelsman (Chapter 8) uses a panel for industrial firms to test the possibility that hold-up problems due to specificity of labour and capital

---

[7]   See Van Ark and Crafts (1996) who discuss a comparison between Maddison's growth accounting work and the extension of Levine and Renelt's (1992) regression analysis.

in the production relationship may explain that wage moderation policies have simultaneously supported productivity and employment growth in the Netherlands. Despite the preliminary nature of his results, Bartelsman finds no reason to reject this possibility, as the number of firms with unusually large investment and TFP growth after the wage moderation agreement of 1982 was higher than before.

5. TECHNOLOGICAL CHANGE AND INNOVATION AS SOURCES OF PRODUCTIVITY GROWTH

The role of technological and organisational change in economic growth has been intensively researched over the past decades. The rise of the new economic history or cliometrics during the second half of the 1960s, including the work of Fogel, North, David, and Temin, has contributed to laying the empirical foundations in linking the study of economic growth to that of technological change, economic institutions and government policies.[8] North's emphasis on institutions as a means to provide and safeguard incentives for individuals to engage in productive activities is fundamental in understanding differences in economic performance across countries (North, 1981).

A second stream of research that provided much empirical evidence on the contribution of technology to growth is from the innovation literature. Much of this research had a strong case study nature, as appears from the pathbreaking work by, for example, Mansfield (1995) and Rosenberg (1994). Many of these industry studies on R&D and patenting have provided a rich empirical foundation to the dynamics of technological change. Freeman and Soete (1997) have been instrumental in providing a theoretical foundation to the economics of technological change and innovation. The microeconomics of innovation deals with the "competitive struggle" of firms due to the professionalization of R&D, and the high uncertainty that firms face in this process. The macroeconomics of innovation deal with the determinants of differences in national systems of innovation that were described above as fundamental in understanding the differences in growth performance across countries. In the third edition of Freeman and Soete's Economics of Industrial Innovation the historical dimension of the book was strengthened as the authors recognized the importance of path dependence in models of evolutionary change.

The first paper in this last section of the volume also looks at technology and knowledge from a historical viewpoint. Mokyr (Chapter 9) develops a

---

[8] A good overview of some original cliometrics work can be obtained from Temin (1973).

theory of knowledge and applies it to explain the timing of the Industrial Revolution. In his view the Industrial Revolution is caused by the scientific revolution in the seventeenth century and the enlightment movement of the eighteenth century. Mokyr makes a distinction between *useful knowledge* and *techniques*. Changes in knowledge equal discoveries whereas changes in techniques represent patented inventions. Clearly techniques require knowledge, but techniques provide feedback to the creation of new knowledge. Applying this concept to the Industrial Revolution, Mokyr concludes that it was not just new knowledge *per se* but better access to knowledge that explains the success of the Industrial Revolution at that specific time.

Nowadays, education and research and development are two of the recognised vehicles to transform knowledge into techniques. Jacobs, Nahuis and Tang (Chapter 10) analyse both drivers for technology diffusion for the Netherlands since 1973. They find that R&D variables systematically have positive effects on productivity growth, whereas human capital variables do not appear to influence TFP growth. These results lead the authors to conclude that innovation driven growth theories better describe the growth process than the human capital based growth process.

The final three chapters go into more detail in measuring the impact of innovation on growth. Lichtenberg's paper (Chapter 11) uses very detailed data on the introduction and utilisation of new products in the pharmaceutical industry mimicking the role of innovation in the process of economic growth. The author finds that pharmaceutical innovation contributes to productivity growth as it reduces the demand for hospitalisation without reducing life expectancy. A more far-reaching implication of these findings is that the effects of pharmaceutical innovations go beyond what is accounted for by GDP as longevity increases with such innovations.

The paper by Fagerberg and Verspagen (Chapter 12) can be most clearly placed in the tradition of the "technology gap" approach. The authors address *how* innovation and diffusion of technology affects productivity growth. Concerning the diffusion of technology they combine a *broad* view (catching up by increasing absorptive capacity) and a *narrow* view (R&D embodied in goods). Whereas the latter is only one mechanism to strengthen productivity growth, they conclude that own R&D is of crucial importance, in particular when it interacts with other variables strengthening the absorptive capacity.

Finally, the paper by Rensman and Kuper (Chapter 13) combines the concepts of the interaction between knowledge and technology and that of absorptive capacity. Following the innovation-driven growth literature (Aghion and Howitt, 1998), the authors combine imperfect competition with innovation-based growth and learning-by-doing in innovation. These forces generate spillovers from industrial research and patenting activity. On the basis of the testing of their model for the U.S., U.K., France and Germany, they conclude that the growth rate of R&D expenditures and the change in the gap with the technology leader (*i.e.*, the U.S.) play a significant role in the explanation of the growth rate of labour productivity. International spillovers do occur, but they do not take place completely or immediately, so that differences in productivity growth persist. Domestic efforts to gain knowledge are thus important as a learning mechanism for the adoption of foreign technology locked up in patents from abroad.

6.   THE UNFINISHED RESEARCH AGENDA

As mentioned above three quarters of a century of research on economic growth, productivity and technological change have brought about a remarkable convergence in viewpoints on the driving forces behind productivity growth. Nevertheless, the papers in this volume show that the research agenda is not quite fulfilled. Many of the issues that need to be resolved require improvements in methodologies and in particular better data. It is not our aim here to outline a complete research agenda, but we wish to call attention to some issues for further research that emerged prominently while evaluating these papers.

Firstly, concerning the sources of growth, many papers deal with the question on the interaction of human capital and technology. Clearly skill-biased technological change suggests complementarity between human capital and R&D at firm level, but at macroeconomic level the complementarity can be compromised by substitution effects between skilled and unskilled labour on both labour and product markets (OECD, 1996). A major research issue will therefore be to gain a better understanding of how technological progress affects the composition of the human capital base. Moreover, in order to better understand the relation between human capital and technology diffusion, more research is needed on how the knowledge base accumulates via learning-by-doing.

Secondly, it appears from many papers that catching up has been a key force in improving the productivity performance, but it also appears that catching up has not been automatic and that in many cases convergence has not gone all the way. The role of "ultimate" sources of growth features dominantly in the explanations for this. Many of the papers have dealt with the role of institutions but, at an even deeper level, there may also be a role for differences in culture, mentality, and preferences of people that affect the institutional rearrangements in different countries, notably between Europe and the United States but also between the European countries themselves. Ultimately, such rearrangements determine the impact of structural reforms in labour, capital and product markets on economic performance. We believe that the role of competition *versus* coordination in stimulating technological and organisational innovations deserves more attention. In this respect the mechanism to safeguard tacit knowledge, including organisational and managerial knowledge is also important.

Finally, the conference we held in September 1998, at which the papers included in this volume were presented, was titled "Productivity and Living Standards." It is fair to say that we have not quite succeeded to make a strong connection between these two. Clearly income per head of the population is not a comprehensive indicator of living standards. Some of the papers do show the importance of the topic. For example, the papers by Gordon (Chapter 2) and Mokyr (Chapter 9) indicate the importance of new inventions for the improvement in living standards. The paper by Lichtenberg (Chapter 11) is most explicit about how innovations in pharmaceutical products reduce hospitalization and eventually increase longevity, which might be one of the most important aspects of the rise in living standards. Strikingly, this evidence from the American papers in the volume is not complemented with evidence on Europe. Furthermore there has been no attention in any of the papers for the role of environmental factors in improving living standards. Future research should try to establish these links in better ways.

REFERENCES

Abramovitz, M. (1956), "Resource and Output Trends in the United States since 1870," *The American Economic Review* 46, pp. 5-23.

Abramovitz, M. (1991), "The Post-war Productivity Spurt and Slowdown: Factors of Potential and Realisation," in: G. Bell (ed.), *Technology and Productivity: The Challenge for Economic Policy*, OECD, Paris, pp. 19-37.

Aghion, P. and P. Howitt (1992), "A Model of Growth through Creative Destruction," *Econometrica* 60, pp. 323-351.

Aghion, P. and P. Howitt (1998), *Endogenous Growth Theory*, Cambridge: MIT Press.

Ark, B. van (ed.) (1997), *Economic Growth in the Long Run. A History of Empirical Evidence*, The International Library of Critical Writings in Economics 76, 3 volumes, Cheltenham: Edward Elgar Publishers.

Ark, B. van and N.F.R. Crafts (eds.) (1996), *Quantitative Aspects of Postwar European Economic Growth*, Paris: CEPR/Cambridge University Press, pp. 84-164.

Barro, R. and X. Sala-i-Martin (1992), "Convergence," *Journal of Political Economy* 100, pp. 223-251.

Baumol, W.J., S.A.B. Blackman and E.N. Wolff (1989), *Productivity and American Leadership, The Long View*, Cambridge Mass.: MIT Press.

1. Introduction   15

Broadberry, S.N. (1997), *The Productivity Race. British Manufacturing in International Perspective, 1850-1990*, Cambridge: Cambridge University Press.
Clark, C. (1940), *Conditions of Economic Progress*, 1st edition, London, MacMillan.
Crafts, N.F.R. (1997), "Endogenous Growth: Lessons for and from Economic History, " in D.M. Kreps and K.F. Wallis (eds.), *Advances in Economics and Econometrics: Theory and Applications*, Volume II, Cambridge: Cambridge University Press, pp. 38-78.
David, P.A. (1975), *Technical Choice, Innovation and Economic Growth: Essays on American and British Experience in the Nineteenth Century*, Cambridge: Cambridge University Press.
David, P.A. (1986), "Understanding the Economics of QWERTY: The Necessity of History," in W.N. Parker (ed.), *Economic History and the Modern Economist*, Oxford: Basil Blackwell, pp. 30-49.
Denison, E.F. (1962), *The Sources of Economic Growth in the United States and the Alternatives Before Us*, CED Supplementary Paper No. 13, New York: Committee for Economic Development.
Denison, E.F. (1974), *Accounting for United States Economic Growth: 1929-1969*, Washington: The Brookings Institution.
Denison, E.F. (1979), *Accounting for Slower Growth: The United States in the 1970s*, Washington: The Brookings Institution.
Denison, E.F. (1985), *Trends in American Economic Growth, 1929-1982*, Washington: The Brookings Institution.
Domar, E.D. (1946), "Capital Expansion, Rate of Growth, and Employment," *Econometrica* 14, pp. 137-147.
Eichengreen, B. (1996), "Institutions and Economic Growth: Europe Since World War II," in N.F.R. Crafts and G. Toniolo (eds.), *Economic Growth in Europe Since 1945*, Cambridge: Cambridge University Press, pp. 38-72.
Freeman, C. and L. Soete (1997), *The Economics of Industrial Innovation*, Cambridge: MIT Press, Third edition.
Gerschenkron, A. (1962), *Economic Backwardness in Historical Perspective*, Cambridge Mass.: Harvard University Press.
Harrod. R.F. (1948), *Towards a Dynamic Economics*, London: MacMillan.
Harberger, A.C. (1998), "A Vision of the Growth Process," *The American Economic Review* 88, pp. 1-32.
Hulten, C.R. (2000), "Total Factor Productivity: A Short Biography, " NBER Working Paper No. W7471, Cambridge Mass.
Jorgenson, D.W. (1995), *Productivity, Volume 1, Postwar U.S. Economic Growth* & Volume 2, *International Comparisons of Economic Growth*, Cambridge Mass: The MIT Press.
Jorgenson, D.W. and K.J. Stiroh (2000), "Raising the Speed Limit: U.S. Economic Growth in the Information Age," *Brookings Papers on Economic Activity* 2, forthcoming.
Kaldor, N. (1957), "A Model of Economic Growth," *The Economic Journal*, vol. 67, pp. 591-624.
Kaldor, N. (1961), "Capital Accumulation and Economic Growth," in: F. A Lutz and D.C. Hague (eds.), *The Theory of Capital*, London: MacMillan.
Kendrick, J.W. (1961), *Productivity Trends in the United States*, Princeton: Princeton University Press.
Kendrick, J.W. (1976), *The Formation and Stock of Total Capital*, NBER General Series 100, New York: Columbia University Press.
Kuznets, S. (1956-1967), "Quantitative Aspects of the Economic Growth of Nations," *Economic Development and Cultural Change*, various issues.

Levine, R. and D. Renelt (1992), "A Sensitivity Analysis of Cross-Country Growth
    Regressions," *The American Economic Review*, 82, pp. 942-963.
Lucas, R.E. (1988), "On the Mechanics of Economic Development," *Journal of Monetary
    Economics* 22, pp. 3-42.
Maddison, A. (1972), "Explaining Economic Growth," *Banca Nazionale del Lavoro Quarterly
    Review*, September.
Maddison, A. (1982), *Phases of Capitalist Development*, Oxford: Oxford University Press.
Maddison, A. (1991), *Dynamic Forces in Capitalist Development*, Oxford: Oxford University
    Press.
Maddison, A. (1995), *Monitoring the World Economy 1820-1992*, Paris: OECD Development
    Centre.
Maddison, A. (1996), "Macroeconomic Accounts for European Countries," in: B. van Ark and
    N.F.R. Crafts (eds.), *Quantitative Aspects of Post-War European Economic Growth*,
    Cambridge: CEPR/Cambridge University Press, pp. 28-83.
Mansfield, E. (1995), *Innovation, Technology and the Economy. The Selected Essays of
    Edwin Mansfield*, two volumes, Aldershot: Edward Elgar Publishers.
Mankiw, N.G., D. Romer and D. Weil (1992), "A Contribution to the Empirics of Economic
    Growth," *Quarterly Journal of Economics*. 107, pp. 407-438.
Nelson, R.R. and S.G. Winter (1982), *An Evolutionary Theory of Economic Change*,
    Cambridge MA: Harvard University Press.
North, D.C. (1981), *Structure and Change in Economic History*, New York: W.W. Norton.
OECD (1996), *Technology, Productivity and Job Creation*, Vol. 2, *Analytical Report*, Paris.
Oliner, S.D. and D.E. Sichel (2000), "The Resurgence of Growth in the Late 1990s. Is
    Information Technology the Story?," Federal Reserve Board, mimeo.
Romer, P.M. (1986), "Increasing Returns and Long Run Growth," *Journal of Political Economy*
    94, pp. 1002-1037.
Romer, P.M. (1990), "Endogenous Technological Change," *Journal of Political Economy*, 98, pp.
    S71-S102.
Rosenberg, N. (1994), *Exploring the Black Box. Technology, Economics and History*,
    Cambridge: Cambridge University Press.
Salter, W.E.G. (1960), *Productivity and Technical Change*, Cambridge: Cambridge
    University Press.
Schumpeter, J.A. (1943), *Capitalism, Socialism and Democracy*, New York: Harper and Row.
Scott, M.F. (1989), *A New View of Economic Growth*, Oxford: Oxford University Press.
Silverberg, G. and B. Verspagen (1995), "Evolutionary Theorizing on Economic Growth,"
    MERIT, mimeographed.
Solow, R.M. (1956), "A Contribution to the Theory of Economic Growth," *Quarterly Journal
    of Economics* 70, pp. 65-94.
Solow, R.M. (1957), "Technical Change and the Aggregate Production Function," *Review of
    Economics and Statistics* 39, pp. 312-330.
Solow, R.M. (1960), "Investment and Technical Progress," in: K. Arrow, S. Karlin and P.
    Suppes (eds.), *Mathematical Methods in the Social Sciences*, Stanford University Press.
Swan, T.W. (1956), "Economic Growth and Capital Accumulation," *Economic Record* 32,
    pp. 334-361.
Temin, P. (ed.) (1973), *New Economic History. Selected Readings*, Harmondsworth: Penguin
    Books.
Tinbergen, J. (1942), "Zur Theorie der Langfristigen Wirtschaftsentwicklung,"
    Weltwirtschaftliches Archiv, 55, pp. 511-549.
Tunzelmann, G.N. von (1995), *Technology and Industrial Progress. The Foundations of
    Economic Growth*, Aldershot: Edward Elgar Publishers.

PART I

UNDERSTANDING GROWTH REGIMES

Chapter 2

Interpreting the "One Big Wave" in U.S. Long-term Productivity Growth

Robert J. Gordon
Northwestern University, National Bureau of Economic Research and Centre for Economic Policy Research

Key words: Economic growth, Productivity, Technical change

Abstract: This paper assesses the standard data on output, labour input, and capital input, which imply "one big wave" in multi-factor productivity (MFP) growth for the United States since 1870. The wave-like pattern starts with slow MFP growth in the late 19th century, then an acceleration peaking in 1928-50, and then a deceleration to a slow rate after 1972 that returns to the poor performance of 1870-1891. A counterpart of the standard data is a mysterious doubling in the ratio of output to capital input when the post-war era is compared with 1870-1929. Three types of measurement adjustments are applied to the standard input data. Following the lead of Denison and Jorgenson-Griliches, adjustments for the changing composition (or "quality") of labour and capital, currently published by the BLS back to 1948, are estimated for 1870-1948. These composition adjustments take into account the shifting mix of the labour force along the dimensions of education and age-sex composition, and of the capital stock between equipment and structures. Further adjustments are made to capital input data to allow retirement to vary with gross investment rather than to follow a fixed pattern depending only on age, and to add types of capital owned by the government that are particularly productive in the private sector. A new MFP series taking account of all these adjustments grows more slowly throughout, and the "big wave" phenomenon is both flatter and extends back further in time to 1891. However, there is no solution to the post-1972 productivity slowdown, and in the new data MFP growth during 1972-96 proceeds at a pathetic 0.1 percent per year. A by-product of the measurement adjustments is to solve completely the previous puzzle of the jump in the output-capital ratio; in the new data this ratio is actually lower in 1996 than in 1870. The primary substantive explanation for the big wave lies in the timing of inventions. MFP growth during the "big wave" period benefited from the diffusion of four great clusters of inventions that dwarf today's information technology revolution in their combined importance. A complementary hypothesis is that the partial closing of American labour markets to immigration and of American goods markets to imports during the big wave period gave an artificial and temporary boost to real wages which fed back into boosting productivity growth, followed by a reopening that contributed to the post-1972 productivity slowdown.

"The change in trend that came after World War I is one of the most interesting facts before us. There is little question about it. . . . the rate of growth in productivity witnessed by the present generation has been substantially higher than the rate experienced in the quarter-century before World War I."

Solomon Fabricant, introduction to Kendrick (1961, p. xliii)

1.   INTRODUCTION

It is now more than 25 years since the growth rate of labour productivity and of multi-factor productivity (MFP) decelerated sharply both in the United States and in most other industrialised nations.[1] This slowdown in productivity growth, or "productivity slowdown" for short, has eluded many attempts to provide single-cause explanations, including fluctuations in energy prices, inadequate private investment, inadequate infrastructure investment, excessive government regulation, and declining educational test scores.[2] The wide variation in productivity slowdowns and accelerations

---

[1]   The data in this paper end in 1996, because this was as far as the U.S. Bureau of Labour Statistics had extended its data on labour and capital composition, and multi-factor productivity, at the time the conference draft of this paper was written. During the 1996-99 period the quarterly data on output per hour indicate a modest acceleration when growth over the recent 1995:Q4-1999: Q1 interval is compared with the slowdown interval 1972:Q2-1995:Q4. Gordon (1999b) argues that this acceleration can be entirely explained by (1) improved measurement of price deflators, (2) normal procyclical effects, and (3) the production of computer hardware, with nothing left over to indicate a structural revival in productivity growth in the 99 percent of the economy engaged in activities other than the manufacture of computers.

[2]   Given that the productivity growth slowdown has continued over the period 1973-96, energy prices are ruled out as a cause, since by the early 1990s real energy prices had returned almost to their 1972 levels. Private investment is ruled out in that the productivity slowdown has occurred not just in output per hour but also in multi-factor productivity, which takes into account the growth of capital input. If private investment in equipment has "super-normal" returns, as argued by De Long-Summers (1991), then a recalculated MFP exhibits an even more severe slowdown than in the official data. The infrastructure

across individual industries also argues against a single-cause explanation.[3] The slowdown has also been immune to multi-faceted explanations, including those of the late Edward F. Denison (1962, 1979, 1985) to quantify the role of a slowdown in the growth of inputs and specific qualitative factors such as the movement out of agriculture and the spread of crime.

1.1   Explaining the "Big Wave"

When an important problem so completely eludes explanation, other possibilities are suggested. Perhaps we have been asking the wrong question. A basic theme of this paper is that slow productivity growth in the past 25 years echoes slow productivity growth in the late nineteenth century. Perhaps both were normal, and what needs to be explained is not the post-1972 slowdown but rather the post-1913 "speedup" that ushered in the glorious half century between World War I and the early 1970s during which U.S. productivity growth was much faster than before or after.

The timing of the productivity "golden age" is different in the U.S. from that in Europe and Japan, where there is no novelty in suggesting that the 1948-73 "golden age" may have been unsustainable, particularly insofar as it contained an element of catching up from lost opportunities during the previous dismal decades of the two world wars and the Great Depression.[4] However, the United States is another story. The low level of productivity and per-capita income in Europe relative to the U.S. in an early post-war year like 1950 reflects not only Europe's poor performance but also the rapid advance of the U.S. prior to that point.[5] Although most casual observers assume that 1948-73 was the "golden age" of U.S. productivity growth as it was in Europe and Japan, the data compiled in this paper suggest that the

---

hypothesis proposed by Aschauer (1989) in research on the aggregate economy has been criticised on the grounds of reverse causation and for failing to explain cross-country productivity differences (Ford-Poret, 1991). Environmental regulation provides only a partial explanation of the productivity slowdown, and only for a few specific industries, *e.g.*, electric utilities. Baily-Gordon (1988) use Bishops' earlier work to argue that declining test scores can explain at best 0.2-0.3 percentage points of the overall productivity growth slowdown.

[3] See Gordon (1998), Tables 3 and 4.

[4] Nordhaus (1982) christened his pessimistic interpretation the "depletion hypothesis," that we were running out of resources and ideas. Abramovitz (1986, 1991) regards the first 25 years after the war as a unique period when simultaneously the production possibility frontier expanded rapidly and as well the possibility of "realisation" of this potential was unusually favourable.

[5] Abramovitz (1991, Table 2, col. 1) shows that mean productivity in Maddison's sample of 15 countries (Europe and Japan) fell from 77 percent of the U.S. level in 1870, to 61 percent in 1913, to 46 percent in 1950, and then recovered to 69 percent by 1973 and 76 percent by 1986.

American golden age began much earlier, around the time of World War I, and that a substantial part of the great leap in the level of multi-factor productivity had already occurred by the end of World War II.

Unlike the common image of a step function, with steady MFP growth through 1973 and a post-1973 step down to a lower level, this paper shows that another image is more appropriate, that of "one big wave." Starting the record at 1870, MFP growth was slow until 1890, then accelerated and reached a crescendo in the five or six decades starting around World War I (1913-72), and then decelerated until in 1972-96 it reached a rate similar to that in 1870-1913.

The big wave image raises at least two big questions, (1) "is it real?" and (2) "what caused it?" Was there indeed a "golden age" of economic growth that spanned the half century between 1913 and 1972, in contrast to a more normal situation of slow growth before and after?[6] If so, why did the big wave occur? Was there a happy coincidence of particular innovations that created unusually rapid MFP growth during this period? If so, are we forced to conclude pessimistically that slow growth since 1972 has been normal and that we may never return to the earlier years of glory?

This paper is about both questions, "is it real?" and "what caused it?" We establish the existence of the big wave in the official U.S. data and then examine numerous measurement issues which could either cut down the peak of the wave or boost its post-1972 wake. We construct and extend previous estimates of changes in the *composition* of labour and capital inputs, which depending on semantics could be considered as errors in the measurement of inputs or explanations of the growth rate in MFP, and in addition make corrections to the quantity of capital input. In explaining the big wave, we give primary attention to the many great inventions of the late 19th and early 20th centuries. Compared with these, the information technology (IT) "revolution", which dates back to the first commercial mainframe computer in 1954, is smaller-scale and less important than the real revolution caused by the earlier cluster of "great inventions." Other hypotheses are also examined, including the idea that immigration and flexible markets made labour cheap both before World War I and in the past two decades, thus driving down real wages and labour's marginal product, whereas during the "big wave" period controls on immigration and the growing influence of labour unions worked in the opposite direction.

---

[6]   Abramovitz (1991, Table 1) cites his own earlier research as indicating that MFP growth was only 0.45 percent per year over the entire nineteenth century, 1800-1905.

1.2   Plan of the Paper

The paper begins in Section 2 by examining data since 1870 on the growth rates of output, labour input, and two types of capital input, namely structures and equipment. We examine some critical relationships that have not received much attention, including the relationship between the big wave in MFP growth and the jump between the 1920s and 1950s in the output/structures ratio. Section 3 turns to existing post-war data on secular changes in the quality of labour and capital and then attempts to extend backwards before World War II estimates of changes in labour quality using a consistent methodology. Section 4 examines several issues in measuring the quantity and composition of capital that relate equally to the inter-war and post-war period, and Section 5 provides new quantitative estimates of the secular growth in labour and capital input and in MFP itself. Section 6 provides an overview of several hypotheses that together are promising in providing an explanation of the big wave. The most important of these is the concurrence of five great clusters of inventions in the late nineteenth and early twentieth century. Complementary explanations involve the closing off of the U.S. economy to immigrant workers and to imported goods between the 1920s and 1960s. Section 7 concludes.

2.   BASIC DATA ON OUTPUT AND INPUTS

2.1   Data Sources and their Main Features

While there are many sources of data on output and input growth in the U.S. economy over the last 125 years, three basic sources remain paramount. The U.S. National Income and Product Accounts (NIPA) provide a consistent set of accounts on the income and product side since 1929. For gross product originating (or value added) by industry the accounts are more difficult to use, since the current methodology has been extended back only to 1977, and previous estimates back to 1948 are based on a methodology that differs in many major and minor aspects. The NIPA also include data on employment and hours of labour input on a consistent basis, and the agency that produces the NIPA (Bureau of Economic Analysis, or BEA) also maintains data on capital stocks by industry since 1925.

Another complementary data set on aggregate output and input, available annually for 1948-96, is maintained by the Bureau of Labor Statistics

(BLS).[7] While the BEA is the basic source for the output and capital input data used by the BLS, and the BLS is the basic source for the labour input data used by the BEA, there are two important differences. First, the BLS data are available only for three sectors – private business, private nonfarm business, and manufacturing. In contrast, the BEA data set is available for roughly 60 two-digit industries.[8] Second, the BLS data incorporate for the period since 1948 the results of extensive research on the composition of labour and capital, inspired in large part by the work of Denison on labour input and of Dale W. Jorgenson and Zvi Griliches (1967) on both labour and capital input, whereas the BEA data contain no information at all on the composition of labour or capital input.

The third data set is the classic work by John Kendrick (1961) which provides time series on output, labour input, and capital input for major (one-digit) industry divisions over the long period between 1870 and 1953. The best match to extend the Kendrick data to the present on a consistent basis is the BEA data set, because it has much more disaggregated detail than the BLS data. Like the Kendrick data, the BEA data contain no compositional adjustments. We will turn in the next section to the BLS composition adjustments and how much they explain of the growth in the Kendrick/BEA MFP series. Subsequently we will explore the possibility of extending back before 1948 similar composition adjustments for labour and capital input.

2.2   MFP Growth and the Output-Capital Ratio Puzzle

This paper ignores inputs of energy and imported materials and considers only inputs of labour and capital. In this context it is obvious that the growth rate of MFP (m) is a weighted average of the growth of average labour productivity $(y\text{-}n)$ and of the average product of capital $(y\text{-}k)$:

$$m = y - \alpha n - (1-\alpha)k = \alpha(y-n) + (1-\alpha)(y-k) \qquad (1)$$

Here α is the share of labour and reflects the standard joint assumptions of constant returns to scale and competitive factor pricing.

In the 1960s, largely as the result of data then newly published by Kendrick (1961) and Kuznets (1961), economists became aware of the puzzling behaviour of the output-capital ratio. If one ignored the years within the 1929-48 interval in which economic relations were distorted by

---

[7]   Since the conference version of this paper was written, the data set described here has been extended to 1996 and will soon be extended to 1998.

[8]   BEA data on hours of labour input are only available at the one-digit industry level while output, employment, and capital stock data are available at the two-digit level.

the Great Depression and World War II, it was clear that between the 1920s and 1950s there had been a sharp one-time leap in the output-capital ratio, *i.e.*, the average product of capital. In terms of Equation (1), the growth rate *(y-k)* was much faster during the decades of the 1930s and 1940s than in any other two-decade period in recorded U.S. history. Clearly, if the average product of labour grew steadily, then measured MFP growth (*m*) would be unusually high during the period of the spurt in (*y-k*).[9]

Figure 1 begins our examination of the "standard" data on output and labour input based on splicing the Kendrick and BEA data sets at their intersection point of 1929. Details of data collection for the standard data are provided in the Data Appendix. Sectoral capital stock data come from Kendrick before 1925 and from the BEA capital stock study since 1925. As discussed below, there is a "rupture" in the BEA data source on capital, in that several data series previously compiled (*e.g.*, capital retirements) have been discontinued, and this has required some improvisation to achieve a consistent historical record.

Figure 1 displays the output/capital ratio separately for equipment and structures in the top frame and for the total capital stock, *i.e.*, equipment and structures together, in the bottom frame. The jump in the output/equipment ratio observed during 1936-44 was transitory. By 1966 the ratio had returned to its level of 1929, and the ratio declined steadily after 1966. But the jump for the output/structures ratio was huge and permanent. The average ratio for 1960-96 (1.13) was almost double the 1929 ratio of 0.59 and more than 2.5 times the average ratio for 1890-99 of 0.42. The ratio of output to total capital (equipment plus structures) in the bottom frame is dominated by structures (which were 5.0 times the constant-dollar value of equipment in 1929).

---

[9] The jump in the output-capital ratio intrigued me sufficiently to devote my Ph. D. dissertation (Gordon, 1967) to explaining it. This paper represents a return to several themes that remained unresolved at that time. My attention to the big wave was drawn by Duménil and Levy (1990), who call attention to this "rupture" in technical change without decomposing it by sector nor providing any link to the several aspects of capital input mis-measurement that in substantial part are responsible for it.

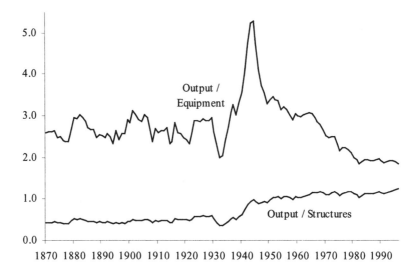

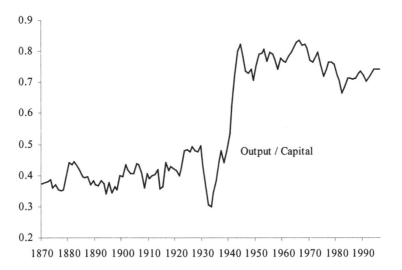

sources: see data appendix

Figure 1. Alternative Ratios of Output to Capital, 1992 Prices, Nonfarm Nonhousing Private Economy, 1870-1996

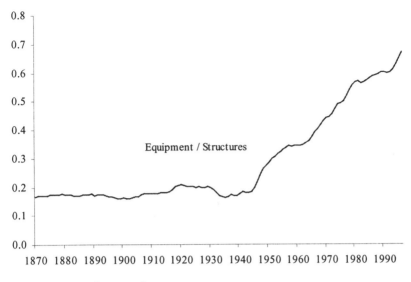

sources: see data appendix

Figure 2. Ratio of Equipment to Structures, 1992 Prices, Nonfarm Nonhousing Private Economy, 1870-1996

As shown in the top frame of Figure 1 the jump in the ratio for structures was permanent but that for equipment was temporary. A corollary is that the ratio of equipment to structures, as shown in Figure 2, exhibits a steady and relentless increase beginning in the mid-1930s from an average of about 0.18 for 1870-1913 to an average of 0.62 for 1990-96. This dramatic feature of the historical record has received surprisingly little attention; clearly there has been a continuous bias toward space-saving innovation in the development of new equipment as compared to the equipment that was in place in the late 1920s.

Figure 3 compares average labour productivity (output per hour, or ALP) with MFP over the full period since 1870. While both ALP and MFP exhibit a high degree of cyclical volatility, the log-linear trends drawn through selected years reveal several features of long-run trends.[10] The first is that the

---

[10] The use of piecewise loglinear detrending implicitly involves the same method of separating trend and cycle as the more formal approach of Blanchard and Quah (1989), and this is to assume that the unemployment rate is stationary in the long run, that output is not, and that demand disturbances can be represented by shocks that occur in common to unemployment and to deviations of output from trend. The years used to identify trends are 1870, 1891, 1913, 1928, 1950, 1964, 1972, 1979, 1988, and 1996. These are "cyclically neutral" years chosen to smooth out the effects of recessions, depressions, and wartime booms. All the years chosen for the post-war have roughly the same

big wave phenomenon is evident for both ALP and MFP, with faster growth
during the middle period (1913-72) than in either the early or late periods.
The second is that the big wave phenomenon is more pronounced for MFP
than for ALP, and in the framework of Equation (1) above this is the
counterpart of the jump in the output-capital ratio in the middle period.

Table 1. Outputs, Inputs, and MFP for Non-farm Non-housing Business GDP, Annual Growth
Rates over Selected Intervals, 1870-1996

Years	Output	Labour	Capital	MFP
1870-1891	4.41	3.56	4.48	0.39
1891-1913	4.43	2.92	3.85	1.14
1913-1928	3.11	1.42	2.21	1.42
1928-1950	2.75	0.91	0.74	1.90
1950-1964	3.50	1.41	2.89	1.47
1964-1972	3.63	1.82	4.08	0.89
1972-1979	2.99	2.38	3.46	0.16
1979-1988	2.55	1.09	3.35	0.59
1988-1996	2.74	1.74	2.26	0.79
Long-term Trends				
Years	Output	Labour	Capital	MFP
1870-1913	4.42	3.24	4.16	0.77
1913-1972	3.14	1.28	2.07	1.60
1972-1996	2.75	1.71	2.98	0.62

Sources: see Data Appendix

Several dimensions of the "big wave" phenomenon evident in Figure 3
are quantified more precisely in Table 1. Here are presented annual
(logarithmic) percentage growth rates for output, inputs, and MFP in the
non-farm non-housing private business sector. The top section of the table
exhibits growth rates for nine medium-term intervals, the same as those used
to draw the log-linear trends in Figure 3. The bottom section identifies long-
term trends by dividing the full period into three intervals split at 1913 and
1972. The middle period has not only the fastest growth rate of MFP but also
the slowest growth rates of labour and capital.[11] We note that the "big wave"

---

unemployment rate, close to 5.5 percent. The long time span between 1928 and 1950 is
intended to eliminate the impact of the Great Depression and World War II. While 1941
would be a possible interim year, distortions in output and labour markets (with rapid
inflation, excess demand, and continuing residual unemployment) might create misleading
results.

[11] The tendency for input growth and MFP growth to be negatively correlated over long time
intervals was observed in Romer (1987).

is roughly symmetric, in that the final 1972-96 period has about the same rate of MFP growth as the initial period 1870-1913.

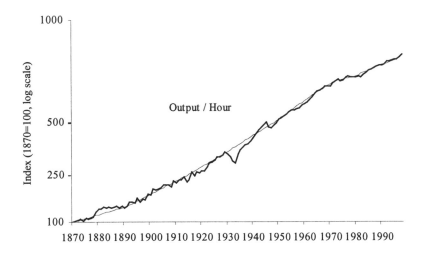

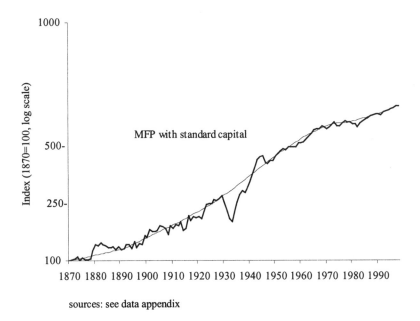

sources: see data appendix

Figure 3. Output per Hour and Multifactor Productivity in the Nonfarm Nonhousing Private Economy, 1870-1996

3.   COMPOSITION ADJUSTMENTS FOR LABOUR AND CAPITAL

Dating from the pioneering work of Denison (1962) and Jorgenson-Griliches (1967), it has been conventional to explain part of the growth in MFP as the result of an improvement in the quality of labour. The BLS has adopted the framework of Jorgenson (1990) and publishes its indexes of labour and capital input, and of MFP, *after* correcting for changes in labour and capital composition.

In the rest of this paper, we shall use the word "composition" in preference to the somewhat misleading alternative label "quality" to describe the resulting adjustments to the growth of inputs. The increased growth in labour input that results from placing greater weight on more highly educated workers, in proportion to the incomes earned by those with higher educational attainments, clearly warrants labelling as an increase in labour quality. However, a decline in the growth rate of labour input, as in the 1970s, that results from rapid growth in the share of females in the labour force and the lower earnings weights attributable to females should not be called a "decline in quality" – this is not only inaccurate, but even offensive. Similarly, the adjustments to the growth in capital input reflect primarily the higher depreciation rate and hence rental price of equipment relative to structures, yielding a faster growth rate of capital input than in the dollar-weighted capital stock when the share of equipment is increasing relative to structures. Again, it is misleading to refer to this as an "increase in capital quality" instead of labelling it for what it is, a "shift to shorter-lived assets."

3.1   The Post-war Impact of Changing Input Composition

The labour composition adjustments are obtained by the BLS by developing Tornqvist-weighted aggregates of the hours worked by all persons, classified by education, work experience, and gender. Weights are shares of labour compensation in each group. Thus an increase in the share of higher-educated or more experienced employees will be interpreted as a positive change in labour composition, whereas an increase in the share of less-experienced teenagers would represent a negative change in labour composition.

The capital composition adjustments are obtained by weighting four types of capital (equipment, structures, inventories, and land) separately within each of 53 industries using estimated rental prices for each asset type. Since the rental price includes both the net return to capital and depreciation, any shift toward short-lived assets would be interpreted as an increase in the composition of capital. As we have seen in Figure 2, there has been a continuous shift from structures to equipment since the 1930s, and this emerges in the Jorgenson-BLS method as implying a continuous upward movement in the composition of capital.

Table 2. Annual percentage growth rates of output, inputs, and MFP, with and without composition adjustments, for non-farm business GDP, 1950-1996

	1950-64	1964-72	1972-79	1979-88	1988-96
Output (*Y*)	4.35	4.23	3.60	3.14	1.98
Labour					
Hours (*H*)	0.99	1.64	2.18	1.85	1.16
Composition	0.40	-0.03	0.00	0.54	0.52
Quality-Adjusted (*L*)	1.38	1.61	2.18	2.39	1.67
Capital					
Stock (*K*)	2.91	3.82	3.23	3.31	1.74
Composition	0.85	1.29	1.23	1.45	0.59
Quality-Adjusted (*J*)	3.76	5.11	4.46	4.76	2.33
MFP					
Based on *H* and *K*	2.69	1.83	1.08	0.84	0.70
Based on *L* and *J*	2.23	1.54	0.75	0.04	0.11
Effect of Quality Adj.	0.46	0.28	0.32	0.80	0.59
Addenda:					
Y/H	3.36	2.59	1.42	1.29	0.83
Y/L	2.97	2.61	1.42	0.75	0.31
Y/K	1.44	0.41	0.37	-0.17	0.25
Y/J	0.59	-0.88	-0.85	-1.63	-0.35

Sources: *Y,L,J*, Adjusted MFP from Multifactor Productivity Trends, 1995 and 1996, BLS, Release USDL 98-187, May 6, 1998.
H,K, and composition effects provided in unpublished e-mails from Michael Harper of the BLS. MFP based on *H* and *K* was calculated by aggregating *H* and *K* using the same implicit weights as are used by the BLS to aggregate *L* and *J*.

The Kendrick and BEA data used to construct Table 1 do not contain any adjustments for labour or capital composition. Now we turn to Table 2 which indicates the magnitude of the composition adjustments. The top line of Table 2 displays growth rates of output, which in the BLS data are more rapid than the BEA data used in Table 1 for 1950-88 but slower for 1988-96.

The next section distinguishes the growth rates of composition-unadjusted hours of labour input (as used in Table 1) from the composition-adjusted growth rates that include the effects of changing composition across education, experience, and gender categories. During 1964-79 it appears that the benefits of increasing educational attainment were cancelled out by a shift toward less experienced teenagers and the rapid inflow of females into the labour force. After 1979 the share of teenagers declined and the female labour force participation rate levelled off, allowing the positive impact of increasing educational attainment to be augmented by a slight increase in workforce experience.

The next section provides the composition adjustments for capital. Somewhat surprisingly, in view of the growing importance of short-lived computer capital, the compositional adjustment for capital grows more slowly in the most recent period (1988-96) than in any of the earlier periods. As a result of this phenomenon and of slower growth in the capital stock, the growth rate of composition-adjusted capital input falls by half when the most recent period is compared to the middle three periods. This helps to explain why composition-adjusted MFP growth ("based on L and J") in the next section of Table 2 is slightly faster in 1988-96 than in 1979-88, despite the fact that ALP growth measured by either Y/H or Y/L declines sharply in the final period.

Because the combined effect of the composition adjustments is greatest in the final two periods, the growth rate of MFP slows more sharply over the post-war period when the composition adjustments are included than when they are excluded, and indeed composition-adjusted MFP growth is barely positive over 1979-96. Similarly, the bottom section of Table 2 shows that ALP growth slows somewhat more from 1950-64 to 1988-96 when the effects of the labour composition adjustment are included. We also note in the bottom section of Table 2 that the output-capital ratio that takes account of capital composition change (Y/J) declines at about one percent per year after 1964. This decline in the average product of capital and the accompanying decline in capital's marginal product may raise a question as to the priority of increasing national saving and investment as a "cure" for the productivity slowdown.[12]

3.2   Changes in Labour Composition, 1913-50

Further to understand the "big wave" phenomenon, we must develop measures of changes in labour composition for years prior to the post-war coverage of the BLS composition adjustments. Fortunately the elements of

---

[12] The decline in the marginal product of capital was noted in this context by Baily and Schultze (1990).

such adjustments back to 1909 have already been developed in Denison's seminal initial book (1962) on the sources of economic growth. However, Denison's techniques and assumptions are not consistent with the current BLS methodology, so in this section we lay out Denison's calculations and compute the changes needed to make them consistent with the BLS data discussed above for the post-war period.

Table 3. Elements of Denison's Quality Corrections to Labour Input, Annual Percentage Growth Rates, Total Economy, 1913-79

	1913-28	1928-50	1950-64	1964-72	1972-79
1. Employment	1.35	1.01	0.64	1.87	2.70
2. Potential hours per employee	-0.38	-0.75	-0.36	-0.63	-0.61
3. Hours of labour input (1+2)	0.97	0.36	0.28	1.24	2.10
4. Labour input (3+5)	1.36	0.78	0.46	1.43	2.23
5. Quality adjustment for hours (4-3)	0.39	0.42	0.18	0.19	0.14
6. Quality adjustment for education	0.57	0.62	0.60	0.67	0.75
7. Quality adjustment for age, gender	0.11	0.02	-0.06	-0.45	-0.47
8. Total quality adjustment (5+6+7)	1.07	1.06	0.72	0.40	0.42
9. Alternative education adjustment	0.49	0.48	0.54	0.71	0.84
10. Alt. total quality adjustment (7+9)	0.60	0.50	0.48	0.25	0.37
Elements of Education Adjustment	1910-30	1930-50	1950-64	1964-72	1972-76
11. Effect of increased years of education	0.30	0.38	0.43	0.56	0.67
12. Effect of increased days per year of education	0.27	0.23	0.17	0.11	0.08
13. Total education adjustment	0.57	0.62	0.60	0.67	0.75

Sources for 1913-28 by line number: (1,2,4): Denison (1962), Table 5, p. 37.: (6,7): Denison (1962), Table 11, p. 85; (9): Line 11 divided by 0.6; (11,12): Denison (1962), Table 9, p. 72.
Sources for 1928-79 by line number (note that 1929 data in sources below are extrapolated backwards from 1929 to 1928 using sources for 1913-28 listed above): (1): Denison (1985), Table 3-1, p. 85, col. 1; (2) Denison (1985), Table 3-2, p. 86, col. 2; (5): Denison (1985), Table 3-1, p. 85, col. 9 divided by potential hours from the source of line 2; (9): Line 11 divided by 0.8; (11): Denison (1979), Table F-5, p. 169, col. 1; (13): Denison (1979), Table F-5, p. 169, col. 3.

Denison made two controversial assumptions in developing his labour composition adjustments. First, he did not use hours as his basic measure of labour input, but rather assumed that effort per hour increased as hours per week decreased from 52.0 in 1909 to 39.8 in 1957. Second, he adjusted downward by 40 percent the effect of increased educational attainment for the assumed contribution of ability to earnings differentials across educational categories. That is, if a college graduate earned 100 percent more than that of a high school graduate, Denison assumed that only 60 percent of this differential represented the contribution of higher education and the remaining 40 percent represented the contribution of the higher assumed innate ability of college graduates.[13]

Table 3 displays the ingredients in Denison's calculations and the changes needed to create a series that is consistent with BLS methodology. Since Denison's adjustments are presented as annual time series, we can calculate logarithmic percentage growth rates over the same intervals that are defined in Tables 1 and 2.[14] Line 1 lists the growth in total employment, while line 2 shows the negative rate of change of "potential" hours per employee (here "potential" is used in the sense of eliminating the effect of the business cycle). Growth in hours of labour input are then computed in line 3 as the sum of the first two lines and contrasted with Denison's computation of total labour input in line 4. The difference between line 4 and line 3, displayed separately in line 5, represents Denison's adjustment for the assumed effect of shorter hours per week on output per hour.

Denison made the assumption that at or above the hours per week prevailing in 1929 (48.6) a given percentage decrease in hours per week would increase productivity per hour by the same amount, *e.g.*, he assumed an elasticity of productivity to weekly hours of -1.0. At the lower level of weekly hours (39.8) reached in 1957, he assumed an elasticity of -0.4, and he interpolated between the 1929 and 1957 values of weekly hours. Stated another way, Denison's approach assumes that a reduction from the 1929 level of weekly hours per employee has no impact on output per employee, while a one percent reduction from the 1957 level of weekly hours per employee reduces output per employee by 0.6 percent. The effect of Denison's approach can be seen in the shifting elasticity of productivity to reductions on hours per employee – the ratio of line 5 to line 2 – which amounts to -1.03 for 1913-28, -0.56 for 1928-50, -0.50 for 1950-64, -0.30 for 1964-72, and -0.23 for 1972-79.[15]

---

[13] Partly stimulated by Denison's assumption, there was a vast outpouring of research on education and ability in the 1960s. As summarised by Griliches (2000), this research found no consistent or significant influence of ability on earnings differentials by educational category.

[14] Denison's 1962 book contained data through 1958 and projections through 1965 and later years. His 1985 book contained data for 1929 through 1982. As stated in the notes to Table 3, we use the 1962 data to cover our 1913-28 period and the 1985 book for 1928-79, backcasting the 1929 data in the 1985 book to 1928 using 1928-29 data as presented in the 1962 book.

[15] The description here of Denison's procedure refers to his first (1962) book. His procedure in his 1985 book is more complex, treats different age-sex cohorts of part-time and full-time workers separately, and chooses somewhat lower elasticities than in the 1962 book.

Denison's adjustment for education involves two changes from the standard Jorgenson/BLS technique of using observed wages by educational attainment category to attribute a productivity gain to increasing educational attainment over time. Denison multiplies the results of this compositional adjustment by 0.6, reflecting his assumption that differences in ability rather than educational attainment explains 40 percent of observed differences in earnings across educational attainment categories. Thus the estimated effect in the first column, line 11, of 0.30 percent per year represents the multiplication of the compositional adjustment of 0.5 by 0.6 to reflect the 40 percent deducation for the assumed ability contribution. Then on line 12 Denison boosts his estimate by assuming that any percentage increase in the number of school days per year has the same effect on productivity as a like percentage increase in the number of school years per person. The total education effect calculated by Denison for decadal intervals is listed on line 13 and translated into an annual series for individual years on line 6.[16]

Denison's final calculation is a compositional adjustment for age and sex, with an additional adjustment for the increased relative earnings of females. This age-sex adjustment as listed on line 7 makes only a small contribution to his final composition adjustment for labour input listed on line 8. Clearly, the Denison methodology leads to a very large labour composition effect, much larger than the BLS composition effect in Table 2 for the overlapping periods of 1950-79.

However, Denison's large adjustments do not correspond to the methodology currently used by the BLS, which does not make any adjustment for the effect of changing hours per week on productivity, any adjustment for changes in school days per school year, nor any adjustment for ability in calculating the impact of increasing educational attainment. To compute a new set of labour composition adjustments for 1913-79 using Denison's data, we eliminate the composition adjustment for changing hours per week. Then for the educational adjustment, we take only the impact of increasing school years per person (line 11) and ignore the impact of increasing school days per year (line 12), and subsequently divide the resulting composition adjustment by 0.6 for 1913-28 and 0.8 for 1928-79 to eliminate the assumed ability adjustment. The resulting "alternative" labour composition adjustment as displayed on line 10 is substantially smaller than the Denison concept on line 8, although the difference shinks through time. The alternative labour composition adjustment is only slightly higher than the BLS adjustment for 1950-64 but much higher for 1964-79.

---

[16] The 40 percent ability offset used in Denison's 1962 book was reduced to 20 percent in the 1985 book, and it is this later figure that is relevant in the columns of Table 3 covering the post-1928 period.

Claudia Goldin (1998, p. 346) provides some additional perspective on changes in education as an explanation of the "big wave": "Human capital accumulation and technological change were to the twentieth century what physical capital accumulation was to the nineteenth century – the engine of growth." She documents the revolution in secondary education attendance in the three decades after 1910, with enrolment rates rising from 18 to 73 percent between 1910 and 1940 and goes further in attributing to the secondary school revolution a substantial part of America's productivity advantage over European nations.[17] Goldin goes further by creating new estimates of graduation rates for 1910 that are substantially lower than implied by the 1940 Census of Population, implying a more rapid growth rate of educational attainment than in the official data. We do not pursue this bias further, because Denison was already aware of this bias and made an adjustment for it. Whether or not Denison's bias correction is consistent with Goldin's new results is a complex issue that lies beyond the scope of this paper.[18]

3.3   Changes in Labour Composition, 1870-1913

Denison's treatment of labour quality begins in 1909 but the current paper computes MFP starting in 1870. In this section we shall ignore changes in age-sex composition, which in table 3 are negligible prior to 1964 and focus on changes in labour composition attributable to education. What information is available to compute a labour quality adjustment for the period 1870-1909? Goldin (1988, Figure 1, p. 348) shows that during the 1890-1910 interval the percentage of those aged 14-17 graduating from secondary school increased only from about 4 to 9 percent and thus had a much smaller effect on the quality of the labour force than the increase from 9 to 52 percent that occurred between 1910 and 1940. Was there an equivalent explosion in elementary school enrolment during 1870-1910 that would have implied an increase in educational attainment comparable to that after 1910?

[17] "But the countries whose per capita incomes were closest to that of the United States in 1910 did not undergo an equivalent transformation at that time. Rather, their high school movements did not materialise for another thirty or more years. . . Not only was the high school movement from 1910 to 1940 a uniquely-American phenomenon, the secondary school as we know it today was a uniquely-American invention" (Goldin, 1998, pp. 349-50).

[18] See Denison (1962), pp. 70-71.

Table 4. Elementary School Enrolment as a Share of Population Aged 5-14, and Illiterate Share of Total Population, Selected Years, 1870-1930

	1870	1890	1910	1930
1. Enrollment in Kindergarten and Grades 1-8 (thousands)	7481	12520	16898	21278
2. Population aged 5-14 (thousands)	8287	12465	16393	21855
3. Percent of Population Enrolled	90.3	100.4	103.1	97.4
4. Illiterate as Percent of Population aged 10 and over	11.5	7.7	5.0	3.0

Source: Historical Statistics of the United States from Colonial Times to the Present, Bureau of the Census, 1960: (Line 1): series H226; (line 2): series A72 plus A73; (line 3) equals line 1 as a percent of line 2; (line 4): series H408.
Note: a. 1871 rather than 1870.

Two measures of educational attainment prior to 1910 are displayed in Table 4. The first line displays enrollment in elementary schools (kindergarten plus grades 1-8), which can be compared with the population aged 5-14, as displayed on the second line. The percent of the population enrolled is displayed on the third line and displays remarkably little increase over the 60 years shown, only from 90 to 97 percent. Consistent with this evidence that elementary education was already standard by 1870 (at least for the white population) is the final line which shows the illiteracy rate for the same years, implying that literacy for whites was already 88.5 percent in 1870, reaching 97.0 percent in 1930.

It remains to translate this information into an estimate of the change in educational attainment. Goldin (1998, Table 1, p. 346) provides a distribution of educational attainment that distinguishes between the percentage distribution in each grade interval (8 or below, 9-11, 12, and over 12) and the mean years of attainment in each interval. This is presented for three cohorts, those born, respectively, in 1886-90, 1926-30, and 1946-50. To estimate years of educational attainment forty years earlier for the cohort born 1846-50, we take Goldin's attainments for the 1886-90 group, cut the percentage in each of the higher three intervals (9-11, 12, and over 12) in half, redistributing them to the 8 and below group, and then cut mean years for the elementary school group by half a year. This yields average attainment for our early cohort of 6.23 years, compared to Goldin's three cohorts of 7.58, 11.46, and 12.82, respectively.

The annual growth rate between our early cohort and Goldin's earliest is 0.49 percent per year, compared with annual growth between Goldin's three cohorts of 1.03 percent and 0.56, respectively. If we take a person aged 42 to be in the midst of working life, then the implication is that the growth rate of educational attainment for adult workers was 0.49 percent per year between 1890 and 1930, 1.03 percent between 1930 and 1970, and 0.56 percent per year between 1970 and 1990.[19] There is a puzzling conflict between Denison's education adjustment (either line 9 or 11 of Table 3), which is most rapid in his final period of 1972-79, and Goldin's attainment series, which reaches its peak growth rate (when applied to the working-age adult population) around 1950 and then falls by half between 1950 and 1980.

The best we can do with our available information is to estimate that the growth of educational attainment in the late nineteenth century was about half that of the mid-twentieth century, which would reduce Denison's 0.54 percent for 1950-64 (Table 3, line 9) to 0.27 percent per annum. However, there is one additional step, which is to convert changes in educational attainment into changes in labour quality by applying earnings differentials across education-attainment groups. Translating changes in the growth rate of educational attainment directly into changes in labour quality would be valid only if the rate of return to increase in education had remained constant over time, which it clearly has not. In fact, Goldin and Katz (1999, Figure 4) estimate that the returns to high school education fell by half between 1914 and 1949, before recovering almost to their previous level. Since the rate of return on increases in high school enrolment were much higher around 1910 than in the middle of the century, this would appear roughly to cancel out the slower growth of educational attainment in the earlier period. As a result, we shall assume in the rest of this paper that labour quality increased during 1870-1913 at 0.5 percent per year, roughly the same as Denison's educational adjustment (Table 3, line 9) over the entire period 1913-64.

4.   ISSUES IN THE MEASUREMENT OF CAPITAL

In addition to the questions raised in the previous section about techniques for computing labour composition adjustments, questions can be raised as well about output and capital input data in every interval. As we go back in time, price deflators on which output and capital input data are based become more problematical, as they rely on thinner and thinner samples of the final products actually sold at the time.

---

[19] For instance, the first growth rate of 0.49 percent per year is between cohorts with a mean birth year of 1848 and 1888, who would be 42-year-old adult workers in 1890 and 1930, respectively. The final growth rate of 0.56 percent per year is between birth cohorts with a mean birth year of 1928 and 1948, who would be 42-year-old adult workers in 1970 and 1990, respectively.

Here we concentrate on issues involving the growth of capital input. The close relationship of capital to the "one big wave" phenomenon is clear in comparing Figures 1 and 3 as discussed above, where the spike in the growth rate of MFP in the 1928-50 interval (the level of which is shown in the lower frame of Figure 3) corresponds to the period when the output-capital ratio (shown in the lower frame of Figure 1) made its one-time permanent jump. In addition to showing that the timing of the big wave and of the sharp jump in the output-capital ratio is identical, Figures 1 and 3 (and the *Y/J* ratio in Table 2) also show that the period of slow productivity growth since the mid 1960s has also been a period of a falling output-capital ratio. The latter phenomenon has been interpreted by Martin Baily and Charles Schultze (1990) as evidence of diminishing returns to capital, supporting the traditional Solow growth model against claims by Paul Romer (1990) and others that measured income shares understate the contribution of capital to output growth.

The purpose of this section is to consider several issues in the measurement of capital that, taken together, may help to explain the sharp jump in the output-capital ratio displayed in the bottom frame of Figure 1. These are the shifting composition of different types of capital, retirement patterns, and the role of government-owned capital in contributing to private production. The following sections introduce each issue and discuss the results of an attempt to provide a step-by-step re-measurement of capital input that deals with each issue in turn.

4.1   Adjustment for Changing Composition

Jorgenson and Griliches (1967) pioneered the use of service price weights for capital, based on the argument that the marginal product of each type of capital, *e.g.*, structures and equipment, is equal at the margin to its service price, and a more refined version of their approach has been adopted by the BLS in the capital composition adjustments displayed in Table 2 above. For instance, the service price of equipment is the relative price of equipment (p^E) times the sum of the real interest rate and depreciation rate ($r+\delta^E$), and similarly for structures. Since the depreciation rate for equipment is roughly four times that for structures, the use of service price weights substantially raises the share of equipment in capital input and diminishes the share of structures.

Since the big wave in MFP growth is related to the 1928-50 jump in the structures-output ratio (Figure 1), a reduction in the weight on structures indirectly dampens the big wave. Thus our task in this paper is to develop an adjustment for the shifting equipment-to-structures ratio (Figure 2) that applies to the period prior to the BLS post-war capital composition adjustments.

Already introduced in Table 2 and repeated in Table 5, column (2), are the capital composition adjustments provided by the BLS for the 1948-96 interval. These are obtained, as stated above, by weighting four types of capital (equipment, structures, inventories, and land) separately within each of 53 industries using estimated rental prices for each asset type. To extend these prior to 1948, our only information is on two types of capital, equipment and structures. Our approach is to create a crude composition index based only on reweighting equipment and structures for 1870-1996 and then compare it to the BLS capital composition index for the overlap period, 1948-96. Our crude index is the ratio of an index (1992=100) of the capital stock of equipment with a weight of three and structures with a weight of one (the "3:1 index") to a standard capital stock index which weights equipment and structures dollar-for-dollar (the "1:1 index"). The growth rate of this ratio is displayed in column (1) of Table 5.

Our capital composition index, that is, the ratio of the 3:1 to the 1:1 index displayed in column (1), grows steadily throughout the post-war period but more slowly than the BLS index shown in column (2) for the period after 1950, presumably because the BLS index contains additional reweighting within categories of equipment and across industries that has the effect of shortening the average lifetime of equipment and raising its service price. For the three intervals between 1950 and 1979, the growth rate of our crude composition index is slightly more or less than one-half the growth rate of the BLS capital composition index for various subperiods, averaging out to 0.56 for the full 1950-79 period.[20] Accordingly, we shall extrapolate the BLS composition index backwards before 1948 by dividing the growth rate of our crude composition index in column (1) by 0.56. Moving backwards, the BLS composition index in Table 2 grows by 1.29 percent per year in 1964-72 and 0.85 percent per year in 1950-64, and our extrapolated BLS index grows at 0.68 in 1928-50, 0.21 in 1913-28, mere 0.07 percent per year during 1870-1913. Thus the capital composition factor becomes important only after 1928, unlike changing labour composition which, at least along the educational dimension, is important throughout the 1870-1996 period. Subsequently we shall examine graphs which display the effects of the capital composition adjustment on the annual behaviour of capital input and of MFP over the 1870-1996 period.

---

[20] We omit the post-1979 period because it is most affected by the growing importance of computers, which play no role prior to 1948. It would make little difference to our results if we were to base the backcasting exercise only on the 1950-64 period; this would change our 0.56 backcasting factor to 0.49.

Table 5. Adjustments to Capital Input, Annual Growth Rates over Selected Intervals, 1870-1996

Years	Reweight Equipment 3:1	Back-cast BLS Comp. Adjustment	Effect of Variable Retirement			Add GOPO	Add High-ways
			Equip-Ment	Structures	Total		
	(1)	(2)	(3)	(4)	(5)	(6)	(7)
1870-1891	0.03	0.06	-.--	-.--	-.--	-.--	-.--
1891-1913	0.04	0.07	-.--	-.--	-.--	-.--	-.--
1913-1928	0.12	0.21	-.--	-.--	-.--	-.--	-.--
1928-1950	0.38	0.68	0.85	0.61	0.66	0.13	0.17
1950-1964	0.42	0.85	-1.11	-0.66	-0.76	-0.06	0.37
1964-1972	0.74	1.29	-0.69	-0.60	-0.64	-0.09	-0.01
1972-1979	0.77	1.23	-0.48	-0.49	-0.49	-0.03	-0.32
1979-1988	0.20	1.45	0.00	0.11	0.06	-0.02	-0.27
1988-1996	0.41	0.59	0.48	0.19	0.40	0.00	-0.13

Long-term Trends

Years							
1870-1913	0.03	0.07	-.--	-.--	-.--	-.--	-.--
1913-1972	0.37	0.68	-0.05	-0.01	-0.03	0.02	0.20
1972-1996	0.43	1.10	-0.02	-0.10	-0.07	-0.02	-0.24

Sources by Column:

(1): Equipment and structures data in 1992 dollars from same sources as Figures 1 and 2. Data shown in this column are the growth rate of the equipment and structures aggregate when each dollar of equipment capital is weighted 3.0 times one dollar of structures, minus the growth rate when equipment and structures are weighted dollar for dollar; (2): 1948-96, unpublished BLS series obtained from Michael Harper. 1870-1948, extrapolated backwards by dividing the growth rate of column 1 by 0.56, which is the average ratio of column 1 to column 2 during 1950-79; (3)-(5): See text and Data Appendix; (6)-(7): See Data Appendix.

Notes: Data listed for 1913-72 in columns (3)-(7) refer to 1925-72.

4.2   Variable Lifetimes

The single most important error in measuring capital input may be the inadequate allowance for quality change, the topic of my book on durable goods prices (1990). Unfortunately, a consistent set of new estimates of investment goods prices is available only for the period covered in that book, 1947-83, and only scattered evidence is available for earlier or later years. In particular, there is no readily available evidence that the bias in the growth rate of official price indexes for investment goods is higher or lower before or after the 1947-83 period than during that period. For the purposes of this paper, a continuous drift in measured price indexes relative to true prices does not have a major impact on the timing of MFP growth by decades. Even if the measurement error were different across decades, this would not skew our MFP calculations in a major way, simply because deflation errors affect both output and capital input growth in the same direction.[21]

Much more important in affecting the timing of capital input and MFP growth across decades is the universal assumption in standard capital data that service lifetimes and retirement patterns are constant. Yet Feldstein and Rothschild (1974) have argued that from a theoretical perspective a fixed retirement pattern is not optimal, and Feldstein and Foot (1971) showed on the basis of firm-level data that retirement patterns are variable and depend on firm cash flow and the state of the economy-wide business cycle. An "eyeball test" suggests that for both structures and equipment retirements occur when new investment occurs. Gross private investment was unusually low between 1930 and 1947 because of the Great Depression and World War II, and standard capital measures assume that buildings were being torn down on schedule during this period (leading to the implication that the annual growth rate of the capital stock dropped to nearly zero during 1928-50).[22] Yet Chicago's Loop and New York's Midtown were not littered with vacant lots during the 1930s and 1940s; the old buildings were still there.[23]

---

[21] For instance, I estimated for the 1947-83 period that the growth rate of capital input had been understated by 1.60 percent per year, but that this caused an overstatement of MFP growth by only 0.17 percent per year over the same 1947-83 period (Gordon, 1990, Table 12.14, column 5). Jorgenson (1966) showed theoretically that the impact of price measurement errors on MFP growth depend on the relative size of the share of investment in GDP and the share of capital in total income.

[22] Our standard capital stock series summarised in Table 1 grows at only 0.04 percent per year between 1929 and 1945. All of its growth rate for 1928-50 shown in Table 1 occurs during 1928-29 and 1945-50.

[23] A vivid example of the cessation in office building construction in the 1930s and 1940s occurs in Chicago, where the tallest building from 1930 to 1957 was the Board of Trade, but after 1957 the title for tallest building changed every year or two until 1973. The story is similar in other cities.

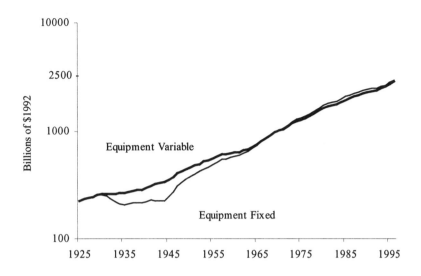

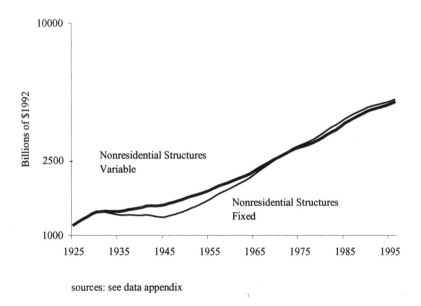

sources: see data appendix

Figure 4. Effect of Variable Retirement Pattern, 1925-1996

A simple way to allow for variable retirement patterns is to make the retirement rate depend on gross investment. This relationship can be derived from the empirical Equation estimated by Feldstein-Foot (1971):

$$\frac{R}{K} = \beta_0 + \beta_1 \left(\frac{F}{K} \right) + \beta_2 \left(\frac{N}{K} \right) + \beta_3 U \tag{2}$$

Here R/K is the ratio of retirements to the capital stock, *i.e.*, the retirement rate, F/K is the cash flow ratio, N/K is the net investment ratio, and U is the unemployment rate. To simplify this Equation for use here, we assume that both the cash flow ratio and unemployment rate depend on the ratio of gross investment to capital:

$$\frac{F}{K} = \alpha_0 + \alpha_1 \left(\frac{G}{K} \right) ; \ U = \gamma_0 + \gamma_1 \left(\frac{G}{K} \right) \tag{3}$$

Using the identity that

$$\frac{N}{K} \equiv \frac{G}{K} - \frac{R}{K}, \tag{4}$$

we can combine (3) and (4) and write a relationship between the retirement rate and the gross investment ratio:

$$\frac{R}{K} = A_0 + A_1 \left(\frac{G}{K} \right). \tag{5}$$

To convert Equation (5) into a specific adjustment in the capital stock series, we begin with BEA data on retirements and the ratio of gross investment to capital, available from 1925 to 1988.[24] No adjustment is performed before 1925, but this omission is not important since the motivation for the adjustment is the delay in retirements in the 1930s and 1940s caused by

---

[24] The basic computation was carried out on BEA gross investment and retirement data for the period 1925-88, as stated in the text. After these computations were carried out in 1992, the BEA changed the format of its historical capital stock data and no longer publishes gross investment or retirements. The current paper is based on the new BEA net investment data and bases its estimate of the effect of variable retirement on the previous results developed from the previous BEA gross investment and retirement data available for 1925-88.

unusually low gross investment during that period. The adjusted retirement rate $(R/K)^*$ is computed from the BEA data as follows:

$$\left(\frac{R}{K}\right)_t^* = \left(\frac{R}{K}\right)_t \frac{(G/K)_t}{\overline{(G/K)}} \tag{6}$$

Thus we simply multiply the BEA's retirement rate by the ratio of G/K in each year to its sample mean over 1925-1996. This procedure implies that retirements are reshuffled among the years between 1925 and 1996, but the average retirement rate over the entire period is maintained at the same level as in the BEA data.

The effect of the variable retirement adjustment is shown in Table 5 for equipment in column (3), for structures in column (4), and for the sum of equipment and structures in column (5). The effect is to make capital input grow faster over the 1928-50 period, as expected, and to grow slower during 1950-79. Over the entire 1925-96 period the effect of this adjustment is negligible, as is intended.

The adjustment is shown for the entire 1925-96 period in Figure 4, with the adjustment displayed for equipment in the top frame and for structures in the bottom frame. The shift to a variable retirement pattern substantially boosts the stock of both equipment and structures between 1929 and 1965 (for equipment) and 1970 (for structures). The ratio of the fixed-retirement capital stock for equipment reaches its low point relative to the variable retirement equipment stock in 1943-44 and for structures in 1945-50. As would be expected, the variable retirement pattern reduces the stock of both equipment and structures after 1975, since there was more capital existing in 1930-65 to be retired.

4.3   Omitted Capital

Part of the sharp rise in output during World War II was made possible by plants and equipment that were owned by the government but operated by private firms to produce goods and services. When the output-capital ratio puzzle was first discussed in the 1960s, the official statistics on capital input in the private sector did not keep track of this government-owned privately-operated (GOPO) capital, and thus the 1940-45 increase in the output-capital ratio (and hence in MFP) was exaggerated. After I studied this phenomenon and estimated its magnitude (1969), the BEA began to keep track of GOPO capital and includes it now as a separate category in its capital stock data bank. Thus we can show the impact of including GOPO capital, as in column

(6) of Table 5, which is to boost the growth rate of capital input during 1928-50 (all of this occurs in 1940-45) and to reduce it after 1950.

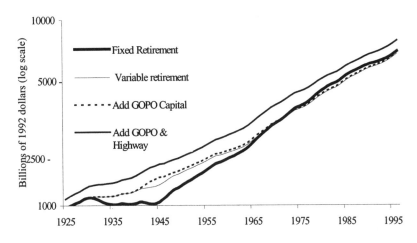

sources: see data appendix

Figure 5. Alternative Nonresidential Fixed Capital Aggregates, 1925-1996

A related issue is that a substantial part of government-owned infrastructure serves as an unmeasured input to production in the private sector. In particular, there has been a gradual shift over time in the transportation sector from privately owned railroad capital to publicly owned highways, airports, and air-traffic control facilities. Sufficient data are available to allow us to add to private capital input two types of government capital, GOPO in column (6) and highway capital in column (7) of Table 5, relying on Fraumeni's (1999) recent estimates of the latter. The effect of adding highway capital is to boost the growth rate of capital input in both the 1928-50 and 1950-64 periods but to reduce it thereafter, which has the effect of explaining a small part of the "big wave" of MFP growth during 1928-64 and a small part of the post-1972 MFP growth slowdown.[25]

The combined impact of changing from fixed to variable retirement, and of adding GOPO and highway capital, is illustrated for the 1925-96 period in Figure 5. Instead of declining by 7.4 percent between 1930 and 1944, total capital input actually increases by 28 percent (not counting the capital composition adjustment). This is clearly an important finding and highly

---

[25] Highway capital data are included only beginning in 1925. To avoid an artificial jump in total capital between 1924-25, the total capital measure including highway capital is ratio-linked in 1925 to avoid having any impact on the growth rate of capital from 1924 (or any earlier year) to 1925.

relevant to the puzzle of how the United States succeeded in producing so much during World War II. Subsequently we will take a broader look at the revised input series over the entire 1870-1996 period.

5.   SUMMARY OF INPUT DATA REVISIONS AND IMPLICATIONS FOR MFP

5.1   Corrections to Labour and Capital Input Data

We now take a tour of several graphs and tables that summarise the implications of our labour and capital composition adjustments, and of our capital quantity adjustments, for the full 1870-1996 period. The tables provide summary information on growth rates over the same intervals specified in Table 1, and the figures provide additional information by displaying all the years individually.

The effects of the labour composition adjustments on the level of labour input is shown in Figure 6 - the more rapid growth of composition-adjusted labour input combines the BLS composition series back to 1948, the Denison series adjusted to correspond with the BLS concept back from 1948 to 1913, and a guesstimate back to 1870 based on scattered evidence on enrolment rates, illiteracy, and the rate of return to high school education. The effects on growth rates over our standard intervals are shown in Table 6, where in column (3) the labour composition adjustment is shown to have about the same impact in raising labour input growth by about 0.5 percent per year in all periods except 1964-72 and 1972-79.

Columns (4) through (6) of Table 6 compare standard capital input with composition-adjusted capital input and with capital input adjusted both for composition and the three quantity adjustments quantified separately in Table 5 and Figure 5, namely the shift from fixed to variable retirement, the addition of GOPO capital, and the addition of highway capital. Unlike the labour composition adjustment, which has a similar effect in all intervals but 1964-79, the effect of the capital composition and quantity adjustments differ radically across intervals. By far the greatest impact is in 1928-50, the core period of the "big wave" in MFP growth, where there is a substantial impact of capital composition and where the other three adjustments (variable retirement, GOPO capital, and highway capital) all have sizeable effects. The combined capital adjustments also have substantial effects of close to one percentage point per year in three of the five post-war intervals, but virtually no impact prior to 1913. Thus the combined capital adjustments have the effect of reducing MFP growth after 1913 relative to pre-1913 MFP growth and reduce MFP most of all in 1928-50, 1964-72, and 1979-96. Figure 7 shows the same adjustments for each year back to 1870 and emphasises that the quantity adjustments had their greatest proportional effect in the 1940s while the composition adjustment made the most difference between 1964 and 1988.

Table 6. Summary of Input Adjustments, Selected Intervals, 1870-1996

Years	Standard Labour Input	Comp. Adjusted Labour Input	Effect of Labour Adjust-ment	Standard Capital Input	Comp. Adjusted Capital Input	Comp. & Quantity Adjusted Capital Input	Effect of Capital Adjust-ment
	(1)	(2)	(3)	(4)	(5)	(6)	(7)
1870-1891	3.56	4.05	0.49	4.48	4.53	4.53	0.05
1891-1913	2.92	3.42	0.50	3.85	3.92	3.92	0.07
1913-1928	1.42	2.01	0.59	2.20	2.41	2.52	0.32
1928-1950	0.91	1.41	0.50	0.66	1.34	2.28	1.62
1950-1964	1.41	1.81	0.40	2.94	3.79	3.52	0.58
1964-1972	1.82	1.86	0.04	4.15	5.44	5.02	0.87
1972-1979	2.38	2.40	0.02	3.46	4.69	4.10	0.64
1979-1988	1.51	1.99	0.48	3.27	4.56	4.31	0.96
1988-1996	1.35	1.93	0.58	2.23	2.90	3.19	0.96
Long-term Trends Years							
1870-1913	3.24	3.73	0.49	4.16	4.22	4.22	0.06
1913-1972	1.28	1.72	0.44	2.06	2.75	3.01	0.95
1972-1996	1.71	2.09	0.38	2.98	4.04	3.87	0.99

Sources by column: (1)-(2): Table 2 and Table 3, line 10, plus text discussion for 1870-1913; (3): column 2 minus column 1; (4):   Same sources as Table 1; (5)-(6): Table 5; (7):   column 6 minus column 4.

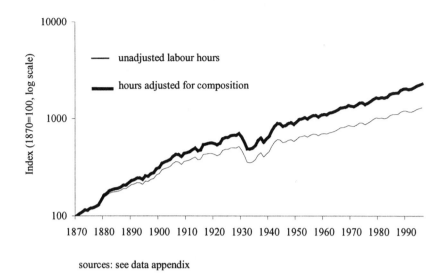

sources: see data appendix

Figure 6. Labour Input With and Without Composition Adjustment, Nonfarm Nonhousing
Private Economy, 1870-1996

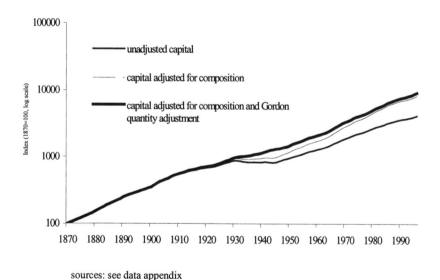

sources: see data appendix

Figure 7. Alternative Measures of Capital Input, Nonfarm Nonhousing Private Economy,
1870-1996

5.2   Implications for MFP Growth

We have now seen that the timing of our three types of input adjustments is quite different. The labour composition adjustment has a uniform effect in boosting labour input growth and reducing MFP growth across all periods except 1964-79. The capital composition adjustment is negligible before 1913 and has its largest effect in boosting capital input growth and reducing MFP growth during the post-war period, especially between 1964 and 1988. We have seen that several quantity adjustments made to the standard capital series have the effect of substantially raising the growth rate of capital input during the 1928-50 "big wave" interval relative to subsequent intervals, and indeed these adjustments reduce the growth rate of capital input in every interval but 1988-96, thus partly offsetting the positive impact on capital growth of the capital composition adjustment.[26]

The effects of these adjustments on MFP are displayed in Table 7 and Figure 8. Comparing the growth rates of MFP based on standard inputs in column (1) with the alternative growth rates of MFP based on fully adjusted inputs in column (4), we see that MFP growth is reduced in every period but by quite a different amount. The capital quantity adjustments have their biggest impact in 1928-50, the period in which MFP growth is reduced the most. The labour composition adjustments are close to zero in 1964-72 and 1972-79, the periods when MFP growth is reduced the least. And the capital composition and quantity adjustments are negligible prior to 1913, when the reduction in MFP is also relatively low. Overall, looking at the long-term trends in the bottom of Table 7, the middle period still has the most rapid MFP growth, although its margin of victory over 1870-1913 is substantially reduced. However the reduction in the growth rate of MFP after 1972 is almost as great as in 1913-72, and thus the contrast between the "big wave" period and the post-1972 "slowdown" period remains intact.

---

[26] Recall that the capital quantity adjustments do not extend before 1918 due to the absence of comparable data.

Table 7. MFP for Non-farm Non-housing Business GDP, Annual Growth Rates for Selected Intervals, 1870-1996

	Standard Inputs	Standard Capital, Labour Composition Adjustment	Labour and Capital Composition Adjustments	L& K Composition Adjustment and Capital Quantity Adjustments	Effect of all Adjustments
Years	(1)	(2)	(3)	(4)	(4)-(1)
1870-1891	0.54	0.22	0.20	0.20	-0.34
1891-1913	1.20	0.87	0.85	0.85	-0.35
1913-1928	1.43	1.03	0.96	0.93	-0.50
1928-1950	1.92	1.58	1.36	1.05	-0.87
1950-1964	1.59	1.32	1.04	1.13	-0.46
1964-1972	1.05	1.02	0.59	0.73	-0.32
1972-1979	0.25	0.24	-0.17	0.02	-0.23
1979-1988	0.73	0.41	-0.02	0.07	-0.66
1988-1996	0.82	0.43	0.21	0.12	-0.70
Long-term Trends					
Years					
1870-1913	0.88	0.55	0.53	0.53	-0.35
1913-1972	1.60	1.30	1.08	0.99	-0.61
1972-1996	0.62	0.37	0.01	0.07	-0.55

Sources: MFP calculated from standard and adjusted input series as listed in Table 6.

Figure 8 exhibits the same alternative MFP series for which the growth rates are displayed in Table 7. The input adjustments do create an important change in timing in contrast to MFP based on standard inputs. Instead of exhibiting a distinct acceleration in 1928-50 as compared to the periods immediately before or after, fully adjusted MFP growth appears as nearly a straight line all the way from 1891 to 1972, and indeed Table 7 shows that the growth rates over the five sub-periods within 1891-1972 vary only between 0.77 and 1.17 percent, a range of 0.40 percentage points compared to the range over the same sub-periods of more than twice as much, 0.87 points, when MFP is based on standard inputs as in column (1) of Table 7.

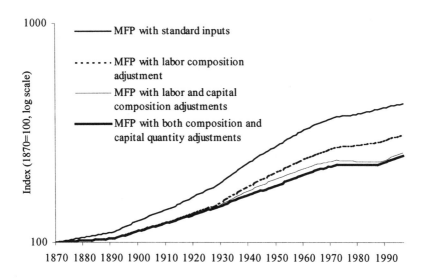

sources: see data appendix

Figure 8. Alternative Measures of MFP, Nonfarm Nonhousing Private Economy, 1870-1996

5.3   Implications for the Output-Capital Ratio

This paper began by pointing to the permanent doubling in the output to capital ratio between the pre-war and post-war eras, as depicted in Figure 1. Does this mysterious jump in the ratio survive the composition and quantity adjustments developed in this paper?

Figure 9 compares the output-capital ratio based on standard and adjusted capital input, while retaining the same measure of real output. It appears that the composition and quantity adjustments to capital input completely eliminate the permanency of this jump, a long-standing feature of the data that has previously resisted a coherent explanation.[27] Indeed when both output and capital input are expressed in 1992 prices, the output/capital ratio is lower in 1996 (0.64) than in 1870 (0.71), in contrast to the doubling that occurs with the standard capital input date (0.37 to 0.74).

---

[27] The jump in the output-capital ratio depicted in Figures 1 and 9 using the standard capital series was the original motivation for my 1967 Ph.D. thesis on problems in measuring real investment.

sources: see data appendix

Figure 9. Alternative Ratios of Output to Capital, 1992 Prices, Nonfarm Nonhousing Private Economy 1870-1996

Two further differences stand out between the adjusted and standard data when shorter periods are examined. First, the increase between 1926 and 1953 in the output- capital ratio is substantially less with the adjusted than with the standard data, 9 percent (from 0.89 to 0.97) instead of by 65 percent (from 0.49 to 0.81). Second, there is a pronounced downdrift in the post-war period in the adjusted data, with the output-capital ratio declining from 0.97 in 1953 to 0.64 in 1996 (a 34 percent decline) in contrast to a much milder decline from 0.81 in 1953 to 0.74 in 1996 (a 9 percent decline). The radical difference in the historical behaviour of the output-capital ratio combines the influence of the steady increase in capital growth created by the composition effect after 1928 with the boost to capital growth in the 1928-50 interval created by the quantity adjustments.

6.   SUBSTANTIVE HYPOTHESES

Now we turn to the task of explaining the "big wave" in U.S. growth in MFP, now expressed with the new data as the much faster growth between 1891 and 1972 than before or particularly after 1972. In discussing substantive explanations of the big wave, we begin with the timing of the great inventions and then proceed to other complementary hypotheses.

6.1   The Great Inventions

In related research (Gordon, 1998) I have argued that the current information-technology revolution does not compare in its quantitative importance for MFP with the concurrence of many great inventions in the late nineteenth and early twentieth century that created the modern world as we know it. There are four major clusters of inventions to be compared with the computer, or chip-based IT broadly conceived. These are:

(1) The first great invention in the "Group of Four" is electricity, including both electric light and electric motors. As shown by Nordhaus (1997), electricity drastically reduced the true price of light. Electric motors, after a developmental period of two or more decades emphasised by David (1990), revolutionised manufacturing by decentralising the source of power and making possible flexible and portable tools and machines. After a somewhat longer lag, electric motors embodied in consumer appliances eliminated the greatest source of drudgery of all, manual laundry, and through refrigeration virtually eliminated food spoilage and through air conditioning made summers enjoyable and opened the southern United States for modern economic development.

(2) Sharing the title with electricity for the most important invention that had its main diffusion in the twentieth century is the internal combustion engine, which made possible personal autos, motor transport, and air transport. Grouped in this category are such derivative inventions as the suburb, interstate highway, and supermarket.[28] Gradually eliminated or greatly reduced were many of the ills of the late nineteenth century, from manure to unplowed snow to putrid air to rural isolation.

(3) The third group of great inventions includes both petroleum and all the processes which "rearrange molecules," including petrochemicals, plastics, and pharmaceuticals. These are largely an independent invention, but some of the innovations were induced by the demands of motor and air transport. They helped to reduce air pollution created by industrial and heating uses of coal, and they made possible many new and improved products, as well as conquering illness and prolonging life.

(4) The final member of the "Group of Four" is the complex of entertainment, communication, and information innovations that were developed before World War II. This set of inventions that made the world smaller can be traced back to the telegraph in 1844 and includes the telephone, radio, movies, television, recorded music, and mass-circulation

---

[28] Bresnahan and Gordon (1997) in their introduction provide a formal analysis of how complementary inventions like supermarkets, suburbs, and highways increase the consumer surplus contributed by new inventions like the internal combustion engine and the motor car.

newspapers and magazines. Television, which was invented in the 1920s and 1930s, is the only one of these innovations that was diffused after World War II. Otherwise, all the rest were well established before World War II and created a quantum leap in the standard of living when a year like, say, 1939 is compared with fifty years earlier.

The "Group of Four" inventions, in turn, created an increase in per capita income and wealth that allowed an improvement in living standards even in those aspects of consumption where inventions did not play a major role, particularly the ability of families to afford many more square feet of shelter (and in the suburbs more land surrounding that shelter) than at the turn of the century.

Has the information revolution spawned by the computer created as great a change in living conditions as any of the four major complexes of early twentieth-century inventions? While retrospective exercises are inevitably subjective, it is interesting to play an expanded version of what I like to call the "New Yorker game." A few years ago the *New Yorker* commissioned a critic to sit in front a television set for an entire week and record his impressions. He had many reactions, but the one most relevant for us is that he was surprised from the reruns of 1950 TV shows how similar were the living conditions of the 1950s Ozzie and Harriet families in comparison to those of today. Clearly living conditions were far better in the 1950s than in the 1890s, in large part because of the "Group of Four" inventions. We can surmise that a hypothetical critic revisiting the 1890s through a time machine would not have the same reaction as the *New Yorker* critic visiting the 1950s from the 1980s. For our purposes, it is a moot point whether life changed more between the 1890s and 1920s or between the 1920s and 1950s. What does seem sure is that society had cured most of the ills of late nineteenth century living conditions by the 1950s and 1960s without any help from computers.

To understand at a deeper level why the computer revolution does not measure up to the earlier great inventions, it is useful to consider some of the ways in which the great inventions created productivity growth. Electric light was a unique invention that extended the length of the day for reading, entertainment, and other pursuits. Both the electric motor and internal combustion engine created faster and more flexible movement, directly raising the productivity of factory workers, housewives, truck drivers, and airline pilots as the machines they powered could rotate ever faster. Petroleum refining, chemicals, plastics, and pharmaceuticals all involve the physical rearrangement of molecules in ways that change materials into more productive forms. The complex of electric and electronic entertainment and information industries arrived in a void in which nothing comparable existed and had, one may safely conjecture, a greater impact on everyday life of the average family than the second and third generation developments, *e.g.*, VCRs, CDs, the first generation of colour TV, and ever-larger TV screens, which provided merely better or more convenient ways of performing the same basic functions.

Some of the output of computers is, in principle, as productivity-enhancing as that of electric motors or motorised transport. From the earliest punch-card sorters, some applications of computer technology have involved movement and speed. Numerically controlled machine tools, robots, and other computer-driven machinery has the same potential for productivity improvement as the earlier great inventions and doubtless accounts for the robust rate of productivity growth still apparent in some (but not all) manufacturing industries. The use of ever-faster computers and peripherals to churn out securities transactions, bank statements, and insurance policies should enhance productivity growth in the finance/insurance sector. And, just as the motor car enormously increased personal mobility and flexibility, so the computer has spawned inventions whose main output is convenience, most notably the ATM machine.

These productivity enhancing aspects of computers suggest that MFP performance in the past two decades would have been even worse than the dismal record of Table 7 without the benefits of computers. Yet the benefits of computers have not been strong enough to bring us back to the rapid rates of MFP advance enjoyed before 1972. In my analysis (1998), the rapid price declines of computer power have resulting in diminishing returns to computers operating with unparalleled force. Just as the elementary textbook example explains diminishing returns as resulting from the application of additional units of labour to a fixed supply of land, so the computer revolution has resulted in the application of vastly multiplied units of computation power to a fixed supply of time and mental power for any given computer user. The computer revolution did not begin with the earliest PCs in the 1980s but with mainframes in the early 1950s. After more than four decades the greatest benefits of computers have been achieved. The newest aspect of the computer revolution, the internet, can be viewed largely as a source of information and entertainment that substitutes for other forms of information and entertainment.

An intriguing connection of the time path of technical innovation with the "big wave" is Kleinknecht's (1987) count of "radically new products," which rises from six during 1850-1920 to 29 during 1920-1950 and then falls to five during 1950-70.[29] Kleinknecht's count is reproduced in Table 8.

---

[29] See Freeman (1986) for a collection of suggestive papers on long swings in design and innovation.

Table 8. Types of Innovations in Ten-Year Periods

	PI[1]	IP[2]	Scientific Instruments	Difficult Cases
1850-59	0	1	0	0
1860-69	1	2	0	1
1870-79	1	5	0	0
1880-89	3	4	0	0
1890-99	0	2	0	0
1900-09	1	5	0	1
1910-19	0	4	0	1
1920-29	6	2	0	0
1930-39	14	4	2	6
1940-49	9	5	4	1
1950-59	2	8	3	4
1960-69	3	4	9	2

[1]PI= Product innovations (radically new products)
[2]IP= Improvement and process innovations
Source: Kleinknecht (1987), p. 66

6.2   Other Substantive Hypotheses

Immigration and the co-dependence of productivity and real wages

Given the timing of the "big wave," it is striking that productivity growth was slow in the late nineteenth century when immigration was important, and then again in the 1970s and 1980s when the baby boom and renewed immigration created rapid labour-force growth. This observation is related to Romer's (1987, Figure 1) demonstration that productivity growth and labour-force growth in U.S. history is negatively correlated over 20-year intervals since 1839. Thinking about immigration may be helpful in explaining why the U.S. MFP growth slowdown in the 1970-90 period has been concentrated in non-manufacturing. My idea (further developed in Gordon, 1997) is that new entrants (teens and adult females in the 1970s and legal and illegal immigrants in the 1980s) have mainly gone into unskilled service jobs and have held down the real wage in services, in turn promoting the lavish use of unskilled labour in such occupations as grocery baggers, busboys, valet parkers, and parking lot attendants, jobs that barely exist in high-wage European economies. In contrast, immigrants in the 1890-1913 period were disproportionately employed in manufacturing, and their prescence probably dampened real wage increases and delayed the introduction of labour-saving equipment.[30] The "big wave" period of rapid productivity growth coincides roughly with the shutting off of mass immigration in the 1920s and the slow labour-force growth of 1930-65.

Real wage convergence and divergence

Goldin and Margo (1992) have recently studied the sharp convergence, *i.e.*, reduction in inequality, of real wages in the 1940s and subsequent divergence, and Goldin and Katz (1999) have shown the same type of V-shaped behaviour for the rate of return to both high school and college education. If relative labour scarcity coincided with a technology that created a high demand for unskilled and semi-skilled workers, then the relatively high wages for low-skill work in the 1940s may have in turn stimulated efficiency improvements that boosted productivity. Wages started diverging after 1950, with a sharp increase in inequality in the 1980s and 1990s that is reflected in a big jump in the rate of return to college education, mainly because the real wages of high school graduates fell. This process is the outcome of a complex process in which changing technology, an increased supply of cheap imported manufactured goods, and immigration interacted to erode the rents previously earned by union members with high school educational attainment. This, in turn, may have reversed the stimulus to higher efficiency that took place in the 1940s. The immigration and convergence stories are related, since Borjas (1992) shows that immigration in 1880-1913 introduced much of the inequality in skills and real wages that Goldin and Margo (1992) show was substantially eliminated in the 1940s.

Growing openness to trade

Trade theory teaches that trade in goods, not just labour mobility, can lead to convergence of incomes. This idea that trade simultaneously promotes convergence but also generates a slowdown of income growth in the leading country is closely related to several recent models, particularly that of Johnson and Stafford (1992). In this context a contribution to the "big wave" may have been a movement away from free trade in the Fordney-McCumber tariffs of 1922 and Smoot-Hawley Act of 1930. This movement away from trade may possibly help to explain some of the "big wave" and also the

---

[30] On the industrial and occupational composition of successive generations of immigrants, see Borjas (1994). On migration and economic development in an international context see Hatton-Williamson (1992) and Williamson (1992).

temporary cessation of convergence among nations in the 1913-1950 period previously noted by Abramovitz (1986, 1991) and many others.[31]

"Heavy" and "Light" technology and the upsurge in the equipment-structures ratio

One of the most striking (and as yet little noticed) features of the historical record appears in the ratio of the capital stock of producers' equipment to that of non-residential structures. This ratio (shown in Figure 2 above) remains constant between 1870 and 1945 and then rises rapidly and steadily by a factor of almost four through 1996.[32] I believe this phenomenon is related to Wright's (1990) emphasis on the raw-materials intensity of U.S. technology in the late nineteenth century, which favoured "heavy" and space-intensive machinery (steel mills, railroad stock and track, *etc.*). Technological innovation beginning with the electric motor allowed a shift to lighter and less space-intensive equipment, so that more and more equipment could be stuffed into a given number of square feet of structures. Space-saving may have been an important part of the big wave, but this particular trend has continued throughout the period of slow MFP growth after 1972. Since computers have many of the same characteristics as electric motors (space-saving, energy-saving, materials-saving), a continuing puzzle is the failure of computers to boost productivity growth as electric motors apparently did.[33]

7.   CONCLUSION

It is interesting that there is no mention of the big wave in recent commentaries on productivity by such prominent authors as Abramovitz (1986, 1991), Baumol-Blackman-Wolff (1989), Maddison (1982, 1987,

---

[31] The idea that protection can raise productivity is related to an idea that emerges from the McKinsey (1992) cross-country study, that West Germany boosts productivity in retailing by regulations that directly limit shop opening hours and indirectly stifle the development of shopping centres (thus creating crowded busy stores in contrast to the U.S. malls that are empty for many of their weekly opening hours).

[32] Figure 2 is based on the "standard" capital series. With variable retirement the equipment/structures ratio rises slowly from 0.200 in 1929 to 0.248 in 1945, whereas with fixed retirement the ratio is 0.200 in 1929 and 0.199 in 1945.

[33] A development related to "heavy" materials and to the "big wave" is that the geographical concentration of U.S. manufacturing rose to a peak in 1940 and then fell (Kim, 1992). The economy may have received a one-time boost in MFP from the dispersion of manufacturing to more efficient locations in the 1940-70 period, made possible by "lighter" materials, motor transport, and the diffusion of air conditioning.

1989), and Nelson-Wright (1992). Most of the focus in the recent literature has been on the world-wide productivity slowdown, on convergence among leading industrial nations, and on catch-up of these nations to the U.S. level of productivity. There has been remarkably little attention to the fact that in the century before 1973 U.S. productivity did not grow at a uniform rate, or at a peak rate during 1948-73, but rather displayed a sharp acceleration at some point after 1913. Yet this fact which makes up the early part of the big wave was evident as soon as Kendrick's (1961) results were computed, and Solomon Fabricant emphasises it in his introduction to Kendrick's book (see the quote at the beginning of this paper). This paper has shown that the standard data on output, labour input, and capital input imply "one big wave" in multi-factor productivity (MFP) growth, with MFP growth exhibiting a symmetric wave that peaks in 1928-50 and slows gradually moving backwards to 1870-91 and forward to 1972-96. Much of this paper has discussed adjustments to MFP growth for changes in the composition of labour and capital input and adjustments to the quantity of capital input to take account of variable retirement, GOPO capital, and highway capital. These adjustments change the symmetry, flatten out the wave, and move it backwards. MFP growth is very slow during 1870-91, relatively steady at roughly one percent per year from 1891 to 1972, and then almost completely disappears in 1972-96. The peak interval for MFP growth is now 1950-64 rather than 1928-50, although the margin is narrow and the 1928-50 period remains in second place despite the extensive data revisions that have the effect of boosting input growth and reducing MFP growth more in the 1928-50 interval than in any other period.

We have argued that previous attention to the post-1972 productivity slowdown is misguided. The question should be recast: why was productivity growth so much faster between 1891 and 1972 than either before or after, and fastest of all between 1928 and 1964? Our preferred hypotheses combine several explanations, most notably the concurrence of a multitude of important inventions occurring simultaneously prior to and at the beginning of the rapid growth period. Two other leading explanations with the correct timing rely on a theoretical connection between open economies and slow growth in incomes, real wages, and productivity. The closing of American labour markets to immigration between the 1920s and 1960s, thus boosting wages and stimulating capital-labour substitution, contributed to the big wave. So in like manner did the combination of high tariffs, depression, and war, in closing off American goods markets from the influence of imports, thus postponing the convergence of incomes with America's trading partners and temporarily boosting wage growth for American workers.

This paper is undeniably pessimistic in its implications. If the big wave resulted from great inventions whose effects have now been fully diffused through the economy, together with a temporary shift towards closed labour and goods markets, the outlook for a revival of MFP growth is not promising. The optimists declare the arrival of a "new economy" in which the benefits of the hi-tech revolution and globalisation will bring about a revival of rapid growth, but in my view the remorseless progression of diminishing returns has left the greatest benefits of the computer age in the past, not awaiting us in the future.

A   DATA

This Appendix lists the sources of output and "standard" labour and capital input. The adjustments for changes in labour and capital composition and for variable retirement are described in the text and the notes to the tables. Sources of GOPO and highway capital are listed here.

BEA tables are cited by the number used in the *Survey of Current Business*, August 1998, and the most recent data are ratio-linked to earlier BEA sources for the same concept that sometimes use different table numbers.

Nonfarm Nonhousing Business Output

1870-1929: Kendrick (1961), Table A-III p. 298 (total output) less Table A-III p. 298, (government) less Table A-III, P298 (farm) less Table A-XV p. 320 (housing).

1929-96: BEA, Table 1.8.

Nonfarm Nonhousing Business Labour Hours

1870-1889: Kendrick (1961), Table A-XXII p.332 (total hours) less Table A-X p.312 (farm). Since the Kendrick data are based on decade averages, in order to get cyclical variation, Kendrick's numbers are fitted by ordinary least squared regression onto Balke-Gordon (1989) output.

1889-1948: Kendrick (1961), Table A-XXIII P.338

1948-96: BEA, Table 6.9C for nonfarm private domestic hours minus hours in real estate from Table 6.8C multiplied by hours per employee in the Finance, insurance, and real estate sector obtained as the ratio of Table 6.9C to Table 6.8C.

Nonfarm Nonhousing Business Capital

1870-1929 Equipment: Kendrick (1961) Table A-XVI p.323 (Equipment) minus Table III, p. 367 (Farm Equipment).

1929-1996 Equipment: BEA Fixed Reproducible Tangible Wealth CD-ROM, Table Tw2a, nonresidential equipment minus farm equipment.

1870-1929 Structures: Kendrick (1961) Table A-XVI P.323 (Nonresidential structures) minus Table III, p. 367 (farm structures). These are both interpolated from decade averages. Because of the unusual behaviour of the Kendrick structures figures for 1890-1900, data from Raymond Goldsmith were substituted instead.

1929-1996 Structures: BEA Fixed Reproducible Tangible Wealth CD-ROM, Table Tw2a, nonresidential structures minus farm structures.

GOPO (Government-owned, privately operated) Capital

1870-1925: It was assumed that most government owned privately operated capital in the early 1920's is merchant vessels built by U.S. shipyards in World War I, and so GOPO is set equal to zero prior to 1918.

1925-1988: BEA wealth data tape.
   Highway Capital

1925-1996: Fraumeni (1999).

REFERENCES

Abramovitz, Moses (1986), "Catching Up, Forging Ahead, and Falling Behind," *Journal of Economic History* 46, pp. 385-406.

Abramovitz, Moses (1991), "The Post-war Productivity Spurt and Slowdown: Factors of Potential and Realisation," in: G. Bell (ed.), *Technology and Productivity: The Challenge for Economic Policy*, OECD, Paris, pp. 19-37.

Aschauer, David A. (1989), "Is Public Expenditure Productive?," *Journal of Monetary Economics* 23, pp. 177-200.

Baily, Martin Neil and Robert J. Gordon (1988), "The Productivity Slowdown, Measurement Issues, and the Explosion of Computer Power," *Brookings Papers on Economic Activity* 19, pp. 347-420.

Baily, Martin Neil and Charles L. Schultze (1990), "The Productivity of Capital in a Period of Slower Growth," *Brookings Papers on Economic Activity: Microeconomics 1990* 21, pp. 369-420.

Balke, Nathan S. and Robert J. Gordon (1989), "The Estimation of Pre-war GNP: Methodology and New Results," *Journal of Political Economy* 97, pp. 38-92.

Baumol, William J., Sue Anne Batey Blackman and Edward N. Wolff (1989), *Productivity and American Leadership: the Long View*, Cambridge MA: MIT Press.

Berndt, Ernst R. and Jack Triplett (1990), *Fifty Years of Economic Measurement: the Jubilee of the Conference on Research in Income and Wealth*, Chicago: University of Chicago Press for NBER.

Blanchard, Olivier J. and Danny Quah (1989), "The Dynamic Effects of Aggregate Demand and Supply Disturbances," *American Economic Review* 79, pp. 655-73.

Borjas, George J. (1994), "Long-run Convergence of Ethnic Skill Differentials: The Children and Grandchildren of the Great Migration," *Industrial Labour Relations Review* 7, pp. 553-73.

Bresnahan, Timothy F. and Robert J. Gordon (eds.) (1997), *The Economics of New Goods*, Chicago: University of Chicago Press for NBER.

David, Paul A. (1990), "The Dynamo and the Computer: An Historical Perspective on the Modern Productivity Paradox", *American Economic Review Papers and Proceedings* 80, pp. 355-61.

De Long, J. Bradford and Lawrence H. Summers (1991), "Equipment Investment and Economic Growth," *Quarterly Journal of Economics* 106, pp. 445-502.

Denison, Edward F. (1962), *The Sources of Economic Growth in the United States and the Alternatives Before Us*, Supplementary Paper no. 13, New York: Committee for Economic Development.

Denison, Edward F. (1979), *Accounting for Slower Economic Growth: The United States in the 1970s*, Washington: Brookings.

Denison, Edward F. (1985), *Trends in American Economic Growth, 1929-82*, Washington: Brookings.

Duménil, Gérard and Dominique Levy (1990), "Continuity and Ruptures in the Process of Technological Change," working paper, CEPREMAP, August.

Feldstein, Martin S. and David K. Foot (1974), "Towards an Economic Theory of Replacement Investment," *Econometrica* 42, pp. 393-423.

Feldstein, Martin S. and David K. Foot (1971), "The Other Half of Gross Investment: Replacement and Modernization Expenditures," *Review of Economics and Statistics* 53, pp. 49-58.

Ford, Robert, and Pierre Poret (1991), "Infrastructure and Private-Sector Productivity," *OECD Economic Studies* 17, pp. 63-89.

Fraumeni, Barbara M. (1999), "Productive Highway Capital Stock Measures," paper written under subcontract to Battelle Memorial Institute, Federal Highway Administration, Department of Transportation, January.

Freeman, C. (ed.) (1986), *Design, Innovation and Long Cycles in Economic Development*, New York: St. Martin's Press.

Goldin, Claudia (1998), "America's Graduation from High School: The Evolution and Spread of Secondary Schooling in the Twentieth Century," *Journal of Economic History* 58, pp. 345-74.

Goldin, Claudia and Lawrence F Katz (1999), "The Returns to Skill in the United States across the Twentieth Century," NBER working paper 7126, May.

Goldin, Claudia and Robert A. Margo (1992), "The Great Compression: The Wage Structure in the United States at Mid-Century," *Quarterly Journal of Economics* 107, pp. 1-34.

Gordon, Robert J. (1967), "Problems in the Measurement of Real Investment in the U.S. Private Economy," Ph. D. Dissertation, M.I.T.

Gordon, Robert J. (1969), "$45 Billion of U.S. Private Investment Has Been Mislaid," *American Economic Review* 59, pp. 221-38.

Gordon, Robert J. (1990), *The Measurement of Durable Goods Prices*, Chicago: University of Chicago Press for NBER.

Gordon, Robert J. (1997), "Is There a Tradeoff between Unemployment and Productivity Growth?," in: D. Snower and G. de la Dehesa (eds.), *Unemployment Policy: Government Options for the Labour Market*, Cambridge UK: Cambridge University Press, pp. 433-63.

Gordon, Robert J. (1998), "Monetary Policy in the Age of Information Technology: Computers and the Solow Paradox," Paper presented to Bank of Japan conference, Monetary Policy in a World of Knowledge-based Growth, Quality Change, and Uncertain Measurement, June 19.

Gordon, Robert J. (1999a), "U.S. Economic Growth Since 1870: One Big Wave?," *American Economic Review Papers and Proceedings* 89, pp. 123-8.

Gordon, Robert J. (1999b), "Has the 'New Economy' Rendered the Productivity Slowdown Obsolete?," Unpublished working paper, Northwestern University, June.

Griliches, Zvi (2000), *Research and Development, Education, and Productivity: A Personal Retrospective*, Cambridge MA: Harvard University Press.

Hatton, Timothy J. and Jeffrey G. Williamson (1992), "International Migration and World Development: A Historical Perspective," NBER Historical Paper no. 41, September.

Johnson, George, and Frank Stafford (1992), "Models of Real Wages and International Competition," unnumbered University of Michigan working paper, July.

Jorgenson, Dale W. (1966), "The Embodiment Hypothesis," *Journal of Political Economy* 74, pp. 1-17.

Jorgenson, Dale W. (1990), "Productivity and Economic Growth," in: Berndt-Triplett (1990), pp. 19-118.

Jorgenson, Dale W. and Zvi Griliches (1967), "The Explanation of Productivity Change," *Review of Economic Studies* 34, pp. 249-83.

Kendrick, John W. (1961), *Productivity Trends in the United States*, Princeton: Princeton University Press for NBER.

Kim, Sukkoo (1992), "Expansion of Markets and the Geographic Distribution of Economic Activities: The Trends in U.S. Regional Manufacturing Structure, 1860-1987," unnumbered UCLA working paper, October 14.

Kleinknecht, Alfred (1987), *Innovation Patterns in Crisis and Prosperity: Schumpeter's Long Cycle Reconsidered*, London: Macmillan.

Kuznets, Simon (1961), *Capital in the American Economy: Its Formation and Financing*, Princeton: Princeton University Press for NBER.

Maddison, Angus (1982), *Phases of Capitalist Development*, New York: Oxford University Press.

Maddison, Angus (1987), "Growth and Slowdown in Advanced Capitalist Economies: Techniques of Quantitative Assessment," *Journal of Economic Literature* 25, pp. 649-98.

Maddison, Angus (1989), *The World Economy in the 20th Century*, Paris: OECD.

McKinsey Global Institute (1992), *Service Sector Productivity*, Washington: McKinsey & Company.

Nelson, Richard R., and Gavin Wright (1992), "The Rise and Fall of American Technological Leadership: The Post-war Era in Historical Perspective," *Journal of Economic Literature* 30, pp. 1931-64.

Nordhaus, William D. (1982), "Economic Policy in the Face of Declining Productivity Growth," *European Economic Review* 18, pp. 131-58.

Nordhaus, William D. (1997), "Do Real-Output and Real-Wage Measures Capture Reality? The History of Lighting Suggests Not," in: Bresnahan and Gordon (1997), 29-66.

Romer, Paul M. (1987), "Crazy Explanations for the Productivity Slowdown," *NBER Macroeconomics Annual 1987*, pp. 163-201.

Romer, Paul M. (1990), "Capital, Labour, and Productivity", *Brookings Papers on Economic Activity: Microeconomics 1990* 21, pp. 337-67.

Williamson, Jeffrey G. (1992), "The Evolution of Global Labour Markets in the First and Second World Since 1830: Background Evidence and Hypotheses," NBER Historical paper no. 36, February.

Wright, Gavin (1990), "The Origins of American Industrial Success: 1879-1940," *American Economic Review* 80, pp. 651-68.

Chapter 3

Surveying Two Centuries of Dutch Growth, 1807-1995
(Dis)equilibrium Growth Regimes in International Perspective

Jan Luiten van Zanden
University of Utrecht

Key words: Economic growth, Growth history, Industrialisation, Catching up

Abstract: Using a new database of the reconstructed national accounts of the
Netherlands two centuries of Dutch economic growth are analysed. During the
19th century this economy was especially in comparison with Belgium as an
equilibrium growth track. A comparison with growth in the United States
revealed that the Netherlands after 1945 went through a phase of
disequilibrium growth.

1.   INTRODUCTION

Over the past decade, a group of economists and economic historians from
Utrecht and Groningen universities has sought to reconstruct the national
accounts of the Netherlands between 1807 and 1913 and realign previously
available estimates of GDP and its prime components for the post-1913
period.[1] These efforts have resulted in what, to our knowledge, at present
constitutes the longest series of annual national income data which complies
with modern conceptual definitions and the measurement standards of national
accounting procedures. Although some problems do remain -especially the
World War II period warrants further exploration and the many standing
measurement revisions between 1948 and the present still pose numerous
problems[2] – this vast database should serve to produce many new insights into

---

[1]   The results have been published in Smits, Horlings and van Zanden (1997); and van Ark
    and de Jong (1996).
[2]   den Bakker *et al.* (1996).

the development of the Dutch economy over the preceding two centuries and allow for the testing of some theories that have more recently become popular in economic thought. Dissertations and papers which so far have been published on the basis of this research have typically focused on particular subperiods, sectors of the economy or sources of expenditure. Extensive work has for instance been published on nineteenth-century capital formation (Groote, 1995), on service sector performance during that same period (Smits, 1995; Horlings, 1995), on World War I economic change (van der Bie, 1995), and on industrial development during the 20th century (1913-1965) (de Jong, 1999).

By contrast, in this paper I aim to delineate the long term development of the economy and confront the underlying statistical evidence with a some basic themes from modern growth theory. The issue on which I focus is whether the concept of a "steady state" of growth, which is central to this branch of economic theorising, can be applied to the long run performance of the Netherlands. Does one find the characteristics of such an equilibrium growth path, or should one think in terms of successive disequilibria to describe what happened in the economy of the Netherlands between 1807 and the present? And what does this tell us of the relevance of growth theory and of the special characteristics of Dutch economic development?

In a classic essay Kaldor has suggested six "stylised facts" for the construction of theoretical models of economic growth.[3] The most convincing among these "stylised facts" are, according to Scott, the facts that over substantial periods of time the growth rate of output, the growth rate of the labour force, the share of investment in output and the share of wages in income tend to remain unchanged.[4] According to Solow the fact that these "leading four" showed stability implied that "the steady state is not a bad place for the theory of growth to start, but may be a dangerous place for it to end."[5] According to Solow, then, when a country shows a more or less stable growth rate of GDP and of the labour force (and, as a result, I add, a stable growth rate of GDP per capita), and a stable share of investment and of wage income in total income, one may perhaps conclude that it shows the features of the equilibrium growth that is at the core of the old and of much of the new growth theory.

The "stylised facts" of equilibrium growth, then, are according to Solow the stability of GDP (per capita) growth, of the investment ratio and of the functional distribution of income. In this paper I will therefore focus on the

---

[3]   Kaldor (1961), pp. 178-9.

[4]   Scott (1989), p. 48; Barro and Sala-I-Martin (1995) p. 5 also state that these four stylised facts "seem to fit reasonably well with the long-term data for currently developed countries."

[5]   Solow (1970), p. 7.

long run development of these three variables. But more can be added. A steady state can continue forever, not only because there is no structural change – because all economic variables by definition grow at the same rate and therefore ratios between capital stock and income, or between profits and capital stock *etc.* remain constant – but also because the expectations of the actors are always realised, so that they will repeat their decisions (to invest, to consume, to supply labour, *etc.*, in certain quantitative proportions). Moreover, special institutions, or government policies do not influence the long run growth of the economy, which is determined by – dependent on the specification of the model – the rate of savings, the productivity of capital, and/or the (exogenous) rate of technological change.[6]

Disequilibrium growth, of course, is fundamentally different. The way growth theory traditionally deals with it, is through the concept of a *traverse*, a movement from one equilibrium growth path to another one – for example the result of the introduction of a superior technology which must be incorporated in the capital stock of the economy concerned.[7] During these transitional dynamics, all structural variables which remain stable during a steady state will change to become consistent with the technological determinants of the new stable growth path (for example, if the new technology would favour human capital, the share of labour in income would have to rise). Moreover, institutions and government policies can either speed up or retard the process, which may, under certain circumstances, also lead to "overshooting" of the new growth path.[8] At the core of this idea of a *traverse* is, however, that after a time period, perhaps after some overshooting followed by a "crisis," a new phase of steady growth begins again.

This way to approach economic growth may for economic historians seem rather unrealistic and not very illuminating. However, economists do use the "stylised facts" of long run economic development to argue in favour of this kind of approach, although they almost always only use data from the United States and/or the United Kingdom to make this point.[9] When they use concepts such as the "steady state," economists tend to think that they correlate to some extent with historical reality. It is probably the duty of the economic historian to find out whether this is correct.

More importantly perhaps is the point that this kind of reasoning is implicit in much of the economic-historical literature. Let us illustrate this by

---

[6] See for example Barro and Sala-i-Martin (1995), p. 144.

[7] Hicks (1973), pp. 81-150.

[8] Ibidem; in a recent book by Amendola and Gaffard (1998) the implications of thinking in terms of "out of equilibrium" growth paths are investigated in a systematic way. Although this book has certainly influenced this paper, we prefer to continue to think in terms of "transitional dynamics."

[9] Explicit statements of this kind can be found in two leading books on the theory of economic growth: Scott, (1989), pp. 45-54 and Barro and Sala-i-Martin (1995), pp. 33-4.

focusing on the two debates that are central to the economic history of the 19th century – the debate on the Industrial Revolution – and of the 20th century – the discussion on catching up and convergence in the world economy.

The Industrial Revolution is in much of the literature interpreted as a sudden change in the technological capabilities of an economy, resulting in a very rapid growth of production and productivity in (small) parts of this economy, i.e. in certain industries.[10] This disequilibrium character of industrialisation results, for example, in rather sudden changes in the demand for (skilled) labour, and therefore in changes in the distribution of income.[11] Gerschenkron's theory of relative backwardness is the most famous attempt to develop a systematic approach towards this pan-European process. In his studies he compared the industrialisation of a country to which modern industry was endogenous (Great Britain) with the experiences of nations which were relatively backward at the beginning of their Industrial Revolution and which therefore had to borrow the new techniques from the English example. He found a pattern of relatively stable (steady state) growth in the English case, whereas in the "backward countries" industrialisation was characterised by huge growth spurt (in many ways similar to Hicks' *Traverse*). One of the fundamental problems of this accelerated industrialisation process was how to generate the funds to invest in the new technology (a problem which is also raised in the recent book on "out of equilibrium" growth by Amendola and Gaffard).[12] New institutions had to be developed to find these funds. Universal banks played this role in Germany and Italy, according to Gerschenkron, whereas the state performed this function in a country which was even more backward, Russia.[13] Where such an institution did not emerge, the traverse was postponed or slowed down – according to Gerschenkron this happened in Austria (Gerschenkron, 1977). The theory of Gerschenkron can therefore to some extent also be interpreted as an "application" of the growth theories sketched, although his work in fact predates much of the relevant theoretical work. And much of the critical work that has been published concerning his approach basically concludes that in many countries industrialisation was an "equilibrium" process, in which these special institutions did not play a large role.[14]

The debate about the process of catching up of the European economies after 1945, can be interpreted in a similar way. It is assumed that one economy, the productivity leader (the US), is on an equilibrium growth path (an idea to

---

[10] See for example Crafts (1985), pp. 7-8, 78-86.

[11] These disequilibrium results of the industrialisation process have been the subject of the research by Williamson (1985).

[12] Amendola and Gaffard (1998), pp. 35-45.

[13] Gerschenkron (1962); see for a critical examination of his work Sylla and Toniolo (1991).

[14] See the contributions to Sylla and Toniolo (1991).

which I will return) and that the experience of the European economies, who as a result of a number of exogenous shocks (World War I and II) have lagged behind, can be interpret as a process of "catching up" in which they incorporate the more advanced technology that has been developed by the productivity leader.[15] This is, by definition, a process of disequilibrium growth that ends when the European economies are able to attain the levels of productivity of the US. Beyond that point rapid growth of the post war period will end and a period of slower equilibrium growth will begin. The role of institutions necessary to profit from the opportunities of catching up (for example to finance the necessary large investments) is also stressed in recent literature (Eichengreen, 1996). Both debates, on industrialisation and on catching up, will be central to our discussion of the development of the Dutch economy between 1807 and 1996.

2. THE EVIDENCE: TWO CENTURIES OF ECONOMIC GROWTH

Investigation of trend rates of growth and their variation over time occupies a central position in economic history. In seeking to examine the behaviour of Dutch long-term economic growth, I accept the criticism by Crafts, Leybourne and Mills (1990) of conventional statistical methods of periodisation, which use arbitrary intervals and compare output estimates containing cyclical components to measure changes in compound growth rates (Crafts, Leybourne and Mills, 1990). As a consequence, in Table 1 and Figure 1,[16] I combine conventional methods to give a practical, comparative longterm view with a graphical representation of annual growth rate estimates derived by applying the structural (Kalman filter) timeseries model used by Crafts, Leybourne and Mills to isolate the structural component in Dutch growth performance. Looking at Figure and Table 1 it is possible to distinguish roughly three periods of economic growth, preceded by a fourth one:[17]

- Before 1820 (and probably since about 1670) the economy of Holland was at best stagnant, following a pattern of development described both by Adam Smith and early nineteenth-century analysts as Keuchenius and Metelerkamp as a "stationary state." The long term growth rate of GDP and, especially within Holland, that of population, was close to zero.[18]

---

[15] The classic paper is Abramovitz (1986).

[16] Unless stated otherwise, the figures in this paper are all based on the database national accounts (see note 1).

[17] These changes in trend growth rates are also found by Smits, de Jong and van Ark (1999).

[18] A more detailed analysis of this "stationary state" in van Zanden and van Riel (2000) chapter 1; see also de Vries and van der Woude (1997), pp. 703-710.

- During the greater part of the 19th century annual growth rates of GDP on average approximated 1.5 to 2.5 percent. More precisely, between 1820 and 1913 the average pace of growth amounted to 1.94 percent. The decades between 1840 and 1860 witnessed a slow down in growth rates, however, whereas after 1900 there was a moderate tendency towards acceleration.
- After a slump in 1916-1918, growth rates went up to about 4 to 5 percent during the 1920s, and again to that level during the "Golden age of European Growth" of 1950-1973. This period of high growth rates was interrupted by the consequences of two external shocks, namely the depression of the 1930s, imported through upheld monetary orthodoxy, and the Second World War.
- Finally, in the years after the mid-seventies, growth rates have reverted to 19th century levels. A growth rate of more than 3 percent is now considered to be exceptionally good, below 1.5 percent as being below average performance. Forecasts for the near future consider 2 to 2.5 percent as "normal." For the next four years the government budget, for example, is planned on the basis of a 2.25 percent growth rate.

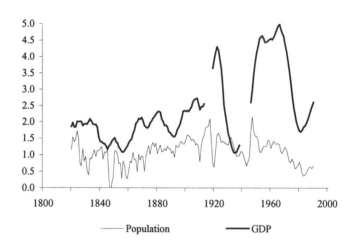

Figure 1. Estimated Trend Growth in Dutch Population and Gross Domestic Product Using the Crafts-Leybourne-Mills Structural Time-series Model, 1820-1990

For the 18th and the 19th century this interpretation of the different phases of growth is essentially consistent with established opinion (although the retardation of the 1840s and 1850s is a new fact, to which I return). There is consensus that the 18th century was characterised by stagnation, and that somewhere in the first half of the 19th century (and our research suggests at about 1820) a switch to another growth regime took place.

Table 1. Long-term Growth Rates in Population, Gross Domestic Product and Labour Productivity, the Netherlands Compared with Northwest Europe and the US, 1820-1990

	Population			GDP		
	NL	NW Europe	US	NL	NW Europe	US
1820-1850	0.94	0.79	2.94	2.06	1.56	4.10
1850-1870	0.76	0.59	2.70	1.61	1.63	4.20
1870-1890	1.14	0.74	2.29	1.97	1.77	3.91
1890-1913	1.35	0.85	1.88	2.38	2.16	3.82
1913-1938	1.38	0.52	1.17	2.44	1.80	1.76
1947-1973	1.29	0.80	1.48	5.07	4.83	3.94
1973-1990	0.63	0.28	0.98	2.19	2.26	2.62
1919-1929	1.34	0.61	1.48	4.56	3.33	3.42
1929-1938	1.23	0.53	0.73	0.33	1.49	-0.59

	GDP per capita			GDP per hour		
1820-1850	1.12	0.77	1.16			
1850-1870	0.85	1.04	1.50			
1870-1890	0.83	1.03	1.62	1.30	1.46	1.57
1890-1913	1.03	1.31	1.94	1.25	1.60	2.20
1913-1938	1.04	1.28	0.58	1.79	1.83	2.11
1947-1973[a]	3.73	3.98	2.43	4.80	4.55	2.74
1973-1990	1.55	1.98	1.63	2.50	2.35	1.15
1919-1929	3.22	2.72	1.94	3.84	3.54	2.78
1929-1938	-0.89	0.96	-1.31	-0.12	1.35	1.55

Note: a: the initial year in the case of GDP per hour is 1950.
Sources: Post-1913 results: van Ark and de Jong (1996), p. 291; Nineteenth- century estimates: Smits, Horlings and van Zanden (1997); Non-Dutch nineteenth century data: Maddison (1995).

The interpretation of 20th century economic growth – the notion that there existed a period of high growth rates between 1920 and the mid 1970s, interrupted by depression and war – is more controversial. The period of 1950-1973 – the Golden Age of European Economic Growth – is usually seen as an exceptional one, characterised by unusual high growth rates which were (at least partly) the result of catching up after 1945. However, a close look at growth rates in the European countries studied by Maddison, shows that a clear acceleration of the 1920s occurred in almost all of them (Table 2). In almost all countries growth rates during the 1920 were much higher than in the period before 1913 and were more or less similar to those realised after 1950. This was the case irrespective of the fact whether they were neutral during the First

World War (Netherlands, Norway, Denmark, Switzerland) or lost a large part of their capital stock during it (Belgium, France).

Table 2. Growth Rates of GDP in Four Periods

	1870-1913	1920-1929	1950-1973	1973-1994
Belgium	2.0	3.4	4.0	1.9
Denmark	2.7	3.6	3.8	1.9
Finland	2.7	5.4	4.9	1.9
France	1.6	4.9	5.0	2.1
Germany	2.8	4.9	6.0	2.2
Italy	1.9	2.9	5.6	2.5
Netherlands	2.2	4.9	4.7	2.1
Norway	2.1	3.2	4.1	3.3
Sweden	2.2	4.1	3.7	1.4
Switzerland	2.4	4.8	4.5	1.1
UK	1.9	1.9	3.0	1.7
Unweight Average	2.2	4.0	4.5	2.0

Source: Maddison (1995).

The fact that this first growth spurt has not attracted the attention it deserves, and has not been recognised as a precursor to the Golden Age after 1950, is due to the many distortions and exogenous shocks that destabilised the economic system during the 1920s and 1930s. Most shocks (for example the forced re-introduction of the gold exchange standard at the pre-war parity) must have lowered growth (in Britain and Scandinavia in this case). The Dutch case is probably exceptional as its return to gold convertibility in 1925 apparently did not harm the economy.[19] Moreover, the profits it reaped from the fact that it was kept out of the First World War made up much of the losses it suffered as a result of growing international protectionism of the 1920s. It may have been one of the few countries which, at least during the 1920s, was actually on its (new) long term growth path.

There is probably greater consensus that since the 1970s the European economies have witnessed lower growth rates of a supposedly lasting nature (Table 2). In recent years the growth performance of most European countries is almost similar to the growth rates that were attained during the (final decades of the) 19th century (Norway, for obvious -oil- reasons is an exception here).

This brief survey of two centuries of growth leads us to ask two questions. Firstly, can economic growth and industrialisation of the Netherlands in the

---

[19]   See van Zanden (1998), pp. 100-105.

19th century be interpreted in terms of "balanced growth" (a term introduced by Griffiths, 1980) or "equilibrium growth?" In this respect I focus on a comparison with the economic evolution of Belgium, a country which went through a period of very rapid industrialisation (between 1840 and 1870), exactly at the same time when growth in the Netherlands slowed down. The second question is related to the 20th century growth experience. Hhow should the two periods of very rapid growth (1920s and 1945-1973) be interpreted, as two (rather short) steady states, or is disequilibrium more characteristic of this hectic period? And how can the return to a regime of slow growth after 1973 be understood? To put the Dutch experience into perspective, at this point a comparison will be made with the growth of the economy of the United States in the 20th century.

3.   SLOW INDUSTRIALISATION IN THE 19TH CENTURY

The starting point is the two (other) "stylised facts" of steady state growth, the share of wages in income and the investment ratio. The estimates for the former variable show that during the 19th century on a macro-economic level the functional distribution of income was remarkably stable, although some changes within the different sectors did occur (see Figure 2). This stability is very striking in view of the violent fluctuations and the changes in its level that occurred during the 20th century (see the next section).

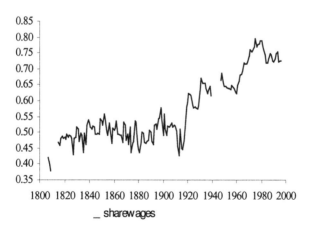

Figure 2. The Share of Wages (including an imputed compensation for self employment) in Net National Income, 1807-1996

For the reconstruction of the share of investments in GDP two different series were estimated, namely investment in capital goods and government expenditure on education (human capital formation). The latter series is the weaker one, because it does not include private expenditure on education (but it covers all levels of governments: the municipalities, the provinces and the central state). To a minor extent expenditure on education overlaps with total expenditure on physical capital goods (investments in schools, for example, are represented in both series). Therefore I did not combine the two series.

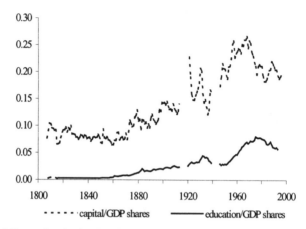

Figure 3. Capital Formation in the Dutch Economy: Expenditure on Physical Capital Goods and Government Expenditure on Education as a Share of GDP, 1807-1996

To answer the question whether the investment ratio remained more or less unchanged, economists usually focus on expenditure on capital goods (the first series). The long run dynamics of this series is quite clear from Figure 3. Levels of investments are relatively small in the 19th century, although they tend to rise somewhat after about 1860/70. Between 1807 and 1860 about 8% of GDP is invested in capital goods (there is a slight tendency of this ratio to fall between ca 1825 and 1860) and less than 1% is spent on education (this may have been somewhat higher as a result of private spending). Capital formation goes up around 1870 (when the level increases to about 10% and almost 2% respectively) and again during the 1890s (investment/GDP moves up to about 12%), but compared by 20th century standards these changes are still rather small.

These results – the near stability of the share of wages in income, of the investment ratio and of the rate of growth of GDP per capita – would certainly suggest that economic development during the 19th century was characterised by a "steady state." This may seem remarkable, because industrialisation is often regarded as a disequilibrium phenomenon. In this respect, a comparison with the industrialisation of Belgium is illuminating. The Netherlands at the beginning of the 19th century was a relatively prosperous country with a GDP per capita not much lower than Great Britain, a relatively small agricultural sector and a large services sector. Belgium, on the other hand, was much more "backward," but – thanks perhaps to its rich deposits of iron ore and coal – its growth potential was higher. Both countries were relatively small, and therefore dependent on the development of international trade.

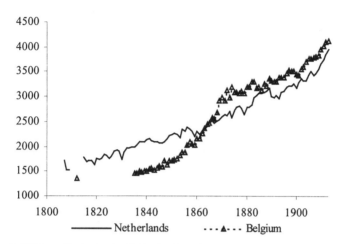

Figure 4. GDP per Capita in the Netherlands and Belgium 1807-1913 (in dollars of 1990)

In the 1840s both small open economies were confronted with an exogenous shock. The liberalisation of international trade after 1842 (the first reforms by Peel) and 1846 (the abolishment of the Corn Laws). In Belgium this ignited a classic industrialisation process, resulting in a very high growth rate of GDP. Whereas between 1812 and 1840 growth in the Netherlands had probably been comparable to that in Belgium, this changed radically after 1840 when the Belgium economy started to grow very rapidly (Figure 4).[20] Driving forces behind this "big spurt" were (a) a strong expansion of industrial exports (b) a very rapid growth of investment activity stimulated by a railway boom and by the export drive and (c) the structural transformation of the economy (because cities boomed, and labourers migrated in large numbers to the new industrialising regions).[21] The disequilibrium features of this growth spurt are that, firstly, economic growth accelerated sharply (but slowed down again after 1870) and, secondly, investments went up from less than 10% in the 1840s to more than 20% at about 1870. Finally, the share of wages in GDP probably fell in the same years (from about 40% in the 1840s to about 30% at about 1870,

---

[20] Horlings and Smits (1997), pp. 103-106.
[21] A recent survey is Buyst and van Meerten (1997), pp. 569 ff. See also Mokyr (1976), pp. 27-40.
[30] Horlings and Smits (1997), pp. 94, 100.

but these data are less reliable).[22] To finance the growth spurt, new banks were set up or old banks began to play a much more important role in the economy. The Generale Bank, for example, set up in 1822, in this period became the first example of an "investment bank" in Europe, controlling large parts of the engineering, metal working and coalmining industries of the country. The government too, played a distinct role in the industrialisation process by, for example, facilitating and subsidising the growth of railways (and of the exports of railways equipment).[23]

Whereas Belgium showed much of the classic features of the "big spurt" of a "backward" country between 1840 and 1870, in the Netherlands economic growth slowed down somewhat during these years, in spite of the fact that one would expect that this small open economy would also profit from the liberalisation of international trade. The big difference with Belgium was, however, that not industry but agriculture (and to a lesser degree, services) was the sector that saw its exports being boosted by these changes. In other words, the Netherlands had, at about 1840, a comparative advantage in the exports of agricultural products (of butter, cheese and livestock products), whereas industry was confronted with increased international competition during the same period. The differences in comparative advantages between the northern and the southern part of the Low Countries are also evident from estimates of the labour productivity in industry and agriculture. Between 1850 and 1870 in the Netherlands labour productivity in agriculture was about 76 to 100% of labour productivity in industry, whereas in Belgium this ratio was only 30 to 45%.[24]

Consequently, after 1840 agricultural exports went up very rapidly, and the price level of foodstuffs rose to international levels, whereas at the same time the deficit on the industrial trade balance grew enormously.[25] Figure 5 shows what happened with the share of wages in value added in industry, services and agriculture (these series combined together result in the stability of Figure 2). Before 1840 the wage share in the three sectors was about equal (this was perhaps a period of true "balanced growth"), but after the mid 1840s the wage share in industry went up sharply (the result of international competition/falling prices) whereas the reverse happened in agriculture and services. The prosperity in agriculture led to a slowing down of the process of structural transformation (why migrate when employment in the countryside expanded rapidly and real wages were probably higher than in the cities?). This, and the stagnation in industrial development, explains the

---

[31] Buyst and van Meerten (1997), 569 ff.
[24] Horlings and Smits (1992), p. 92.
[25] For more details: van Zanden and van Riel (2000), chapter 6. See also Knibbe (1993), p. 129.

low (and somewhat declining) level of capital formation during these years. These contrasting developments are also clear from a comparison of the composition of GDP (Table 3). In Belgium the share of industry increased from 29% (1812) to 49% (1870) whereas the share of agriculture declined to a comparable degree. In the Netherlands the share of industry fell (32% in 1836 to 24% in 1870) whereas agriculture became more important.[26] All in all, Dutch economic growth was rather slow in this period in which the economy tended to specialise on agricultural commodities.

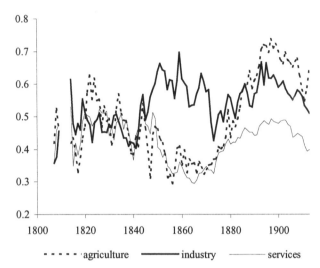

Figure 5. The Share of Wages in Gross Value Added of the Three Sectors 1800-1913

During the 1860s this export boom ended. When the agricultural depression of the post 1873 period set in, the position of the primary sector became much weaker, which stimulated the process of structural transformation (see Figure 5 and Table 3). These changes suggest that the image of a process of balanced growth – or of equilibrium growth – may be a accurate description of the most salient features of Dutch economic development during the 19th century – especially when a comparison with Belgium is made – but that a more detailed analysis also uncovers behind this surface a more complex story of the interaction of different sectors, which is important to understand the dynamics of growth.

[26] Horlings and Smits (1997), p. 87.

Table 3. The Shares of the Three Sectors in GDP (in current prices) in Belgium and the Netherlands 1808/12-1910.

	1808/12	1836	1850	1870	1890	1910
Belgium						
Agriculture	30	20	21	14	11	10
Industry	29	37	38	49	43	40
Services	41	42	41	37	45	50
Total	100	100	100	100	100	100
Netherlands						
Agriculture	25	22	26	30	21	19
Industry	30	32	26	24	32	31
Services	45	46	48	46	47	50
Total	100	100	100	100	100	100

Source: Horlings en Smits (1997), p. 87.

4.   CATCH-UP DURING THE 20TH CENTURY

One of the fundamental issues of 20th century economic history is to understand the processes of divergence and convergence that occurred in this period. The US, the productivity leader of the "convergence club," is almost always used as the reference point – a standard practice which I willadopt. Therefore this section begins with comparing the long run performance of the US economy with that of the Netherlands.

The figures of the development of GDP per capita in both countries during the past 175 years shows two countries following very different trajectories.[27] What strikes most in Figure 6 is the fact that the long run growth rate of US GDP per capita is almost perfectly stationary – in logarithmic form it is almost a straight line. Crafts and Mills using structural component time series analysis have recently tested this remarkable stationarity of the GDP per capita growth rate of the US, showing, for example, that trend growth rates of per capita GDP between 1870 and 1914 were essentially the same as those in the post 1950 period.[28] There are two interrelated deviations from the trend, namely the depression of the 1930s and the enormous expansion during the first half of the 1940s, both the result of large exogenous shocks.

I discussed already in the previous section that a comparable equilibrium growth path can be found for the Dutch economy in the 19th century, of which the trend is clearly lower than in the US (as a result of which the US overtakes

---

[27] The Dutch series are again based on the results of a project to reconstruct the national accounts for the Netherlands; see note 1; the US series are derived from Maddison (1995) and Weiss (1994), p. 13 (for the period 1820-1850).

[28] Crafts and Mills (1996), p. 425.

the Netherlands in the 1870s according to the Maddison estimates). At two occasions did the Dutch economy achieve a higher growth path to profit from the catch up potential that resulted from its slower growth during the 19th century. Directly after 1918 growth was much faster than before the Great War, but the depression of the 1930s broke off this first experiment in catching up. Nevertheless, the rapid growth during the 1920s already closed the gap with the US to a substantial extent. After 1945 a second acceleration occurred. Between 1945 and 1973 the gap between the two economies narrowed rapidly, but in the past two decades the difference has stabilised as both economies grew at about the same pace. The retardation of growth after 1973 cannot be interpreted as a return to a long term economic growth path – *i.e.* the pre 1913 "steady state" – that was interrupted by wars and depression (which is known in the German literature as the "Jánossy hypothesis").[29] The levels and the rates of economic expansion after 1973 are clearly unrelated to what happened before 1913, and growth rates between 1945 and 1973 were much higher than is consistent with a return to the pre 1913 "steady state."[30]

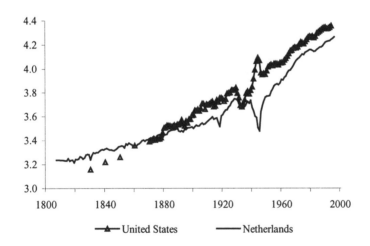

Figure 6. GDP per Capita in the US and in the Netherlands 1820-1995 (1990 dollars)

Equally instructive is what happened with levels of capital formation. Figure 7 contains estimates of the share of investment in GDP which show that in the US this share was almost perfectly constant in the long run (the 1930s and 1940s being the exceptions again).[31] The highest average per decade (the

[29] See Crafts and Toniolo (1996), pp. 16-7.
[30] See also Crafts and Mills (1996), pp. 421-5, who use old data for pre 1913 Dutch economic growth which tend to underestimate growth in the 19th century however.
[31] The US data are from Maddison (1992).

1970s: 19.4%) was only three points above the level at the beginning of the period (1870s: 16.2%), and in recent years the levels of the 19th century are barely surpassed. Compared with the almost completely stable relationship between capital formation and GDP in the US, the Netherlands show a strong increase in this ratio, from about 8% before 1870, 10-12% in the years before 1913, 17% in the 1920s to a peak of almost 25% in the 1960s. The two accelerations of growth (after 1918 and after 1945) are clearly related to much higher levels of capital formation than in the past, and the post 1973 deceleration of growth is also accompanied by a decline to a lower level (of about 20% presently).

The third "stylised fact" concerns the share of wages in total income (Figure 8). For the US three different series were linked, which all show a more or less constant wage share. Only during the depression of the 1930s do wages as a share in income go up much, but in the long run the changes in this structural parameter have been relatively small.[32] In the Netherlands, however, there has been a strong rise of the wage share during the two phases of rapid growth, i.e. the early 1920s and again during the 1960s and first half of the 1970s. After about 1980 a decline in the share of wages sets in, however.[33] The explanation for the stability of the income distribution of the US seems to be that (a) real wages increased at the same pace as labour productivity, (b) technical change was labour augmenting (or Harrod neutral) and (c) capital productivity (the ratio between the capital stock and output) was more or less constant with an equally constant long term real rate of interest.[34]

This comparison suggests that the US – following the criteria formulated by Solow – was on a remarkable stable growth path during the greater part of the 19th and the 20th century, with almost constant growth rates of GDP per capita and almost perfectly constant shares of investment and of wages in income. Much of the old and new growth theory is based on these phenomena, which are however peculiar to the US (and possibly to some extent to the UK too).[35]

---

[32] Johnson (1954), pp. 178-9; and Scott (1989), pp. 551-2. I linked the series of King (1850-1900), Johnson (1900-1930) and Scott (1930-1985) which were all calculated in a slightly different way. The data before 1930 refer to five-years averages.

[33] See also Amendola and Gaffard (1998), p. 253, who found comparable swings in the share of wages in GDP in western European countries between 1970 and 1995, and almost no change in the US.

[34] See the discussion in Burda and Wyplosz (1997), pp. 117-8.

[35] See Scott (1989), pp. 45-54; Barro and Sala-i-Martin (1995), pp. 33-4.

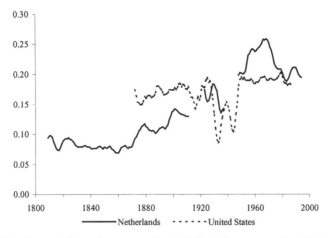

Figure 7. The Share of Gross Investment in GDP (both in current prices) in the US and the Netherlands, 1830/1870-1990 (five year moving averages)

The Netherlands followed a comparable stable growth path during the 19th century, but after 1920 and again after 1945 economic growth accelerated sharply, investment went up and also radical changes in the distribution of income occurred. It is obvious that the growth path of the 20th century is at odds with the "stylised facts" of steady state growth.

Two explanations for the disequilibrium character of Dutch economic development in the period 1913-1973 may be suggested. The first explanation focuses on the impact of the two great shocks, the First and the Second World War. During the First World War, when the Netherlands remained neutral, the economy was pulled from its slow growth path and new opportunities for much more rapid growth after the war were created (during the war the economy contracted somewhat, but the capacity to produce was certainly enlarged as a result of large investments in a number of basic industries). Rapid growth in the 1920s was a result of this "profiting" from its neutral status, and from the fact that neighbouring countries, who had been at war, managed to grow rapidly too, but from a much lower starting point (Table 2). However, the exogenous shock of the depression of the 1930s – there were, as far as we know, no domestic causes for the downturn of the economy after 1929 – ended this phase of rapid growth.

The consequences World War II, during which the country was occupied by the Germans, are much more complex. In 1945 the capacity to produce was curtailed, but the opportunities to profit from US-technology were much larger than in 1918, and new institutions were indeed set up to profit from these new opportunities (for example, wage moderation, the result of a new institutional settlement, was probably rather successful).[36] Rapid reconstruction created a very favourable climate for accelerated economic growth, which became a self-reinforcing process.[37] The 1960s and 1970s saw the "overshooting" of this rapid growth regime, resulting, amongst others, in large tensions on the labour market, (too) rapid increases in real wages, inflation, a strong expansion of the welfare state and a resulting strong decline in the profitability of industry (which undermined its financial structure). During the 1970s, when the convergence process was completed – the remaining difference in GDP per capita with the United States is largely the result of a relatively low labour input head of the Dutch population – a number of shocks ended the high growth regime (i.e. the collapse of the Bretton Woods system and the oil price hike of 1973). The transition to the equilibrium growth of the 1980s and 1990s was as a result of the problems created during the 1960-1973 period accompanied by the necessary restructuring of industry which resulted in increased unemployment, but these problems seem to be solved during the 1990s.

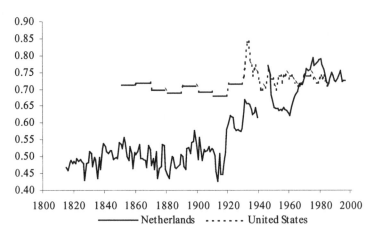

Figure 8. The Share of Wages (including imputed wages of self employed) in total income, 1820/1850-1995

Another approach would be to see the changes between 1914 and 1973 as being part of one process of transition from an equilibrium growth regime during the 19th century – based say on the technology of the first Industrial Revolution – to another steady state beginning in the 1980s. What is striking in Figures 6, 7 and 8, is that the features of the Dutch 19th century growth regime

---

[36]   Eichengreen (1996), p. 45.
[37]   More details of this interpretation are presented in van Zanden (1999).

are very different from those of the US. Growth was much slower and the share of investment in GDP and of wages in income was much smaller than in the productivity leader. But during the 20th century traverse – between 1914 and 1973 – these structural differences have disappeared and the characteristics of the Dutch growth regime have, at the end of this century, become very similar to those of the US (again the "overshooting" during the 1960s and 1970s is evident from this point of view). It may perhaps be argued that this traverse was caused by a protracted movement towards the technology of the second Industrial Revolution (which was, if these statistics are correct, and more human-capital intensive, because the share of labour in income increased, and needed larger quantities of capital goods, because the investment ratio went up), a switch which was interrupted and delayed by the exogenous shocks of World War I and II.

5.   CONCLUSION

In this paper I have attempted to show that it may be useful to approach the issue of historic economic growth with the concept of growth regime, an extended periods of time in which economic growth shows more or less stable characteristics. On the basis of modern growth theory, two types of growth regimes were distinguished, steady state or equilibrium growth and disequilibrium growth, which was analysed in terms of a traverse between two different steady states. In my view this distinction clarifies the very different behaviour of the Dutch economy in the 19th and the 20th century. The first period was characterised by steady state growth – whereas Belgium went through a real Industrial Revolution which shows the features of a traverse (consistent with the Gerschenkron interpretation of industrialisation in a "backward" country). The backgrounds of these divergent growth path during the 19th century were briefly analysed. Slow growth in the Netherlands is probably related to the fact that (after 1840) is specialised on the production of agricultural products (and services), whereas Belgium had a comparative advantage in (semi-finished) industrial products. Growth in the 20th century, especially during the Golden Age of European economic growth (1945-1973) had all the features of a disequilibrium growth path, which resulted in "overshooting" during the 1960s and early 1970s (when growth had become too fast to be sustainable and led to strong tensions on the labour market which undermined the financial structure of the economy).[38] This contrasts sharply with the balanced growth path that is apparently characteristic for the economy of the United States in this period. The more general point I try to make is that long run economic growth can probably best be understood as a succession of growth regimes which show a certain degree of path dependency: once an economy is on either a low or a fast growth track, the interplay of demand and supply forces – and of expectations – seem to keep the economy at this particular trajectory.

This phenomenon, which may perhaps be called the persistence of growth regimes, can again be illustrated with some examples from the Dutch growth record. In more conventional explanations of the successive phases of economic growth, supply factors dominate the picture. The acceleration of growth after 1913 or 1918, for example, is explained by the fact that the Second Industrial Revolution, and especially the introduction and spread of electricity, made possible large advances in productivity, resulting in Gordon's "big wave" of fast productivity growth.[39] One of the problems of such an interpretation is the timing of the acceleration of growth. Whereas the spread of electricity began in the 1880s, and accelerated sharply after 1900 – in 1913 already about 45 per cent of the capacity of power sources in manufacturing and construction consisted of electric motors[40] – GDP growth was hardly going up before the 1920s. Perhaps the economy needed the shock of World War I to begin to grow more rapidly after the persistence of slow growth during the preceding decades (during which the GDP-per capita gap with the productivity leaders the US and the UK had increased markedly). This leads to the hypothesis that accelerations of GDP growth are not "normal," *i.e.* they occur very infrequently and perhaps only, as in the Dutch case, after wars when the economy has contracted severely and rapid growth is made possible because of this previous contraction.

---

[38] An important difference between the two disequilibrium growth regimes analysed in this paper should be mentioned: in the Netherlands after 1945 the growth of the demand for labour outstripped its supply, which resulted in very rapid increases in wage costs and declining profitability after 1961, which undermined the long term prospects of growth; in Belgium between 1840 and 1870 the share of wages in income did not increase but declined, which probably implies that the labour supply was much more elastic (thanks to the sharp contraction of the labour force in agriculture). As a result Belgian industrialisation did not "overshoot" and the growth spurt was not followed by a protracted depression after 1873.

[39] Gordon (2000). A similar explanation is put forward by Smits, de Jong and van Ark (1999).

[40] Albers (1998), p. 209.

In a similar way it can be argued that high growth rates tend to persist, as the economic development between 1960 and 1973 suggests. On the basis of the interpretation that focuses on supply factors alone, which sees the 1913-1973 period as one phase of rapid growth caused by the productivity advances made possible by the technology of the Second Industrial Revolution, one would expect a gradual slowing down of productivity growth during the years in which the new technologies became mature, the 1960s and early 1970s (and one would expect this to happen much earlier in the United States). I would argue that the persistence of the high growth regime of the post 1945 period was a major cause behind the high productivity growth during the period until 1973 (the sharply increasing real wages and the tensions on the labour market forced capitalists to invest in labour saving equipment. High rates of investment brought about a rapid renewal of the capital stock, *etc.*). Similarly, the sudden decline of productivity growth after 1973 is probably to a large extent caused by the slow growth in the following decades.

These different growth regimes, which are, of course, partially determined by the possibilities for technological change, determine the extent to which actual growth is in line with the productivity advances made possible by technological change. One might argue that the Dutch economy, which was on a slow growth trajectory during the 19th century, tended to "underperform," because output and productivity growth was relatively slow and it was, in terms of GDP per capita, overtaken by the US and Belgium. The rather unorthodox conclusion might be that GDP growth was not sufficient to profit from the new opportunities of the first (and the second) Industrial Revolution. In a similar way one can argue that during the 1960s the Dutch economy "overperformed," that the high growth regime forced a too high level of productivity growth on the economy, which is perhaps just another way of expressing the fact that it was "overshooting." If these conclusions are warranted, it becomes important to understand much more in detail the inherent dynamics of growth regimes and the switches from one regime to another. The series of the reconstructed national accounts for the Netherlands will, I hope, be an important instrument for studying these processes in the future.

REFERENCES

Abramovitz, M. (1986), "Catching up, Forging Ahead and Falling behind," *Journal of Economic History* 46, pp. 385-406.

Albers, R.M. (1998), *Machinery Investment Dynamics and Economic Growth*, dissertation Groningen University, Groningen.

Amendola, M. and J.L. Gaffard (1998), *Out of Equilibrium*, Oxford: Clarendon Press.

Ark, B. van, and H.J. de Jong (1996), "Accounting for Economic Growth in the Netherlands since 1913," *Economic and Social History in the Netherlands* 7, pp. 199-242.

Bakker, G.P. den, J. de Gijt and R.A.M. van Rooijen (1996), "New Revision Policies for the Dutch National Accounts," *Economic and Social History in the Netherlands* 7, pp. 243-260.

Barro, R.J. and X. Sala-i-Martin (1995), *Economic Growth*, New York: McGraw-Hill.

Bie, R. van der (1995), *Een doorlopende groote roes. De economische ontwikkeling van Nederland, 1913/21*, Amsterdam: Thesis Publishers.

Burda, M. and C. Wyplosz (1997), *Macroeconomics. A European text*, Oxford: Oxford University Press.

Buyst, E. and M. van Meerten (1997), "De Generale Maatschappij en de economische ontwikkeling van België," in E. Buyst *et al.* (eds.), *De Generale Bank 1822-1997*, Tielt: Lannoo.

Crafts, N.F.R. (1985), *British Economic Growth during the Industrial Revolution*, Oxford: Clarendon Press.

Crafts, N.F.R., S.J. Leybourne and T.C. Mills (1990), "Measurement of Trend Growth in European Industrial Output Before 1914: Methodological Issues and New Estimates," *Explorations in Economic History* 27, pp. 442-67.

Crafts, N. and T.C. Mills (1996), "Europe's Golden Age: An Econometric Investigation of Changing Trend Rates of Growth," in B. van Ark and N. Crafts (eds.), *Quantitative Aspects of Post-war Economic Growth*, pp. 415-431, Cambridge: Cambridge University Press.

Crafts, N. and G. Toniolo (1996), "Postwar Growth: and overview," in N. Crafts and G. Toniolo (eds.), *Economic growth in Europe since 1945*, Cambridge: Cambridge University Press, pp. 1-37.

Eichengreen, B. (1996), "Institutions and Economic Growth: Europe after World War II," in N. Crafts and G. Toniolo (eds.), *Economic Growth in Europe since 1945*, Cambridge: Cambridge University Press, pp. 38-72.

Gerschenkron, A. (1962), *Economic Backwardness in Historical Perspective*, Cambridge (Mass), Harvard University Press.

Gerschenkron, A. (1977), *An Economic Spurt that Failed*, Princeton: Princeton University Press.

Gordon, R.J. (2000), "Interpreting the "One Big Wave" in U.S. Long-term Productivity Growth," this volume.

Griffiths, R.T. (1980), *Achterlijk, achter of anders?*, Inaugural Lecture, Free University, Amsterdam.

Groote, P. (1995), *Kapitaalvorming in infrastructuur in Nederland 1800-1913*, Capelle aan den IJssel: Labyrint Publication.

Hicks, J. (1973), *Capital and Time*, Oxford: Clarendon Press.

Horlings, E. (1995), *The Economic Development of the Dutch Service Sector, 1800-1850. Trade and Transport in a Premodern Economy*, Amsterdam: Neha.

Horlings, E. en J.P.H. Smits (1997), "A Comparison of the Pattern of Growth and Structural Change in the Netherlands and Belgium, 1800-1913," *Jahrbuch für Wirtschaftsgeschichte*, pp. 83-106.

Johnson, D.G. (1954), "The Functional Distribution of Income in the United States, 1850-1952," *Review of Economics and Statistics* 34, pp. 175-82.

Jong, H.J. de (1999), *De Nederlandse industrie 1913-1965. Een vergelijkende analyse op basis van de productiestatistieken*, Amsterdam: Neha.

Kaldor, N. (1961), "Capital Accumulation and Economic Growth," in F.A. Lutz and D.C. Hague (eds.), *The Theory of Capital*, London: Macmillan.

Knibbe, M. (1993), *Agriculture in the Netherlands 1851-1950*, Amsterdam: Neha.

Maddison, A. (1992), "A Long-run Perspective on Saving," *Scandinavian Journal of Economics* 94, pp. 181-96.

Maddison, A. (1995), *Monitoring the World Economy, 1820-1990*, OECD, Paris.

Mokyr, J. (1976), *Industrialisation in the Low Countries, 1795-1850*, New Haven: Yale U.P.

Scott, M.F. (1989), *A New View of Economic Growth*, Oxford: Clarendon Press.

Smits, J.P.H. (1995), *Economische groei en structuurveranderingen in de Nederlandse dienstensector 1850-1913*, Ph-D thesis, Free University, Amsterdam.

Smits, J.P.H., E. Horlings and J.L. van Zanden (1997), "The Measurement of Gross National Product and its Components. The Netherlands, 1800-1913," Research memorandum N.W. Posthumus Institute 97-1, Utrecht.

Smits, J.P.H., H. de Jong and B. van Ark (1999), "Three Phases of Dutch Economic Growth and Technological Change, 1815-1997," Research Memorandum, Groningen Growth and Development Center GD-42.

Solow, R.M. (1970), *Growth Theory: an exposition*, Oxford: Clarendon Press.

Sylla, R., and G. Toniolo (eds.) (1991), *Patterns of European Industrialisation*, London: Routledge.

Vries, J. de, and A. van der Woude (1997), *The First Modern Economy. Success, Failure and Perseverance of the Dutch Economy, 1500-1815*, Cambridge: Cambridge University Press.

Williamson, J.G. (1985), *Did British Capitalism breed Inequality?*, Boston: Allen & Unwin.

Weiss, Th. (1994), "Economic Growth before 1860: Revised Conjectures," in Th. Weiss and D. Schaefer (eds.), *American Economic Development in Historical Perspective*, pp. 11-28, Stanford: Stanford University Press.

Zanden, J.L. van (1998), *The Economic History of the Netherlands 1914-1995*, London: Routledge.

Zanden, J.L. van, and A. van Riel (2000), *Nederland 1780-1914. Staat, economie en instituties*, Amsterdam: Balans.

Zanden, J.L. van (1999), "Post War European Economic Development as an Out of Equilibrium Growth Path. The Case of the Netherlands," paper presented at seminar Northwestern University, May.

Chapter 4

Institutions and Economic Growth in Postwar Europe
Evidence and Conjectures

Barry Eichengreen and Pablo Vazquez*
George C. Pardee and Helen N. Pardee Professor of Economics and Political Science, University of California, Berkeley; and University of Santander and Office of the Spanish Prime Minister, Madrid, respectively.

Key words: Economic growth, Institutions

Abstract: This paper seeks to shed light on the economics of Europe's post-World War II "golden age," fleshing out the role of institutions in the postwar growth process. It argues that the institutional arrangements inherited from Europe's prior history were particularly well-suited to the macroeconomic and technological imperatives of economic growth following World War II. Corporatist labour relations encouraged the wage moderation and high levels of investment needed to reproduce American-style industrial production on a massive scale. Relatively centralised structures were well suited to the incremental technical changes needed to adapt American technologies for European circumstances. And the institutions of European and global integration went some way towards creating the mass market in consumer goods and the open market raw materials needed to support the transplantation of American technologies.

*   An earlier version of this paper was presented at the conference on Productivity and Living Standards, Groningen, September 1998. We are grateful for the organisers of that conference (also the editors of this volume) for helpful suggestions.

91

1.   INTRODUCTION

It is now conventional to refer to the post-World War II era of rapid growth ending around 1971 as the "golden age." Quibbles about dates and magnitudes notwithstanding, there is no question that the first postwar quarter century was a period in which output, employment and productivity grew rapidly relative to what came before and what followed.

There is no shortage of explanations for the golden age.[1] The one with which we are concerned in this paper emphasises the role of institutions in solving commitment and co-ordination problems.[2] The argument goes as follows. In a postwar context characterised by severe capital shortage and a backlog of unexploited technologies, investment was the one indispensable ingredient for growth. Net investment rates in 1950-1970 were nearly twice as high as in 1920-40. This was a period of "extensive growth," not in the narrow sense that additions to output were associated exclusively with additions to the stock of capital and labour inputs, but in the broad sense that returns to capital and labour were not strongly diminishing and that productivity advance could be achieved by emulating best practice in the United States.

But this additional investment had to be financed, and once financed it had to be sensibly allocated. Here wage moderation and export growth were key. Wage moderation stimulated investment by enhancing its profitability and making available the resources to finance it. The opening of the European economies, whose exports expanded even faster than their output, provided an incentive to allocate investment to sectors where the returns were highest – to those sectors, in other words, in which the country had a comparative advantage. It allowed capacity to be expanded without being constrained by domestic demand.

This is where institutions came into play. Europe's postwar growth benefited from institutions that solved commitment and co-ordination problems in whose presence neither wage moderation nor the rapid

---

[1] Two compendia of these are Crafts and Toniolo (1996) and Dumke (1997).

[2] See Eichengreen (1996). Analyses in a similar spirit include Landesmann and Vartianen (1993), Hargreaves Heap (1994) and Przeworski and Wallerstein (1982). Part of the difficulty of relating this paper to kindred work is that similar concepts are referred to by different names. Where we refer to "commitment and co-ordination problems," for example, Hargreaves Heap uses the phrase "prisoner's dilemma and co-ordination games." Przeworski and Wallerstein refer to bargains between capital and labour as "class compromises" and stress the need for capitalists to "consent to institutions that would make it reasonably certain that wages would increase as a function of profits according to some rule..." (p.218). Boyer and Mistral (1992) uses the term "Fordism" to refer to the cooperative structure of industrial relations and equitable division of productivity gains in Europe after World War II.

expansion of trade would have been possible. Domestically, institutions disseminated information and monitored the compliance of economic interest groups with the terms of their agreement to moderate wage claims and boost investment. They created bonds that would be lost in the event that any party reneged and co-ordinated the terms of the agreement across sectors of the economy. Internationally, institutions co-ordinated the restoration of current account convertibility across countries and cemented national governments' commitment to openness, encouraging countries to restructure along export-oriented lines and more fully exploit their comparative advantage.

In this paper we report new evidence that speaks to this interpretation. We utilise newly-developed measures of the structure of labour-management relations and of the institutional commitment to external opening. The results are consistent with the importance of investment and exports for growth, of international institutions for the expansion of exports, and of the institutions of labour-management relations for the wage moderation that supported the investment.

In addition, we extend this interpretation in new directions, developing its implications for technology policy. Building on work by Kitschelt (1991) and others, we suggest that Europe's postwar institutions were better adapted to absorbing the backlog of existing technologies available after World War II than they were to supporting innovation.[3] If the 1971-73 watershed can be seen as a transition to "intensive growth," not in the narrow sense that all growth in output per worker was now rooted in domestically-generated technological progress but in the broad sense that growth now depended more heavily on innovation than it had in the preceding quarter of a century, then it appears that the institutions inherited by the Europe of the 1970s were less than ideally suited to the task. Similarly, labour market institutions that were well suited to the high-growth 1950s and 1960s functioned less well in the less buoyant 1970s and 1980s.

No single paper can verify all these conjectures. This paper is best read as one in a series, each of which adds colour to a larger canvas.[4]

---

[3] Soskice (1996), while also emphasising the institutional prerequisites for technological change, takes a rather different approach to the same issues, mainly because he focuses on a later period.

[4] In addition to the above-mentioned paper, see Eichengreen (1994) and Eichengreen (1998).

2.   FACTS

Table 1 provides an eagle-eye's view of Europe's growth. The most striking feature of the top panel, which reports GDP growth for various sub-periods, is that between 1950 and 1971 the 12 Western European economies grew by 4.7 per cent per annum, more than twice as fast as over the century and a half since 1820.[5] Over the second sub-period from 1973 through 1992, growth averaged 2.2 per cent per annum, almost exactly the average over the entire 172 years since 1820. Aside from the golden age, only in 1870-1913, the last period of marked internationalisation when the growth of foreign trade, foreign investment and international migration outstripped the growth of production, did output growth in Western Europe also reach the 1820-1992 averages.

Table 1. Phases of Growth, 1820-1992 (annual average compound growth rate)

	1820-70	1870-1913	1913-50	1950-73	1973-92	1820-1992
				GDP		
Western Europe	1.7	2.1	1.4	4.7	2.2	2.2
Southern Europe	1.0	1.5	1.3	6.3	3.1	2.1
Eastern Europe	1.6	2.4	1.6	4.7	-0.4	2.0
World	1.0	2.1	1.9	4.9	3.0	2.2
				GDP per capita		
Western Europe	1.0	1.3	0.9	3.9	1.8	1.5
Southern Europe	0.6	1.1	0.4	4.9	1.7	1.4
Eastern Europe	0.7	1.0	1.2	3.5	1.1	1.1
World	1.3	1.3	0.9	2.9	1.2	1.2

Source: Maddison (1995).

The same fluctuations are evident in Southern Europe, where the pattern of acceleration and deceleration is if anything even more dramatic.[6] While growth over the entire period since 1820 is essentially the same as in Western Europe, the postwar acceleration is more pronounced. Growth is fully three times as fast in 1950-73 as over the period as a whole. While Southern Europe also experienced the post-1973 slowdown, growth there is still 50 per cent faster in 1973-92 than the period average.

---

[5]   Austria, Belgium, Denmark, Finland, France, Germany, Italy, the Netherlands, Norway, Sweden, Switzerland and the UK.

[6]   Greece, Portugal, Spain, Turkey and Ireland (following Maddison, who groups economies as much by their initial economic structure — by, inter alia, the importance of agriculture and initial income — as by proximity to the Equator).

Even more than in Western Europe, then, the second half of the 20th century, and especially the 1950-73 period, stands out.[7]

Table 2. Per Capita Real GDP Growth in 56 Countries, 1820-1992 (annual average compound growth rates)

	1820-70	1870-1913	1913-50	1950-73	1973-92
12 Western European Countries					
Austria	0.7	1.5	0.2	4.9	2.2
Belgium	1.4	1.0	0.7	3.5	1.9
Denmark	0.9	1.6	1.6	3.1	1.6
Finland	0.8	1.4	1.9	4.3	1.6
France	0.8	1.5	1.1	4.0	1.7
Germany	1.1	1.6	0.3	5.0	2.1
Italy	0.6	1.3	0.8	5.0	2.4
Netherlands	1.1	0.9	1.1	3.4	1.4
Norway	0.5	1.3	2.1	3.2	2.9
Sweden	0.7	1.5	2.1	3.1	1.2
Switzerland.	n.a	1.5	2.1	3.1	0.8
United Kingdom	1.2	1.0	0.8	2.5	1.4
Arithmetic avg.	0.9	1.3	1.2	3.8	1.8
5 South European Countries					
Greece	n.a.	n.a.	0.5	6.2	1.5
Ireland	1.2	1.0	0.7	3.1	2.7
Portugal	n.a.	0.5	1.2	5.7	2.1
Spain	0.5	1.2	0.2	5.8	1.9
Turkey	n.a.	n.a.	0.8	3.3	2.6
Arithmetic avg.	n.a.	0.9	0.7	4.8	2.2
7 Eastern European Countries					
Bulgaria	n.a.	n.a.	0.3	5.2	-1.4
Czechoslovakia	0.6	1.4	1.4	3.1	-0.1
Hungary	n.a.	1.2	0.5	3.6	0.0
Poland	n.a.	n.a.	n.a.	3.4	-0.6
Romania	n.a.	n.a.	n.a.	4.8	-1.6
USSR	0.6	0.9	1.8	3.4	-0.4
Yugoslavia	n.a.	n.a.	1.0	4.4	-0.5
Arithmetic avg.	n.a.	1.2	1.0	4.0	-0.8

Source: Maddison (1995).

---

[7] Figures are also provided for Eastern Europe, although this region is not the subject of the present paper. There is also some evidence of the operation of the extensive-growth model there, although the figures for the region should be taken with several grains of salt. The bottom panel of Table 1 compares the growth of output per capita in the different regions. Here, Western Europe compares even more favourably, since it consistently featured the lowest rate of population growth.

Table 2 disaggregates by country. It shows that extensive growth was fastest in Germany, Austria and Italy, reflecting Germany's postwar *Wirtschaftswunder*, Austria's economic and geographic proximity to its larger neighbour, and (Northern) Italy's success in catching up with the continent's high-income regions. It was slowest in the United Kingdom, a problem that by the 1970s had given rise to a literature on that country's "economic failure." While the U.K. continued to underperform the Western European average after 1973 (with the economy's dismal performance in the 1970s swamping its improved performance in the 1980s), the change in per capita income was every bit as slow in Switzerland, Sweden and the Netherlands. In Southern Europe, meanwhile, the golden age was brightest in Greece and Iberia, least so in Turkey and in Ireland, while the post-1973 slowdown was least dramatic in these last two countries.[8]

Table 3. The Contribution to Growth of Gross Domestic Product in Nine Western European Countries of Labour, Capital, and Technical Progress, 1949-59

Country	Labour Force	Capital Stock	GDP Trend	Estimated Contribution to Growth of GDP of:			
				Labour	Capital	Technical progress	ICOR
	(1)	(2)	(3)	(4)	(5)	(6)	(7)
			(Compound annual percentage rate of growth)				
Western Germany[1]	1.6	6.0	7.4	1.1	1.8	4.5	2.6
Italy	1.1	3.2	5.9	0.8	1.0	4.1	2.1
Yugoslavia	1.1	4.9	5.5	0.8	1.5	3.2	2.5
Netherlands	1.2	4.8	4.8	0.8	1.4	2.6	4.0
France	0.1	3.4	4.5	0.1	1.0	3.4	2.9
Norway	0.3	4.6	3.4	0.2	1.4	1.8	8.5
Sweden	0.5	2.0	3.4	0.3	0.6	2.5	4.1
Belgium	0.3	2.6	3.0	0.2	0.8	2.0	2.8
United Kingdom	0.6	3.1	2.4	0.4	0.9	1.1	3.7

Source: Extract from United Nations (1964). [1]1950-59.

Table 3 decomposes growth into the contributions of capital, labour and technological change.[9] Germany's position in the 1950s at the top of the growth league reflects the rapid growth of inputs (fast growth of the labour

[8]   Indeed, Ireland and Turkey were the best performers in Southern Europe in the years of intensive growth.

[9]   Based on a Cobb-Douglas production function with a coefficient of 0.7 for the labour force.

supply and high investment rates), but also the rapid growth of productivity. Technological progress is also rapid in Italy, reflecting that country's success at closing the productivity gap vis-à-vis Europe's high-income countries. Britain's poor performance is seen to reflect both low investment rates and disappointing productivity growth. France stands out for the stagnation of its labour force.[10]

Table 4. Growth of Real GDP and Its Components 1960-69

Country	Labour Force	Capital Stock[3]	Real GDP	Estimated contribution to growth of GDP by:		
				Labour	Capital	Technical Progress
			(Annual Percentage Rate of Growth)			
Greece	-0.9	6.6	6.8	-0.7	2.0	5.5
Italy[2]	-0.3	5.3	5.6	-0.2	1.6	4.2
France	0.8	5.4	5.3	0.6	1.6	3.2
Belgium[1]	0.3	5.2	4.7	0.2	1.6	3.0
Germany	0.4	6.0	4.7	0.3	1.8	2.6
Sweden[1]	0.5	4.1	4.3	0.3	1.2	2.8
Norway[1]	1.0	3.9	4.1	0.7	1.2	2.2
Finland[1]	0.2	4.9	4.0	0.1	1.5	2.4
U.K.	0.3	4.4	3.1	0.2	1.3	1.6

Sources: OECD Economic Outlook database; OECD Flows and Stocks of Fixed Capital; IMF *World Economic Outlook.*
Notes on Capital Stock:
[1] Belgium, Finland, Norway, Sweden: average over 1963-69.
[2] Italy: average over 1961-69.
[3] Net total capital stock at constant prices for all countries except Sweden (gross total capital stock at constant prices).
Note: growth rates calculated as the difference of the log of the levels.
Note on Estimated contributions to growth of GDP:
Contribution by Labour = 0.7 * Average annual growth rate of the labour force
Contribution by Capital = 0.3 * Average annual growth rate of the capital stock
Contribution by Technical Progress is calculated as a residual

Growth accelerated further in the 1960s.[11] The rate of growth of output per employed person jumped from 3.6 per cent per annum in the 'fifties to

[10] While French policymakers were much concerned about this "Malthusian" problem, Table 3 suggests that the country's impressive productivity performance (behind that of only Germany and Italy) sustained more-than-respectable rates of output growth.

[11] We should entertain the possibility that causality ran in the opposite direction, from faster growth enjoyed for independent reasons to willingness to participate in a free-trade area. Lamfalussy (1963) considers this question and concludes in favour of the interpretation in the text. We return to this issue below.

4.2 per cent in the 'sixties (Table 4).[12] Investment was maintained at high levels, and the countries of Western Europe remained net importers of capital.[13] Much of this foreign investment from the United States was associated with technology transfer in chemicals, computers and transport equipment. Investment ratios rose further, although much of the additional outlay was needed to make up for depreciation of the now-larger capital stock and was devoted to housing and consumer durables spending by now-wealthier households. Meanwhile, labour force growth was sustained by the movement of workers to the industrial regions from Mediterranean Europe and North Africa. Only in Austria and West Germany, where growth had been fastest, was there a clear slowing down between the 'fifties and the 'sixties. In Belgium, Denmark, France and Norway, all relatively poor performers in the 1950s, there was an acceleration.[14]

In Southern Europe, growth accelerated to even higher levels as Greece, Portugal and Spain began the process of liberalising and opening to Europe and the world. In Spain, the pivotal event was the tariff of 1960, under which half of all barriers to imports from OECD countries were removed.[15] For Portugal the pivotal event was joining EFTA. Greece negotiated an association agreement with the EEC (as did Spain). Rather than shunting these countries into the agricultural backwater, opening was associated with rapid growth of labour-intensive manufactures.[16] In Spain industrial production expanded at an annual rate of 10.2 per cent, the service sector by 6.7 per cent and agriculture by 2.3 per cent per year from 1960 through 1973, as labour was shifted from low-productivity agriculture to high-productivity manufacturing, and as capital goods were imported from

---

[12] The acceleration GDP growth was more modest, rising from 4.5 to 4.7 per cent per annum, reflecting the falling rate of growth of employment.

[13] With the exception of the U.K. and, toward the end of the period, West Germany and Italy.

[14] Norway finally reaped returns on expensive infrastructure investments undertaken in earlier years. France, previously saddled by controls, cartels and public enterprises, benefited disproportionately from the liberalisation of trade. Denmark, where trade liberalisation in the 1950s had created serious problems for an industrial sector which had been generously protected since the 1930s, now reaped the benefits of industrial rationalisation (inefficient firms closed and their more efficient counterparts merged, leading to increased productivity and a greater ability to reap economies of scale), allowing increased production and exports of engineering and electrical equipment and of the products of the brewing industry.

[15] Spain was the only country where the growth of exports lagged the growth of output in the 1950s.

[16] In part this reflected the fact that trade in agriculture was less than free. Among the first concrete achievements of the EEC was its Common Agricultural Policy, under which trade in foodstuffs was restrained, and the EFTA agreement was initially limited to industrial goods.

abroad.[17] With Austrian and German growth declining from higher levels and the pace picking up in these other countries, the norm became expansion by 4.5 per cent per annum, fully twice the historical average. Only Britain failed to share in the phenomenon, output per worker there growing per annum by a meagre 2.5 per cent.[18]

All in all, this review of the record confirms that there is indeed a golden age to be explained.

3.   HYPOTHESES

Lancaster (1973), Grout (1984) and van der Ploeg (1987) model a dynamic game between capital and labour. Welfare is maximised when capitalists and workers agree to trade current compensation for future gains. Workers moderate their wage claims in order to make profitable investments in capacity modernisation and expansion. Capitalists restrain dividend payout in order to reinvest. Investment stimulates growth, raising the future incomes of both capitalists and workers. In the cooperative equilibrium in which workers and capitalists exercise restraint, the costs of foregoing current consumption are dominated by the benefits of the future increase in incomes.

This cooperative equilibrium may be impossible to sustain, however, for the sequencing of events renders it time inconsistent. If investment requires liquidity and liquidity requires profits, then workers must restrain their wage demands now in order to make profits available to capitalists for investment later. But once the wage restraint has occurred, capitalists are even better off if they renege on their agreement to invest, paying out profits as dividends instead. Since investment is no higher than if they had failed to moderate their wages, workers have no incentive to exercise restraint. Even if workers can be convinced of capital's willingness to invest, unions may be tempted to recontract after the investment has taken place. If workers renege and appropriate the surplus created by the additional investment, profits will be no higher than if management had failed to invest, and management has no incentive to plow profits into investment. In the noncooperative equilibrium, workers pursue wage increases and management pays out profits, causing investment and growth to lag.

---

[17] Harrison (1993), p.23.

[18] Growth was also disappointing in Ireland and Denmark, in part because both countries were dependent on the slowly growing British export market. But the fact that the incremental capital-output ratio was so high in Ireland suggests that supply-side problems existed there as well. These can be attributed to the kind of fragmented industrial relations system also familiar in the U.K. (see the discussion to follow). In addition, the fact that Ireland and Denmark were heavily agricultural meant that they encountered particular difficulties in penetrating the protected domestic markets of other countries.

A contract that binds capitalists to invest and workers to restrain wages can therefore leave both groups better off. The social and economic institutions developed in Europe after World War II can be thought of as serving this function.[19] Institutions worked to monitor the compliance of capitalists with their deferred contribution to the bargain and to disseminate evidence of noncooperation; by reducing the likelihood that shirking would go undetected, these mechanisms reduced the temptation to indulge in noncooperative behaviour. Institutions were used to create "bonds" that would be lost in the event of reneging, "bonding" the participants and providing a further deterrent to shirking. By committing capital to invest the profits made available by wage restraint, they provided labour the incentive to moderate their wage claims. By committing labour to continue to exercise restraint rather than "scooping" profits, they provided capital the incentive to invest. Long-term contracts, pacts between the social partners and government, and statutory wage and price controls can all be thought of as precommitting unions to wage moderation and inducing management to invest. Unemployment, health and retirement programs – the institutions of the welfare state, in other words – served as bonds that would be jeopardised if labour reneged.

The centralisation and concertation of sectoral wage negotiations further encouraged wage moderation. Insofar as one firm's earnings could pass through the capital market and finance another's investment, the benefits of wage moderation by any one group or union accrued to other workers. Since the level of wages affected economy-wide determinants of investment like the interest rate, there was a need to coordinate wage demands across sectors to render a bargain to moderate wage claims attractive to each party to the accord.[20]

On the employer side, any one firm contemplating investment had to worry that its decision to invest would encourage its workers to raise their wage demands in order to appropriate the extra profits generated by the investment. But if wages were determined in economy-wide rather than enterprise-level negotiations, an individual firm's investment decision would no longer affect the wages it had to pay. In these circumstances, centralised wage negotiations led to a higher level of investment and, insofar as productivity was raised, to higher wages in equilibrium.[21]

For deferring consumption to be worthwhile, investment had to be productive. For investment to stimulate growth, in other words, there had to

---

[19]   A la North (1993) and North and Weingast (1989).

[20]   Otherwise a prisoner's dilemma could arise in which any one sectoral bargaining unit would agree to moderate its demands only if it expected others to do the same, but in the absence of an agreement to harmonise demands no one had an incentive to be moderate.

[21]   These possibilities are modelled by Hoel (1990).

be a market for the goods produced by industries whose capacity was augmented and whose efficiency was enhanced. Here the post-World War II expansion of trade was key. International trade – for European countries intra-European trade in particular – allowed countries to specialise in sectors in which they had a comparative advantage without regard to limits on the demand for their products at home. It allowed them to rely on cheap foreign inputs that were impossible or uneconomical to produce domestically.

But reallocating resources along lines of comparative advantage could turn out to be a costly mistake if one's trading partners reneged on their commitment to openness. Encouraging the expansion of steel production on the assumption that coal and iron ore could be imported from abroad, for example, could be a costly error if foreign supplies were not forthcoming. Augmenting the capacity of such industries would not pay if other countries refused to reduce their tariffs. Before encouraging the rationalisation of domestic production along lines of comparative advantage, governments consequently had to be convinced that their partners' turn to openness was permanent.

Here again institutions solved commitment and co-ordination problems. The European Coal and Steel Community created monitoring and surveillance technologies that guaranteed the French steel industry access to German coal and German industry access to French iron ore. A Joint High Authority monitored the compliance of participating countries to the terms of their agreement. The European Payments Union (EPU) co-ordinated the simultaneous move of European countries to currency convertibility for intra-European current-account transactions and committed the participants to a sequence of trade liberalisation measures. The EPU Managing Board monitored the policies of member countries in order to discourage them from reneging on their commitments.[22] Compared to unilateral convertibility, then, the payments union was a more credible commitment mechanism.[23]

---

[22] The participants contributed currency and credit to the EPU's central fund; access to these resources was contingent on their adherence to the EPU agreement, which thereby served as a bond.

[23] How, it might be asked, does our thesis that the institutions of European integration and industrial relations helped to solve commitment and co-ordination problems that would have otherwise prevented Europe from achieving the wage moderation, high investment and rapid export growth that were key ingredients of its postwar growth process differ from previous work? Most previous analyses of corporatist labour relations (e.g. Crouch 1985, Bruno and Sachs 1985) have concentrated on short-run wage and employment dynamics (the response of wages and unemployment to supply shocks in more and less corporatist economies, for example). Our focus, in contrast, is on wage, employment and output trends over the intermediate run. Similarly, previous work on regional trade arrangements has concentrated on short-run trade creation and trade diversion; our concern, in contrast, is with the implications for medium-term export performance.

4.   EVIDENCE ON LABOUR- AND TRADE-
RELATED INSTITUTIONS

Institutions were not equally well adapted to the imperatives of postwar growth in all European countries. The U.K. and Ireland essentially failed to develop the requisite arrangements while France and Italy did so only with delay. In these countries, wage pressure was intense, and investment was stifled. Some countries, of which France is a prime example, were slow to restructure along export-oriented lines and to capitalise on opportunities for export-led growth.

This section exploits the fact that institutional arrangements differed to analyse their connection with growth performance more systemically.

4.1   Output

No consensus exists among macro-econometricians on the importance of institutions for economic growth. Two recent studies, Crafts (1992) and Grier (1993), reach broadly negative conclusions about the importance of institutionalised bargaining. Yet other studies which consider a broader range of institutions, *viz.* Knack and Keefer (1995, 1996) and La Porta *et al.* (1997), report rather more supportive conclusions. It is fair to say that the jury is still out.

To maximise comparability with previous studies, we take the data and specification in Grier (1993) as our starting point. Grier uses data for 24 OECD countries for the period 1950-88.[24] We follow him by drawing output data from the Heston-Summers Penn World Tables (in our case Version 5.5), but drop Iceland, Luxembourg and Turkey as special cases unlikely to shed much light on the dynamics of European growth.[25]

Grier relates the rate of growth of GDP to output per capita at the start of the period (per capita GDP in dollars at purchasing power parity), the rate of population growth, the standard deviation of inflation, and the ratio of government consumption to GDP.[26] Per capita output should enter negatively if catch-up is important. Population growth should enter

---

[24] The 24 countries are Australia, Austria, Belgium, Canada, Denmark, Finland, France, Germany, Greece, Japan, Iceland, Ireland, Italy, Luxembourg, the Netherlands, New Zealand, Norway, Portugal, Spain, Sweden, Switzerland, Turkey, the U.K. and the U.S. Grier takes five-year averages of country data (except for a three year average for 1985-88) and pools the cross sections.

[25] Data on the volume and value of exports (including re-exports) are taken from the OECD's *National Accounts Statistics* and *Statistical Bulletin*. The share of exports destined for European and OECD countries is drawn from the *Statistics of Foreign Trade* of the OECD (Series A).

[26] We include fixed effects for periods in each of the equations reported.

positively, since the dependent variable is the rate of growth of aggregate output. While growth should decline with the variability of inflation, the sign of the coefficient on the average inflation rate is not obvious a priori.[27] Government consumption should enter negatively if it crowds out more productive uses of resources.

In most of our regressions we include both the investment/GDP ratio at the start of the period and the period-average rate of growth of investment, anticipating positive signs on both.[28] We consider several measures of exports: the export/GDP ratio at the start of the period, the growth rate of total exports, the growth of exports going to EU countries, and the growth of exports to all of (OECD) Europe.[29]

The first equation in Table 5, estimated by ordinary least squares, replicates Grier's basic result.[30] Most of the variables enter with the anticipated signs and with coefficients that differ significantly from zero at standard confidence levels. Initial GDP enters negatively as predicted by the catch-up hypothesis. The growth of government consumption is negative, as if it crowds out other more productive forms of spending. The investment ratio is positive and significant, as anticipated. The variance of inflation is negative and significant, population growth positive and significant.[31]

---

[27] Motley (1994) suggests that inflation may depress growth by diverting resources into unproductive uses such as changing wages and prices more frequently, economising on holdings of non-interest-bearing assets, etc. Grier measures average inflation as the first difference of the period average on the grounds that first differences are more likely to isolate the unexpected changes in inflation that may be important for output. The results we report here take the more straightforward approach of using the period average rate of inflation.

[28] Grier measures investment by its share of GDP. Since including the rates of growth of investment and exports in the output equation creates the possibility of simultaneity bias, we in general treat all our investment and export variables as endogenous.

[29] For our purposes, OECD Europe includes in addition to members of the EEC/EU (depending on time period), Austria, Finland, Norway, Sweden, and Switzerland.

[30] t-statistics reported in this paper are calculated using heteroskedastic-consistent standard errors.

[31] Aside from some of the fixed effects, average inflation is the one variable whose coefficient does not differ from zero at standard confidence levels. We measure this variable as the period average of the annual log difference of the purchasing-power-parity price level in each country plus the annual log difference in the U.S. GDP deflator, since the Heston-Summers PPP price level is measured relative to the U.S. price level. Levine and Zervos (1994) and Motley (1994) similarly fail to find that inflation is significantly related to growth.

Table 5. Determinants of GDP Growth 1950-1988

	EQ1	EQ2	EQ3	EQ4	EQ5
Constant	3.17	1.21	0.88	1.15	0.51
	(5.61)	(1.35)	(0.80)	(1.06)	(0.57)
Population Growth	0.74	0.62	0.75	0.76	0.94
	(4.32)	(2.96)	(3.12)	(3.22)	(4.07)
GDP per capita	-0.28	-0.34	-0.25	-0.22	-0.28
	(6.26)	(6.65)	(3.25)	(3.58)	(4.32)
Average Investment/GDP	0.10	0.20			
	(5.63)	(6.17)			
Inflation Variability	-0.07	-0.09	-0.10	-0.09	-0.16
	(2.39)	(2.62)	(3.02)	(2.59)	(3.03)
Growth Gov. Cons./GDP	-0.44	-0.45	-0.09	-0.03	-0.26
	(7.17)	(7.22)	(0.99)	(0.33)	(2.49)
Inflation	-0.03	-0.08	-0.05	-0.03	-0.09
	(1.03)	(1.80)	(1.09)	(0.83)	(1.66)
Investment Growth			0.53	0.50	0.41
			(6.65)	(6.26)	(5.16)
Initial Investment/GDP			0.08	0.05	0.12
			(1.85)	(1.09)	(2.75)
Export Growth			0.17	0.13	-0.02
			(2.56)	(1.67)	(0.26)
Growth of Intra-EEC Trade				0.07	
				(1.15)	
Growth of Intra-Europe Trade					0.14
					(2.48)
N	192	168	168	168	168
R^2	0.67	0.65	0.64	0.66	0.66
s.e.	1.12	1.22	1.35	1.33	1.35

Table 6. Determinants of GDP Growth 1950-70 and 1971-1988

	EQ1		EQ2		EQ3		EQ4		EQ5	
	1950-70	1971-88	1950-70	1971-88	1950-70	1971-88	1950-70	1971-88	1950-70	1971-88
Constant	4.55 (6.14)	2.49 (2.54)	4.13 (4.29)	0.95 (0.86)	2.38 (2.06)	3.97 (3.01)	2.09 (1.60)	3.14 (2.41)	2.48 (2.40)	2.25 (1.29)
Population Growth	1.19 (4.41)	0.79 (3.71)	1.34 (4.31)	0.59 (2.14)	1.48 (5.70)	0.21 (0.75)	1.48 (5.73)	0.20 (0.70)	1.67 (5.85)	0.48 (1.42)
GDP per capita	-0.52 (7.77)	-0.20 (3.45)	-0.64 (8.24)	-0.28 (4.58)	-0.48 (4.75)	-0.30 (3.71)	-0.47 (4.51)	-0.25 (3.55)	-0.53 (5.59)	-0.28 (3.83)
Average Investment/GDP	0.09 (3.96)	0.10 (4.92)	0.13 (3.95)	0.19 (5.50)						
Inflation Variability	-0.16 (2.94)	-0.07 (1.89)	-0.19 (3.36)	-0.10 (2.18)	-0.22 (3.88)	-0.05 (1.39)	-0.21 (3.65)	-0.08 (1.99)	-0.29 (4.51)	-0.12 (1.83)
Growth Gov. Cons./GDP	-0.37 (5.77)	-0.44 (4.21)	-0.34 (5.41)	-0.51 (4.88)	-0.04 (0.55)	-0.33 (3.03)	-0.04 (0.51)	-0.32 (3.04)	-0.20 (2.52)	-0.37 (3.00)
Inflation	-0.16 (2.01)	-0.01 (0.31)	-0.18 (2.24)	0.04 (0.86)	-0.14 (1.38)	-0.10 (1.74)	-0.15 (1.41)	-0.07 (1.37)	-0.15 (1.65)	-0.12 (1.97)
Initial Investment					0.06 (1.90)	0.14 (3.11)	0.07 (1.87)	0.12 (2.71)	0.08 (2.14)	0.14 (2.97)
Investment Growth					0.30 (3.47)	0.41 (6.60)	0.32 (3.44)	0.37 (5.73)	0.24 (3.48)	0.34 (4.26)
Export Growth					0.20 (3.84)	-0.05 (0.50)	0.18 (2.40)	-0.05 (0.49)	0.06 (1.09)	-0.15 (1.27)
Growth of intra-EEC Exports							0.02 (0.56)	0.05 (1.61)		
Growth of intra-Europe Trade									0.10 (2.27)	0.13 (1.53)
N	84	84	84	84	84	84	84	84	84	84
R^2	0.62	0.50	0.65	0.55	0.70	0.59	0.70	0.63	0.72	0.57
s.e.	1.16	1.02	1.19	1.11	1.16	1.09	1.16	1.02	1.15	1.18

Since growth plausibly encourages investment as well as investment encouraging growth, we re-estimated using instrumental variables.[32] The results, shown in the second column, differ little. One noteworthy difference is that the coefficient on inflation now differs from zero at the 90 per cent confidence level.

Equation 3 adds two measures of capital formation – the rate of growth of investment at constant prices and the initial investment ratio – along with export growth. All three coefficients are significantly greater than zero at the 90 per cent level or better, consistent with our hypothesis of the proximate sources of Europe's growth. The importance of exports for growth is consistent with Edwards' (1998) review of the literature linking openness to economic growth.

We also tested whether the growth of exports to the countries that committed to regional trade liberalisation by forming the European Coal and Steel Community (ECSC) and the European Economic Community was more important than exports to the rest of the world.[33] While ECSC and EEC members may have been willing to liberalise trade more quickly than other countries by virtue of the success of European institutions in solving commitment and co-ordination problems (in which case our measures of the effects of the ECSC and EEC below should have a significant impact on the expansion of exports), there is no obvious reason why exports to specific markets should have been particularly conducive to growth. Thus, when the growth of both total and intra-EEC exports is included, as in Equation 5, it is total exports, not intra-EEC exports, that matter for overall economic growth.[34]

In Table 6 we split the period into the 1950s-1960s and 1970s-1980s. The effects of catch-up are more pronounced in the first subperiod, as expected. Export growth also plays a more important role in the first subperiod, consistent with the hypothesis that trade was a particularly important engine for growth in the golden age. The larger coefficient on inflation (in absolute

---

[32] As instruments we use the exogenous variables employed in our investment, export and wage equations below. The other equations reported subsequently are also estimated using instrumental variables.

[33] The relative importance of intra-European trade was measured as the percentage change in the value of exports to ECSC/EEC markets (EEC markets for short) relative to the percentage change in the value of total exports. We allowed the countries included in this subcategory to change with time as additional countries joined the EEC. Henrekson, Torstensson and Torstensson (1997) also consider the impact of EC and EFTA membership on GDP growth, reporting a positive effect of European integration on long-run growth rates.

[34] Interestingly, when we add exports to all European markets, this term dominates the other export measures.

value terms) is consistent with the emphasis we place on wage moderation for supporting the postwar growth miracle.[35]

Table 7. Determinants of Export Growth 1950-1988

	EQ1	EQ2	EQ3	EQ4	EQ5	EQ6
Constant	2.32	0.50	2.16	-1.85	1.05	1.18
	(1.79)	(0.22)	(1.77)	(0.84)	(0.48)	(0.92)
GDP Growth	1.07	1.14	1.00	1.13	1.10	0.99
	(4.57)	(4.62)	(3.39)	(4.33)	(5.09)	(3.89)
Inflation	-0.25	-0.26	-0.24	-0.21	-0.22	-0.24
	(1.80)	(1.91)	(1.75)	(1.59)	(1.72)	(1.72)
Inflation Variability	0.30	0.31	0.31	0.32	0.32	0.37
	(2.29)	(2.63)	(2.43)	(2.96)	(2.68)	(2.92)
ECSC/EEC	2.70		2.46	1.58	0.80	
	(3.32)		(2.88)	(1.90)	(1.59)	
EPU/CONV.		1.75				
		(0.92)				
ART. VIII			0.80			
			(0.60)			
Conv. (1958-)				-0.66	-0.77	
				(0.33)	(0.06)	
EPU (1951-57)				5.97	2.05	
				(2.73)	(0.91)	
ECSC						7.34
						(2.83)
EEC (1958 -)						0.97
						(1.16)
N	168	168	168	168	168	168
R^2	0.35	0.40	0.40	0.39	0.42	0.40
s.e.	3.65	3.66	3.65	3.69	3.56	3.66

4.2   Exports

The next step in our argument involves the link from domestic and international institutions to the export growth and investment that fuelled the postwar growth miracle. Two arrangements affecting exports were the European Payments Union which preceded the restoration of current account convertibility, and the European Coal and Steel Community (ECSC) which developed into the European Economic Community (EEC). We construct a dummy variable for countries which belonged to the ECSC and/or the EEC,

---

[35] We would have also expected larger coefficients on the investment terms in the first subperiod than the second; this is the one expectation that is disappointed.

denoted "EEC," and a second for countries which participated in the EPU or whose currencies were convertible for current account transactions, denoted "EPU."[36]

Previous studies have tended to find some effect of European economic and monetary integration on the pattern of trade. Frankel (1992) includes a dummy variable for EC member states in his gravity equations for bilateral flows, finding that membership encouraged intra-EC trade even after controlling for income, population, distance and contiguity, but without discouraging trade between EC members and the rest of the world. Eichengreen (1993), in an analogous exercise for the EPU in the 1950s, obtains similar results. Aitken (1973), also utilising a gravity framework, finds that EEC membership significantly stimulated trade between member countries starting in the early 1960s. He detects little sign that membership in the European Coal and Steel Community boosted trade in the 1950s, however. De Grauwe (1988) similarly considers bilateral trade flows among ten industrial countries since the 1960s. He finds that EC membership significantly increased trade among the six founding members in the 1960s but no longer had a discernible effect in the 1970s, a contrast which he attributes to increased trade diversion following the admission of three new members in 1973. He does, however, find a strong trade-stimulating effect of membership in the 1970s for the three new entrants themselves.

Table 7 summarises the results of regressing the growth of export volumes on the growth of GDP, population growth and the stance of domestic and international policies.[37] In Equation 1, the coefficient on ECSC and EEC membership (captured by the composite variable "EEC") is positive and significant at the 95 per cent level, supporting the notion that the institutions of European integration solved commitment and co-ordination problems hindering the expansion of trade. In addition, the growth of exports depends, as expected, on the growth of GDP.

---

[36] Information on the latter was drawn from the *IMF's Exchange and Trade Restrictions Yearbooks*.

[37] We focus on total exports as our dependent variable, although we also analysed the determinants of intra-European exports. The results do not differ significantly. Given the importance of exports for GDP growth, the latter is treated as endogenous. A related issue is whether it is appropriate to also treat our EEC and EPU dummies as endogenous. There are good reasons to think so: the level of trade with other participants may well influence the attractiveness of joining a regional arrangement. Countries which trade more heavily with one another may want to establish institutionalised relations to lock in those benefits. How the growth rate of trade may affect the decision to join is not entirely clear: rapid growth that foreshadows an even higher trade ratio in the future may magnify the benefits just described, but lagging trade growth may also heighten the perceived need to join in an institutional arrangement so as to reverse the slump in trade. While these arguments do not predict that endogeneity will bias OLS coefficients in a particular direction, they all suggest treating the EPU/convertibility variable as endogenous, as we do below.

Table 8. Determinants of Export Growth 1950-1970 and 1971-1988

	EO1		EO2		EO3		EO4		EO5		EO6	
	1950-70	1971-88	1950-70	1971-88	1950-70	1971-88	1950-70	1971-88	1950-70	1971-88	1950-70	1971-88
Constant	-0.96 (0.49)	6.30 (2.51)	-4.74 (1.36)	6.30 (2.51)	-1.15 (0.58)	4.51 (3.00)	-4.78 (1.41)	6.30 (2.51)	-4.04 (1.51)	5.25 (2.34)	-1.19 (0.58)	6.30 (2.51)
GDP Growth	1.27 (3.93)	-0.49 (2.22)	1.49 (4.35)	0.49 (2.22)	1.17 (3.10)	0.50 (2.42)	1.47 (4.17)	0.49 (2.22)	1.50 (4.77)	0.50 (2.30)	1.25 (3.82)	-0.49 (2.22)
Inflation	0.07 (0.19)	-0.18 (1.45)	0.17 (0.43)	-0.18 (1.45)	0.15 (0.41)	-0.19 (1.72)	0.18 (0.46)	-0.18 (1.45)	0.13 (0.38)	-0.19 (1.50)	0.10 (0.25)	-0.18 (1.45)
Inflation Variability	0.68 (3.01)	-0.05 (2.87)	0.76 (3.42)	0.20 (1.87)	0.73 (3.11)	-0.20 (1.58)	0.75 (3.39)	0.20 (1.87)	0.70 (3.38)	0.19 (1.73)	0.70 (2.96)	-0.05 (2.87)
ECSC/EEC	4.08 (3.36)	-0.39 (0.56)	3.29 (2.74)	-0.39 (0.56)	3.95 (3.38)	-0.14 (0.20)	3.18 (2.64)	-0.39 (0.56)	1.92 (2.28)	-0.07 (0.13)		
EPU/CONV.			3.17 (1.39)	-2.22 (1.02)								
ART. VIII					0.07 (0.83)	-0.33 (0.30)						
Conv. (1958-)							2.32 (0.87)	-2.22 (1.02)	2.60 (1.43)	-1.13 (0.59)		
EPU (1951-57)							3.62 (1.65)		3.08 (1.51)			
ECSC											4.80 (2.40)	
EEC (1958-)											3.40 (2.28)	-0.39 (0.56)
N	84	84	84	84	84	84	84	84	84	84	84	84
R²	0.41	0.27	0.42	0.27	0.41	0.26	0.44	0.27	0.27	0.27	0.42	0.27
s.e.	4.08	2.81	4.08	2.81	4.11	2.82	4.03	2.81	2.79	2.80	4.08	2.81

We also include the level and variability of inflation as two measures of domestic economic policies which might have crowded out exports. Average inflation enters with the expected negative sign, but inflation variability, unexpectedly, enters positively.

Equation 2 adds the dummy variable for countries which were EPU members or whose currencies were convertible on current account.[38] Its coefficient is insignificantly different from zero at standard confidence levels, while the coefficient for ECSC/EEC membership retains its size and significance.[39]

The insignificance of the EPU/convertibility measure could conceivably reflect imprecision in how we have dated the restoration of convertibility. In Equation 3 we therefore substitute the date when countries accepted Article VIII of the IMF Articles of Agreement. This fails to alter the finding.

To test whether the effects of the EPU differed from those of the unilateral restoration of convertibility, we include in Equation 4 separate proxies for EPU membership and current account convertibility. The results are striking: EPU membership has a strong positive effect on trade (consistent with results obtained in Eichengreen 1993, using an entirely different methodology), while the adoption of current account convertibility at the end of 1958 has a negligible effect. Again, this is consistent with the emphasis placed in our interpretation on the role of collective European institutions (in this case, the European Payments Union) in solving commitment and co-ordination problems in the first postwar decade.

We can similarly distinguish the relative importance of the ECSC before 1959 and the EEC subsequently by including separate variables for the participation in the ECSC and the EEC, as in Equation 6. While both positively influence the volume of trade, the ECSC dummy is larger, and only it differs significantly from zero at standard confidence levels. Again this points to the critical role of European institutions in the immediate postwar years.

Table 8 breaks the sample at 1970. With the smaller samples, the coefficients on the institutional variables of interest are less precise. But there are still some suggestive contrasts. Equation 4 confirms that it is EPU membership and not current account convertibility that does most of the work and that the effect of these variables is evident only in the earlier subperiod. Similarly, Equation 6 shows that the effects of the ECSC and

---

[38] We identified the date when current-account convertibility was restored using the IMF's *Exchange and Trade Restrictions* volumes.

[39] Thus, when convertibility is measured as in Equation 1, only the coefficient on the Coal and Steel Community is significantly greater than zero at standard confidence levels. When convertibility is measured by acceptance of the IMF's Article VIII, in contrast, only post-1958 EEC membership is significant.

EEC membership (which were negligible in equations for the full sample period) are pronounced in the 1950s and 1960s.

Together, then, the results of this section confirm the significance of the EPU and the ECSC in promoting the growth of Europe's trade in the first postwar decade.

4.3   Investment

The next step is to consider the determinants of investment. We are especially interested in the relationship between labour's share of national income and the investment rate.

Our investment equation follows Barro (1991) and Wolf (1995), who analyse investment in a cross section of countries. Barro focuses on the effects of initial GDP per capita, human capital, government consumption as a share of national income, and various proxies for relative price distortions (the average price of investment goods relative to other goods and services, and the standard deviation of that ratio).[40] Wolf considers tax rates, interest rates, Tobin's q, and political conditions. We add labour's share of GDP as the (inverse of the) measure of profitability suggested by the neo-classical model.[41]

The estimates in Table 9 support our emphasis on labour's share as a determinant of investment.[42] This variable consistently enters with a negative sign which differs from zero at the 99 per cent confidence level.

The other variables generally affect investment in plausible ways. For example, investment is negatively related to the growth of the share of government consumption. In two of the three models it is negatively associated with the real interest rate (the rate on government bonds adjusted for the change in the CPI deflator), while the change in Tobin's q (the market valuation of capital relative to its replacement cost, as measured by the percentage change in share prices relative to the percentage change in wholesale prices) has its expected positive effect.

---

[40] Barro also includes revolutions and assassinations per capita as measures of political instability; we exclude these on the grounds that they are mainly applicable to the developing countries in his sample.

[41] For discussion, see Clark (1979) and Kashyap, Stein and Wilcox (1993). We construct our labour income variable using the OECD National Accounts volumes and the International Labour Organisation's *Yearbook of Labour Statistics* (various years).

[42] Labour costs are computed as labour income per member of the labour force.

Table 9. Determinants of Investment Growth 1950-1988

	EQ1	EQ2	EQ3	EQ4
Constant	1.67	1.88	3.26	3.53
	(2.61)	(2.41)	(3.45)	(3.54)
GDP per Capita	-0.93	-0.10	-0.23	-0.24
	(1.06)	(1.08)	(2.18)	(2.35)
Growth Gov.Cons./GDP	-0.38	-0.38	-0.34	-0.33
	(3.05)	(3.04)	(2.70)	(2.69)
Growth of Labour's share	-0.48	-0.48	-0.47	-0.44
	(3.89)	(3.93)	(3.91)	(3.57)
Growth of Corporate tax rate	-13.93	-14.02	14.31	14.39
	(3.77)	(3.77)	(3.81)	(3.91)
Growth of Tobin's q	5.05	5.02	4.81	4.70
	(2.37)	(2.38)	(2.32)	(2.26)
Inflation	0.06	0.06	0.04	0.04
	(1.10)	(1.08)	(0.69)	(0.70)
Political Instability		-0.25	-0.22	-0.26
		(0.56)	(0.51)	(0.59)
Real Interest Rate		1.97	-0.15	-0.14
		(2.15)	(2.22)	(2.09)
Variability of Labour costs				-0.20
				(0.84)
N	155	155	155	155
R^2	0.51	0.51	0.51	0.52
s.e.	2.31	2.14	2.16	2.16

Breaking the sample into subperiods, as in Table 10, suggests that while the change in labour's share has mattered throughout the postwar period, its coefficient is consistently larger for the 1950s and 1960s than for the 1970s and 1980s. The variability of labour costs similarly appears to have a negative impact on investment in the first subperiod but not the second.[43]

Overall, then, the results tend to support our emphasis on the importance of wage restraint for sustaining the high levels of investment that were a crucial ingredient of Europe's postwar growth recipe.

---

[43] In addition, we find that investment was driven by government spending and political instability in the first period, but by corporate taxes, Tobin's q, and real interest rates in the second. This makes it tempting to argue that investment depended more heavily on politics and public policies in the first period but more heavily on financial-market conditions in the second.

Table 10. Determinants of Investment Growth 1950-1970 and 1971-1988

	EQ1		EQ2		EQ3		EQ4	
	1950-70	1971-88	1950-70	1971-88	1950-70	1971-88	1950-70	1971-88
Constant	3.28	0.21	4.38	-0.39	4.24	2.15	4.99	2.67
	(3.76)	(0.12)	(4.13)	(0.22)	(3.41)	(0.98)	(3.75)	(1.13)
GDP per capita	-0.18	-0.80	-0.22	-0.78	-0.21	-0.20	-0.25	-0.25
	(1.35)	(0.56)	(1.63)	(0.54)	(1.49)	(0.46)	(1.84)	(0.43)
Growth Gov. Cons./GDP	-0.26	-0.18	-0.50	-0.23	-0.50	-0.15	-0.49	-0.14
	(4.43)	(0.57)	(4.71)	(0.72)	(4.72)	(0.46)	(4.62)	(0.43)
Growth of Labour's share	-0.81	-0.53	-0.86	-0.52	-0.86	-0.52	-0.64	-0.55
	(3.94)	(2.62)	(4.57)	(2.60)	(4.60)	(2.63)	(4.71)	(2.66)
Growth of Corporate tax rate	-4.51	-21.4	-4.92	-21.4	-4.90	-21.9	-6.25	-22.38
	(1.64)	(5.24)	(1.91)	(5.13)	(1.89)	(5.22)	(2.43)	(5.21)
Growth of Tobin's q	1.60	7.82	1.70	7.95	1.72	7.72	-0.12	7.62
	(0.40)	(3.38)	(0.48)	(3.42)	(0.48)	(3.46)	(0.03)	(3.46)
Inflation	0.08	0.04	0.04	0.03	0.04	0.01	0.06	0.01
	(0.55)	(0.67)	(0.28)	(0.65)	(0.30)	(0.26)	(0.42)	(0.17)
Political Instability			-1.16	0.89	-1.19	0.70	-1.28	0.68
			(2.67)	(1.36)	(2.59)	(1.04)	(2.78)	(0.98)
Real Interest Rate					0.02	-0.14	-0.05	-0.16
					(0.21)	(2.13)	(0.49)	(2.31)
Variability of Labour costs							-0.66	0.07
							(1.61)	(0.29)
N	75	80	75	80	75	80	75	80
R^2	0.44	0.54	0.47	0.55	0.48	0.55	0.49	0.55
s.e.	2.00	2.13	1.95	2.12	1.96	2.15	1.95	2.17

4.4   Wages

A large literature is concerned with the role played by labour-management relations in macroeconomic outcomes (see for example Bruno and Sachs, 1985; Calmfors and Driffill, 1988; Crouch, 1985), much of it emphasising the connection between corporatist governance and wage bargaining. While fewer authors focus on the connection between the centralisation of bargaining and labour-market outcomes, our interpretation suggests that centralisation can serve as an alternative to (or possibly complement) corporatism in solving co-ordination problems.

Table 11. Determinants of Wage Growth 1950-1988

	EQ1	EQ2	EQ3	EQ4	EQ5
Constant	0.03	0.06	0.05	0.06	0.06
	(3.69)	(3.05)	(3.19)	(5.50)	(5.07)
Growth of GDP per worker	0.93	0.60	0.01	0.01	0.01
	(3.46)	(1.85)	(3.70)	(4.36)	(4.29)
Labour Force Growth	-0.78	-0.46	-0.80	-0.48	-0.43
	(1.18)	(0.68)	(1.23)	(0.71)	(0.64)
Investment Growth	-0.76	-0.54	-0.82	-0.94	-0.94
	(2.80)	(2.00)	(2.93)	(3.47)	(3.45)
Inflation	0.16	0.37	0.20	0.26	0.26
	(1.52)	(1.47)	(1.76)	(2.39)	(2.41)
Demand pressure	-0.55	-0.42	-0.65	-0.92	-0.92
	(2.80)	(1.44)	(3.12)	(4.28)	(4.31)
Crouch Index		-0.03			
		(2.57)			
Corporation Index			-0.02		0.01
			(1.87)		(0.84)
Centralisation				-0.06	-0.06
				(4.94)	(4.14)
N	168	168	168	168	168
R^2	0.45	0.48	0.45	0.48	0.48
s.e.	0.03	0.03	0.04	0.03	0.03

A limitation of much of this work is that it uses snapshots of corporatist structures at a point in time, generally the late 1970s and early 1980s, to analyse bargaining rounds stretching over several decades, when the relevant institutions in fact changed markedly over time. For the present study, in contrast, we constructed indices of corporatism and the centralisation of bargaining separately for each five-year period.

Our specification relates the rate of growth of money wages to inflation, demand pressure (the deviation of log output from trend), the growth of real GDP per worker (as a measure of labour productivity), the growth of the labour force, and the rate of growth of investment.[44] Table 11 confirms that wages grew more slowly where investment grew quickly, as predicted by our analytical framework. Wage growth was slower where the growth of the labour force was faster, consistent with Kindleberger's (1967) elastic-labour-supplies hypothesis. Not surprisingly, wages increase with productivity and inflation.

Table 12. Determinants of Wage Growth (I) 1950-1970 and 1971-1988

	EQ1		EQ2		EQ3		EQ4	
	1950-70	1971-88	1950-70	1971-88	1950-70	1971-88	1950-70	1971-88
Constant	0.04	0.15	0.04	0.15	0.03	0.15	0.03	0.14
	(5.10)	(6.21)	(4.45)	(5.99)	(3.23)	(6.38)	(5.20)	(6.05)
Growth of GDP	0.69	0.41	0.67	0.57	0.63	0.47	0.67	0.39
per worker	(3.16)	(0.72)	(3.35)	(1.01)	(2.88)	(0.82)	(3.17)	(0.70)
Labour Force	-0.98	-0.02	-0.01	-0.02	-0.01	-0.02	-0.97	-0.02
Growth	(1.49)	(1.88)	(1.57)	(1.66)	(1.59)	(1.94)	(1.47)	(2.04)
Investment	-0.35	-0.45	-0.31	-0.54	-0.28	-0.47	-0.34	-0.46
Growth	(1.80)	(1.39)	(1.73)	(1.62)	(1.41)	(1.45)	(1.74)	(1.43)
Inflation	0.52	-0.61	0.49	0.12	0.47	0.21	0.53	-0.33
	(2.44)	(0.05)	(2.25)	(0.10)	(2.24)	(0.19)	(2.69)	(0.28)
Demand	-0.14	-0.01	-0.14	-0.01	-0.41	-0.01	-0.15	-0.01
pressure	(0.70)	(3.99)	(0.65)	(4.02)	(0.21)	(3.96)	(0.83)	(3.87)
$Corp_1$	-0.01	-0.02						
	(1.43)	(1.20)						
$Corp_2$			-0.01	-0.50				
			(1.02)	(1.94)				
$Corp_3$					-0.54	-0.03		
					(0.30)	(1.28)		
$Corp_4$							-0.06	-0.07
							(2.16)	(1.48)
N	84	84	84	84	84	84	84	84
R^2	0.40	0.50	0.40	0.51	0.39	0.40	0.41	0.50
s.e.	0.02	0.04	0.02	0.04	0.02	0.03	0.03	0.04

We include in these equations two measures of corporatism, one based on our own reading of primary sources (newspaper accounts, trade union reports, *etc.*) and one based on Colin Crouch's. (Specifically, this quantifies Crouch's (1993) description of changes in labour relations since the 1950s.) In the first equation of Table 11, the coefficient on the Crouch index is negative and significant, consistent with the notion that more corporatist economies were characterised by more moderate wage growth. In the second

---

[44] Investment is again treated as endogenous.

equation, which instead uses our own index, the relevant coefficient is still negative but now significant only at the 90 as opposed to the 95 per cent confidence level. The third equation substitutes a measure of the centralisation of wage bargaining, since Section 3 suggested that corporatism and centralisation were alternative means of solving commitment and co-ordination problems. The coefficient on this index has the anticipated negative sign and is strongly significant.

Table 13. Determinants of Wage Growth (II) 1950-1988

	EQ1	EQ2	EQ3	EQ4
Constant	0.05	0.05	0.05	0.04
	(3.95)	(4.05)	(3.43)	(3.73)
Growth of GDP per worker	0.01	0.01	0.01	0.01
	(3.88)	(4.04)	(3.54)	(3.82)
Labour Force Growth	-0.47	-0.35	-0.58	-0.59
	(0.66)	(0.47)	(0.84)	(0.87)
Investment Growth	-0.93	-0.97	-0.87	-0.53
	(3.20)	(3.26)	(2.92)	(1.81)
Inflation	0.23	0.23	0.23	-0.01
	(2.01)	(1.98)	(2.13)	(3.47)
Demand pressure	-0.66	-0.77	-0.59	-0.61
	(3.09)	(3.28)	(2.87)	(3.04)
$Corp_1$	-0.03			
	(2.09)			
$Corp_2$		-0.04		
		(2.40)		
$Corp_3$			-0.03	
			(1.51)	
$Corp_4$				-0.08
				(2.58)
N	168	168	168	168
R^2	0.44	0.43	0.44	0.44
s.e.	0.04	0.04	0.03	0.03

When we include both centralisation and corporatism, as in the fourth equation, centralisation dominates. When we break the sample at 1970, we find that centralisation matters throughout the postwar period. Interestingly, there is support for the importance of corporatism (however measured) mainly in the second subperiod.

Table 13 is an exercise in sensitivity analysis. In the first equation corporatism is measured using a version of the Bruno and Sachs index (denoted $Corp_1$); it is taken as the sum of a vector of zero-one variables measuring union centralisation, employer centralisation, low shop floor autonomy, and works councils.[45] This variable enters with a significant negative sign.

The second equation measures corporatism as the product rather than the sum of its four constituents in an attempt to test whether its effects hinge on the presence of all four components; this index, $Corp_2$, also enters with a significant negative coefficient. The third equation measures corporatism as the average of $Corp_2$ and the share of the labour force unionized; this measure, $Corp_3$, is negative but not significant at standard confidence levels. Finally, the fourth equation measures corporatism as the average of $Corp_3$ and a measure of the stringency of incomes policies ranging from zero to one; this measure, $Corp_4$, is significantly negative. Tables 12 and 14, which breaks the sample, suggests that unionism and incomes policy were particularly effective in allowing European economies to coordinate on equilibria that involved wage moderation in the golden age as opposed to the post-1970 period.

To see which elements of labour-management arrangements were most important for restraining wage inflation, we also entered the components of these indices separately. Consistent with previous findings, measures of worker and employer centralisation appear to have been relatively important in supporting wage moderation. Table 14 does not suggest significant differences in their impact in the first and second subperiods.

Thus, evidence derived using various different measures of the institutionalisation of labour-management relations supports the hypothesis that centralisation and perhaps also corporatisation played a significant role in moderating wage demands.

5.   INSTITUTIONS AND TECHNICAL CHANGE

Previous sections have emphasised the institutional determinants of output, investment, exports, and wages. But institutions mattered not just for macroeconomic outcomes but for the microeconomics of technical change as well. In this section we develop this other dimension, offering some conjectures about institutional determinants of technical change.

---

[45] Normalized to range from zero to one. All of the other indices we construct below are similarly normalised to the zero-one range.

Table 14. Determinants of Wage Growth (II) 1950-1970 and 1971-1988

	EQ1		EQ2		EQ3		EQ4		EQ5	
	1950-70	1971-88	1950-70	1971-88	1950-70	1971-88	1950-70	1971-88	1950-70	1971-88
Constant	0.03 (4.70)	0.14 (6.11)	0.04 (2.55)	0.19 (6.26)	0.04 (4.26)	0.17 (6.37)	0.05 (6.28)	0.16 (7.08)	0.05 (5.57)	0.16 (6.33)
Growth of GDP per worker	0.62 (2.89)	0.39 (0.69)	0.37 (1.59)	0.10 (0.17)	0.65 (3.17)	0.44 (0.80)	0.71 (3.51)	0.57 (1.11)	0.69 (3.47)	0.57 (1.11)
Labour Force Growth	-0.01 (6.13)	-0.02 (2.18)	-0.72 (1.14)	-0.02 (1.81)	-0.01 (1.70)	-0.03 (2.40)	-0.97 (1.53)	-0.02 (1.92)	-0.91 (1.43)	-0.02 (1.90)
Investment Growth	-0.26 (1.32)	-0.41 (1.31)	-0.50 (0.31)	-0.68 (0.27)	-0.29 (1.47)	-0.41 (1.31)	-0.37 (1.90)	-0.50 (1.67)	-0.36 (1.98)	-0.50 (1.66)
Inflation	0.45 (2.27)	-0.50 (0.44)	0.27 (0.85)	0.15 (0.60)	0.45 (2.25)	-0.67 (0.06)	0.53 (2.67)	0.62 (0.57)	0.55 (2.83)	0.61 (0.57)
Domestic pressure	-0.22 (0.12)	-0.01 (3.86)	0.21 (0.95)	-0.01 (2.79)	-0.61 (0.33)	-0.01 (4.46)	-0.35 (1.90)	-0.01 (4.72)	-0.38 (2.19)	-0.01 (4.63)
Crouch			-0.54 (0.38)	-0.08 (3.59)						
Corporation Index					-0.01 (0.82)	-0.04 (2.05)			0.01 (0.90)	0.97 (0.03)
Centralisation Index							-0.03 (3.20)	-0.06 (3.43)	-0.04 (3.13)	-0.06 (2.84)
N	84	84	60	60	84	84	84	84	84	84
R^2	0.39	0.49	0.33	0.57	0.39	0.51	0.43	0.54	0.44	0.54
s.e.	0.02	0.04	0.02	0.04	0.02	0.04	0.02	0.03	0.02	0.03

5.1   Institutions and Technology Transfer

Johnson and Stafford (1998) offer the following characterisation of post-World War II technology. In the immediate postwar years, an increasing number of market organisations applied the techniques of scientific management to their operations. Tasks were simplified by an extensive division of labour, increasing the demand for unskilled and semi-skilled labour and levelling the distribution of income. Technologies making intensive use of heavy machinery, raw materials and less-skilled labour and presupposing the existence of a large domestic market, developed in the United States in the course of previous decades, could be "taken off the shelf" by producers in other countries seeking to expand capacity and raise productivity.[46]

As emphasised by Wright (1990), the U.S. economy's dependence on material-using technologies and goods produced for the mass market increased continuously from 1880 through World War II. And as argued by Kogut (1992), the concept and practice of professional management originated in the United States, circa 1900. Similarly, staffing large firms with a cadre of professional middle managers was almost exclusively an American phenomenon. This American recipe for industrial success was epitomised by the automobile industry which, following Henry Ford, produced for a mass market using an extensive division of labour and heavy inputs of steel and energy.

While the automobile industry was perhaps the most dramatic case where the United States opened up a productivity lead in the years preceding World War II, that productivity advantage was general. According to Maddison (1996), labour productivity in Europe was a mere 40 per cent of U.S. levels in 1950.[47] The gap did not reflect any intrinsic inefficiency of European labour: insofar as Europe possessed Abramovitz's capability for catch up, the gap could be closed by importing the latest U.S. techniques, which in practice meant mass-production, scientific-management-based techniques, and by equipping European workers with U.S. levels of capital equipment. This is not just an historian's interpretation. It was the view of contemporaries, notably of the U.S. officials who made visits by European bureaucrats, industrialists and trade unionists to American factories an obligatory part of the Marshall Plan in order that they might observe the techniques of mass production and scientific management on the shop floor. European officials acknowledged this by giving priority in early postwar

---

[46] On the nature of American technological leadership in this period, see Nelson and Wright (1992).

[47] Denison's early estimates are consistent with Maddison's. In addition, Denison suggests that the gap in total factor productivity was nearly as large. See Denison (1967).

planning to iron and steel, transport equipment, and non-electrical machinery, sectors in which capital intensity and scientific management were particularly important. And national trade unions and employers associations were, for the reasons described in Section 3 above, ideally suited for delivering the wage moderation and high investment needed to support the expansion of capacity in these sectors.

5.2   Institutions and Incremental Innovation

To be sure, it would be an exaggeration to say that Europe's task was simply to emulate the U.S. example. American technology had to be adapted to European circumstances, notably shorter production runs and more costly raw materials. The liberalisation of intra-European trade could loosen the market-size constraint but not eliminate it. Similarly, the liberalisation of trade in raw materials could weaken America's comparative advantage in raw-material-intensive activities without overturning it. Adaptation to European conditions was still required.

Here too institutions had a role. Perrow (1984, 1986) and Kitschelt (1991) have suggested that certain institutional arrangements are particularly conducive to the kind of incremental innovation that was important in the early postwar years. Industries like iron and steel tend to be characterised by "tight coupling," "linear" technology and low uncertainty, in their parlance. Tight coupling means that each step or component of the production process is difficult to separate from the others. Linearity means that it is easy to understand the system's operation, to learn from feedback signals, and to keep outputs under control. In tightly-coupled, linear systems, innovation will tend to be global (since coupling discourages localised change) and incremental (since the linear nature of the process encourages continuous adaptation). Global innovation requires a heavy dose of capital for investment and concertation among stakeholders, all of whom must agree to the changes affecting the entire system. Again, in the immediate postwar period European institutions fit the bill. The wage moderation needed for high investment and the concertation needed for global adaptation were facilitated by corporatist arrangements and centralised bargaining. The skills needed to adapt and incrementally modify existing technologies could be conveyed through Northern European countries' existing systems of technical education and apprenticeship training. Cohesive employers associations discouraged firms from poaching workers, preventing skills with industry-wide applicability from being undersupplied. The absence of high-powered incentives within the firm implied a preference for bank rather than securitised finance of the sort that Europe's bank-based financial system was in a position to supply. The need for consensus decision making to support global innovation implied that long-term financing via stable shareholding and bank-delegated monitoring worked better than securitised finance.[48] For all these reasons, then, innovation in the industries most important to Europe's growth in the 1950s and 1960s was facilitated by the institutions the continent had in place.

In contrast, new industries like computers, semiconductors, software and biotechnology were characterised by loose coupling, complex interactions, and high uncertainty. Loose coupling encourages innovations with the capacity to radically transform a part of the production process while leaving the rest unchanged. Complexity means that innovation depends on trial-and-error learning. And high uncertainty means that the risks associated with innovation have to be compensated for with high returns. In this environment, the institutions most conducive to technical change are decentralised structures that facilitate the exchange of information by blending cooperation with competition. Technical progress depends less on high levels of capital formation than on the creation of an environment conducive to loosely-coupled innovative activities, among the elements of which will be high-powered financial incentives. This is hardly the sort of innovation that would have been facilitated by the relatively centralised institutional structures in place in Europe after World War II.

The implication is that productivity could rise quickly for several decades after World War II because Europe's institutions were well suited to the kind of global, incremental, capital-using adaptations needed for technical progress in industries like iron and steel, heavy machinery and transport equipment, but that growth decelerated once the problem became to develop complex, radical innovations. Europe's economy thrived in the era of the steel mill, in other words, but stumbled in the age of the microchip.[49]

---

[48] See Soskice (1996). To underscore the message of an earlier footnote, it is important to note that the way these ideas are applied here differs significantly from the way Soskice himself develops the argument.

[49] This view must be reconciled with Europe's revealed comparative advantage in sectors producing high quality consumer goods and speciality inputs, the so-called "flexibly specialised" industries of Piore and Sabel (1984). It is not necessary to deny the continent's success in these sectors or to shoe-horn them into one of the two technological categories described above, for their case would appear to be captured by a third type of technological system, characterised by loose coupling, linear technology and low uncertainty, also identified by Perrow. In this type of system, change can be incremental because coupling is loose, but wage compression poses no particular barrier to innovation because uncertainty is low. Thus, there is no reason why a significant fringe of flexibly-specialised producers could not coexist throughout the period alongside Europe's more capital-intensive, large-enterprise-based heavy industries.

5.3   The Institutional Foundations of R&D

Nelson and Wright (1992) posit a second foundation for American technological leadership in the post-WWII period along with the country's lead in the development of scientific-management-based mass-production manufacturing. This was America's large investment in research and development. In the 1950s and 1960s, the share of American workers engaged in R&D and with scientific or engineering credentials was double or triple British, German and French levels.[50] The U.S. dominated trade in high-technology products throughout the period.[51] Again, this is not just the historian's imputation. European leaders betrayed considerable anxiety over America's lead in computers and semiconductors. The OECD published a series of studies on Europe's R&D gap.

America's heavy investment in R&D reflected the contributions of both the public and private sectors. Public-sector spending was stimulated by the Cold War, notably the Sputnik shock. By 1963 the fraction of business R&D financed by direct government funds was 70 per cent higher in the U.S. than the U.K., and the gap vis-à-vis Continental Europe was even larger.[52] Funding for the National Science Foundation, the National Institutes of Health, the Department of Defense, and the Atomic Energy Commission encouraged universities to increase their capacity to supply scientists and engineers. Subsidies for education (through, inter alia, the G.I. Bill), together with high per capita incomes and a relatively even income distribution, encouraged individuals to invest in secondary and post-secondary education to an extent that significantly exceeded the levels reached in Europe.

But a key foundation of America's comparative advantage in R&D was that the country possessed institutions conducive to the activity. It inherited from the 19th century a system of land grant universities designed to provide practical scientific education.[53] Already at the turn of the century U.S. university students per 1,000 primary students was two to three times European levels. Professionally-managed American enterprises, following the lead of General Electric, DuPont, AT&T and Kodak, were early to establish their own in-house research laboratories. When the time came to expand the supply of engineers and scientists, the U.S. had the capacity in place, and when it came time to place them with large firms, the latter

---

[50] Expenditure on R&D as a percentage of GDP may have differed by less across countries but was still significantly higher in the United States.

[51] Verspagen (1996) provides a number of additional R&D indicators for the period.

[52] Verspagen (1996), Table 5.3.

[53] Land grant universities were coupled with cooperative agricultural extensive services, whose staff were encouraged to provide practical knowledge of scientific advances in such fields as soil, chemistry, plant biology, and animal husbandry.

already possessed the in-house research infrastructure needed to put them to work.

Europe's institutes of technical training were better adapted to incremental changes in machinery design and machine building than to the development of radical new technologies. Freeman (1997) traces the Northern European constellation of R&D-related institutions back to the 19th century. For example, under the influence of Friedrich List, the Prussian government set up training institutes to produce skilled craftsmen, subsidised the dissemination of technical advice and assistance, and rebated duties on imports of machinery. It sought to promote a cooperative, corporatist attitude on the part of employers toward the training of their workers. Again, the point is that this constellation of institutions, which encouraged incremental, global innovation rather than radical, localised advances, had roots deep in European history.

The absence of U.S.-style institutions did not prevent Europe from building up its R&D capacity after World War II. By the 1970s European countries had gone a considerable way toward closing the gap in terms of R&D spending vis-à-vis the United States. Rather, the point is that this particular constellation of institutions gave the U.S. a head start. It contributed to the gap that existed after the war in labour and total-factor-productivity, particularly in mass-production, scientific-management-based industries. It heightened America's comparative advantage in the new "high-tech" industries of the second post-WWII quarter century, although it took some time, until the 1990s in fact, for this last advantage to manifest itself in improving U.S. competitiveness.

This section is necessarily more speculative than its predecessors, since internationally comparable estimates of R&D expenditures have only become available in recent years. Table 15 reports some exploratory regressions of the importance of various types of R&D for labour productivity. These regressions are necessarily exploratory because the sample is small (concentrating on the latter part of the 1970s and the 1980s). Nonetheless, the importance of R&D spending comes through clearly, whether measured as total R&D or R&D in non-electrical machinery. By implication, it reinforces the weight we attach to the institutional framework for innovation.

Table 15. Determinants of Labour Productivity

	EQ1	EQ2	EQ3	EQ4	EQ5	EQ6	EQ7	EQ8	EQ9
Constant	-0.67	-0.02	-0.59	-2.40	-2.54	-2.12	-0.63	-2.89	-4.30
	(0.63)	(0.02)	(0.56)	(3.07)	(3.51)	(2.63)	(0.81)	(4.13)	(5.01)
Real Interest Rates	0.10	0.11	0.10	0.17	0.16	0.14	0.07	0.19	0.28
	(1.47)	(1.54)	(1.49)	(3.32)	(3.37)	(2.47)	(1.27)	(3.95)	(3.95)
Growth in Tobin's q	3.17	3.47	3.16	3.70	3.89	4.72	5.64	3.80	3.28
	(2.70)	(2.76)	(2.82)	(3.88)	(4.27)	(4.80)	(5.45)	(4.26)	(2.52)
R&D in manufacturing as a share of investment	11.30	9.86	11.59	15.34	13.63			13.99	20.16
	(3.91)	(3.73)	(3.85)	(6.88)	(6.84)			(6.92)	(6.34)
Corporatism index	1.73		2.26	2.05	1.75	1.07	0.89	0.66	2.59
	(2.08)		(2.69)	(2.75)	(2.42)	(1.41)	(1.17)	(0.85)	(2.33)
Centralisation index		0.32	-0.68	-0.78	-0.71	-0.49	-0.53	0.03	-0.62
		(0.46)	(0.93)	(1.23)	(1.08)	(0.66)	(0.75)	(0.04)	(0.83)
Export Growth				0.21	0.18	0.18	0.13	0.20	0.13
				(5.07)	(4.81)	(4.92)	(2.93)	(5.35)	(4.09)
Growth of Capital Stock per worker					22.60	29.51	28.67	19.62	-4.02
					(2.02)	(2.75)	(2.59)	(1.73)	(0.23)
Total R&D as a share of investment						10.59			
						(4.46)			
R&D in non-electrical machinery as a share of investment							3.69		
							(3.89)		
Average years of higher schooling in the total population over age 25								1.07	
								(2.56)	
Number of Students in Universities as % of total population									1.88
									(2.75)
N	45	45	45	45	45	45	45	45	45
R^2	0.49	0.45	0.49	0.65	0.68	0.77	0.56	0.74	0.74
s.e	1.10	1.15	1.11	0.94	0.91	1.00	1.07	0.85	0.99

6. A PERSPECTIVE ON THE ACCELERATION AND SLOWDOWN

This paper has sought to shed light on the economics of Europe's post-World War II "golden age." It has offered new measures, new tests, and new stories designed to flesh out the role of institutions in the postwar growth process.

The argument is that the institutional arrangements Europe inherited from its prior history were particularly well-suited to the macroeconomic and technological imperatives of economic growth following World War II. Corporatist labour relations encouraged the wage moderation and high levels of investment needed to reproduce American-style industrial production on a massive scale. The fact that Europe lacked the institutions to develop an R&D capacity comparable to America's was of relatively little moment so long as the problem was to exploit existing technologies as much as it was to develop new ones. In fact, European countries' relatively centralised institutions were well suited to the incremental technical changes needed to adapt American technologies to European circumstances. And the institutions of European and global integration went some way toward creating the mass market in consumer goods and the open market in raw materials needed to support the transplantation of American technologies.

Any satisfactory explanation for the post-World War II acceleration in European growth must have implicit in it an explanation for the post-1971 slowdown. The perspective developed here suggests the following account. Europe's institutions were particularly well suited to an environment in which there existed a backlog of known technologies. Although that backlog was extensive in the wake of World War II, Europe's very success in exploiting it undermined the basis for the golden age. By the 1970s that backlog had been exhausted, and the problem became to undertake more radical innovation. At this point, Europe's institutional inheritance of centralised structures, wage compression and bank rather than securitised finance became more a handicap rather than an advantage. Some countries, most notably France, attempted to compensate with heavy government investment in high technology but with incomplete success.

One can argue further that the depletion of Europe's opportunities for catch-up growth itself undermined the bargain between capital and labour in which wage moderation was traded for high investment. The argument, as developed in Eichengreen (1996), goes like this. While workers and capitalists are both best off if they agree to defer current consumption in return for future gains which take the form of additional investment that results in higher productivity and incomes for all concerned, neither is willing to agree to defer without an assurance that the other will do the same.

This is the problem that corporatist institutions are designed to solve. But assume now a decline in the rate of return on deferring current consumption because, for example, of a fall in the return on investment and in the underlying rate of productivity growth. The incentive to resist the temptation to renege is correspondingly reduced, and institutions that were adequate to contain this temptation previously may no longer suffice. The exhaustion of the technological backlog and the end of the catch-up phase of Europe's growth could have played this role by reducing the return on investment and weakening the inventive for capital and labour to adhere to their agreement to defer current consumption in return for what were now more meagre future gains. The hot summer of 1968 and the wage explosion that followed had many causes, to be sure, but this perspective suggests that the internal dynamics of the catch-up process were at least one of them.

REFERENCES

Abramovitz, M. (1986), "Catching Up, Forging Ahead, and Falling Behind," *Journal of Economic History* 46, pp. 385-406.

Aitken, N. D. (1973), "The Effect of the EEC and EFTA on European Trade: A Temporal Cross-Section Analysis," *American Economic Review* LXIII, pp. 881-92.

Barro, R. J. (1991), "Economic Growth in a Cross Section of Countries," *Quarterly Journal of Economics* CVI, pp. 407-43.

Boyer, R. and J. Mistral (1992), *Accumulation, Inflation, Crises*, Paris: PUF.

Bruno, M. and J. Sachs (1985), *The Economics of Worldwide Stagflation*, Cambridge: Harvard University Press.

Calmfors, L. and J. Driffill (1988), "Centralisation of Wage Bargaining and Economic Performance," *Economic Policy* 6, pp. 13-61.

Clark, P. (1979), "Investment in the 1970s: Theory, Performance and Prediction," *Brookings Papers on Economic Activity* 1, pp. 73-113.

Crafts, N.F.R. (1992), "Institutions and Economic Growth: Recent British Experience in an International Context," *Western European Politics* 15, pp. 16-38.

Crafts, N.F.R. and G. Toniolo (1996), *Economic Growth in Europe since 1945*, Cambridge: Cambridge University Press.

Crouch, C. (1993), *Industrial Relations and European State Traditions*, Oxford: Clarendon Press.

Crouch, C. (1985), "The Conditions for Trade Union Restraint," in L. Lindberg and C. Maier (eds.), *The Politics of Inflation and Economic Stagnation*, Washington, D.C.: The Brookings Institution, pp. 103-39.

De Grauwe, P. (1988), "Exchange Rate Variability and the Slowdown in the Growth of International Trade," *Staff Papers* 35, pp. 63-84.

Denison, E. (1967), *Why Growth Rates Differ*, Washington, D.C.: The Brookings Institution.

Dumke, R. (1997), "Reappraising the Post-War Economic System in Germany: Is the Social Market Economy Passe?," unpublished manuscript, IFO Institute.

Edwards, S. (1998), "Openness, Productivity and Growth: What Do We Really Know?," *Economic Journal* 108, p. 383-98.

Eichengreen, B. (1993), *Reconstructing Europe's Trade and Payments: The European Payments Union*, Manchester and Ann Arbor: Manchester University Press and University of Michigan Press.

Eichengreen, B. (1994), "Institutional Prerequisites for Economic Growth: Europe After World War II," *European Economic Review*, 38, pp. 883-90.

Eichengreen, B. (1996), "Institutions and Economic Growth: Europe Since World War II," in N.F.R. Crafts and G. Toniolo (eds.), *Economic Growth in Europe Since 1945*, Cambridge: Cambridge University Press, pp. 38-72.

Eichengreen, B. (1998), "Innovation and Integration: Europe's Economy Since 1945," in M. Fulbrook (ed.), *The Short Oxford History of Europe in the 20th Century*, Oxford: Oxford University Press (forthcoming).

Europa Publications (various years), *Europa World Yearbook*, London: Europa Publications.

Frankel, J. (1992), "Is a Yen Bloc Forming in Pacific Asia?" in R. O'Brien (ed.), *Finance and the International Economy*, Oxford: Oxford University Press.

Freeman, C. (1997), "The National System of Innovation in Historical Perspective," in D. Archibugi and J. Michie (eds), *Technology, Globalization and Economic Performance*, Cambridge: Cambridge University Press, pp.24-49.

Grier, K., B. (1993), "Governments, Unions and Economic Growth," unpublished manuscript, George Mason University.

Grout, P.A. (1984), "Investment and Wages in the Absence of Binding Contracts: A Nash Bargaining Approach," *Econometrica* 52, pp. 449-60.

Hargreaves Heap, S. P. (1994), "Institutions and (Short-run) Macroeconomic Performance," *Journal of Economic Surveys* 8, pp. 35-56.

Harrison, J. (1993), *The Spanish Economy: From the Civil War to the European Community*, London: Macmilllan.

Hayward, J.E.S. (1966), "Interest Groups and Incomes Policy in France." *British Journal of Industrial Relations* 4, pp. 165-200.

Henrekson, M., J. Torstensson and R. Torstensson (1997), "Growth Effects of European Integration," *European Economic Review* 41, pp. 1537-557.

Hoel, K. (1990), "Local Versus Central Wage Bargaining with Endogenous Investments," *Scandinavian Journal of Economics* 92, pp. 453-69.

Johnson, G. and F. Stafford (1998), "Technology Regimes and the Distribution of Real Wages," unpublished manuscript.

Kashyap, A.K., J. C. Stein and D. W. Wilcox (1993), "Monetary Policy and Credit Conditions: Evidence from the Composition of External Finance," *American Economic Review* 83, pp. 78-98.

Kindleberger, C. P. (1967), *Europe's Postwar Growth*, New York: Oxford University Press.

Kitschelt, H. (1991), "Industrial Governance Structures, Innovation Strategies, and the Case of Japan: Sectoral or Cross-National Comparative Analysis?," *International Organization* 45, pp. 453-93.

Knack, S. and Ph. Keefer (1995), "Institutions and Economic Performance: Cross-Country Tests Using Alternative Institutional Measures," *Economics and Politics* 7, pp. 207-28.

Knack, S. and Ph. Keefer (1996), "Institutions and the Convergence Hypothesis: The Cross National Evidence," *Public Choice* 87, pp. 207-28.

Kogut, B. (1992), "National Organizing Principles of Work, and the Erstwhile Dominance of the American Multinational Corporation," *Industrial and Corporate Change* , pp. 285-326.

Lamfallusy, A. (1963), *The European Union and the Six*, Homewood, Ill.: Irwin.

Lancaster, K. (1973), "The Dynamic Inefficiency of Capitalism," *Journal of Political Economy* 81, pp. 1092-110.

Landesmann, M. and J. Vartiainen (1993), "Social Corporatism and Long-term Economic Performance," in J. Pekkarinen, M. Pohjola and B. Rowthorn (eds.), *Social Corporatism*, Oxford: Oxford University Press, pp. 210-42.

La Porta, R., F. Lopez-de-Silanes, A. Schleifer and R. Vishny (1997), "Legal Determinants of External Finance," *Journal of Finance* 52, pp. 1131-150.

Levine, R. and S. Zervos (1994), "What We Know About Policy and Growth from Cross-Country Analysis," in L. Pasinetti and R. Solow (eds.), *Economic Growth and the Structure of Long-term Development*, New York: St. Martin's Press, pp. 22-44.

Maddison, A. (1996), "Macroeconomic Accounts for European Countries," in B. van Ark and N. Crafts (eds.), *Quantitative Aspects of Post-War European Economic Growth*, Cambridge: Cambridge University Press, pp. 27-83.

Motley, B. (1994), "Growth and Inflation: A Cross-Country Study," unpublished manuscript, Federal Reserve Bank of San Francisco.

Nelson, R. (1993), *National Innovation Systems*, New York: Oxford University Press.

Nelson, R. and G. Wright (1992), "Rise and Fall of American Technological Leadership: The Postwar Era in Historical Perspective," *Journal of Economic Literature* 30, pp. 1931-964.

North, D. C. (1993), "Institutions and Credible Commitment," *Journal of Institutional and Theoretical Economics* 149, pp. 11-23.

North, D. C. and Barry Weingast (1989), "Constitutions and Commitment: The Evolution of Institutions Governing Public Choice in Seventeenth Century England," *Journal of Economic History* 49, pp. 803-32.

Perrow, C. (1984), *Normal Catastrophes*, New York: Basic Books.

Perrow, C. (1986), *Complex Organisations*, New York: Random House, 3rd edition.

Piore, M. and C. Sabel (1984), *The Second Industrial Divide: Possibilities for Prosperity*, New York: Basic Books.

Ploeg, F. van der (1987), "Trade Unions, Investment and Employment: A Non-Cooperative Approach," *European Economic Review* 31, pp. 1465-492.

Przeworski, A. and M. Wallerstein (1982), "The Structure of Class Conflict in Democratic Societies," *American Political Science Review* 76, pp. 215-38.

Rokkan, S. and J. Meyriat (1969), *International Guide to Electoral Statistics, Volume 1: National Elections in Western Europe*, Paris: Moulton.

Soskice, D. (1996), "German Technology Policy, Innovation, and National Institutional Frameworks," WZB Discussion Paper 96-319.

Taylor, C. L. and M. C. Hudson (1983), *World Handbook of Political and Social Indicators*, New Haven: Yale University Press.

United States Department of State (various years), *World Strength of Communist Parties*, Washington, D.C.: Government Printing Office.

Verspagen, B. (1996), "Technology Indicators and Economic Growth in the European Area: Some Empirical Evidence," in B. van Ark and N. Crafts (eds.), *Quantitative Aspects of Post-War European Economic Growth*, Cambridge: Cambridge University Press, pp. 215-43.

Wolf, H. (1995), "Postwar Germany in the European Context: Domestic and International Sources of Growth," in B. Eichengreen (ed.), *Europe's Postwar Recovery*, Cambridge: Cambridge University Press, pp. 323-52.

Wright, G. (1990), "The Origins of American Industrial Success, 1879-1940," *American Economic Review* 80, pp. 651-68.

PART II

DETERMINANTS OF PRODUCTIVITY

Chapter 5

The Interaction between Business Cycles and Productivity Growth
Evidence from US Industrial Data

James R. Malley, V. Anton Muscatelli, and Ulrich Woitek
University of Glasgow

Key words: Manufacturing, Total Factor Productivity, Growth, Business cycles,
               Opportunity cost, Learning by doing

Abstract: In this paper, we employ total factor productivity data adjusted for factor
               utilisation over the cycle, to model the dynamic interaction between TFP and
               employment. Our data spans twenty 2-digit SIC code manufacturing sectors in
               the US. There are two key results. First, we show that the impact of technology
               shocks on employment cycles is much weaker than suggested by real business
               cycle-type models, and that in a number of cases employment responds
               negatively to technology shocks. Second, in examining the impact of
               employment shocks on TFP, we find some evidence for both opportunity cost
               and learning-by-doing effects.

1.   INTRODUCTION

Policy-makers in OECD economies are increasingly focusing on the
determinants of long-run productivity growth. Indeed, institutional reforms
in a number of countries[1] have attempted to ensure a more stable
macroeconomic environment on the grounds that this is conducive to long-
run growth (see Balls, 1998). The key to understanding how business cycles
impact on long-run growth comes from recent theoretical research in

---

[1]   There have been monetary and fiscal policy reforms in a number of countries: not only
      moves to granting central banks greater independence, but in addition a number of
      economies have attempted to limit the fiscal actions of governments (cf. recent UK
      reforms and the Stability Pact for prospective EMU members).

endogenous growth. There are numerous theoretical contributions which highlight the implications of this linkage for the desirability of stabilisation policy (see, for instance, Stadler, 1990; Martin and Rogers, 1995; Muscatelli and Tirelli, 1998).

However, very little is known at the empirical level about the extent to which long-run productivity growth depends on fluctuations in output and/or employment. Economic theory has identified various potential channels through which recessions and booms can affect productivity growth, but empirical work in this area is still quite rare (see Saint-Paul, 1997 for a survey). Existing empirical work also suffers from serious shortcomings. As Saint-Paul points out, one of the key problems is the lack of reliable data on total factor productivity growth. Standard constructions of total factor productivity (TFP) ignore considerations pertaining to market power, returns to scale and variations in factor utilisation over the cycle. A second problem is that existing work commonly uses VAR models with just-identifying assumptions which involve imposing strong (and often arbitrary) *a priori* causal links on the interactions between business cycles and TFP growth. A final problem is that the vast majority of existing studies are conducted on aggregate data, and so ignore the possibility of serious aggregation bias.

This paper addresses these problems, and investigates the dynamic interaction between employment cycles and TFP growth using US manufacturing data from the NBER productivity database. Our main results are as follows. First, there seems to be little evidence of a significant impact of temporary employment shocks on the level of TFP at the aggregate manufacturing level. This is consistent with existing aggregate economy studies which only occasionally find significant effects of business cycles on long-run productivity. Second, we find that the use of cyclically-adjusted TFP series dramatically alters the results normally obtained using standard Solow residuals. Third, we find that our adjusted TFP data also shed some light on the separate but related issue of how technology shocks affect employment.[2] We find that the impact of technology shocks on employment varies considerably between sectors, in contrast to existing results obtained using unadjusted TFP data. This result suggests that technology shocks are less important in driving aggregate employment fluctuations than assumed in standard real business cycle models. Finally we provide evidence that technology shocks have temporary or even permanent negative effects on employment. This last result can be explained by sticky-price general-equilibrium macroeconomic models and the presence of "creative destruction" effects.

The rest of the paper is divided as follows. Section 2 provides a brief survey of the theoretical literature which underpins our empirical models,

---

[2]   For recent empirical work on this issue, see Gali (1999) and Malley and Muscatelli (1996).

and surveys the existing empirical literature. Section 3 sets out the methodology which we follow in constructing cyclically-adjusted TFP. Section 4 describes our modelling approach and our econometric results, and Section 5 concludes.

2. THE INTERACTION BETWEEN BUSINESS CYCLES AND GROWTH: TECHNOLOGY AND EMPLOYMENT SHOCKS

In examining the interaction between business cycles and growth we have to allow for the possibility of bi-directional causal links. We first consider how business cycles (employment shocks[3]) affect TFP. Here the central issue is whether cyclical downturns are periods of opportunity or waste. Indeed the debate on the impact of business cycles on growth goes back to Keynes, Robertson and Schumpeter. A useful survey of the various theoretical models which address this issue is provided by Saint-Paul (1997), we only provide a summary here. One general approach in this literature is to argue that productivity-enhancing activities are most likely to occur in periods of cyclical upswing, through learning-by-doing effects (LBD) whereby individual productive units tend to generate new ideas and design better ways of organising production whilst they are actually engaged in productive activities (see Arrow, 1962; Argote and Epple, 1990; Solow, 1997). Similarly, it is argued that where R&D expenditures have to be financed from retained profits, R&D activity is more likely to take place in booms than in recessions (see Stiglitz, 1993).

An alternative approach is to argue that reorganisation activities usually take place within firms during recessions, when the opportunity cost (OC) in terms of lost production is lower (see Bean, 1990; Hall, 1991). In addition, firms may respond to greater financial discipline in downswings by resorting to innovation, and resource reallocation may take place between firms in recessions as the least efficient productive units exit from the industry (see Caballero and Hammour, 1994). The notion that there is a process of "Darwinian Selection" in recessions is also at the heart of the Schumpeterian approach to cycles and growth.

However, empirical evidence on the links between cycles and long-run productivity growth is still extremely thin. There are only a handful of econometric studies which analyse the impact of cyclical shocks on TFP levels in the long-run (Gali and Hammour; 1991, Saint-Paul, 1993; Malley and Muscatelli, 1999). All of these studies estimate bivariate semi-structural

---

[3] The issue of why we focus on employment shocks rather than output shocks in examining the impact of business cycles on productivity growth is dealt with below.

VARs for variations in employment and TFP to detect the link between demand shocks and productivity, be it labour productivity or TFP. They examine the impulse responses of TFP levels to temporary employment shocks, and find some support for the "opportunity cost" approach, suggesting that cyclical downturns tend to have a positive impact on total factor productivity in the long run.

It is notable that all these studies use variations in employment to identify business cycle shocks, rather than a measure of output. The advantage of employment as a measure of cyclical disturbances is that OC or LBD effects are more likely to be correlated with actual changes in a firm's production organisation (which often comes with variations in employment or job reallocation) than with variations in production levels. Davis and Haltiwanger (1990, 1992) show that the job destruction cycle does not quite match the output cycle, and therefore identifying business cycle shocks with employment fluctuations may provide a more accurate measure of the mechanism through which organisational capital is accumulated.[4]

We should also point out that, in concentrating on bivariate VARs which are specified in variations of employment and TFP we are not able to differentiate between aggregate demand shocks, and other real shocks (*e.g.* shocks to labour supply or taxation policy) which might cause employment to vary. Thus, when we assert that these models are designed to pick up the interaction between business cycles and growth, we are *not* restricting ourselves to a particular source of cycles in employment.

All the previous studies cited above (with the exception of Malley and Muscatelli, 1999) use aggregate macroeconomic data, as opposed to industry-level data whilst the phenomena described above may clearly differ considerably across industrial sectors. Intuitively we might expect OC effects to be predominant in some sectors, and LBD effects in others. In addition, it may be easier to obtain a more accurate measure of TFP at a more disaggregated level.

Furthermore, none of these studies make any systematic allowance for the mis-measurement of TFP due to factor utilisation, market power and returns to scale effects over the cycle. It is now recognised that this is an extremely important issue (see Hall, 1990; Burnside *et al.*, 1995; Basu, 1996), in that factor mis-measurement may be up to 20% of the total change in measured factor use (see Basu, *op cit.*).

Finally, the VAR models estimated in previous work have generally used the standard Choleski decomposition approach to just-identifying the

---

[4] Although not reported here, we find that using an industry output measure as our cyclical variable does not lead to significant OC or LBD effects for any industries in the long run. Again, this suggests that most of the effect of business cycles shocks on TFP occur through variations in employment levels.

impulse responses of TFP to employment shocks, or an alternative just-identifying assumption based on assuming a particular lagged impact of employment shocks on TFP. The problem with these just-identifying restrictions is that they involve imposing a causal structure on the model which cannot be tested.

Next, we turn our attention to the way in which shocks to TFP (technology shocks) affect employment. The study of the impact of technology shocks on employment has generally been the domain of real business cycle models, and more recently of sticky-price general equilibrium models (see, *inter alia*, King and Watson, 1995; Gali, 1999). The effect of technology shocks on employment in these models is due to a standard shift effect on labour demand and the accompanying impact on capital accumulation. But in general such models do not focus on the long-run effects of technology shocks on employment.[5]

Labour market search theory has also analysed the impact of productivity growth on employment. These models (see Mortensen and Pissarides, 1994; Aghion and Howitt 1991, 1994) have focused on how changes in the growth rate of productivity can affect inflows and outflows from unemployment, and hence the equilibrium unemployment/employment rate. Whether technology impacts positively or negatively on employment depends partly on whether a positive technology shock leads to the destruction of low-productivity jobs, the creation of new jobs in new firms as technological innovation fosters firm creation, or capital-labour substitution effects. The strength of these effects may again differ markedly between sectors, and this provides an additional incentive to estimate industry-level VARs. Direct empirical evidence on these effects is again difficult to find, but at the *aggregate* level, there seems to be evidence that technology shocks cause employment to fall (at least temporarily).[6]

Of course there is nothing to rule out RBC type shocks co-existing with a labour market search based propagation mechanism. Indeed, recently Den Haan *et al.* (1997) have shown using a calibrated model that job destruction dynamics may play an important role in explaining the persistence of output effects arising from technology shocks. Ultimately, one cannot rule out a permanent effect of technology shocks on employment (or unemployment). If a unit root is present in the employment data, this may be partly due to shifts in agent preferences or in wage and price-setting mechanisms, but one

---

[5] Also, it is important to note that long-run LBD or OC effects are ruled out by assumption in such models. In fact VAR models based on RBC models or dynamic sticky price models generally assume that the unit root in productivity is due solely to productivity shocks (see Gali, 1999).

[6] See Forni and Reichlin (1995), Blanchard *et al.* (1995), Gali (1999), Malley and Muscatelli (1997).

cannot rule out *a priori* the effect of technology shocks in driving the trend in employment.

In Section 4 we shall return to the issue of how our econometric methodology allows us to capture the dynamic interrelationship between TFP and employment, and the response of these variables to demand and technology shocks. We now turn our attention to the construction of adjusted TFP series.

3.   TOTAL FACTOR PRODUCTIVITY: SOLOW RESIDUALS AND ADJUSTED SERIES

In virtually all empirical work employing the growth accounting framework (including the studies cited in Sections 1 and 2), TFP growth is measured as in Solow (1957). However, it is well know that the Solow residual may not be an accurate measure of "true" multi-factor productivity since it ignores considerations pertaining to market power, non-constant returns to scale and variable factor utilisation over the cycle (see Hall, 1991; and Basu, 1996). Clearly any research which hopes to accurately gauge the link between employment cycles and growth requires a measure of TFP which, at least, accounts for the points raised by Hall and Basu.[7] Accordingly, in the VAR analysis which follows in the next Section, we will use cyclically adjusted TFP based on the measure developed in Basu (1996).[8]

In order to illustrate the relationship between the traditional Solow residual and the Basu measure of TFP, it is convenient to start by restating the standard definitions which are commonly used in the literature. First, consider the following production function:

$$Y_t = \Theta_t F\left[N_t, M_t, K_t\right] \tag{1}$$

where, Θ_t represents an index of Hicks neutral technical progress; F is a homogenous production function of some degree, γ; Y_t is real gross output; and N_t, M_t and K_t are labour and real material and capital inputs respectively.

Taking logs of both sides of (1) and then differentiating with respect to time gives

$$\frac{\dot{Y}}{Y} = \frac{\dot{\Theta}}{\Theta} + \frac{\Theta F_N N}{Y}\left(\frac{\dot{N}}{N}\right) + \frac{\Theta F_M M}{Y}\left(\frac{\dot{M}}{M}\right) + \frac{\Theta F_K K}{Y}\left(\frac{\dot{K}}{K}\right) \tag{2}$$

---

[7]   This point is also forcefully made by Saint-Paul (1997).

[8]   Note that Basu's measure is an extension of Hall (1991) and hence allows for the possibility of both market power and non-constant returns to scale.

where, ΘF_N, ΘF_M and ΘF_K are the marginal products of labour, material inputs and capital respectively. The firm is assumed to minimise the following cost function in order to determine the optimal levels of capital and labour to employ,

$$C = wN + P_m M + rK \tag{3}$$

subject to the production constraint in (1). The symbols w, P_m and r are defined as the nominal wage per worker, the price of material inputs and the rental rate of capital respectively.

The first-order conditions resulting from minimising (3) subject to (1) are

$$\Theta F_N = \frac{w\gamma}{\lambda}, \Theta F_M = \frac{P_m \gamma}{\lambda} \text{ and } \Theta F_K = \frac{r\gamma}{\lambda} \tag{4}$$

where, the Langrangian multiplier λ is defined as marginal cost.

3.1   Revenue Based Total Factor Productivity

The original Solow (1957) residual is derived assuming (i) constant returns to scale and (ii) perfect competition in the factor and product markets. To measure marginal cost, Solow assumes that it is *observable* at the market price of output, P. Accordingly the marginal products of capital and labour in (4) can be rewritten as

$$\Theta F_N = \frac{w}{P}, \Theta F_M = \frac{P_m}{P} \text{ and } F_K = \frac{r}{P} \tag{5}$$

Substituting the marginal products in (5) back into (2) gives

$$\frac{\dot{Y}}{Y} = \alpha_t^n \left(\frac{\dot{N}}{N} \right) + \alpha_t^m \left(\frac{\dot{M}}{M} \right) + \alpha_t^k \left(\frac{\dot{K}}{K} \right) + \frac{\dot{\Theta}}{\Theta}, \text{ where} \tag{6}$$

$$\alpha_t^n = \frac{wN}{PY}, \alpha_t^m = \frac{P_m M}{PY}, \text{ and } \alpha_t^k = 1 - \alpha_t^n - \alpha_t^m = \frac{rK}{PY}$$

The discrete time approximation to (6) is given by (see Diewert, 1976)

$$\Delta y_t = \tilde{\alpha}_t^n \Delta n_t + \tilde{\alpha}_t^m \Delta m_t + \tilde{\alpha}_t^k \Delta k_t + \Delta \theta_t, \text{ where}$$

$$\Delta y_t = \log\left(\frac{Y_t}{Y_{t-1}}\right), \Delta n_t = \log\left(\frac{N_t}{N_{t-1}}\right), \Delta m_t = \log\left(\frac{M_t}{M_{t-1}}\right), \Delta k_t = \log\left(\frac{K_t}{K_{t-1}}\right),$$

$$\Delta \theta_t = \log\left(\frac{\Theta_t}{\Theta_{t-1}}\right), \tilde{\alpha}_t^n = \frac{\alpha_t^n + \alpha_{t-1}^n}{2}, \tilde{\alpha}_t^m = \frac{\alpha_t^m + \alpha_{t-1}^m}{2}, \tilde{\alpha}_t^k = \frac{\alpha_t^k + \alpha_{t-1}^k}{2}.$$

(7)

Total factor productivity growth or the Solow residual is therefore derived as the difference between output growth and weighted input growth, e.g.

$$\%\Delta TFP_{Solow} = \Delta \theta_t + \varepsilon_t = \Delta y_t - \tilde{\alpha}_t^n \Delta n_t - \tilde{\alpha}_t^m \Delta m_t - \alpha_t^k \Delta k_t. \tag{8}$$

Note that a random term, ε_t has been added in (8) to reflect the stochastic nature of productivity growth. Under this view, TFP growth is the sum of a constant underlying growth rate, $\Delta \theta_t$ plus a random component, ε_t.

3.2   Cost Based Total Factor Productivity

To address the problems of mis-measurement associated with imposing constant returns to scale, Hall (1990) derives an alternative measure of TFP which does not require an assumption regarding competition. In contrast to Solow, Hall assumes that marginal cost, λ is not observable as the market price of output, P. Instead of measuring each input's shares in revenue, (PY) he uses their shares in cost.[9]

Using the cost-shares, the marginal products in (5) can be rewritten as

$$\Theta F_N = \frac{w\gamma Y}{wN + P_m M + rK}, \Theta F_M = \frac{P_m\gamma Y}{wN + P_m M + rK}, \text{ and}$$

$$\Theta F_K = \frac{r\gamma Y}{wN + P_m M + rK}.$$

(9)

Again, output growth is found by substituting (9) into (2) and solving for Δy_t, e.g.

$$\Delta y_t = \gamma\left(\tilde{\alpha}_t^{n'} \Delta n_t + \tilde{\alpha}_t^{m'} \Delta m_t + \tilde{\alpha}_t^{k'} \Delta k_t\right) + \Delta\theta_t' + \varepsilon_t, \tag{10}$$

---

[9]   Note that the cost shares are defined as ($C=wN+PmM+rK$). Further note that if $PY>C$, due to pure monopoly profits, then Solow's revenue shares will underestimate the elasticity of output with respect to all inputs.

where the α' denote cost shares,

$$\tilde{\alpha}_t^{n'} = \frac{\alpha_t^{n'} + \alpha_{t-1}^{n'}}{2}, \tilde{\alpha}_t^{m'} = \frac{\alpha_t^{m'} + \alpha_{t-1}^{m'}}{2}, \tilde{\alpha}_t^{k'} = \frac{\alpha_t^{k'} + \alpha_{t-1}^{k'}}{2},$$

$$\alpha_t^{n'} = \frac{wN}{C}, \alpha_t^{m'} = \frac{P_m M}{C}, \alpha_t^{k'} = 1 - \alpha_t^{n'} - \alpha_t^{m'} = \frac{rK}{C}; C = wN + P_m M + rK.$$

Using the cost-based shares, TFP growth (adjusted for non-constant returns and market power) can now be expressed as

$$\%\Delta TFP_{Hall} =$$
$$\%\Delta TFP' - \left\{ (\gamma - 1) \left(\tilde{\alpha}_t^{n'} \Delta n_t + \tilde{\alpha}_t^{m'} \Delta m_t + \alpha_t^{k'} \Delta k_t \right) \right\} \equiv \Delta \theta_t' + \varepsilon_t \tag{11}$$

Note that if $\gamma = 1$ and $PY = C$ then $\%\Delta TFP_{Hall} = \%\Delta TFP' \equiv \%\Delta TFP_{Solow}$.

3.3   Cost-Based (Utilisation Adjusted) Total Factor Productivity

Building directly on Hall's cost-based measure, Basu (1996) provides a method for obtaining a measure of TFP growth which is net of cyclical changes in factor utilisation. Basu's proposed adjustment relies on using data on material inputs as an indicator of cyclical factor utilisation. The argument he puts forward is that unlike employment and capital, material inputs do not have an utilisation dimension, and hence one can use relative changes in the input of raw materials and other measured factor inputs (capital and labour) to deduce the extent to which factor utilisation changes over the cycle.

In contrast to (1), we follow Basu and employ the following production function

$$Y_t = \Theta_t F[(G_t \cdot N_t), M_t, (Z_t \cdot K_t)] \tag{12}$$

where, G and Z are the levels of labour and capital utilisation. Using the same methods as employed in (2)-(9) the following alternative cost-based Solow residual, net of factor utilisation, can be derived

$$\%\Delta TFP_{Basu} =$$
$$\underbrace{\Delta y_t - \gamma \left(\tilde{\alpha}_t^{n'} \Delta n_t + \tilde{\alpha}_t^{m'} \Delta m_t + \tilde{\alpha}_t^{k'} \Delta k_t \right)}_{\%\Delta TFP_{Hall}} - \gamma \underbrace{\left(\tilde{\alpha}_t^{n'} \Delta g_t + \alpha_t^{k'} \Delta z_t \right)}_{u_t} \tag{13}$$

where the shares are defined as in Hall.

In other words, $\%\Delta\text{TFP}_{Basu}$ in (13) is equal to $\%\Delta\text{TFP}_{Hall}$ net of changes induced by capacity utilisation. Note however, that the problem with (13) in its current form is that this measure of TFP growth cannot be calculated since some of the components of u_t are *unobservable* (*i.e.* Δg and Δz). To derive the relationship between *unobserved* capital and labour inputs and *observable* or measured material inputs Basu makes use of the following more restricted production function

$$Y = \Theta F\big[V\big\{(G \cdot N), (Z \cdot K)\big\}, H\{M\}\big]$$ (14)

where the value-added function, V and the material costs functions, H are assumed to have constant returns to scale. Note that the function F, however, still has the same properties as set out in (1). Log-linearising (14) and using the first-order conditions for cost minimisation the growth rate in value added, Δv_t can be expressed as

$$\Delta v_t = \Delta m_t - \sigma\big(\Delta p_{v_t} - \Delta p_{m_t}\big)$$ (15)

where, Δm is material cost growth, $\sigma \geq 0$ is the (local) elasticity of substitution between value-added and materials (with $\sigma = 0$ representing the Leontief case and $\sigma = 1$ the Cobb-Douglas unit-elastic case), and $\Delta p_v, \Delta p_m$ measure value-added and materials inflation, respectively.[10]

The growth in value-added can next be expressed as a Divisia index in terms of the growth in observed capital and labour input and unobserved utilisation, *e.g.*

$$\Delta v_t = \frac{\tilde{\alpha}_t^{n'}\big(\Delta n_t + \Delta g_t\big) + \tilde{\alpha}_t^{k'}\big(\Delta k_t + \Delta z_t\big)}{\tilde{\alpha}_t^{n'} + \tilde{\alpha}_t^{k'}}$$ (16)

Substituting (16) into (15) for Δv_t, rearranging and substituting the resulting expression, which is equal to $u_t(=\tilde{\alpha}_t^{n'}\Delta g_t + \tilde{\alpha}_t^{k'}\Delta z_t)$, into (13) gives

$$\%\Delta TFP_{Basu} = \Delta y_t - \gamma\big(\Delta m_t - \sigma\big(\tilde{\alpha}_t^{n'} + \tilde{\alpha}_t^{k'}\big)\big(\Delta p_{v_t} - \Delta p_{m_t}\big)\big) + \varepsilon_t$$ (17)

---

[10] Bruno (1984) reviews a number of papers and reports a consensus range for σ between 0.3-0.4. A more recent study by Rotemberg and Woodford (1992) provide an estimate σ of 0.7 (which is the baseline value used by Basu (1996)).

Note that unlike (13), TFP growth in (17) is defined in terms of only *observable* magnitudes.

3.4   Estimating Cyclically Adjusted TFP

To derive the utilisation adjusted measure of TFP growth, we next (using U.S. manufacturing data from 1959-91) undertake instrumental variable (*IV*) estimation of (17) to identify γ and hence $\%\Delta\text{TFP}_{Basu}$. *IV* estimation is required in this context due to the obvious endogeneity of the regressors. We will employ the same set of instruments proposed by Ramey (1989) and Hall (1990) and augmented by Caballero and Lyons (1992) and Basu (1996).[11]

Table 1 reports the results of estimating (via 3SLS) returns to scale for aggregate manufacturing and two major sub-aggregates. The results of Table 1 indicate for the chosen aggregations that (i) returns to scale are decreasing (but in an economic context, not far from constant) and (ii) the estimates are extremely robust to alternative values of σ.

Table 1. Estimates of Return to Scale for Alternative Values of σ

	Manufacturing	Durables	Non-Durables
$\sigma=0.0$	0.94	0.92	0.92
$\sigma=0.3$	0.95	0.93	0.94
$\sigma=0.5$	0.95	0.94	0.95
$\sigma=0.7$	0.96	0.94	0.95
$\sigma=1.0$	0.96	0.95	0.96

Note that the above estimates are obtained by applying *3SLS* to the relevant industries comprising a particular aggregation. Based on standard *t-tests*, all of the above estimates are significantly different from zero at less than the 1% level. Finally note that, based on standard *Wald-tests*, all of the above estimates are significantly different from unity.

Tables 2 and 3 provide several different views on the extent to which the Basu measure has succeeded in removing cyclical variation in Solow based TFP. For example, Table 2 reveals, regardless of the value of σ, that the correlation of the Basu measure with alternative measures of the cycle is uniformly lower than the Solow residual.

---

[11] These include the growth rate of Military Spending; the growth rate of the World Price of Oil (deflated by both the price of Manufacturing Durables and Non-Durables); and the Political Party of the President. Note that the instruments have been chosen as ones which can cause important movements in employment, material costs, capital accumulation and output but are orthogonal with the random component of TFP growth.

Table 2. Correlation between TFP and Output/Hours Growth

	Solow	Basu				
		$\sigma=0$	$\sigma=0.3$	$\sigma=0.5$	$\sigma=0.7$	$\sigma=1$
Manufacturing Output	0.95	0.24	0.19	0.16	0.16	0.17
Durable Output	0.95	-0.09	-0.19	-0.24	-0.28	-0.32
Non-Durable Output	0.92	0.43	0.40	0.38	0.36	0.33
Manufacturing Hours	0.84	0.25	0.16	0.12	0.09	0.08
Durable Hours	0.84	-0.02	-0.13	-0.20	-0.25	-0.31
Non-Durable Hours	0.79	0.41	0.37	0.34	0.32	0.28

Note, that based on standard *t-tests*, the bi-variate correlation coefficients which tested significantly different from zero at the 5% level include the Solow residuals and the Basu residuals for Non-Durable Output when $\sigma=0$, 0.3, 0.5 and 0.7 and for Non-Durable Hours when $\sigma=0$ and 0.3).

Additionally, Table 3 shows that the variance of TFP relative to alternative measures of the cycle is uniformly lower for the Basu based measure. This lower correlation of the adjusted TFP measure and the cycle implies smaller technology shocks and therefore has been interpreted by some as a problem for real-business cycle (RBC) type models. However, a lower variance of TFP shocks might still correlate well with output and employment cycles. This would depend on the strength of the propagation mechanism. Our VAR results in the next section will offer some insights into this issue.

Table 3. Variance of TFP to Variance Output/Hours Growth

	Solow	Basu				
		$\sigma=0$	$\sigma=0.3$	$\sigma=0.5$	$\sigma=0.7$	$\sigma=1$
Manufacturing Output	0.52	0.02	0.02	0.02	0.03	0.03
Durable Output	0.39	0.02	0.02	0.02	0.02	0.02
Non-Durable Output	0.71	0.14	0.14	0.14	0.14	0.15
Manufacturing Hours	0.50	0.02	0.02	0.02	0.02	0.03
Durable Hours	0.42	0.02	0.02	0.02	0.02	0.02
Non-Durable Hours	0.71	0.14	0.14	0.14	0.14	0.15

Finally Table 4 reports estimates of returns to scale for twenty 2-digit industries over the period 1959-1991. Not surprisingly, given the limited degrees of freedom relative to the 3SLS estimations, returns to scale are not significantly different from unity for nearly all industries.[12]

---

[12] This confirms earlier results obtained using a different method by Burnside *et al.* (1995). They use electricity consumption as a proxy for capital utilisation. For a comparison of the two techniques see the discussion to Burnside *et al.* (1995).

Table 4. Estimates of Return to Scale, $\hat{\gamma}_{i=20...39}$ for Alternative Values of σ

	Durable Goods Industries				
		$\sigma=0$	$\sigma=0.3$	$\sigma=0.5$	$\sigma=0.7$	$\sigma=1$
sic24	Lumber and wood	0.97	0.98	0.98	0.99	1.00
sic25	Furniture and fixtures	1.00	1.02	1.02	1.03	1.04
sic32	Stone, clay and glass	0.90	0.92	0.93	0.94	0.96
sic33	Primary metals	0.99	0.98	0.96	0.95	0.94
sic34	Fabricated metals	1.12	1.12	1.12	1.12	1.13
sic35	Industrial machinery & equipment	0.96	0.95	0.94	0.94	0.93
sic36	Electronic & electric equipment	1.18	1.16	1.15	1.13	1.11
sic37	Transportation equipment	0.83	0.84	0.85	0.86	0.87
sic38	Instruments & related products	1.12	1.10	1.08	1.07	1.05
sic39	Miscellaneous industries	1.03	1.04	1.04	1.05	1.06

	Non-Durable Goods Industries				
		$\sigma=0$	$\sigma=0.3$	$\sigma=0.5$	$\sigma=0.7$	$\sigma=1$
sic20	Food and kindred products	1.20	1.20	1.21	1.21	1.22
sic21	Tobacco products	1.44	1.41	1.39	1.37	1.34
sic22	Textile mill products	1.08	1.09	1.09	1.09	1.09
sic23	Apparel & other textile	0.91	0.93	0.94	0.95	0.96
sic26	Paper & allied	1.21	1.19	1.17	1.16	1.14
sic27	Printing & publishing	0.85	0.89	0.91	0.95	1.00
sic28	Chemicals & allied	1.25	1.22	1.20	1.18	1.15
sic29	Petroleum & coal products	1.11	1.10	1.09	1.08	1.06
sic30	Rubber & misc. plastics products	1.11	1.11	1.11	1.11	1.10
sic31	Leather & leather products	1.33	1.32	1.32	1.32	1.31

Note that, based on standard *t-tests*, all of the above IV estimates of $\hat{\gamma}_i$, are significantly different from zero at less than the 1% level except for sic21. Further note that, based on standard *Wald-tests*, none of the estimates of $\hat{\gamma}_i$ are significantly different from unity except sic26 and sic37.

4.   THE ECONOMETRIC MODEL AND RESULTS

4.1   Econometric Methodology

As explained in the introduction, previous empirical verification of the relationship between business cycles and growth (Gali and Hammour, 1991; Saint-Paul, 1993; and Malley and Muscatelli, 1999) has used semi-structural VAR analysis. Consider the following p^{th}-order structural or primitive VAR for TFP growth, Δz_{it}, and the percentage change in total employment, Δl_{it}, for each sector i,

$$\mathbf{x}_{it} = \begin{bmatrix} \Delta z_{it} \\ \Delta l_{it} \end{bmatrix} :$$

$$\mathbf{x}_{it} = \sum_{j=1}^{p} \mathbf{A}_j \mathbf{x}_{i,t-j} + \mathbf{u}_{it} ; t = 1,\ldots T \tag{18}$$

where $\mathbf{x}_{it}$ is the (2x1) vector of dependent variables, $\mathbf{A}_j$, $j = 1,\ldots,p$ are the (2x2) parameter matrices,[13] and $\mathbf{u}_{it}$ is an (2x1) vector of disturbances, following the usual assumptions: $E(\mathbf{u}_{it}) = \mathbf{0}$, $E(\mathbf{u}_{it}\mathbf{u}'_{it}) = \Sigma$, $E(\mathbf{u}_{it}\mathbf{u}'_{it'}) = \mathbf{0}$ $\forall\, t \neq t'$.

From our discussion in Section 2, the structural disturbance corresponding to the TFP variable (Δz_{it}) corresponds to technological shocks to TFP growth, and the structural disturbance corresponding to the employment variable (Δl_{it}) captures demand-side or business cycle disturbances.

However, a number of issues have to be addressed. The first concerns the long-run properties of the model. Our VAR is specified in differences. Given that both TFP and employment will display a stochastic trend, then our LBD and OC theories suggest we should not restrict the model so as to rule out the possibility of employment shocks driving the stochastic trend in the TFP variable (in contrast to standard RBC models). Vice-versa, as discussed in Section 2, we have to allow for the possibility of technology shocks driving the trend in employment. This is especially important when using sectoral data, as in some industries technology shocks may have helped to drive negative trends in employment (labour substitution effects), or positive trends (labour complementarity effects). This has implications for the identification of the VAR. Unlike VAR modelling approaches where long-run effects are constrained *a priori* by theoretical considerations (*e.g.* Blanchard and Quah, 1989), the questions posed by OC and LBD theories require no long-run restrictions to be imposed on the effects of technology and business cycle shocks.

Let us now consider the identification issue in more detail. Provided that the above model is stationary, it has an infinite MA representation

---

[13] The order of the VAR is decided using the AIC criterion; the maximum lag is fixed at 2, the minimum at 1. To ensure that the estimated system is stationary, we computed the roots of the characteristic polynomial $|A-\lambda I|=0$, where A is the system matrix of the VAR(1) representation of equation (18), and checked whether the moduli are inside the unit circle (see Lütkepohl (1991), p. 9-13; results are available on request).

$$\mathbf{x}_{it} = \sum_{j=0}^{\infty} \mathbf{B}_j \mathbf{u}_{i,t-j}; \mathbf{B}_0 = \mathbf{I}_n; \mathbf{B}_j = \sum_{k=1}^{p} \mathbf{A}_k \mathbf{B}_{j-k}; j = 1,2,\ldots \qquad (19)$$

If the error variance-covariance matrix Σ is diagonal, the parameter matrices of the MA representation can be interpreted as responses of the system to past shocks. However, if Σ is not diagonal, the VAR is not identified. To solve this problem, orthogonalised impulse responses can be derived by using, amongst others, the Cholesky (see Sims, 1980) or the Blanchard and Quah (1989) decompositions.

As already noted the Blanchard-Quah identification is inappropriate to our case because we wish to test the long-run impact of employment and technology shocks. Most previous authors (see Gali and Hammour, 1991; Malley and Muscatelli, 1996) have used a Choleski decomposition, or an alternative restriction on the short-run impact of shocks (Saint-Paul, 1993). However, all of these procedures require the imposition of *a priori* knowledge regarding the contemporaneous or the long-run dynamic interaction of the variables. The economic implications of the Choleski identification might seem reasonable in our context, given that effects considered in LBD or OC models (e.g. reorganisation, on-the-job training, the introduction of new techniques, R&D activity) typically only impact TFP with a lag. However, this restriction might be inappropriate, especially when using annual data if reorganisation effects following employment shocks feed on to productivity improvements within a year (see Saint-Paul, 1993). An alternative Choleski just-identifying restriction would reverse the assumption regarding contemporaneous causation, thus assuming that productivity shocks do not impact immediately on employment levels. But again, this seems an arbitrary restriction.

Here we pursue an alternative identification scheme which overcomes these problems, and which has recently been proposed by Pesaran and Shin (1998) and Koop *et al.* (1996). If we interpret the impulse response function at lag h as the difference between a h-step VAR forecast assuming a shock on the variable j, δ_j, and a VAR forecast without a shock, we obtain generalised impulse (GI) responses (Ω_{t-1} is the information set available at time t)

$$\mathbf{GI}(h,\delta_j,\Omega_{t-1}) = \mathrm{E}\left(\mathbf{x}_{t+h}\middle|\mathbf{u}_{t,j} = \delta_j,\Omega_{t-1}\right) - \mathrm{E}\left(\mathbf{x}_{t+h}\middle|\Omega_{t-1}\right). \qquad (20)$$

In order to compute the forecasts for the other variables i, $i \neq j$, we need starting values at time t, conditional on the fact that there is a shock to series j. To obtain these starting values, we use the contemporaneous relationship between the error terms given by the estimated error variance covariance matrix. The assumption of a multivariate normal distribution of the error terms leads to the following expression for the starting value in series i

$$E\left(u_{t,i}\middle|u_{t,j}=\delta_j\right)=\frac{\sigma_{ij}}{\sigma_{jj}}\delta_j. \tag{21}$$

i.e. we make use of the expected values for $u_{t,i}$, $i = 1, \dots , n$, conditional on the shock on variable j. Setting δ_j equal to the standard deviation of $\mathbf{u}_j$, we obtain for the generalised impulse responses

$$\psi_{j,h}^{G} = \mathbf{B}_h \begin{pmatrix} \sigma_{1j} \\ \vdots \\ \sigma_{ij} \\ \vdots \\ \sigma_{nj} \end{pmatrix} \frac{\delta_j}{\sigma_{jj}} = \left.\frac{\mathbf{B}_h \Sigma \mathbf{e}_j}{\sqrt{\sigma_{jj}}}\right|_{\delta_j=\sqrt{\sigma_{jj}}}, \tag{22}$$

where $\mathbf{e}_j$ is an $(n \times 1)$ vector of zeroes with unity as jth element. The generalised long-run multiplier is defined as

$$\psi_{j,\infty}^{G} = \sum_{k=0}^{\infty}\psi_{j,k}^{G} = \frac{\sum\limits_{k=0}^{\infty}\mathbf{B}_k\Sigma\mathbf{e}_j}{\sqrt{\sigma_{jj}}}. \tag{23}$$

Finally, the generalised forecast error decomposition is defined as

$$\theta_{k,j}(h) = \frac{\sum\limits_{l=0}^{h-1}\sigma_{jj}^{-1}\left(\mathbf{e}_k'\mathbf{B}_l\Sigma\mathbf{e}_j\right)^2}{\sum\limits_{l=0}^{h-1}\left(\mathbf{e}_k'\mathbf{B}_l\Sigma\mathbf{B}_l'\mathbf{e}_k\right)} ; k, j = 1,\dots,n. \tag{24}$$

The above expression is calculated as the percentage decrease in the forecast error variance of variable k, due to conditioning on the innovations to variable j by using the contemporaneous relationship between the variables given by equation (24) (see Pesaran and Shin, 1998).

4.2   Results

We now present the results from our VAR analysis. We have estimated the VAR model (18) using both aggregate manufacturing data, and disaggregated data for twenty two-digit SIC code industries comprising the aggregate. We report estimates using both the standard Solow measure for TFP as set out in (8), and the adjusted Basu TFP measure in (17). For reasons of space, we only tabulate the results for the case where $\sigma = 0.5$.[14]

Table 5. Aggregate Series - Impulse Responses

	Solow									
	Technology → N					N → Technology				
	Horizon					Horizon				
	0	1	2	3	∞	0	1	2	3	∞
Aggregate	0.026**	0.010**	-0.004	-0.006	0.027**	0.021**	-0.012**	-0.014*	-0.004	-0.004
Durables	0.034**	0.019**	-0.010	-0.009	0.035**	0.026**	-0.011**	-0.023**	-0.011	-0.017
Non-Durables	0.016**	0.005	-0.001	-0.001	0.019**	0.015**	-0.009**	-0.007**	-0.002	-0.002
	Basu (σ=0.5)									
	Technology → N					N → Technology				
	Horizon					Horizon				
	0	1	2	3	∞	0	1	2	3	∞
Aggregate	0.004	0.002	0.000	0.000	0.006	0.001	0.000	0.000	0.000	0.000
Durables	-0.007	-0.009	0.000	0.003	-0.012	-0.001	0.004*	0.002	0.002	0.005*
Non-Durables	0.005	0.006	0.002	0.000	0.012**	0.003	-0.003	-0.001	0.000	-0.002

Note that a superscript **/* indicates that the impulse responses are significant at the 5%/10% level respectively. Further note that the confidence intervals are obtained by employing the bootstrap method using 1000 replications for each step.

First, let us turn to the aggregate data for manufacturing, and to a basic disaggregation into durable and non-durable product industries. Tables 5 and 6 show the cumulated impulse responses and the forecast error decompositions for these three cases using the Solow and Basu measures. There are two important points to note about the impulse responses. The first is that, although the Solow case confirms the results in favour of the OC hypothesis found in earlier work, the total effect of employment shocks on

---

[14] Note, however, that these results, like those in Tables 5-8 are robust to changes in σ from 0 to 1. The VAR results pertaining to alternative values of σ are available on request from the authors.

the level of TFP[15] is insignificant. The second important point to note is that the results using the Basu measure of TFP are, generally, weaker for aggregate manufacturing. For the durable sector a significant LBD effect can be detected, and for non-durables we have a negatively-signed long-run effect, but this is not statistically significant at the 10% level. These disaggregated results cast some doubts on the validity of earlier evidence on the prevalence of OC effects (see Saint-Paul, 1997), and suggest much greater variability across different sectors. Note also that our disaggregated models are also given greater statistical weight since the forecast error decompositions indicate that our aggregate models generally explain a smaller proportion of the total forecast variance than the industry results examined below.

A natural reaction to these results is to examine a finer disaggregation of the data. There is no reason to expect that OC or LBD-type effects or the impact of technology shocks on employment are likely to be the same in different industries, given their different susceptibility to the economic cycle, differences in technology, and the differing degree of labour reallocation and re-organisation within each sector. As noted in the introduction aggregation bias is likely to be an important issue when testing for LBD and OC effects.

Table 6. Aggregate Series - Forecast Error Decomposition

	Solow							
	Technology $\rightarrow$ N Horizon				N $\rightarrow$ Technology Horizon			
	1	2	3	∞	1	2	3	∞
Aggregate	0.663	0.689	0.655	0.658	0.663	0.637	0.703	0.699
Durables	0.683	0.741	0.736	0.738	0.683	0.679	0.776	0.789
Non-Durables	0.541	0.561	0.551	0.551	0.541	0.562	0.597	0.598
	Basu (σ=0.5)							
	Technology $\rightarrow$ N Horizon				N $\rightarrow$ Technology Horizon			
	1	2	3	∞	1	2	3	∞
Aggregate	0.013	0.014	0.014	0.014	0.013	0.014	0.015	0.015
Durables	0.023	0.052	0.048	0.052	0.023	0.255	0.283	0.344
Non-Durables	0.055	0.120	0.124	0.124	0.055	0.118	0.130	0.130

The impulse responses using the 20 two-digit SIC industries are tabulated in Table 7, and the forecast error decompositions in Table 8. The first key point to note by comparing the results using the Solow and Basu definitions of TFP is that adjusting the TFP data for factor utilisation over the cycle

---

[15] To be more precise, the cumulated growth rate of TFP.

tends to change the impulse response analysis markedly. Looking first at the impact of employment shocks on long-run TFP, we see that using Solow TFP there is an initial positive impact, which is probably due to increasing factor utilisation.[16] Then OC-type effects seem to set in, so that the long-run multipliers are negative. This seems to confirm the results in the earlier literature, except that for all but one industry the 95% confidence intervals for the impulse responses include zero. The Basu TFP measure takes account of factor utilisation effects, and in this case the contemporaneous impact on TFP of employment shocks is no longer positive for all industries.

Interestingly, a variety of different significant long-run effects can be found. There seems to be clear evidence of LBD effects in the case of three industries (SIC 23, 25, and 37), and OC effects in the case of three industries (SIC 24, 30 and 38). For some industries there seem to be some temporary impacts on changes in TFP, but no significant long-run effect on the level of TFP. This result suggests that the OC effects detected in earlier work might have been the by-product of using pro-cyclical TFP data.

The second point to note, looking at the reaction of employment to technology shocks using the Solow TFP measures, is that we see a significant positive short- and long-run response. The short-run response is typical of the results predicted by RBC-type models. However, results based on the using the Basu measures again produce a variety of different results, with a prevalence of short-run negative employment effects following technology shocks. These short-run negative effects cannot be explained through standard RBC labour demand shifts. Instead the explanation must lie in technology shocks causing either greater factor utilisation and a fall in employment in the presence of sticky prices (see Gali, 1999), or technology shocks inducing labour-substitution effects.

---

[16] Note that in earlier papers (Gali and Hammour, 1991; Saint-Paul, 1993; and Malley and Muscatelli, 1999), the impact effect of employment shocks is set at zero or reduced through the use of the Choleski identification scheme or an alternative scheme putting a low weight on impact effects.

Table 7. Industry VARs - Impulse Responses (continued on next page)

	Solow									
	Technology → N					N → Technology				
	Horizon					Horizon				
Ind.	0	1	2	3	∞	0	1	2	3	∞
20	0.006**	-0.001	0.005**	-0.001	0.009**	0.008**	-0.007**	-0.001	0.000	0.001
21	0.008	0.006	0.002	0.001	0.018	0.010	-0.003	-0.002	-0.001	0.004
22	0.016**	0.021**	-0.001	-0.004	0.043**	0.012**	-0.016**	-0.018**	0.000	-0.026
23	0.019**	0.013	0.006	-0.004	0.044	0.014**	-0.004	-0.008*	-0.007	-0.022
24	0.018*	0.013	0.006	-0.006	0.029**	0.013*	-0.016**	-0.022**	-0.001	-0.015
25	0.032**	0.025**	-0.019**	-0.013	0.036**	0.023**	-0.002	-0.015**	-0.003	0.008
26	0.018*	0.002	-0.006	0.001	0.016	0.020*	-0.018**	-0.011	0.004	-0.006
27	0.015**	0.004	0.000	0.000	0.019*	0.007**	-0.008	-0.002	0.000	-0.003
28	0.009**	0.010**	0.004	0.000	0.021**	0.021**	-0.015**	-0.013**	-0.005	-0.010
29	0.019**	-0.010**	0.006	0.010*	0.025**	0.026**	-0.007	-0.005	-0.017	-0.021
30	0.036**	0.016	-0.023**	-0.009	0.028**	0.025**	-0.007	-0.024**	-0.016*	-0.013
31	0.017*	0.017**	0.004	0.001	0.039**	0.014*	-0.005	-0.002	0.000	0.007
32	0.028**	0.009*	-0.004	-0.006	0.027**	0.021**	-0.012**	-0.015**	-0.006	-0.007
33	0.052**	0.025*	-0.010	0.001	0.067**	0.057**	-0.015	-0.021	-0.006	0.006
34	0.036**	0.023**	-0.004	-0.011*	0.047**	0.025**	0.000	-0.014**	-0.007	0.010
35	0.039**	0.018**	0.003	-0.004	0.049**	0.024**	-0.013**	-0.021**	-0.015*	-0.027**
36	0.038**	0.026**	0.002	-0.006	0.057**	0.021**	-0.005	-0.008*	-0.003	0.007
37	0.038**	0.017*	-0.003	-0.005	0.047**	0.042**	-0.023**	-0.017*	0.000	0.006
38	0.014**	0.023**	0.008	-0.007	0.034**	0.008**	-0.001	-0.009**	-0.004	-0.001
39	0.026**	0.011	0.003	-0.006	0.031**	0.020**	0.005	-0.022**	-0.004	0.006

Note that a superscript **/* indicates that the impulse responses are significant at the 5%/10% level respectively.

Thus, the initial intuition in Basu (1996) that adjustments for factor utilisation might weaken the role for technology shocks, seems to be borne out by our VAR models. Our results are also consistent with the findings in other papers, such as Blanchard *et al.* (1995) in that they support a sticky-price non-RBC interpretation of business cycles. Our findings of a significant long-run negative impact of technology shocks in a small number of industries seems indicative of "creative destruction" type-effects.

Table 7. Industry VARs - Impulse Responses (continued)

Basu (σ=0.5)

| | Technology → N | | | | | N → Technology | | | | |
| | Horizon | | | | | Horizon | | | | |
Ind.	0	1	2	3	∞	0	1	2	3	∞
20	0.001	-0.004	-0.001	0.000	-0.004	0.002	0.001	0.000	0.000	0.002
21	0.002	0.002	0.000	-0.013*	-0.004	0.002	0.009	-0.003	0.005	0.011
22	-0.007	0.009	-0.001	0.001	0.001	-0.003	0.001	0.000	0.000	-0.003
23	0.017*	-0.006	-0.003	-0.001	0.008	0.008*	0.002	0.000	0.000	0.010*
24	-0.020**	0.008	0.001	0.000	-0.010	-0.006	-0.004	0.000	0.000	-0.009*
25	0.017*	0.000	0.000	0.000	0.017	0.005*	0.002	0.000	0.000	0.007**
26	-0.010**	0.009**	0.003	-0.005	-0.003	-0.004**	0.002	-0.001	-0.001	-0.004
27	-0.002	-0.004	-0.001	0.000	-0.006	-0.001	0.001	0.000	0.000	0.000
28	-0.006**	0.002	0.003	0.001	0.001	-0.009**	-0.011	0.009**	0.005	-0.003
29	-0.001	-0.004	0.000	0.000	-0.006	-0.001	-0.016*	0.000	-0.001	-0.019
30	-0.023*	-0.009	0.012	0.008	-0.019**	-0.010*	-0.008**	0.011*	0.005	-0.007**
31	-0.029*	-0.008	-0.009	-0.004	-0.057**	-0.021*	-0.001	0.012**	0.005	-0.010
32	0.006	0.003	0.001	0.000	0.011	0.002	-0.001	0.000	0.000	0.000
33	0.007	0.008	0.000	0.000	0.015	0.002	-0.002	0.000	0.000	0.000
34	-0.015**	-0.012	-0.003	0.003	-0.025*	-0.005**	-0.003	0.005**	0.005**	-0.001
35	-0.012	-0.007	-0.002	-0.001	-0.022	-0.004	0.001	0.000	0.000	-0.002
36	-0.034*	-0.024*	0.014	0.008	-0.045*	-0.015*	0.003	0.012*	0.005	0.002
37	0.019	-0.001	0.002	-0.002	0.018	0.004**	0.003	0.005**	-0.002	0.011*
38	-0.027*	-0.007	-0.003	-0.001	-0.040*	-0.022*	0.006	-0.001	0.000	-0.016**
39	-0.001	-0.003	0.000	0.000	-0.005	-0.001	-0.002	0.000	0.000	-0.003

Finally, the forecast error decompositions in Table 8 are much larger than those calculated for the aggregate series, suggesting that disaggregation leads us to explain a greater percentage of the forecast error. Once again, this suggests that our VARs fit the disaggregated data better. Overall, our industry-level results seem to suggest that the results in the existing literature may be seriously distorted by a failure to measure true productivity shocks in the presence of factor utilisation effects. Also, it appears clear that LBD and OC effects may prevail in different measures in different industries and that previous studies on aggregate data may suffer from severe aggregation bias.

Table 8. Industry VARs - Forecast Error Decomposition (continued on next page)

	Technology → N				N → Technology			
	Horizon				Horizon			
Industry	1	2	3	∞	1	2	3	∞
20	0.241	0.233	0.331	0.331	0.241	0.323	0.324	0.322
21	0.071	0.102	0.107	0.108	0.071	0.068	0.070	0.070
22	0.220	0.448	0.421	0.403	0.220	0.408	0.541	0.477
23	0.358	0.423	0.407	0.383	0.358	0.376	0.424	0.462
24	0.113	0.164	0.131	0.136	0.113	0.227	0.380	0.393
25	0.691	0.658	0.701	0.711	0.691	0.514	0.556	0.551
26	0.409	0.411	0.435	0.435	0.409	0.546	0.582	0.584
27	0.115	0.121	0.121	0.121	0.115	0.218	0.225	0.225
28	0.221	0.346	0.364	0.363	0.221	0.294	0.344	0.347
29	0.481	0.517	0.528	0.589	0.481	0.460	0.443	0.544
30	0.628	0.634	0.701	0.659	0.628	0.640	0.748	0.734
31	0.142	0.238	0.243	0.243	0.142	0.157	0.158	0.158
32	0.659	0.648	0.585	0.583	0.659	0.538	0.603	0.609
33	0.754	0.781	0.786	0.786	0.754	0.735	0.756	0.759
34	0.713	0.778	0.774	0.783	0.713	0.671	0.722	0.724
35	0.611	0.649	0.643	0.630	0.611	0.573	0.666	0.705
36	0.537	0.632	0.612	0.614	0.537	0.490	0.524	0.522
37	0.520	0.563	0.550	0.552	0.520	0.548	0.575	0.573
38	0.155	0.388	0.407	0.428	0.155	0.154	0.255	0.264
39	0.284	0.310	0.291	0.301	0.284	0.289	0.463	0.465

Another interesting aspect of our results is the implication for the response of employment to technology shocks. Early work on TFP adjustment (see Basu, 1996) seemed to suggest that factor utilisation could account for a large amount of the covariation between technology and the business cycle. Our VAR analysis shows that in fact, for a number of industries, technology shocks produce reasonably persistent responses in employment.

This is consistent with technology shocks accounting for aggregate fluctuations in a number of industries. Moreover, the negative impact of technology shocks on employment in a number of industries is suggestive that variants of RBC models embodying job destruction effects in the propagation mechanism (see Den Haan *et al.*, 1997) may be well-founded empirically.

Table 8. Industry VARs - Forecast Error Decomposition (continued)

	Basu (σ=0.5)							
	Technology → N				N → Technology			
	Horizon				Horizon			
Industry	1	2	3	∞	1	2	3	∞
20	0.011	0.099	0.102	0.102	0.011	0.013	0.013	0.013
21	0.005	0.010	0.010	0.171	0.005	0.048	0.050	0.060
22	0.031	0.078	0.079	0.079	0.031	0.030	0.030	0.030
23	0.237	0.236	0.239	0.240	0.237	0.254	0.254	0.254
24	0.096	0.107	0.108	0.108	0.096	0.130	0.130	0.130
25	0.096	0.096	0.096	0.096	0.096	0.105	0.105	0.105
26	0.135	0.211	0.217	0.247	0.135	0.151	0.127	0.132
27	0.002	0.010	0.010	0.010	0.002	0.004	0.004	0.004
28	0.094	0.071	0.082	0.085	0.094	0.188	0.246	0.262
29	0.001	0.017	0.017	0.017	0.001	0.106	0.106	0.106
30	0.242	0.253	0.264	0.267	0.242	0.332	0.441	0.483
31	0.386	0.349	0.370	0.368	0.386	0.381	0.431	0.451
32	0.027	0.032	0.033	0.033	0.027	0.032	0.034	0.034
33	0.013	0.027	0.027	0.027	0.013	0.026	0.026	0.026
34	0.117	0.159	0.156	0.155	0.117	0.142	0.225	0.287
35	0.049	0.062	0.062	0.063	0.049	0.055	0.055	0.055
36	0.441	0.508	0.524	0.538	0.441	0.422	0.540	0.558
37	0.115	0.107	0.106	0.106	0.115	0.148	0.254	0.262
38	0.417	0.403	0.403	0.402	0.417	0.426	0.426	0.426
39	0.000	0.005	0.005	0.005	0.000	0.004	0.005	0.005

5.   CONCLUSIONS

In this paper we have extended the recent empirical literature on the interaction between business cycles and growth by tackling some of the key difficulties in earlier work (see Saint-Paul, 1997). The key difficulties include obtaining an accurate measure of TFP over the cycle and the problem of identifying business cycle and technology shocks in the absence of any obvious *a priori* theoretical identifying restrictions which can be imposed on the basic VAR model. Our results shed light on the effect of technology shocks on employment, an issue which is central to both RBC-type models and labour search models.

Our results tend to show that the interaction between employment and TFP growth is much more diverse in different industries than might appear at first sight. The common practice of including Solow residuals in VARs picks up an artificial correlation over the cycle between TFP and employment which arises due to factor utilisation effects. Such correlations have the effect of creating an artificial homogeneity across sectoral VARs. The use of Basu TFP measures shows instead that business cycles (employment shocks) have very different effects across different industries. This runs counter to all existing empirical evidence in this area (see Saint-Paul, 1997). Also, the apparently uniform positive response of employment to technology shocks found using Solow residuals disappears. This new evidence points against the usual real business cycle mechanism, and favours alternative interpretations for the propagation of technology shocks, which include a role for sticky prices.

One possible future extension of our work is to examine the interaction between TFP, output fluctuations and labour re-allocation at the industry level. As shown in Davis *et al.* (1997), most labour re-allocation between firms takes place within industrial sectors rather than between sectors. Using data on job creation and job destruction at the 2-digit SIC level it might be possible to examine the role played by labour reallocation in production-enhancing activities. One might expect to find that labour reallocation plays a role for those industries where OC effects are found.

Finally, another potential extension would be to carry out a comparison similar industries in different OECD economies. If the presence of LBD or OC effects is, as we suspect, a function of the industry technology, one might expect similar patterns to emerge across different countries.

A   DATA

The following data are provided by Bartelssman and Gray (1994), NBER Manufacturing Productivity Database (see http://www.nber.org/productivity.html):

N total employment (1,000s)
w nominal wage per employee (mill., $)
Hp hours of production workers (mill. of hours)
M real cost of materials inputs (mill., $1987)
K real capital stock (start of year); (mill., $1987)
Y real shipments (mill., $1987)
P price deflator for value of shipments (1987=1)
P_m price deflator for value of materials (1987=1)

GDP (bill chained $1992) is taken from the May 1997 Survey of Current Business (SCB), BEA, U.S. Department of Commerce. Defence Spending (bill chained $1992) from 1959 is taken from the May 1997 SCB. Based on quantity indexes 1992=100, provided by the Department of Commerce, movements in the quantity index series were spliced to the billions of chained 1992 dollar series to obtain 1958. The World Price of Oil from 1965 onwards is taken from 1995 International Financial Statistics Yearbook Average Crude Price, spot (US$/barrel). It is calculated using UK Brent (light), Dubai (medium) and Alaska North Slope (heavy), equally weighted. Prior to 1965 it is taken from 1983 International Financial Statistics Yearbook. Average price (US$/barrel) is calculated as a weighted average of the three oil prices listed: Saudi Arabia; Libya from 1961; and Venezuelan. Following Jorgenson and Sullivan (1981), Hall (1990), Cabellero and Lyons (1992), Nadiri and Mamuneas (1994), and Basu (1996) the rental price of capital, *r* is calculated as follows[17]:

$$r_i = \left(R + \delta_{K,i}\right)\left[\frac{1 - i_K - u_c z}{1 - u_c}\right]PK_i,$$

where *i* refers to industries the two-digit industries {20, 21...39},

$$z = \frac{\rho\left(1 - \omega \cdot i_K\right)}{R + \rho},$$

PK_i is the individual industry physical capital deflator and is taken from the BEA Fixed Reproducible Tangible Assets Database (FRTA).

R is the discount rate (10-year Treasury Notes) and is taken from the 1997 Economic Report of the President (ERP).

$\delta_{K,i}$ is the individual industry physical capital depreciation rate and is taken from BEA's FRTA.

i_K is the investment tax credit and is taken from Jorgenson and Sullivan (1981) until 1980. Following Naadiri and Mamuneas (1994); for 1981 8% is used and for 1982 to 1986 7.5% is used. Post 1986 the rate is set to 0 due to tax code changes in the U.S..

u_C is the corporate income tax rate and is taken from Jorgenson and Sullivan (1981) and Auerbach (1983) up to 1983. Following Nadiri and Mamuneas (1994) the rate is set to 0.46 after 1983.

z is the present value of capital consumption allowances.

ρ is the capital consumption allowance rate obtained by dividing adjusted capital consumption allowances by the capital stock and is obtained from the 1997 ERP.

ω is a dummy variable which takes the value of 0.5 in 1962-63 and 0 elsewhere. Under the Long Amendment (1962-63) firms were required to reduce the depreciable base of their assets by half the amount of the investment tax credit (see Nadiri and Mamuneas, 1994).

REFERENCES

Aghion, P. and P. Howitt (1991), "Unemployment: a symptom of stagnation or a side-effect of growth? ", *European Economic Review* 35, pp. 535-541.

Aghion, P. and P. Howitt (1994), "Growth and unemployment", *Review of Economic Studies*, vol. 61, pp. 477-494.

Argote, L.and D. Epple (1990), "Learning curves in manufacturing", *Science* 247, pp. 920-924.

Arrow, K.J. (1962), "The economic implications of learning by doing", *Review of Economic Studies* 28, pp. 155-173.

---

[17]   Note however that our measure additionally incorporates individual industry for data for several key components of the user cost.

Auerbach, R. (1983), "Corporate Taxation in the United States," *Brookings Papers on Economic Activity* 2, pp. 451-513.

Balls, E. (1998), "Open Macroeconomics in an Open Economy," *Scottish Journal of Political Economy*.

Basu, S. (1996), "Procyclical Productivity: Increasing Returns or Cyclical Utilization?," *Quarterly Journal of Economics* 111, pp. 719-751.

Bean, C.R. (1990), "Endogenous Growth and Procyclical Behaviour of Productivity," *European Economic Review* 34, pp. 355-363.

Bernstein, J. and M. Nadiri (1991), "Product Demand, Cost of Production, Spillovers, and the Social Rate of Return to R&D," *NBER Working Paper n. 3625*.

Blanchard, O., R. Solow and B.A. Wilson (1995), "Productivity and Unemployment," mimeo, MIT.

Blanchard, O.J. and D. Quah (1989), "The Dynamic Effects of Aggregate Demand and Supply Disturbances," *American Economic Review* 79, pp. 655-673.

Bruno, M. (1984), "Profits, and the Productivity Slowdown," *Quarterly Journal of Economics* 99, pp. 1-30.

Burnside, C., M. Eichenbaum, and S. Rebelo (1995), "Capital Utilization and Returns to Scale," *NBER Macroeconomics Annual*, Cambridge MA.

Caballero, R. and M.L. Hammour (1994), "The Cleansing Effect of Recession," *American Economic Review* 84, pp. 1075-1084.

Caballero, R. and R. Lyons (1992), "External Effects in U.S. Procyclical Productivity," *Journal of Monetary Economics* 29, pp. 209-226.

Davis, S. and J. Haltiwanger (1990), "Gross Job Creation and Destruction: Micro-economic Evidence and Macroeconomic Implications," *NBER Macroeconomics Annual*, Cambridge MA.

Davis, S. and J. Haltiwanger (1992), "Gross Job Creation, Gross Job Destruction and Employment Reallocation", *Quarterly Journal of Economics* 107, pp. 819-863.

Davis, S., J. Haltiwanger, and S. Schuh (1997), *Job Creation and Destruction*, Cambridge MA: MIT Press.

Den Haan, W.J., G. Ramey and J. Watson (1997), "Job Destruction and the Propagation of Shocks," *NBER Working Paper no. 6275*, Cambridge Ma.

Diewert, W.E. (1976), "Exact and Superlative Index Numbers," *Journal of Econometrics* 4, pp. 115-146.

Forni, M. and L. Reichlin (1995), "Let's Get Real: a Dynamic Factor Analytical Approach to Disaggregated Business Cycles," *CEPR Discussion Paper no. 1244*, London

Gali, J. (1999), "Technology, Employment, and the Business Cycle: Do Technology Shocks Explain Aggregate Fluctuations?," *American Economic Review* 89, pp. 249-271.

Gali, J. and M.L. Hammour (1991), "Long-run Effects of Business Cycles," mimeo, Columbia University, New York.

Hall, R. (1988), "The Relation between Price and Marginal Cost in U.S. Industry," *Journal of Political Economy* 96, pp. 921-947.

Hall, R. (1990), "Invariance Properties of Solow's Productivity Residual," in P. Diamond (ed.), *Productivity and Unemployment*, Cambridge MA: MIT Press.

Hall, R. (1991), "Recessions as Re-organizations," *NBER Macroeconomics Annual*, Cambridge MA.

Jorgenson, D. and M. Sullivan (1981), "Inflation and Corporate Capital Recovery," in C. Hulten (ed.), *Depreciation, Inflation and the Taxation of Income from Capital*, Washington D.C.: Urban Institute,

King, R.G. and M. Watson (1995), "Money, Prices, Interest Rates and the Business Cycle," *Review of Economics and Statistics* 58, pp. 35-53.

Koop, G., M.H. Pesaran, and S.M. Potter (1996), "Impulse Response Analysis in Nonlinear Multivariate Models," *Journal of Econometrics* 74, pp. 119-147.

Lütkepohl, H. (1991), *Introduction to Multiple Time Series Analysis*, Heidelberg: Springer.

Malley, J. and V.A. Muscatelli (1997), "The Impact of Productivity Shocks on Employment in the U.S.: Evidence from Disaggregated Data," *Economics Letters* 57, pp. 97-105.

Malley, J. and V.A. Muscatelli (1999), "Business Cycles and Productivity Growth: are Temporary Downturns Productive or Wasteful?," *Research in Economics*, forthcoming.

Martin, P. and C.A. Rogers (1995), "Stabilisation Policy, Learning by Doing and Economic Growth," *CEPR Discussion Paper n. 1130*.

Mortensen, D.T. and Pissarides, C.A. (1994), "Technological Progress, Job Creation and Job Destruction", *CEPR Discussion Paper no. 264*, London

Muscatelli, V.A. and P. Tirelli (1998), "Monetary Policy Design and Credibility in a Model of Growth," *Oxford Economic Papers* 50, pp. 644-662.

Nadiri, M. and T. Mamuneas (1994), "The Effects of Public Infrastructure and R&D Capital on the cost Structure and Performance of U.S. Manufacturing Industries," *Review of Economics and Statistics* 76, pp. 22-37.

Pesaran, M. H., and Y. Shin (1998), "Generalised Impulse Response Analysis in Linear Multivariate Models," *Economics Letters* 58, pp. 17-29.

Ramey, V. (1989), "Inventories as Factors of Production and Economic Fluctuations," *American Economic Review* 89, pp. 338-354.

Rotemberg, J. and M. Woodford (1992), "The Effects of Energy Price Increases on Economic Activity", *MIT manuscript*.

Saint-Paul, G. (1993), "Productivity Growth and the Structure of the Business Cycle," *European Economic Review* 37, pp. 861-890.

Saint-Paul, G. (1997), "Business Cycles and Long-run Growth," *CEPR Discussion Paper no. 1642*, London.

Sims, C. (1980), "Macroeonomics and Reality," *Econometrica* 48, pp. 1-49.

Solow, R (1957), "Technical Change and the Aggregate Production Function," *Review of Economics and Statistics* 39, pp. 312-20.

Solow, R. (1997), *Learning from 'Learning by Doing'*, Stanford CA.: Stanford University Press.

Stadler, G.W. (1990), "Business Cycle Models with Endogenous Technology," *American Economic Review* 80, pp. 763-78.

Stiglitz, J. (1993), "Endogenous Growth and Cycles," *NBER Working Paper no 4286*, Cambridge MA.

Chapter 6

Productivity, Income and Technological Change in the Netherlands: Causes and Explanations of Divergent Trends

Bart van Ark and Jakob de Haan
Department of Economics, University of Groningen

Key words: Economic growth, Productivity, Technological change

Abstract: This paper reviews the sources of the acceleration of economic growth in the Netherlands since the early 1980s. In particular the paper focuses on the downside of this growth acceleration, which is the slowdown in productivity growth. We argue that transitory shifts towards a greater share of lower productive employees and lower productive (service) sectors do not provide a full explanation. Hence we investigate to what extent the productivity growth slowdown can be explained from a slow diffusion of technology. Again we find only limited evidence for this hypothesis. We argue that human capital creation and structural reforms in labour and product markets are key elements to exploit the potential for a productivity acceleration in particular in services.

159

1.   INTRODUCTION

Since the late 1980s, the Dutch economy has outperformed neighbouring countries in several respects (see Table 1). It has achieved higher employment and GDP growth in combination with low inflation, and it had the lowest long-term interest rates in the European Union (EU). Dutch per capita GDP growth, which was well below the Northwest European average during the first half of the 1980s, is now almost back to that average. The economy of the Netherlands also suffered less than other European economies from the recessions in 1992-93 and 1995. This performance represents a marked turnaround from the early 1980s, when the country faced a deep recession, the profitability of firms was close to zero, unemployment had risen sharply, and the fiscal deficit amounted to 9½ percent of GDP. Indeed the turnaround has been so remarkable that it has been referred to as a "Dutch miracle" (or the "Delta model") by parts of the media.

In earlier papers we have argued that in fact there has been no miracle (van Ark and de Haan, 1999, 2000).[1] In our view, the recent growth performance of the Netherlands has primarily been the result of a correction of the below-average growth during earlier decades, *i.e.* the 1970s and early 1980s. In van Ark and de Haan (1999) we showed that two fundamental changes in the Dutch economy, namely a policy of almost continuous wage cost moderation since 1982 (the time of the "Wassenaar agreement" between employers, unions and the government in 1982) and a substantial increase in the labour supply (especially caused by a higher participation rate), accounted for the recovery. In van Ark and de Haan (2000) we extended the argument further by formally analysing the effect of wage moderation on the change in employment. In the latter paper we also discussed in more detail labour market reforms and the creation of a more effective wage negotiation structure since the "Wassenaar agreement."

In our earlier papers we also observed another striking feature of the recovery since the 1980s, namely that the acceleration in per capita income went together with a slowdown in labour productivity growth (see Table 1). Whereas during the late 1970s and 1980s per capita income growth had slowed down to well below the average Northwest European growh rate, it accelerated substantially during the late 1980s and early 1990s. In contrast, productivity growth has been faster than per capita income growth between 1973 and the mid 1980s, but the opposite appeared to be the case since then.

---

[1]   For a more long-term view, covering the period since 1913, see van Ark and de Jong (1996).

In this paper we go more deeply into the divergent trends in productivity and per capita income. There are a number of hypotheses that explain these opposite trends in income and productivity performance in the Netherlands.

Table 1. Growth of GDP and GDP per Capita, 1960-1997

	GDP (constant prices)				GDP per Capita			
	Nether-lands	North-west Europe (a)	Euro-pean Union (b)	OECD (c)	Nether-lands	North-west Europe (a)	Euro-pean Union (b)	OECD (c)
1960-1997	3.2	2.9	3.3	3.4	2.4	2.2	2.8	2.8
1960-1973	4.9	4.5	5.3	5.3	3.6	3.5	4.6	4.4
1973-1979	2.6	2.3	2.7	2.8	1.9	1.7	2.1	2.1
1979-1987	1.5	2.0	1.9	2.2	0.9	1.5	1.6	1.8
1987-1997	2.9	2.1	2.4	2.4	2.2	1.3	2.0	1.9

	Total Number of Hours Worked				GDP per Hour Worked			
	Nether-lands	North-west Europe (a)	Euro-pean Union (b)	OECD (c)	Nether-lands	North-west Europe (a)	Euro-pean Union (b)	OECD (c)
1960-1997	0.1	-0.2	-0.2	0.1	3.2	3.2	3.6	3.5
1960-1973	0.3	-0.4	-0.5	0.0	4.5	4.9	5.8	5.3
1973-1979	-0.5	-0.5	-0.3	0.0	3.2	2.8	3.0	2.8
1979-1987	-1.3	-0.2	-0.4	0.1	2.8	2.3	2.3	2.1
1987-1997	1.1	0.2	0.3	0.4	1.7	1.9	2.1	2.0

(a) unweighted average for Austria, Belgium, Denmark, West Germany, Finland, France, Netherlands, Norway, Sweden, Switzerland and United Kingdom; (b) excluding Luxembourg; (c) unweighted average for 20 OECD member states (pre-1995 membership, excluding Luxembourg, Iceland, New Zealand and Turkey)
Source: 1960-1990 (except Netherlands) from Maddison (1995), linked to 1990-1997 from OECD *National Accounts 1960-1996* (Paris, 1998) and OECD *Economic Outlook* (Paris, June 1998). Netherlands from CBS, *Nationale Rekeningen 1997* (and previous issues) and *Arbeidsrekeningen 1997* (and previous issues). Trend in working hours 1960-1987 are for contractual hours from CBS (unpublished).

One explanation concerns the changing contribution of labour input to growth. Whereas labour force participation fell during the 1970s and 1980s, thus reducing the capacity of the economy to expand, it improved since the late 1980s. The decline in the labour force participation in the 1970s and 1980s went hand in hand with high labour productivity growth, as less productive workers lost their jobs. Many of those workers shifted to early retirement or disability schemes. Under the new labour market regime since the 1980s new cohorts of workers entered the labour market, including long-term unemployed, low skilled workers and women

A second hypothesis, which may be related to the first one, is that the share of lower-productivity service industries in the economy has increased due to deindustrialisation. This negative shift-effect occurs when service sectors have not only experienced slower real output growth, but also have lower productivity levels relative to commodity sectors, in particular industry.

In our earlier papers we found only limited evidence for these two transitional sources of the productivity slowdown, *i.e* shifts to lower productive people and lower productive sectors. This paper therefore further develops the third explanation, namely that the productivity growth within individual sectors and industries slowed down. This is a more serious scenario than the explanations mentioned above, because a "within-industry" productivity slowdown will affect per capita income growth in the long run, even though it may be temporarily offset by an increased activity/non-activity ratio.

The structure of the paper is as follows. In Section 2 of the paper we will review how much of the recent improvement in GDP per capita in the Netherlands can indeed be traced to increased labour participation. We then look in some greater detail at the productivity performance at the macro level, including total factor productivity growth, the role of physical and human capital in the growth process, and the performance of R&D as a typical technology variable. In Section 3 we shift the attention to the industry level. We review the evidence on the impact of shift effects on productivity growth, and then continue by focusing on the slowdown in total factor productivity growth by industry. This evidence tells us whether the slowdown has been across the board, or that it was concentrated in particular sectors of the economy, for example in services.

Finally, in Section 5 we will investigate the factors that are most closely associated with the technology performance of the Dutch economy, including the change in human capital intensity, R&D intensity and the intensity of investment in new technologies. We will argue that on the basis of these indicators no evidence can be found of lack of investment in intangible capital. Nevertheless we argue that to turn around the productivity slowdown, human capital creation needs to be brought in better balance with other intagible investment, so that a shift towards new and higher productivity activities can be more easily realised. We also argue that structural reforms in labour and product markets are needed to support high productivity activities in particular in the services sector.

2. LABOUR INPUT AND ITS IMPACT ON THE RISE IN INCOME AND SLOWDOWN IN PRODUCTIVITY GROWTH

The relatively rapid acceleration of growth in the Dutch economy is confirmed by a comparison of growth rates of GDP and GDP per capita vis-à-vis to the averages for Northwest Europe, the European Union and the OECD (Table 1). Compared to Northwest Europe, growth of real GDP and GDP per capita in the Netherlands has been 0.9 percentage points higher between 1987 and 1997. Table 2 presents corresponding figures in terms of relative levels. Whereas GDP per capita in 1997 was still around 4 percent below the Northwest European average it came up from a level of 11 percentage points below the Northwest European level in 1987. In 1987 Dutch GDP per capita was at the bottom of the league of the 11 Northwest European countries, whereas in 1997 it was in 8th place behind Norway, Switzerland, Denmark, Belgium, Austria, France and Germany, although the differences between the latter five countries and the Netherlands were within a range of 1.5 percentage points.[2] The estimates lead to the conclusion that between 1987 and 1997 the Netherlands has been in the process of making up for what it had lost in terms of relative income per capita compared to the rest of Northwest Europe between the late 1970s and 1980s.

The increase in labour input has been one of the main components of the acceleration in GDP growth. Table 3 decomposes the growth of the total number of hours worked since 1960 into the contribution of employment and

---

[2] The internationally comparative national accounts measures in Tables 1, 2, 4 and 5 are according to the System of National Accounts 1968 and purchasing power parities for the year 1993. In 1999 most OECD countries introduced revised GDP measures using the new System of National Accounts 1993 (or, for Europe, the European System of Accounts 1995) and purchasing power parities for 1996. We have not yet used these latest estimates in this paper, partly because the periods for backward extrapolation are not equal across countries, and partly because it is not clear why the most recent purchasing power parities show rather different results in particular relative to the USA than the earlier PPPs for 1990 and 1993. See the Groningen Growth and Development Centre Database (http://www.eco.rug.nl/ggdc/Dseries/dataseries.html) for the most recent updates. However, in the second half of this paper we use the revised Dutch national accounts figures since 1995. The perspective of a per capita income acceleration and productivity slowdown in the Dutch economy has not changed according to these new measures. The selection of the subperiods in Tables 1, 2, 4 and 5 is based on the identification of turning points in an international comparative perspective (see Maddison, 1995). For the Netherlands, the periodical distribution of GDP grwoth between peak-to-peak points in the cycle might have been as follows: 1960-1976: 4.5%; 1976-1989: 2.0%; 1989-1997: 2.9%. This reduces the growth differentials between subperiods somewhat, but does not fundamentally change the perspective of a change towards faster output growth since the 1980s (see Tables 7 and 8).

average hours worked. The number of persons employed has accelerated to 1.8 percent per year on average since 1987, which is equivalent to an increase by almost 1.2 million people. The growth in total working hours has been slower (1.1 percent per year on average), because of the decline in average annual hours per person.

Table 2. Relative Level of GDP per Capita, Northwest Europe=100

	Netherlands	Northwest Europe (a)	European Union (a)	OECD (a)
1960	96	100	79	87
1973	95	100	85	92
1979	95	100	86	93
1987	89	100	85	93
1997	96	100	89	95

(a) See Table 1 for definitions
Source: see Table 1. GDP in national currencies converted to US$ with EKS PPPs for 1993.

Table 3. Labour Input Indicators, Netherlands, 1960 to 1997

	Total hours worked	Employ-ment	Average hours worked		Employ-ment-Population (15-64) ratio (%)	Average hours worked
	(annual compound growth rates)					
1960-1997	0.1	1.3	-1.2	1960	61.9	2,051
				1973	56.2	1,751
1960-1973	0.3	1.6	-1.2	1979	53.3	1,611
1973-1979	-0.5	0.9	-1.4	1987	58.6	1,387
1979-1987	-1.3	0.6	-1.9	1992	64.5	1,344
1987-1997	1.1	1.8	-0.7	1997	67.5	1,297

Source: CBS, *Arbeidsrekeningen 1997* (and previous issues); Maddison (1995); OECD, *Employment Outlook*, various issues

Since 1987 the average number of hours per person employed declined at 0.7 percent a year in the Netherlands. In 1997 the average number of hours per person employed that were actually worked (*i.e.* hours which are paid *and* worked) was less than 1,300 hours per person in the Netherlands compared to approximately 1,540 hours for Northwest Europe as a whole. This low level for the Netherlands is mainly caused by the extraordinary rapid increase in part-time labour from 21.2 percent of total employment in 1983 to 36.5 percent in 1996. The participation rate, defined as persons employed as a percentage of the working age population from 15-64 years old, has gone up from less than 55 percent by the end of the 1970s to 67.5 percent in 1997.

The 1997 participation rate is only marginally lower than the average of 68.1 percent for Northwest Europe. Only Norway, Denmark, Sweden, Switzerland and the United Kingdom still have higher employment/population ratios.[3]

The rise in labour force participation is mainly caused by an increase in the female participation ratio (women employed as a percentage of the female population from 15-64 years) from 30.5 percent in 1975 to about 49.9 percent in 1996.[4] This increase accounts for about two thirds of the rise in employment since the early 1980s. All other effects on employment growth are much smaller. Only since the mid 1990s some decline in the number of people with unemployment benefits or social assistance can be observed. There has not been much decline in the relatively large number of persons on disability benefit except for a brief once-for-all effect following medical re-examinations of persons in this scheme during the early 1990s. Recent estimates suggest that there are still almost 900 thousand people receiving a disability benefit, which is still as much as one third of all people on inactivity benefits (including unemployment benefit, sickness benefit, pre-pension schemes and social assistance). Finally, an important remaining group of unemployed persons concerns those older than 55 years in the Netherlands. In 1997, labour force participation of this group was 32.7 percent compared to an unweighted average of 47.7 percent for the 11 Northwest European countries.[5]

Table 4. Contribution of Labour Input Growth to Real GDP and GDP per Capita Growth

	Netherlands		Northwest Europe	
	%-contribution of hours worked		%-contribution of hours worked	
	to change in real GDP	to change in real GDP per capita	to change in real GDP	to change in real GDP per capita
1960-1997	1	-18	-4	-24
1960-1973	5	-18	-7	-28
1973-1979	-19	-62	-21	-55
1979-1987	-78	-180	-16	-43
1987-1997	37	22	7	-49

(a) See Tables 1 and 3 for definitions and sources

Table 4 shows that between 1987 and 1997 the increase in total hours worked contributed as much as 37 percent to overall GDP growth and 22 percent to the rise in GDP per capita. For both variables this represented a major turnaround compared to the strongly negative contribution of slow

---

[3] See, OECD, *Employment Outlook* (June 1998, Table B).
[4] Sociaal Cultureel Planbureau, *Sociale en Culturele Verkenningen 1997*, Table 2.5, Rijswijk.
[5] Sociaal Economische Raad, *Advies Sociaal-economisch beleid 1998-2002*

labour input growth to per capita income growth during the late 1970s and early 1980s. It is also striking that, in comparison with Northwest Europe, the much larger negative contribution of labour input growth in the Netherlands between 1979 and 1987 turned into a much larger positive contribution between 1987 and 1997.

In van Ark and de Haan (2000) we have argued that the policy of moderation of wage costs, that started in the beginning of the 1980s has been an important factor explaining the increase in labour input. The obvious next step is to consider the impact of wage cost moderation and the consequent rise in labour input on productivity.

Figure 1a shows that between 1973 and 1985, labour productivity grew substantially faster than per capita income, whereas it has increased at a slower rate than per capita income since 1985, and in particularly during the 1990s (Figure 1b; see also Table 1). Table 5 shows labour productivity levels in an international comparative perspective. Between 1973 and 1987 the level of labour productivity in the Netherlands moved ahead of the average Northwest European level by 7 percentage points to 115 percent. However, after 1987 the gap narrowed again by 3 percentage points to 112 percent in 1997.

Table 5. Relative Level of GDP per Hour Worked, Northwest Europe=100

	Netherlands	Northwest Europe (a)	European Union (a)	OECD (a)
1960	112	100	81	94
1973	108	100	89	94
1979	110	100	90	94
1987	115	100	90	93
1997	112	100	92	93

(a) See Table 1 for definitions
Source: see Table 1. GDP in national currencies converted to US$ with EKS PPPs for 1993.

On the basis of this evidence, one might hypothesise that there is a negative relation between the acceleration in employment growth and the deceleration in productivity growth. One possibility is that lower labour costs have caused a substitution of labour for capital and a corresponding decline in capital intensity and total factor productivity growth. To test this we specify a translog production function, in which the growth of labour productivity is decomposed into the contribution of human capital, physical capital, the stock of research and development and total factor productivity. In a discrete time perspective this translog production function can be formulated as:

$$\ln \frac{P_{t+1}}{P_t} = w^l \ln \frac{h_{t+1}}{h_t} + w^k \ln \frac{k_{t+1}}{k_t} + w^r \ln \frac{r_{t+1}}{r_t} + \ln \frac{A_{t+1}}{A_t} \qquad (1)$$

with P as output per hour worked, h as human capital per person employed, k as the physical capital stock per hour worked, r as the stock of research and development per hour worked, A as total factor productivity, and w^l, w^k and w^r as the weights for labour, physical capital and R&D capital, respectively; t and $t+1$ represent time.

Table 6 shows that for the total economy, growth in value added per hour worked (P) slowed down from 4.5 percent between 1960 and 1973 to 1.7 percent between 1987 and 1997. The human capital stock estimates are based on a weighted average of years of primary, secondary and tertiary schooling of the working population, which shows a moderate increase over the period. The estimates of the physical capital stock are constructed with the perpetual inventory method, which implies an accumulation of gross investment using assumptions on the average life times of nonresidential structures and machinery and equipment.[6] In contrast to the human capital intensity, the growth rates of physical capital intensity indeed declined very rapidly over the past four decades. The stock of R&D is constructed on the basis of accumulating R&D investment by private business, research institutes and universities using a life time of R&D investment of 15 years.[7] The decline in R&D intensity is very substantial.

Table 6 shows three concepts of total factor productivity, ranging from considering only nonresidential capital as an input, to also treating human capital and the R&D stock as separate inputs. The contributions of human and physical capital to output growth are based on the factor share of labour and capital in the national product, with an imputation for the labour compensation of self-employed persons. The weight for the R&D stock is assumed to be 0.05 on top of the average factor shares for labour and capital.[8] According to all three TFP concepts a substantive slowdown in TFP growth occurred over the period as a whole.

The bottom panel of Table 6 shows the percentage contribution of each factor to labour productivity growth. Whereas the contribution of physical capital declined slightly, the contribution of human capital rapidly increased, and the contribution of R&D capital halved between the subperiods 1960-73 and 1987-97. Meanwhile the contribution of total factor productivity growth (excluding the contribution of the R&D stock) to labour productivity growth declined from 41 percent during the subperiod 1960-73 to 27 percent during 1987-97.

---

[6] Updates from Groote, Albers and de Jong (1996)

[7] Updated from Minne (1995)

[8] See sources of Table 6 and van Ark and de Jong (1996) for details of the calculations

Table 6. Labour Productivity, Capital Intensity and Various Concepts of Total Factor Productivity, Netherlands, 1960-1997

	1960-73	1973-79	1979-87	1987-97
Value Added per Hour Worked (a)	4.5	3.2	2.8	1.7
Nonresidential Capital Stock per Hour Worked (b)	5.5	4.4	3.6	1.7
Human Capital Stock per Hour Worked (c)	1.0	1.4	1.4	1.6
R&D Stock per Hour Worked (d)	10.8	5.4	3.9	1.5
Total Factor Productivity (e)				
- incl. Nonresidential (NRS) Capital	2.8	2.1	1.7	1.1
- incl. NRS Capital and Human Capital	2.4	1.5	1.1	0.5
- incl. NRS Capital, Human Capital and R&D	1.8	1.2	1.0	0.4
Percentage Contribution to Growth Rate of Value Added per Hour Worked of:				
1) nonresidential capital stock	38	35	39	34
2) human capital stock	9	19	21	36
3) total factor productivity, incl. R&D stock	53	46	41	31
Total contribution (1+2+3)	100	100	100	100
4) R&D stock	12	8	7	4
5) total factor productivity, exl. R&D stock	41	38	34	27

Source notes:

(a) Value added per hour worked, see Table 1.

(b) Capital stock based on perpetual inventory method from Groote, Albers and de Jong (1996) for 1938-50. Investment was accumulated on the basis of 39 and 14 years life assumptions for nonresidential structures and machinery and equipment, respectively

(c) Human capital stock was constructed on the basis of estimates from Maddison (1987, 1991 and 1996) and OECD (1998). These estimates represent educational attainments of the working-age population (15-64 years) distinguished according to primary, secondary and tertiary education, which were weighted at 1.0, 1.4 and 2.0, respectively in line with evidence on relative earning differentials

(d) R&D stock was constructed on the basis of R&D expenditure deflated at the GDP deflator, and accumulated on the basis of a 15-year life time for each R&D investment.

(e) TFP estimates were obtained by applying a translog index based on a Solow-type production function, using average factor shares for each current year and the previous year as weights. Labour compensation weights were augmented with labour compensation for selfemployed persons on the basis of imputed employee compensation. TFP 'incl. NRS capital, Human Capital and R&D' is derived by taking into account the change in the R&D stock using a weight of 0.05 on top of the average factor share. For details, see van Ark and de Jong (1996).

These results suggest that despite the decline in labour cost, the contribution of physical capital to labour productivity growth did not fall much and the human capital contribution even increased. If R&D and TFP are interpreted as technology variables, the cause of the slowdown in labour productivity would be due to a slowdown in innovation. This hypothesis will be further analysed in the next two Sections which looks at the productivity and technology performance by industry.

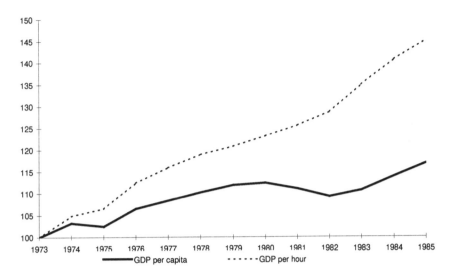

Figure 1a. GDP per Capita and GDP per Hour Worked, Netherlands 1973-85 (1973=100)

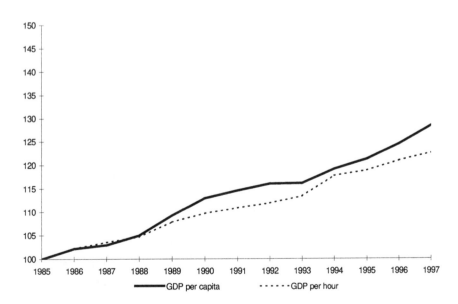

Figure 1b. GDP per Capita and GDP per Hour Worked, Netherlands 1985-97 (1985=100)

3. PRODUCTIVITY PERFORMANCE BY INDUSTRY

On the basis of the evidence from the previous section, one might hypothesise that at the macro level there is a negative relation between the acceleration in employment growth and the slowdown in productivity growth. This might have been caused by a net expansion of labour in industries which are characterised by an above-average share of low-skilled labour or which, for any other reason, have lower productivity growth rates than the average for the economy as a whole. Even with similar growth rates between industries, productivity growth for the economy as a whole might slow down when an increased concentration of economic activity occurs in activities with low productivity levels.

To measure the effect of labour input shifts on the overall productivity growth, one may express the productivity for the economy as a whole as the productivity level by sector weighted by the sectoral employment shares:

$$P_m = \frac{Y_m}{L_m} = \sum_{k=1}^{n}\left(\frac{Y_k}{L_k}\right)\left(\frac{L_k}{L_m}\right) = \sum_{k=1}^{n}(P_k S_k) \qquad (2)$$

with Y and L representing output and labour input by sector ($k=1..n$) and the total economy (m), P representing productivity (Y/L) and S representing the sectoral labour input share (L_k/L_m). In a time perspective this expression can be rewritten as:

$$\Delta P_m = \sum_{k=1}^{n}(\Delta P_k * S_k) + \sum_{k=1}^{n}(P_k * \Delta S_k) + \sum_{k=1}^{n}(\Delta P_k * \Delta S_k) \qquad (3)$$

The first term on the right-hand side of Equation (3) represents the intrasectoral productivity growth, which is the part of the overall productivity change due to productivity growth within each of the sectors. The second term is the net shift or static effect, which measures the effect of the change in sectoral employment shares on overall productivity growth. The net shift effect may also be called "static" because it measures the effects due to higher or lower productivity levels between sectors. This effect is positive when labour moves into sectors with higher levels of productivity. In contrast, the second term is negative when the new activities have lower productivity. The third term is the interaction or dynamic effect, which represents the joint effect of changes in employment shares and changes in sectoral productivity growth. This effect may be called "dynamic" because it measures the effect due to higher or lower productivity growth rates between sectors. The interaction effect can be either negative or positive, depending on whether sectors with a falling (rising) share show rising (falling) productivity (then it is negative) or sectors with a falling (rising) share show falling (rising) productivity (then it is positive).[9]

Table 7 shows the percentage contributions of the three effects to the overall labour productivity growth for ten sectors.[10] We chose the sub-periods according to the peak points in the business cycles in the Netherlands. When looking at the first subperiod (1976-1989) we find that 85 percent of productivity growth is explained by growth within each sector. However, the net shift effect accounted for 18 percent of productivity growth during this period. This positive static effect is in particular the result of higher productivity levels in financial and business services for which the share in employment rose. The dynamic effects are very small during this period.

During the second sub-period (1989-1998) the positive effect due to the increased importance of financial and business services was even stronger, but this was offset by an equally strong outflow of labour from other high productivity sectors, such as manufacturing and government services. Hence the net shift was small at the level of the economy as a whole.[11] Together with the small interaction effect, this implies that "within sector"-productivity growth was the dominant driving force behind the (slower) productivity growth at macro level during the second sub-period.

Hence the conclusion from Table 7 is that there is little support for the view that the slowdown in productivity growth is related to an increase in low-productivity activities. The positive sign of the net shift effect during the first sub-period helped productivity to accelerate instead of to decelerate. This perhaps somewhat counterintuitive result can be explained by the fact that, even though productivity *growth* in many service sectors was *slower* than in commodity sectors, the absolute *level* of value added per hour in

---

[9]   See van Ark (1996) and Timmer (2000) for details on the shift-share method.

[10]   Compared to our previous work (van Ark and de Haan, 1999, 2000) we refined our shift-share calculations following Timmer (2000). The refinement allows us to show the percentage contribution of each effect by sector. In our previous estimates we showed larger positive static and negative dynamic effects for both subperiods, but these were largely offsetting each other, in particular during the second period. The dominant role of intrasectoral effect is clear from both methods.

[11]   When excluding government from the calculations, the net shift from 1989 to 1998 turns negative to minus 7 percent, which in combination with an interaction effect of minus 4 percent, would suggest that both shift effects together take 0.1 percent per year of the productivity growth rate in the market sector. See also CPB (1998a) which shows a small negative net shift effect from sectoral reallocations. However, like in this study, the main explanation for the productivity slowdown according to the CPB study is the decline in "within-sector" growth rates.

finance and business services and other market services was *higher* than in agriculture or manufacturing.

Table 7. The Percentage Contribution of Intra-Sectoral Effect, Net-Shift Effect and Interactive Term by Sector to Growth Rates of Labour Productivity, Netherlands, 1976-89 and 1989-98

	Intra-Sectoral Effect	Net shift Effect	Interaction Effect	Total %-Contribution
		1976-1989		
Agriculture (a)	11.4	-2.1	-0.2	9.2
Mining	-11.4	8.4	-1.0	-4.1
Manufacturing	37.2	-17.0	-0.7	19.4
Public utilities	1.9	-0.9	-0.1	0.9
Construction	8.0	-8.0	-0.6	-0.6
Wholesale and retail trade	20.9	-0.5	-0.1	20.3
Transport and communication	10.9	0.9	0.0	11.8
Finance, insurance and business services (b)	-1.3	24.5	-0.1	23.1
Other market services	-2.7	9.5	-0.2	6.7
Government services	10.3	3.0	-0.1	13.3
Total sectors	85.3	17.9	-3.1	100.0
Productivity growth rate (c)	1.6	0.3	-0.1	1.9
		1989-1998		
Agriculture (a)	11.0	-6.8	-0.4	3.8
Mining	4.3	-2.6	-0.2	1.5
Manufacturing	37.7	-25.4	-1.0	11.2
Public utilities	6.1	-4.3	-0.3	1.4
Construction	-2.6	-2.3	0.0	-4.9
Wholesale and retail trade	12.1	6.9	0.0	19.0
Transport and communication	20.5	-0.9	-0.1	19.6
Finance, insurance and business services (b)	-4.5	43.9	-0.6	38.8
Other market services	2.4	8.7	0.0	11.1
Government services	14.9	-16.1	-0.4	-1.6
Total sectors	101.8	1.1	-2.9	100.0
Productivity growth rate (c)	1.4	0.0	0.0	1.4

(a) includes forestry and fisheries; (b) excluding real estates; (c) the estimates of value added per hour worked in this table are based on sectoral accounts, which differ slightly from those for the total economy (Tables 1 and 6 and Figures 1a and 1b). Firstly, the sectoral accounts use the trend in GDP and labour input for 1995-1998 based on the most recent national accounts revision. Secondly, the accounts here exclude the letting and sale of real estate. Thirdly, the trend in sectoral estimates of working hours, which are based on the change in contractual hours, suggests a somewhat more moderate decline of working hours than the trend in actual hours which we used for the economy as a whole.
Source: Up to 1995 from CBS, *Nationale Rekeningen 1997* and *Arbeidsrekeningen 1997* (and previous issues). From 1995 onwards from CBS, *Nationale Rekeningen 1998.* Trend in working hours 1960-1995 are for contractual hours from CBS (unpublished).

However, further research is required to settle the issue of the shift-share effect. Firstly, as will be discussed in more detail below, measurement problems may lead to an understatement of productivity growth in services with substantial technological or organisational changes. Secondly, the assessment of the productivity slowdown may be expanded to measuring the impact of variables other than the distribution of employment by sector. For example, CPB (1997a, 1998b) also accounted for shift effects from changes in composition of educational levels, age, sex and the share of part-time labour in the labour force. These estimates suggest some small negative shift effects for the 1980s (in particular in services). However, since 1990 the shift towards more highly trained people and a more experienced labour force positively contributed to labour productivity growth.

The most important message that follows from the foregoing analysis is that the productivity slowdown has been across the board. This is confirmed by Table 8, which shows that with the exception of mining, public utilities, transport and communication and government services, labour productivity growth during the period 1989-98 was slower than during the period 1976-89. The slowdown was particularly large in construction, trade and other market services. The finance, insurance and business services sector, which was the sector with the most rapid increase in labour input, had negative labour productivity growth during both subperiods.

To some extent the slow or even negative productivity growth in services is related to measurement problems, in particular in sectors in which the share of new or improved products, for which the output growth is difficult to measure in real terms, increased. For example, the negative productivity growth rates registered in the banking sector are strongly affected by measurement problems. Traditionally, real output growth in banking has been calculated on the basis of the sum of the real value of intermediate inputs and labour cost, thus implicitly imposing productivity growth on the output indicators. Recent experimental calculations by Statistics Netherlands, based on weighted volume indicators, which represent interest margins and procuration, suggest an increase in labour productivity in the banking sector of 3.6 percent per year over the period 1987-1995 (CBS, 1997; Hogenboom and van de Ven, 1998).[12] However, it seems unlikely that corrections for mismeasurement will be as large for other service sectors. The traditional method for banking appeared to miss a particularly large amount of innovation and efficiency improvement in the sector. Recent studies for other sectors, such as business services, do not suggest the same kind of improvements (CPB, 1998c; van der Wiel, this volume).

---

[12] These corrections have been integrated in the most recent national accounts of Statistics Netherlands but have not yet been worked back for years before 1995.

Table 8. Sectoral Labour Productivity, Capital Intensity and Total Factor Productivity Growth, Netherlands, 1976-1989 and 1989-1998

	Value added per hour worked		Nonresidential Capital per hour worked		Total Factor Productivity	
	1976-89	1989-98	1976-89	1989-98	1976-89	1989-98
Agriculture (a)	5.3	4.3	5.5	3.0	3.4	3.1
Mining	-3.3	1.0	1.3	2.6	-4.5	-1.9
Manufacturing	3.6	3.1	3.2	2.8	2.8	2.1
Public utilities	1.4	4.7	0.1	3.2	1.4	2.6
Construction	2.1	-0.7	3.3	1.2	1.8	-0.9
Wholesale and retail trade	2.6	1.1	3.6	1.5	1.9	0.7
Transport and communication	2.7	3.8	2.4	1.7	2.0	3.2
Finance, insurance and business services (b)	-0.3	-0.5	-0.4	-0.7	-0.2	-0.6
Other market services	-0.4	-1.0	1.0	0.7	0.2	0.7
Government services	1.4	2.0	(c)	(c)	(c)	(c)
Total sectors (d)	1.9	1.5	2.2	1.1	1.4	1.1

(a) includes forestry and fisheries; (b) including real estates; (c) included in other market services; (d) productivity growth rates for the total GDP differ slightly from those reported at the aggregate level as explained in Table 7.

Source: GDP and labour input, see Table 7. Capital stock based on perpetual inventory method as calculated by Ronald Albers (DNB) and Joost Beaumont (UvA) using investment in nonresidential capital stock from CBS for 1921-38 and from 1950 onwards, and from Groote, Albers and de Jong (1996) for 1938-50. Investment was accumulated on the basis of 39 and 14 years life assumptions for nonresidential structures and machinery and equipment, respectively. TFP on the basis of translog production function with changing sectoral labour compensation weights averaged derived from CBS, *Nationale Rekeningen* (various issues), augmented with labour compensation for self-employed persons on the basis of imputed employee compensation.

Sectoral estimates of the capital stock are still difficult to obtain for the Netherlands because of serious data problems concerning the time series on investment. The capital stock figures used for the construction of total factor productivity estimates in Table 8 are based on the perpetual inventory method.[13] The figures in Table 8 show that the accumulation of fixed capital per hour worked and total factor productivity growth slowed down in most sectors since 1989.

[13] These estimates have been kindly supplied by Ronald Albers (Netherlands Central Bank) and Joost Beaumont (University of Amsterdam) who (mainly) used official investment data from Statistics Netherlands (CBS). These estimates are subject to revision in particular because the official investment figures pre-1987 and post-1987 are not fully consistent and require further adjustment (see CPB, 1998a). For the post-1995 period only the trend in investment is used, not the level.

Slow total factor productivity growth should not be interpreted rightaway as a sign that the Dutch economy suffers from slow technological progress. Firstly, it has been well established that TFP growth, as obtained from Tables 6 and 8, is not an adequate measure of technological change because it is derived as a residual from deducting the change in capital intensity from the change in labour productivity. Hence, the residual reflects the impact of growth from quality change of production factors (including education and training of the labour force), and from a variety of other factors ranging from the impact of research and development, managerial skills, entrepreneurial innovation, externalities and scale economies.[14] In contrast, a substantial part of investment in physical and human capital may be interpreted as embodied technological change.[15]

Secondly, even if we accept that TFP growth rates can serve as proxies for technological change, a striking observation is that, during the period 1989-1998, a dichotomy arose between the performance of the sectors. On the one hand, even though agriculture, manufacturing, public utilities and transport and communication experienced slower capital intensity and TFP growth than during the previous period, they continued to increase at a rate higher than the economy-wide growth rate. On the other hand, major parts of services (including trade, finance, insurance and business services, other market services and government services) were characterised by below-average growth of capital intensity and TFP. On the basis of a stylised distinction, one might argue that the first group typically represents sectors which can be characterised as "technology creators" whereas the second group consists of typical "technology users".[16] This suggests that the explanation behind the productivity slowdown may come from inadequate technology use rather than lack of invention and innovation. This hypothesis will be further investigated in the final section of the paper by looking into the role of indicators of technology and human capital creation.

---

[14] See, for example, Maddison (1987) and Abramovitz (1991).

[15] See, for example, Jorgenson (1995).

[16] See, for example, Papaconstantinou, Sakurai and Wyckoff (1996) who, on the basis of input-output analysis of purchases of intermediate and capital inputs determine clusters mainly consisting of service industries as being typical technology users, whereas manufacturing industries are typically classified as technology performers. This distinction does not imply that innovation in services is unimportant. Instead it suggests that the positive productivity effect from innovation in these sectors strongly depend on their ability to successfully use technology from elsewhere.

4.   THE ROLE OF INVESTMENT IN INTANGIBLE CAPITAL IN TECHNOLOGY DIFFUSION

Technological change is often equated with invention and innovation. In this line of thinking expenditure on research and development, licensing and patenting are mostly taken as variables to proxy the dynamics of the process of technology creation. Various scholars have argued that the process of diffusing new technologies and adapting these to local circumstances and within firms are crucial to reap substantial productivity gains from technological change.[17] The improvement of skills of the labour force is an important driving force behind the technology diffusion process. "Upskilling" and "reskilling" are seen as necessary conditions for productivity growth, either through the ability of workers to apply new productivity-enhancing technologies or through their greater capacity to improve work organisation.[18]

Table 9 shows the total investment in intangible capital since 1975 and its percentage distribution across various categories. When looking at formal education, government expenditure declined from 6.3 percent of GDP in 1975 to 4.6 percent in 1997. This decline in expenditure on education is partly determined by demographic developments. However, even after a correction for the decline in the share of 0-19 years olds in the population, the share of expenditure on primary and secondary education in GDP still shows a decline of 0.5 percentage points compared to the late 1970s. Meanwhile the share of all intangible investment in GDP remained relatively constant at between 10 and 11 percent until the beginning of the 1990s. Since then it has risen by a full percentage point. This implies the increased importance of other types of intangible investment, including R&D, licenses, software as well as marketing and technical services and consultancy, in both relative and absolute terms.

---

[17] See, for example, Stoneman (1983, 1987) and Dosi, Pavitt and Soete (1990). For a more historical account of the importance of technology diffusion see, for example, Mansfield (1968) and David (1975).

[18] See, for example, Nelson and Phelps (1966), Bartel and Lichtenberg (1987), Benhabib and Spiegel (1994) and OECD (1997, 1998). For a discussion of this relation more specifically focussed on a comparison of the Netherlands and Germany, see Cörvers, de Grip and Orbon (1995). However, the relation between human capital, technology use and productivity growth is a complex one, in particularly in services. Whereas the direct relation between these factors may be a positive one, there may also be a more neutral effect as the rise in technology and productivity raises income and therefore increases demand for relatively low-skilled services jobs. See also Jacobs, Nahuis and Tang (in this volume) for a more negative view on the complimentarity of human capital creation and technology diffusion.

Table 9. Investment in Intangible Capital and Percentage Contribution of Individual Components, 1975-1997

	1975	1979	1982	1987	1991	1997 (a)
Total Human Capital Investment (mln. DFL)	23,015	34,315	39,505	47,715	59,541	83,551
as a % of GDP:						
- only education	6.3	6.5	6.1	5.2	4.8	4.6
After adjustment for change in share of 0-19						
Year olds in population since 1975 (b)	*6.3*	*6.9*	*6.8*	*6.6*	*6.4*	*6.4*
- all intangible investment	10.5	10.9	10.7	10.8	11.0	11.8
	Share in Total Human Capital Investment (%)					
Education (c):	59.8	59.8	56.5	48.1	43.3	38.8
Universities	6.3	6.1	4.3	4.1	3.9	3.8
Other High Education	4.3	4.9	4.5	3.8	4.1	3.8
Primary and Secondary Education	45.2	44.6	43.3	35.4	29.9	26.9
Company Training	4.0	4.3	4.5	4.8	5.3	5.6
Technology:	25.8	25.0	27.8	34.6	35.7	40.5
Research and Development:	19.3	17.3	18.4	21.0	17.4	18.0
Business	10.1	8.7	9.4	12.3	9.2	9.8
Public Research Institutes	4.9	4.5	4.4	4.4	4.1	3.2
Universities	4.3	4.1	4.7	4.3	4.1	4.9
Software	4.2	4.4	4.9	5.8	8.2	10.5
Licenses	2.3	3.3	4.4	7.8	10.1	12.1
Other:						
Marketing	14.0	14.9	15.4	16.9	19.1	20.2
Technical Services and Consultancy	0.5	0.4	0.3	0.4	0.6	0.5

(a) provisional estimates.

(b) assuming an unchanged share of 0-19 year olds in the total population since 1975.

(c) only current expenses on education, excluding public subsidies for students.

Source: Estimates up to 1991 from Minne (1995), Annex A; extrapolated to 1997 estimated, mostly on the basis of sources quoted by Minne (1995) derived from Statistics Netherlands. GDP and population distribution also from Statistics Netherlands.

In the remainder of this section we will look in some more detail at three crucial components of intangible investment. Firstly, we will examine human capital creation in more detail. Secondly, we will focus on a typical indicator of technology creation, *i.e.* the investment in research and development. Finally, we will concentrate our attention on technology use, and more specifically on whether service sectors have made sufficiently use of new technologies to create new service concepts. In this framework we will also discuss the role of investment in information and communication technology.

Table 10. Skill Proportions of the Workforce, Netherlands, UK, Germany and USA

	Netherlands			UK	USA	Germany
	Total Economy	Exposed Sector (a)	Sheltered Sector (b)	Total Economy	Total Economy	Total Economy
	1979	*1979*	*1979*	*1978/79*	*1978/79*	*1978/79*
Low skills	52.4	65.2	57.4	71.5	72.8	34.5
Intermediate skills	32.5	28.0	34.7	21.8	11.4	58.5
High skills	15.1	6.8	7.9	6.8	15.8	7.0
	1993	*1993*	*1993*	*1993*	*1993*	*1993*
Low skills	34.6	44.6	38.4	55.7	60.4	27.8
Intermediate skills	42.8	41.2	45.2	30.9	17.5	60.7
High skills	22.5	14.0	16.3	13.5	22.1	11.4

(a) refers to agriculture, industry, public utilities and transport and communication.
(b) refers to trade, finance, insurance and business services, "other" market services and households.
Higher skills are defined as "degree and above," for the Netherlands all higher education; intermediate skills are "vocational qualifications above high school but below degree," for the Netherlands advanced general secondary education (havo and vwo above 4 years) intermediate vocational qualifications (mbo) and most apprenticeship education; low skills is the remainder, for the Netherlands including only primary education, lower vocational education (lbo), lower general secondary education (mavo) and schools for less-abled pupils.
Source: Netherlands from CBS (1996); UK, USA and Germany from O'Mahony (1998)

The human capital measures which are used for the growth accounting approach in Tables 6 and Table 9 for the distribution of expenditure are necessarily crude, as they only distinguish between primary, secondary and tertiary education, and do not reflect differences in the educational levels of the various schooling systems. Moreover, these measures relate to the total working age population. In particular, differences in the organisation of general education vis-à-vis vocational education are insufficiently reflected. Table 10 therefore provides an international comparison of skills of employees between the Netherlands, Germany, the United Kingdom and the United States.[19] The table clearly shows that the Dutch labour force is relatively well-educated. In 1979, the share of the labour force with high skills, *i.e.* higher vocational education or university, was almost as high as in the United States, and in 1993 it was even higher. Intermediate skills, which include a large share of employees with intermediate vocational skills, were better represented in the Netherlands than in the United Kingdom and the

---

[19] The measures are somewhat at odds with those used by the OECD, which are based on the International Standards Classification of Education (ISCED). The latter refers mainly to years of study and age associated with an educational cycle, rather than actual contents (OECD, 1998).

United States, but lower than in Germany. These figures reflect the large share of vocationally trained people in the Dutch and German labour force relative to the other two countries, even though there are also important differences between the German and Dutch systems of vocational education. Whereas the German system is characterised by an extensive dual schooling system, combining learning in schools with in-company training, the Dutch system relies to a much larger extent on full-time vocational training in schools with only relatively short periods of practice. Indeed, in 1994 as much as 55 percent of pupils in upper secondary education in Germany were classified as apprentices against 25 percent in the Netherlands. The German apprenticeship system has been praised by many scholars[20], but others have criticised it for its very high cost and for its lack of flexibility in an environment of a rapid structural change.[21]

One might expect that the greater reliance of the United States and the United Kingdom on general rather than vocational education is compensated by a greater amount of job-related training. Indeed, the International Adult Literacy Survey suggests that 46 and 52 percent of workers in the United States and the United Kingdom, respectively, spend about 100 hours on job-related training during the first twelve months in a new job. In the Netherlands, the percentage of new workers in training during the first year is lower (only 32 percent), but they spend more than 150 hours on training.[22]

When looking at the sectoral distribution of skills in the Netherlands, it also appears that not only the technology-creating industries, but also the technology-using industries are characterised by high skill levels. The shares of high and intermediate skilled people in the sheltered sector, which mainly consists of services, are even higher than in the exposed sector, which includes agriculture, manufacturing, public utilities and transport and communication. Furthermore, participation in company training is higher than average in transport and communication (52 percent) and financial services (84 percent), but lower in business services, where the percentage is 31 percent (CBS, 1996a). This evidence does not support the hypothesis that there is a technology use problem due to human capital shortages.

The share of R&D expenditure in GDP has shown an interesting pattern since the mid 1970s. R&D intensity by business and government together increased to about 2.2% by the late 1980s. This was lower than in other Northwest European countries, which is mainly due to the relatively small share of typical high-tech industries (such as pharmaceuticals, electronics,

---

[20] See, for example, CPB (1997b), pp. 319-329.

[21] See OECD (1994) and Paqué (1998).

[22] See OECD (1998), Table A3.4. According to CBS (1996a) 35 percent of all workers in 1993 followed company training, of which about 60% was offered externally and 40% internally.

etc.) in Dutch manufacturing. Since the late 1980s business R&D intensity declined for about a decade whereas government R&D intensity remained fairly constant. Since 1992 total R&D intensity has begun to accelerate once again up to more than 2 percent in 1997. Strikingly much of the recovery in R&D intensity is due to a rise in R&D in services, in particular in business services.[23]

Technological and organisational innovations in services are becoming increasingly important overall performed as the share of this sector in GDP and total employment rises. R&D expenditures are only a very crude indicator of services innovation, but fortunately recent innovation surveys provide evidence on other innovation measures, such as investments in design, licenses, marketing and training. Table 11 compares the percentage of firms in manufacturing and services that innovate, the share of each innovation activity in total innovation expenses, and the innovation intensity of each activity in both sectors. Even though innovation intensity in services is still much lower than in manufacturing (colum 3), an equal percentage of firms (namely 89%) in manufacturing and services are engaged in innovative activities (colum 1). The distribution of innovation expenses is quite different, as service firms spend more in relative terms on anything else than R&D (colum 2).[24]

As the innovation surveys are harmonised across European countries by Eurostat, it is possible to compare innovation efforts in services with those in other countries. Such comparisons suggest that the Netherlands is somewhat behind the European on average services innovation (Foyn, 1999). For example, the percentage of services firms that has introduced new or improved products or processes is 36 percent for the Netherlands compared to an EU average of 41 percent. In financial services the gap is bigger at 40 percent for the Netherlands compared to 55 percent for the EU average In contrast the number of innovating firms in manufacturing is reported to be higher in the Netherlands than in the EU as a whole, namely 62 percent of all firms against 53 percent.

Much of the innovation activities in services are related to expenditure on and investment in information and communication technology (ICT). Table 12 shows the share of services in intermediate use of and investment in ICT goods and services from 1990 to 1998. Whereas the share of intermediate use in services of ICT goods has declined somewhat, the use of ICT services increased beyond the share of services in GDP. Similarly investment in ICT goods and in particular ICT services increased rapidly.

---

[23] See, for example, OECD (1999) . It should be emphasized that part of this rise is due to the fact that R&D in services was not properly measured before.

[24] See also van Ark, Broersma and de Jong (1999).

Table 11. Innovators and Innovation Expenses in Manufacturing and Services, Netherlands, 1996

	Percentage of Firms making Innovation Expenses	Share in Total Innovation Expenses	Innovation Expenditure as % of Value Added
	(1)	(2)	(3)
Investment in equipment destined for innovation			
Manufacturing	61	33	3.7
Market Services	64	44	1.3
R&D expenditure with own personnel			
Manufacturing	67	46	5.2
Market Services	46	17	0.5
Purchased R&D			
Manufacturing	30	7	0.8
Market Services	26	5	0.2
Technical design and other development costs			
Manufacturing	20	3	0.3
Market Services	31	8	0.2
Licenses, consultancy, software not related to R&D			
Manufacturing	10	1	0.1
Market Services	23	8	0.2
Marketing			
Manufacturing	23	4	0.5
Market Services	24	5	0.2
Training			
Manufacturing	42	6	0.7
Market Services	53	12	0.4
All Innovation Activities			
Manufacturing	89	100	11.2
Market Services	89	100	3.0

Services include trade, hotels and restaurants, transport and communication, financial and business services and other market services

Source: CBS (1996a), CBS (1998)

Table 12. Share of services in total ICT expenditure and investment, 1990-1998 (%)

	1990	1995	1998
Intermediate use of ICT goods and services in the service sectors			
ICT goods	40	29	31
ICT services	75	80	79
Investment of ICT goods and services in the service sector			
ICT goods	n.a	72	74
ICT services	n.a	67	76(a)

(a) 1997

Services include trade, hotels and restaurants, transport and communication, financial and business services and other market services and government. The definitions of ICT goods and services have changed somewhat between 1990 and 1995-98. ICT goods roughly include computers and telecommunication equipment. ICT services include ICT services and software producers.

Source: CBS (1996b, 1999)

In conclusion, the evidence from this section does not strongly point towards an underperformance in terms of intangible investment in services. This, however, does not yet answer the question on how the average investment performance can be related to the relatively slow productivity growth in services. One reason might be that a better balance between technological change and improvement in human capital is needed. Hence, from a policy perspective, the slowdown in the GDP share of educational investment to 4.6 percent, which is also lower than the average education share in GDP of 5.1 percent in the EU in 1995, is a matter of concern.[25] Moreover, as the human capital theory also points to high "consumption value" of education, these investments also contribute directly to a better use of ICT by consumers.

5.   CONCLUSION AND DIRECTIONS FOR FURTHER RESEARCH

This paper started form the observation of the strikingly divergent trends in income per capita and productivity in the Netherlands since the mid 1980s. We show that the acceleration in per capita income and the slowdown in labour productivity growth is related to a strong increase in labour force participation. As much as 37 percent of the growth rate of real GDP (and 22

[25] See OECD (1999), table 2.1.11

percent of the growth rate of GDP per capita) since 1987 is due to the rise in labour input. As shown in earlier papers (van Ark and de Haan, 1999, 2000) the policy of wage moderation since the early 1980s has contributed to the strong employment creation.

In this paper we focused on explanations for the downside of the growth acceleration story, which is the slowdown in productivity growth. We show that the (combined) effect of changes in the composition of the labour force and a greater concentration of labour in services, which are typically characterised by lower productivity growth, explains little of the productivity slowdown. Even though there is some evidence of an underestimation of productivity growth in services (in particular in the banking sector), the slowdown in productivity growth is unlikely to be explained entirely by measurement problems.

Measures of total factor productivity growth show that that despite a slower growth of capital capital intensity, the contribution of capital intensity to labour productivity growth has only slightly declined. Hence the claim that wage moderation led to a fall in capital-output ratios seems unjustified.

We also found that the productivity slowdown affected all sectors of the economy, and that this concerns both labour productivity and total factor productivity. Sectoral analysis, however, shows that the productivity growth rates in typical technology-using industries, such as trade, finance, insurance and business services, were below the economy-wide growth rate. In contrast, growth rates in typical technology-creating industries, such as manufacturing and agriculture, also show a slowdown, but these were still above the economy-wide average. As the diffusion and use of technology is related to the performance of human capital as a production factor, we analysed the hypothesis that the contribution of human capital to growth might have faltered. This hypothesis is again not confirmed by the evidence. Most of our evidence points to the contrary. The human capital intensity, in particular in services, has substantially improved.

However, we do find shifts in the composition of intangible capital, showing that the share of investment in software, licenses, marketing and (most recently) even R&D has risen at the expense of the share of investment in education. This may have slowed the capability to develop new products and processes in services. For example, we find that the innovative capability of the service sector is somewhat below the average European performance. Other studies have pointed towards the possibility of substantive X-inefficiencies in service sectors and a lack of organisational innovation.[26] Further research on micro-data from production and innovation statistics is needed to shed light upon how widespread these problems are.

---

[26] See, for example, CPB (1998b, 1998c) and the contribution by van der Wiel (2000) to this volume.

In earlier papers (van Ark and de Haan, 1999, 2000) we also looked at the possible contribution of structural reforms to employment growth and found that the evidence is inconclusive. We also noted that various measures concerning liberalisation of product markets, including the extension of opening times of shops, privatisation of public transport services and the abolition of regulations etc. in many areas of services, have mostly been taken in recent years, and that it is unlikely that such measures will have a large impact on growth in the short term. However, Koedijk and Kremers (1996) find a significant relation between productivity growth and product market regulation for 11 EU member states over the period 1980-94. Hence a further monitoring of the effects of product market regulation and deregulation is another fruitful avenue for further research.

REFERENCES

Abramovitz, M. (1991), *Thinking about Growth*, Cambridge: Cambridge University Press.

Ark, B. van (1996), "Sectoral Growth Accounting and Structural Change in Post-War Europe," in B. van Ark and N.F.R. Crafts (eds.), *Quantitative Aspects of Post-War European Economic Growth*, Cambridge: CEPR/Cambridge University Press, pp. 84-164.

Ark, B. van and J. de Haan (1999),"A Miracle or Not? Recent trends in the Growth Performance of the Dutch Economy," in P.A.G. van Bergeijk, J. van Sinderen and B.A. Vollaard (eds.), *Structural Reform in Open Economies: a Road to Success?*, Cheltenham/ Northampton: Edward Elgar, pp. 157-179.

Ark, B. van and J. de Haan (2000), "The Delta-Model Revisited: Recent Trends in the Structural Performance of the Dutch Economy," *International Review of Applied Economics*, forthcoming.

Ark, B. van and H.J. de Jong (1996), "Accounting for Economic Growth in the Netherlands since 1913," *The Economic and Social History in the Netherlands* 7.

Ark, B. van, L. Broersma and G. de Jong (1999), "Innovation in Services. Overview of Data Sources and Analytical Structures," *Research Memorandum GD-44*, Groningen Growth and Development Centre (downloadable from http://www.eco.rug.nl/ggdc/pub/)

Bartel, A.P. and F.R. Lichtenberg (1987), "The Comparative Advantage of Implementing New Technology," *Review of Economics and Statistics* 69, pp. 1-11.

Benhabib, J. and M.M Spiegel (1994), "The Role of Human Capital in Economic Development. Evidence from Aggregate Cross-Country Data," *Journal of Monetary Economics* 34, pp. 143-173.

CBS, *Nationale Rekeningen*, various issues, Voorburg.

CBS, *Arbeidsrekeningen*, various issues, Voorburg.

CBS (1996), *Tijdreeksen Arbeidsrekeningen 1969-1993. Ramingen van het Opleidingsniveau, een Tussenstand*, Voorburg.

CBS (1996a), *Kennis en economie 1996*, Voorburg.

CBS (1996b), *ICT-markt in Nederland 1990-1995*, Voorburg.

CBS (1997), "Een volume-index voor de productiewaarde van het bankwezen op basis van hoeveelheidsindicatoren," October, mimeographed.

CBS (1998), *Kennis en economie 1998*, Voorburg.

CBS (1999), *ICT-markt in Nederland 1995-1998*, Voorburg.

Cörvers, F., A. de Grip and J-P Orbon (1995), "Concurrentiekracht, productiviteit en human capital: een vergelijking tussen Nederland en Duitsland," *Maandschrift Economie* 59, pp. 221-241.

CPB (1997a), "Meer laagbetaald werk, minder arbeidsproductiviteitsgroei?," *Macroeconomische Verkenningen 1998*, section VI.I, pp. 107-117.

CPB (1997b), *Challenging Neighbours. Rethinking Dutch and German Economic Institutions*, Berlin: Springer Verlag.

CPB (1998a), "Sectorale productiviteitsgroei in Nederland," Interne notitie, Den Haag, 6 april.

CPB (1998b), "Recent Trends in Dutch Labour Productivity: The Role of Changes in the Composition of Employment," *Werkdocument no. 98*, Den Haag.

CPB (1998c), *Centraal Economisch Plan 1998*, The Hague.

David, P. (1975), *Technical Choice, Innovation and Economic Growth*, Cambridge: Cambridge University Press.

Dosi, G., K. Pavitt and L. Soete (1990), *The Economics of Technical Change and International Trade*, New York: Harvester Wheatsheaf.

Foyn, F. (1999), "Community Innovation Survey 1997/1998," *Statistics in Focus*, Eurostat, Theme 9, 2.

Groote, P., R.M. Albers and H.J. de Jong (1996), "A Standardised Time Series of the Stock of Fixed Capital in the Netherlands," *Research Memorandum GD-25*, Groningen Growth and Development Centre.

Hogenboom, R. and P. van de Ven (1998), "Heeft het Nederlandse bankwezen een productiviteitsprobleem?," *Bank- en Effectenbedrijf*, May, pp. 30-33.

Jacobs, B., R. Nahuis, and P.J.G. Tang (2000), "Human Capital, R&D, Productivity Growth and Assimilation of Technologies in the Netherlands," this volume.

Jorgenson, D.W. (1995), *Productivity, Volume 1*, Cambridge Mass: MIT Press.

Koedijk, K. and J.J.M. Kremers (1996), "Market Opening, Regulation and Growth in Europe," *Economic Policy* 23, pp. 443-467.

Maddison, A. (1987), "Growth and Slowdown in Advanced Capitalist Economies: Techniques of Quantitative Assessment," *Journal of Economic Literature* 25, pp. 649-698.

Maddison, A. (1991), *Dynamic Forces in Capitalist Development. A Long-Run Comparative View*, Oxford: Oxford University Press.

Maddison, A. (1995), *Monitoring the World Economy, 1820-1992*, OECD Development Centre, Paris.

Mansfield, E. (1968), *The Economics of Technological Change*, New York: W.W. Norton.

Minne, B. (1995), "Onderzoek, ontwikkeling en andere immateriele investeringen in Nederland," *Research Memorandum No. 116*, Centraal Planbureau, The Hague.

Nelson, R.R. and E.S. Phelps (1966), "Investment in Human Capital, Technological Diffusion, and Economic Growth," *American Economic Review* 65, pp. 69-75.

OECD, *Economic Outlook*, various issues, Paris

OECD, *Employment Outlook*, various issues, Paris

OECD, *National Accounts, Volume I*, various issues, Paris

OECD, *Purchasing Power Parities and Real Expenditures*, various issues, Paris

OECD (1994), *OECD Economic Surveys Germany, 1994*, Paris.

OECD (1997), *Technology and Industrial Performance*, Paris.

OECD (1998), *Human Capital Investment. An International Comparison*, Centre for Educational Research and Innovation, Paris.

OECD (1999*), Science, Technology and Industry Scoreboard 1999*, Paris.

O'Mahony, M. (1999), *Britain's productivity performance, 1950-1996*, National Institute of Economic and Social Research, London

Papaconstantinou, G, N. Sakurai and A. Wyckoff (1996), "Embodied Technology Diffusion: An Empirical Analysis for 10 OECD Countries," *STI Working Papers 1996/1*, OECD, Paris.

Paqué, K-H (1998), "Het Duitse model raakt uit de tijd," *Economisch Statistische Berichten* 83, pp. 84-87.

Stoneman, P. (1983), *The Economic Analysis of Technological Change*, Oxford: Oxford University Press.

Stoneman, P. (1987), *The Economic Analysis of Technology Policy*, Oxford: Oxford University Press.

Timmer, M. (2000), *The Dynamics of Asian Manufacturing. A Comparative Perspective, 1963-1993*, Cheltenham/Northampton: Edward Elgar.

Wiel, H. van der (2000), "Labour Productivity Growth in Dutch Business Services: the Role of Entry and Exit," this volume.

Chapter 7

Labour Productivity Growth in Dutch Business Services
The Role of Entry and Exit

H.P. van der Wiel
CPB Netherlands Bureau for Economic Policy Analysis, The Hague

Key words: Exit and entry, Business services

Abstract: Labour productivity growth in Dutch business services has been lacking in recent years. Using a unique firm-level data set of Dutch business services, this paper analyses the effect of enterprise demographics for labour productivity growth. Special attention is given to the contribution of entering and exiting firms to productivity growth. The study shows that entering firms are less productive than incumbents are. Remarkably, entering firms are equally as productive as exiting firms are. Since many new firms entered the market of business services in the period investigated, aggregate productivity growth did not improve. Moreover, incumbents' productivity hardly changed over time, though a wide dispersion in firm productivity growth rates exists.

1.   INTRODUCTION

Labour productivity growth is essential to maintain and improve standards of living. Recent developments in the Netherlands, however, have been discouraging. Although market services show an impressive track record in generating jobs during the 1990s, the track record in productivity is rather poor (see Figure 1). While labour productivity growth in the manufacturing industry improved gradually, in the 1990s compared to the second half of the 1980s, productivity growth in market services dropped sharply, especially in business services. As a result, overall labour productivity growth in the market sector declined further in the first half of the 1990s (van der Wiel, 1998). Moreover, Dutch performance is quite disappointing compared with

187

other OECD countries since the mid-1980s. This could signal that inputs in services are used inefficiently, possibly due to a lack of competitive pressure in the Dutch market services. However, a clear view of forces behind the poor productivity performance is still lacking.

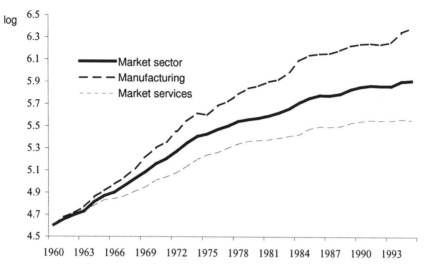

Figure 1. Labour Productivity in the Netherlands, 1960-1995

In order to assess the meagre productivity performance of Dutch services industries, business services have been selected for further research. As the share in employment of business services increases continuously, the need for understanding productivity of services is essential. Business services have emerged as one of the most dynamic industries in Dutch economy in the recent past. This sector which includes branches such as accountancy, computer services, and economic consulting agencies, features noticeable increases in output and employment. In fact the industry realised the highest growth rates of all Dutch industries during the 1980s and early 1990s. The number of firms that entered or exited the business services market was also remarkable in this period. The number of start-ups in the period 1987-1995 was approximately twice as much as the number of existing firms in 1987. High entry and exit rates of firms point to low entry barriers and suggest a high degree of competition. It is generally thought that this combination stimulates efficient management. Yet, labour productivity growth in business services did not improve. Taking into account the government's policy of stimulating entrepreneurship and promoting market forces, this result is puzzling indeed.

Using an internationally unique firm-level data set of the Dutch business services for the period 1987 to 1995, this paper documents the link between productivity performance and firm turnover in order to shed some light on the poor productivity performance of the services industries. The available data provide the opportunity to go beyond the industry level and to descend into the heart of the economy, *i.e.* the firm. Special attention is paid to the contributions of incumbents, entering and exiting firms to labour productivity growth. At this stage of research, the paper aims mainly to be descriptive. Therefore, no conclusive answers can be given. Nonetheless, some conjectures are put forward that could explain the modest productivity growth reasonably well. A lack of competition in buoyant markets, accompanied by a shift in demand towards new products is the most promising one. However, further research is clearly needed to get a better view on the causes of the poor productivity performance.

The remainder of this paper proceeds as follows. Section 2 briefly sketches the data and measurement issues of the firm-level data set of the Dutch business services. Section 3 stresses the importance of enterprise demographics for productivity growth and elucidates the decomposition methodology of productivity growth into the contribution of incumbents, and entering and exiting firms. This Section also discusses the results of the decomposition of labour productivity at two different levels of aggregation of the unit of analysis; *i.e.* business services as a whole, and industries within business services. The next Section tries to disentangle the results by looking for similarities among similar groups of firms. It also puts forward some conjectures that could explain the sluggish labour productivity growth in business services. Finally, Section 5 summarises the main findings of this paper and illustrates areas for further research.

2.   DATA AND MEASUREMENT ISSUES

2.1   Data

The available firm-level data set of the Dutch business services covers the period 1987-1995. The data set is based on a yearly survey undertaken by Statistics Netherlands (CBS), among enterprises with their main activity in business services. This survey forms the basis of the Census of Production. The available data set contains approximately 48,000 observation units for the whole period investigated.

This paper uses gross real output per persons employed (including self-employed) is used as a measure of labour productivity.[1] At a disaggregated

---

[1]   Although one would expect that the greatest part of new jobs consists of part-timers, this has not been confirmed by the sample. The productivity results based on full-time equivalents, therefore, hardly differ and are not reported in this paper.

level, the use of gross output is more appropriate for productivity measurement, because gross output allows symmetrical treatment of capital, labour and intermediate inputs. Gross output is measured as net total sales at market prices. Labour input is measured as the number of people employed (excluding temporary employment). As both variables are derived from the same source, internal consistency of output and inputs is probably guaranteed. Finally, the 3-digit CBS National Accounts deflator for the industry in which the firm is classified deflates gross output.

Main characteristics of business services

Table 1 presents the branches of industries in business services included in this paper. Appendix A contains a full list of all branches engaged in producing business services including those branches which are not analysed in this paper. The short string will be used in tables with lower levels of aggregation. Table 2 lists some basic characteristics of the industries of business services. With regard to output and employment, the most important branch of industry within the business services, is "engineers and architects." Based on gross output per number of people employed, "publicity and advertising agencies" account for the highest productivity level, whereas "press and other business services" have the lowest productivity level. The intermediate input intensity displays huge diversity, pointing to heterogeneity of input use. "Publicity and advertising agencies" use an enormous amount of intermediate input to produce output. In contrast, "accountancy" uses almost no intermediate inputs.

Table 1. Branches of Industries in Business Services

Name	Short string	SBI[a]
Auditors, accountants and tax-experts	Acc	84.2
Computer services	Comp	84.3
Engineers, architects and other technical designing and consulting agencies	Eng	84.4
Publicity and advertising agencies	Publ	84.5
Economic consulting agencies	Econ	84.6
Press and news agencies and other business services	News+obs	84.7 and 84.9

[a] Dutch Standard Industrial Classification 1974 (in Dutch: Standaard BedrijfsIndeling)

All firms in business services are small compared to the average size of manufacturing firms. Most firms in business services have, on average, no more than six employees, whereas the average size of manufacturing is approximately 100 employees. The small scale of firms in business services suggests the absence of economies of scale. New firms can remain small without being confronted with a scale disadvantage.

Table 2. Some Main Economic Indicators of Business Services, 1992

	Acc	comp	eng	Publ	econ	news+obs	Total[d]
Sales per employee (NLG)	108,500	183,750	141,000	319,500	125,000	95,250	144,500
Value added per employee (NLG)	105,250	141,250	109,250	107,250	107,000	70,750	104,750
Output share (%)	16	18	24	19	9	13	100
Employment share (%)	22	14	25	9	11	20	100
Intermediate input intensity[a] (%)	3	23	22	66	15	26	27
Number of firms (x1000)	9.7	5.9	9.8	7.3	11.7	9.5	53.9
Average firm size[b]	6.6	7.1	7.6	3.5	2.7	6.2	5.5
Gross fixed investment rate[c] (%)	5.7	5.4	6.0	9.0	5.1	12.3	6.8

[a] Intermediate input as a percentage of gross value added.
[b] Number of people employed divided by number of firms.
[c] As a percentage of gross value added.
[d] Business services excluding legal services and securities, and temporary employment agencies.
Source: CBS (1994): *Business services; Summarised Overview 1992* (only in Dutch: *Zakelijke dienstverlening; Samenvattend overzicht 1992*)

Another inference drawn from Table 2 is that the gross fixed investment rate, *i.e.* gross fixed investments as percentage of gross value added, does not differ much among the branches. Finally, the investment rate is small compared to the 15 percent in manufacturing in recent years. The investment figures suggest that low amounts of capital will suffice to start-up a viable firm in business services.

Limitations of data

Although the survey of CBS is unique and provides a rich set of variables available, it is certainly not ideal because of issues related to sampling, coverage, status of the firms, and missing variables. Table 3 presents aggregate statistics for the survey compared to the Census of Production.[2]

The annual CBS survey provides a complete coverage of firms with at least 20 employees, while firms with fewer than 20 employees are sampled. Since business services consist of many small firms, most of them are not included in the survey. According to the survey, the mean size of firms is

---

[2] Appendix B contains a comparison between the results of the micro data set and the National Accounts.

almost 35 employees, whereas the average firm's size in the Census of Production is less than 6 employees. Therefore, to estimate the actual contribution of these small firms to the overall, sample weights are used by CBS.

Table 3. Summary Statistics Census of Production versus Sample, 1987

	Census of production	Survey	coverage (in %)
Firms (x1000)	25.9	2.2	8.4
Output (billions NLG)	23.2	15.0	64.6
Employment (x1000)	149.9	75.2	50.2
Average firm size	5.6	34.7	

In theory it is a straightforward task to decompose the growth in labour productivity into its three components of continuing, entering and exiting firms, by weighing each firms labour productivity level with their respective labour share in the industry (see Section 3). However, in practice this decomposition is not straightforward, because not all firms that are actually present are surveyed and included in the data set. Therefore, the correct status of the firms is not always known. As Table 4 illustrates, eight different situations can be distinguished.[3] In this paper, observations of the firms have been matched over 1987 and 1995. In that way, three types of firms can be distinguished: *incumbents* (those firms that are sampled in both years); *exits* (those firms that are sampled only in 1987); and *entrants* (those firms that are sampled only in 1995).[4] The fifth column of Table 4 shows the status of a firm in this paper.

Table 4. Correct Classification versus Chosen Classification of Firms

	Period 1	Period 0	correct classification	chosen classification
1	Present and sampled	Present and sampled	incumbents	Incumbents
2	Present and sampled	Present, not sampled	incumbents	Entrants
3	Present and sampled	Not present	entrants	Entrants
4	Present, not sampled	Not present	entrants	not covered
5	Present, not sampled	Present and sampled	incumbents	Exits
6	Present, not sampled	Present, not sampled	incumbents	not covered
7	Not present	Present and sampled	exits	Exits
8	Not present	Present, not sampled	exits	not covered

Remarkably, additional linked CBS information on birth and death of firms suggests that the number of entrants is probably overestimated in this paper. In a booming market, this is an odd result. Alternative estimates

---

[3] Obviously, the situation not present in both periods is not interesting.

[4] It should be noticed that if a merger or take-over results in a new unique code, mergers are seen as firms that are exiting in period *t*- and the merged firm is seen as an entrant in *t*.

suggest high entry rates in Dutch business services, and therefore does not point to an overestimation of the number of entrants in this paper.[5]

Unfortunately, several interesting variables for productivity research are missing in the micro data set. For instance, data on total labour input are obtainable, but no data are available on differences in labour quality. Firms' prices are also missing. Therefore, if price (or product) differentiation exists, productivity measures will be biased. Finally, capital stocks or capital flows are neither directly collected from firms and must be constructed. However, lacking time series of investments at firm level complicates this construction. Therefore, only capital stocks for incumbents will be constructed (see Section 4). Finally, it is not known how much noise there is in the micro data. However, as can be seen later, variables in the data set correlate with other variables. Moreover, low productivity firms are more likely to exit.

3. THE ROLE OF ENTRY AND EXIT IN BUSINESS SERVICES

3.1 Theory of Productivity Growth; Representative Firms versus Heterogeneity of Firms

Labour productivity is determined by the available technology, scale economies, labour skill, capital intensity and organisation of functions and tasks. Growth in labour productivity results, in part, from the adoption of technical innovations in process and products, which pushes the production frontier upward. Alternatively, capital deepening and improvements in labour quality can also enhance labour productivity growth.

To analyse sources of productivity growth, most studies apply the growth accounting framework based on Solow (1957). This approach assumes that each plant or firm within the same industry shares a single technology relating output to inputs. More recently, however, the availability of micro data has led to a number of studies that stress the importance of heterogeneity in the performance and behaviour of the firm. This second approach emphasises cross-firm differences in productivity and the importance of resource reallocation between firms. Representative firms do not actually exist. Instead, firms focus on various types of output markets and use different technologies with divergent degrees of success. Furthermore, firms differ in their organisation of functions and tasks.

---

[5] Bais, Bangma and Verhoeven (1997).

Therefore, at any point in time, intra-industry differences in performance exist.

Theoretical models of industry dynamics (by, for example, Jovanic, 1982; and Hopenhayn, 1992) study an industry's behaviour over time. These models try to explain the divergent paths of the growth and failure of firms. Likewise all these dynamic models start with the assumption that firms (or producers) within the same industry are heterogeneous, *i.e.* firms differ in their productive efficiency. Idiosyncratic shocks (internal or external) and uncertainty will also affect firms differently. Consequently firms will make varied kinds of decisions regarding entry, growth and exit.

Another characteristic of these dynamic models is that the existence of supra-normal profits and low entry barriers attract new firms to the market and influence productivity performance. High entry rates suggest a competitive and efficient market that exerts pressure on inefficient firms to exit. In theory, entry and exit tend to eliminate excess profits and reduce X-inefficiency, thereby eventually stimulating economic growth. However, in a competitive market with rapidly growing demand, existing firms can earn supra-normal profits, and such profits are likely to persist for as long as it takes for capacity to adjust to demand (see Geroski, 1991). Incumbents will not extend their capacity beyond the efficient scale. Entrants will then fill the gap in unanticipated demand.

3.2   Decomposition Methods of Productivity

To quantify the effect of firm demographics on labour productivity growth, one has to weigh the productivity of individual firms (i) by their market share in employment and add them to the average productivity (P):

$$P = \frac{Y}{L} = \sum_i \frac{Y_i}{L_i} \frac{L_i}{L} = \sum_i P_i S_i \tag{1}$$

with Y is gross output, L is employment, P is labour productivity, and S is the share of firm's employment in total industry. In growth rates, one can rewrite expression (1) as:

$$\frac{\Delta P}{P_0} = \frac{P_1 - P_0}{P_0} = \frac{\sum_i S_{i,1} P_{i,1} - \sum_i S_{i,0} P_{i,0}}{P_0} \tag{2}$$

To measure the effect of entry and exit on productivity between time periods 1 and 0, expression (2) can be rearranged in several arbitrary ways (see, for example, Baldwin, 1995). Only two alternative decomposition methodologies are used here to measure the effect of entry and exit.

Decomposition method 1

The first decomposition methodology is as follows:

$$\frac{\Delta P}{P_0} = \frac{\sum_{i \in I_{c;o,1}}(S_{i,1}P_{i,1} - S_{i,0}P_{i,0})}{P_0} + \frac{\sum_{i \in I_{e,1}}S_{i,1}P_{i,1} - \sum_{i \in I_{x,0}}S_{i,0}P_{i,0}}{P_0} \qquad (3)$$

with I_c are incumbents, I_e entrants and I_x are exits. The overall growth in productivity is determined by two terms. The first term on the right-hand side of (3) features labour productivity growth of incumbents. The second term on the right-hand side represents the net effect of entry and exit on productivity growth. The contribution of incumbents can be further decomposed into a "within" firm effect, and two reallocation effects: an employment-share effect, and a cross term:

$$\sum_{i \in I_{c;o,1}}\Delta P_i S_{i,0} + \sum_{i \in I_{c;o,1}}P_{i,0}\Delta S_i + \sum_{i \in I_{c;o,1}}\Delta P_i \Delta S_i \qquad (4)$$

Since labour productivity may be different across firms, reallocation of employment shares also affects overall productivity growth.

Decomposition method 2

The results obtained by the first decomposition methodology provide little information on the impact of competition. As the productivity level is an indicator of this efficiency, the impact of competition can be more extensively visualised by considering individual productivity levels in relation to the industry average. Rearranging Equation (3) and adding the following term, which is by definition zero:

$$\left(\left(\sum_{i \in I_{c;0,1}}S_{i,1} + \sum_{i \in I_{e,1}}S_{i,1}\right) - \left(\sum_{i \in I_{c;0,1}}S_{i,0} + \sum_{i \in I_{x,1}}S_{i,0}\right)\right)\overline{P_0} \qquad (5)$$

a new decomposition of contributions is at our disposal:

$$\Delta P = P_1 - P_0 = \sum_{i \in I_{c;0,1}} S_{i,0} \Delta P_i + \sum_{i \in I_{c;0,1}} \Delta S_i \left(P_{i,0} - \overline{P}_0 \right) + \sum_{i \in I_{c;0,1}} \Delta S_i \Delta P_i$$
$$+ \sum_{i \in I_{e,1}} S_{i,1} \left(P_{i,1} - \overline{P}_0 \right) - \sum_{i \in I_{x,0}} S_{i,0} \left(P_{i,0} - \overline{P}_0 \right) \tag{6}$$

The bar above the productivity level indicates an average level of the initial period. Again, productivity growth for incumbents is decomposed into respectively, a within effect (the first term on the right-hand side), a reallocation effect and a covariance term. The reallocation effect, *i.e.* the second term, reflects changing market shares, weighted by the deviation of initial firm productivity from the *average productivity level*. Notice that this reallocation effect differs from the reallocation effect of the first decomposition methodology. If incumbents raise their share, they positively contribute to the overall productivity only if they have higher productivity than average initial productivity for the industry. The third term on the right-hand side is a cross term that can be either negative or positive. If an existing firm raises both its market share and productivity level, this effect will be positive.

Additionally, the fourth and fifth terms tell us more about the probable impact of competition from entry and exit. The fourth term shows that entrants with productivity levels above (below) the industry's average provide a positive (negative) contribution. The fifth term indicates that if exiting firms with productivity levels below (above) the industry's average leave the market then overall productivity level will increase (decrease). Hence the effect of entry and exit on productivity is accounted for separately in the second method, whereas in the first method the contribution of turnover is a net effect.

Further decomposition of continuing firms

Baily, Bartelsman and Haltiwanger (1995) have shown that cross-sectional differences between so called upsizing firms and downsizing firms can be important. Following their idea, in terms of success and failure in boosting productivity, combined with whether or not employment increased (up-sized) or decreased (down-sized) continuing firms can be decomposed into four types of firms:
– Successful up-sizers
– Successful down-sizers
– Unsuccessful down-sizers
– Unsuccessful up-sizers

The first types of firm are *successful up-sizers*. Successful up-sizers improve both employment and labour productivity over time. These firms face increasing demand for their products combined with economies of scale or capital deepening. Alternatively, these firms have realised technological progresses that, in turn, make it possible to set prices are falling relative to those of their competitors. Successful up-sizers can extend their market share.

The second types of firm are classified as *successful down-sizers*. Although successful down-sizers improve their labour productivity, their employment shrinks. Downsizing is generally a strategy consciously adopted by firms to improve the efficiency of the organisation and to raise their profit margins. This strategy could be a reaction to a decline in demand. Also, it could be a response to fierce competition.

Firms that both decrease their labour productivity level and their employment level are *unsuccessful down-sizers*. These firms may have also (deliberately) chosen for a strategy of downsizing or are forced to engage in such a strategy, but without success. The number of workers is insufficiently adjusted to decreasing output. This could be due to labour hoarding or to a productivity penalty induced by changing the scale of operations.

Finally, there are firms whose employment increases while labour productivity decreases; *i.e. unsuccessful up-sizers*. Apparently, these firms have changed their production technology. They experience high set-up costs or face diminishing returns. A change in production technology could be observed by a relative fall in wages compared to other firms, which hints at a shift to workers with lower levels of productivity. On the other hand, quality improvements could have altered the product variety, while these quality changes are insufficiently reflected in price deflators, thus suggesting a downward bias in measured output.

3.3   Productivity Decomposition Results

Table 5 shows that a booming demand challenged business services during the period 1987-1995. Gross output expanded by 7 percent per annum, expressing the growing importance of business services in the economy. This remarkable output growth was mainly due to the entry of new firms. Incumbents expanded their activities at an average rate of 2½ percent per year only. At first glance, this result suggests that incumbents were not able to extend their activities beyond a certain scale.

Table 5. Summary Statistics of Dutch Business Services[a] 1987-1995

	1987 level	1995 level	1988-1995 annual percentage change
Labour productivity (x1000)[b]			
All	135.8	135.2	0
Incumbents	144.7	145.0	0
Entrants		132.9	
Exits	132.4		
Employment (x1000)			
All	137.8	239.3	7
Incumbents	37.5	45.4	2½
Entrants		193.9	
Exits	100.3		
Gross output (billion)[c]			
All	18.7	32.3	7
Incumbents	5.4	6.6	2½
Entrants		25.8	
Exits	13.2		
Labour share in firm's income[d]			
All	35.8	33.9	-¾
Incumbents	40.7	44.1	1
Entrants		33.1	
Exits	34.0		
Number of firms[e]			
All	1857	5640	
Incumbents	337	337	
Entrants		5303	
Exits	1520		

[a] Including acc, comp, publ, econ, and news+obs.
[b] Gross output per employee in terms of 1987 guilders.
[c] Gross output in terms of 1987 guilders.
[d] Labour costs as a percentage of gross output.
[e] Actual (unweighted) number of firms in sample.

The forceful economic growth in business services was accompanied by job creation on a considerable scale. This employment growth, moreover, was primarily due to job creation by new firms. A remarkable feature of this industry is that the surge in jobs went hand-in-hand with the growth in output, so that overall labour productivity did not improve on average in the period 1987-1995. Hence, the firm-level data confirm the overall picture of sluggish productivity growth in Dutch market services. Moreover, it should be noted that incumbents failed to increase their labour productivity over time. On top of this, Table 5 shows that the average labour productivity level of firms that disappeared was below the level of incumbents, but virtually equal to that of entrants. Note, however, that there is a time-span of eight years between the figures entrants and exits. One would expect that after eight years the overall productivity levels have increased, including that of entrants.

Measured by labour costs as a percentage of gross output, entrants and exiting firms had lower labour costs on average than incumbents. This is mainly due to the lower wages paid by entering and exiting firms compared to their counterparts.

Finally, firms that exited and entered accounted for a substantial fraction of total output and employment. In 1987, exits accounted for 70 percent of the total output. In 1995, entrants shared more than 80 percent. The importance of entry and exit is confirmed by the high numbers of entering and exiting firms. There is a lot of turnover in Dutch business services. Average output per firm declined due to the high entry rates in the period 1987-1995.

Table 6 contains the contribution of the fourfold classification types of incumbents as well as the net effect of entry and exit to aggregate labour productivity growth. Neither successful up-sizers, *i.e.* firms with increasing employment and labour productivity, nor successful down-sizers (improving productivity/ shrinking employment) contributed to labour productivity growth in business services between 1987 and 1995. Despite their productivity improvements, both types of firms lost market shares because of the enormous number of new competitors that were attracted to the market. This reallocation effect is huge and entirely explains the negative contribution of continuing firms to overall performance.

Results of the second decomposition methodology of productivity are summarised in Table 7. Compared to the results in Table 6, the negative reallocation effect in the second decomposition method is almost absent and the net contribution to productivity growth of entry and exit shrank to zero. The difference in results between both methodologies is due to the fact that the second method compares productivity levels of firms with the average initial productivity. As Table 5 illustrates, differences in productivity between entering and exiting firms are negligible. The second decomposition method ensures that net entry does not raise aggregate productivity solely because the share of entrants is greater than the share of exiting firms. In the remainder, I will only apply the second decomposition method.

Table 6. Contribution of Incumbents, Entrants and Exits to Overall Labour Productivity Growth,[a] 1988-1995 (decomposition methodology 1)

	total	Contribution of incumbents		
		within-effect	Reallocation	Cross term
	Annual percentage changes			
All firms	0			
Incumbents	-1¼	¼	-1½	0
o.w. Successful up-sizers	0			
Successful down-sizers	-½			
Unsuccessful down-sizers	-½			
Unsuccessful up-sizers	-¼			
Entry and exit	1¼			

[a] Including acc, comp, publ, econ, and news+obs.

Table 7. Contribution of Incumbents, Entrants and Exits to Overall Labour Productivity Growth,[a] 1988-1995 (decomposition methodology 2)

	total	contribution of incumbents		
	Annual percentage changes	within-effect	reallocation	Cross term
All firms	0			
Incumbents	0	¼	-¼	0
o.w. Successful up-sizers	¼			
Successful down-sizers	¼			
Unsuccessful down-sizers	-¼			
Unsuccessful up-sizers	-¼			
Entry	-¼			
Exit	¼			

[a] Including acc, comp, publ, econ, and news+obs.

Incumbents in business services, on average, did not succeed in improving their productivity between 1987 and 1995. However, successful up-sizers and successful down-sizers in business services expanded their labour productivity by 3-5 percent annually, which proves that not all firms in market services face a productivity problem (see Figure 2). By contrast, labour productivity of unsuccessful firms diminished by 3-4 percent per year. Hence the allocation of the four types determined the labour productivity performance of continuing firms as a whole.

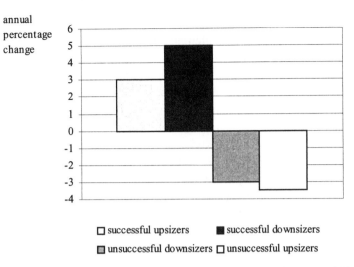

Figure 2. Labour Productivity Growth of Incumbents in the Netherlands, 1988-1995

On average, only 25 percent of all incumbents engaged in producing business services realised both an increase in labour productivity and in employment over time. Again, another 25 percent of the incumbents improved their productivity level, but at the cost of lower levels of employment. Consequently, the remaining 50 percent of survivors were unsuccessful firms. These types of firms counterbalanced the excellent performance of the successful incumbents. The following Section pays special attention to the cause of this diversity among groups of incumbents.

Benchmarking Dutch business services

Assessing the labour productivity performance of Dutch business services by comparing the performance with that of other countries could indicate as to where the weakness lies. Unfortunately, because of data problems and lack of comparable micro-level data for the services sector, international comparison is tricky. Results of sector studies suggest, however, that the rate of labour productivity growth in Dutch market services lags behind that of the USA, the UK and Germany (see O'Mahony, 1999; and van der Wiel, 1998).

Using longitudinal firm-level data, Foster, Haltiwanger and Krizan (1998) recently stated that there is tremendous reallocation of activity across service-sector firms in the US. Much of this reallocation in the selected services industries is generated by entry and exit, which dominate productivity growth. For example, the exit of very-low-productivity plants was the primary contributor to the productivity growth of the USA automobile repair shop industry between 1987 and 1992. This finding does not correspond with that of the Dutch business services.

The demographic performance of Dutch business services can also be compared with Dutch manufacturing. Bartelsman *et al.* (1995) analysed the effect of firm turnover on the productivity performance of Dutch manufacturing. At least two results of his analysis substantially differ with the results in this paper. First, the productivity level of entrants in manufacturing was considerably higher than that of exiting firms. Due to this factor, the effect of firm turnover is positive, and appeared to account for one-third of the productivity growth in Dutch manufacturing between 1980 and 1991. Second, more incumbents in manufacturing succeeded in raising their productivity levels than did their counterparts in the services sector. In fact, more than 60 percent of all Dutch continuing firms in manufacturing realised an increase in productivity, whereas only one out of two incumbents in business services accomplished a rise in productivity. These results suggest that the intensity of competition in business services is less fierce than it is in manufacturing. The role of competition will be further discussed in Section 4.

3.4   Disaggregating Productivity

It could be quite misleading to draw inferences from aggregate data to characterise what has been happening within business services. Aggregate numbers can conceal broad disparities in output and labour productivity performance among various branches of business services. In this regard, Table 8 presents some disaggregated summary statistics on output, employment and labour productivity growth, including those of incumbents.

Some results are striking. First, at a lower level of aggregation, the results are diverse. Huge variations in output and employment growth exist among the industries between 1987 and 1995. Production in "accountancy" grew by approximately 5 percent yearly. However, growth in "economic agencies" was twice as much as realised in "accountancy." Even so all industries within business services performed better than the whole economy. Growth rates of labour productivity also differ widely. Labour productivity in "computer services" and "economic consulting agencies" diminished, whereas it slightly improved in most other branches. Additionally, slow labour productivity growth is not typically of all firms or industries within business services. Two branches, news agencies and accountancy, attained productivity growth rates that come close to growth rates of most manufacturing industries in the same period.

Second, labour productivity of continuing firms improved in most of the industries in the period 1987-1995. Again "computer services" and "economic consulting agencies" are exceptions, although they were the most dynamic branches of business services according to the growth rates of output and employment.

Finally, the numbers of "publicity" and "economic consulting agencies" are also striking. The growth rates of aggregate output and those of the continuing firms differ enormously. Total output in both industries grew substantially, whereas incumbents' output contracted noticeably.

Table 8. Output, Employment and Labour Productivity Growth in the Netherlands, 1988-1995

	Total			Incumbents		
	Output	Employ-ment	Labour productivity	Output	Employ-ment	Labour productivity
	Annual percentage changes					
Acc	4½	3½	1	4¾	3½	1¼
Comp	8¾	10½	-1½	4¼	5¼	-1
Eng [a]	5	5	0	½	-1¼	1¾
Publ	6¼	6	½	-5¾	-7½	1¾
Econ	9¼	14½	-4½	-1¾	0	-1¾
News + obs	7¾	6	1¾	4¾	3	1¾
Business services[b]	7	7	0	2½	2½	0

[a] Period 1989-1995.
[b] Including acc, comp, publ, econ, and news+obs.

Let us now turn to the decomposition of the productivity performance within business services. Table 9 presents the contribution of firm turnover to productivity growth according to the second decomposition methodology. Some remarks can be made.

First, in spite of the fact that continuing firms mostly improved their productivity and that their initial productivity level was above the industries' aggregate, their declining market shares counterbalanced this effect. The latter result is a pattern common to most branches within business services. New entrants gained market shares at the expense of the more productive incumbents. As a result the contribution of incumbents to productivity growth is generally modest on a disaggregated level, and absent at an aggregated level. These results suggest that the strong shift of resources between firms have all but enhanced aggregate productivity growth at the industry level, except for "publicity and advertising." In this context the term reallocation is confusing. In fact, what really happened was that growth of total market demand in business services outstripped the considerable output growth of incumbents. In other words, it was not a reallocation of market shares, but rather the fact that entrants picked up the gap in demand.

Table 9. Contribution to Overall Labour Productivity Growth of Incumbents, Entering and Exiting Firms in Business Services, 1988-1995

	Incumbents				Entry	Exit	Total
	total	within effect	reallocation effect	cross-effect			
	(annual percentage change)						
Acc	½	½	0	0	¼	½	1
Comp	-¼	-¼	0	0	-1½	¼	-1½
Eng [a]	½	1	-¼	-¼	-1¼	¾	0
Publ	½	½	¼	-¼	½	-½	½
Econ	-½	-½	-¼	¼	-4½	¼	-4½
News + obs	¼	¾	-¼	-¼	0	1½	1¾
Business services[b]	0	¼	-¼	0	-¼	¼	0

[a] Period 1989-1995.
[b] Including acc, comp, publ, econ, and news+obs.

Second, the contribution of entry to industries' aggregate productivity growth differs according to industry. Firms that entered the market of economic consulting agencies substantially depressed the overall productivity growth. Although many new firms penetrated this branch, their productivity levels were significantly below the average level of the industry.

Finally, the contribution of exiting firms to productivity growth is only negative in publicity and advertising. Exiting firms in this branch originally had a higher than average productivity level. This peculiar result could be caused by mergers and take-overs. However, this could have led to market power by some firms reflected in a rise of the concentration rate. Nevertheless the concentration rates in this branch did not increase (see Figure 3) and the modest contribution of entrants to productivity growth does not confirm this hypothesis.

In summary, firm-level data suggest that the absent of labour productivity growth in business services is due to the performance of incumbents as well as the net effect of turnover. Changes in market shares, relatively low productivity levels of entrants and a lack of productivity improvements by too many incumbents are important factors that held back labour productivity growth in business services. At a disaggregated level, the story is more discriminating. Apparently the overall sluggish labour productivity growth in business services is due to two industries, computer services and economic consulting agencies. Nevertheless although some remarkable differences appear among industries, common facts seem to hinder labour productivity growth within business services to boost.

4. SLUGGISH PRODUCTIVITY GROWTH: SOME CONJECTURES

4.1 Explanations Productivity Slowdown: Notions versus Facts

This section analyses the results of the previous section in more detail by looking separately at the performance of incumbents, and entrants and exiting firms. At this stage of research the main aim is to exploit the firm-level data. The paper therefore is primarily descriptive and its findings should be viewed as exploratory. Some conjectures and interesting facts pop up that could contribute to an explanation of the poor productivity performance in Dutch business services. Before doing this, notions of the productivity slowdown from literature are confronted with the available facts in business services in the Netherlands so far.

Both this study and the recent growth accounting analysis by van der Wiel (1998) have shown that if a labour productivity problem exists, it is not endemic to the whole market services or to every firm in business services. But is there really a problem? Roughly speaking the literature has put forward four notions to explain the lower productivity growth rates in market services compared to that in manufacturing industry (see, for example, Maclean, 1997):

1. Measurement problems
2. Lack of economies of scale and capital deepening
3. Management and lack of labour skills
4. Lack of competition

Measurement problems

Measurement problems with regard to output and quality changes probably result in an underestimation of service sector output since traditional price measurements partly fail to capture improvements in the quality of services and the effect of new services. As a result labour productivity growth in services could be underestimated. However, some facts and trends in the Netherlands indicate that measurement problems in business services could be less severe than in other service industries.

First, the value of output in business services is apparently less understated than the value of output in many other services for which surveys are lacking. The value of output in business services is measured by CBS firm-level. Second, quality improvements or innovations may be mistreated as pure price increases, thus creating a downward bias in real output and labour productivity. An indication for price measurement errors could be a complete divergence between productivity growth and profitability trends. As will be seen later on, this divergence did not occur. The profitability of firms with worsening productivity declined considerably in the period 1987-1995, whereas the wage rate slightly improved.

There is another reason why it is hard to believe that nowadays measurement errors more severely affect productivity growth in Dutch business services than they did previously when there was no census of production at all. A measurement explanation of the productivity slowdown in services requires mismeasurement to get worse over time, which has not yet been proven. In addition, how can these errors explain the lagging productivity growth in Dutch business services compared to those in the United Kingdom or Germany? Are measurement errors in the Netherlands worse than those in other developed countries?

An issue that I neglect out of necessity is the role of within industry price dispersion and product differentiation. In this paper, 3-digit CBS gross output deflators are used to deflate current output values into real values of output. Micro-level prices or (quality adjusted) quantities are lacking in the data set. Under perfect competition it is legitimate to deflate each firm's output with one price because the price per output should be the same across firms. However, if product differentiation exists or competition is non-perfect, prices may differ between firms. In that case productivity measures are biased, and therefore the contribution of incumbents entering and exiting firms to productivity could be mismeasured.

Lack of economies of scale and capital deepening

The potential for productivity improvements in services by economies of scale and capital deepening is limited. Services generally have less scope for reaping economies of scale than manufacturing industry has. Manufacturing features a higher capital intensity than most service industries.

Business services are being dominated by small-sized firms. This suggests that no increasing returns to scale are at stake. Apparently new firms in business services can remain small without being confronted with substantial cost disadvantage. On the other hand, recent developments of (new) information technology should have eased standardisation of procedures in those branches that extensively use computers. A tendency to scale up exists, in particular, in accountancy. Regarding to global players in this branch, competition forces them to increase in scale by mergers or take-overs.

In this regard Table 10 shows the breakdown of some branches by firm size. In 1995 the labour productivity level of large firms was considerably higher than that of small firms in most branches, except in "economic consulting agencies." On the other hand the differentials in productivity levels between medium and large firms are mostly modest and in favour of medium firms. These observations suggest that economies of scale are not very important beyond a certain scale. Simple regression analysis does not reject this hypothesis. The elasticity between firm size and labour productivity is very small, but positive and significant.

Table 10. Labour Productivity by Firm Size in Dutch Business Services[a], 1995

	Small	Medium
	productivity large firms = 100	
Acc	54	94
Comp	52	100
Publ	42	106
Econ	118	133
News + obs	53	59

[a] Large firms have more than 100 employees; small firms are firms with less than 20 employees and medium firms are firms with 20 to 100 employees. Labour productivity is measured as output per full-time equivalent.

Capital deepening is another way to increase productivity. New machines like computers provide the opportunity to raise output per employee. Unfortunately capital stocks are difficult to construct with the available data set, given the absence of direct measures and the time series of investments required. At this stage of research. I use two crude measures to construct capital stocks for survivors at an aggregated level. First, the capital stock of an industry is based on the total value of depreciation. Assuming a mean life of capital of twenty years, the capital stock of incumbents is simply the value of depreciation times twenty. Additionally, the second estimate for the capital stock is derived by applying the perpetual inventory method by using investment series and an initial capital stock based on the value of depreciation in a base year.

Both crude measures of capital stocks suggest that productivity improvement by capital deepening in business services is missing. The capital stock hardly increased over time. Remarkably, incumbents' nominal investments as percentage of total nominal output declined over time. Even if computers are properly deflated, since prices of computers dropped dramatically the last decades, the share of total investments in real terms has worsened. As will be shown later on entrants show the same investment tendency. Both results are remarkable given the fact that output of business services is booming.

Management and lack of labour skills

A radically different view on sluggish productivity growth in services explains it from management and its organisation of functions and tasks. Several studies stressed the possibility of an inadequate management and deficient organisation of tasks. Recently Biema and Greenwald (1997) pointed to the amazing results attainable if senior executives would pay more attention to how work is actually done. Leading edge service companies in the United Sates attained performance levels that outstripped those of their competitors and, moreover, they realised magnificent progress. Additionally, McKinsey-studies have revealed that the major share of productivity differentials between identical firms can be attributed to the way functions and tasks are organised. Rough indicators such as (material) input as a percentage of output suggest that inefficient (*i.e.* the inputs are relatively high) existing firms do not succeed in improving their productivity level.

Scrutinising the role of labour quality like managerial ability is problematic because data on labour quality are not directly available in the micro data set. According to the results there seems to be a link between wages and productivity. A firm that pays higher wages than average is also more productive than average. The link between wages and productivity will be discussed further below.

Lack of competition

To what extent are the lower productivity growth rates in business services due to a lack of competition? Competition reallocates production and profits from inefficient to efficient firms. Therefore lower rates of productivity growth in services might reflect a lack of competition. The lack of competition could be due to a higher level of regulation and/or to less exposure to international competitors.

This section analyses several indicators, including market concentration rates, standard deviation of productivity levels, entry and exit rates, entry barriers, and profit margins, that could have an impact on productivity or could give an impression of the competitive pressure in business services.

The *market concentration rate*, defined as the gross output of the ten largest firms related to the overall output, is an indicator for measuring the intensity of the competitive process. A rise in market concentration rates could point to less competition. A higher concentration rate can be supposed to result in more monopoly power and higher price-cost margins, because dominant positions of firms on a market yield higher mark-ups.

According to Figure 3, the concentration rate is relatively stable among branches over time. It increased only in computer services. The stable pattern suggests that the effect of mergers and take-overs on the productivity level is negligible, or that the effect on the concentration rates was counterbalanced by high entry rates. The degree of concentration is below 30 percent in most parts of the business services. Broadly speaking, a dichotomy in concentration rates occurs. On the one hand concentration rates are high in accountancy, computer services and news agencies. On the other hand concentration rates are low in the remaining branches. The degree of concentration is remarkably lower than what is found in most industries within Dutch manufacturing.

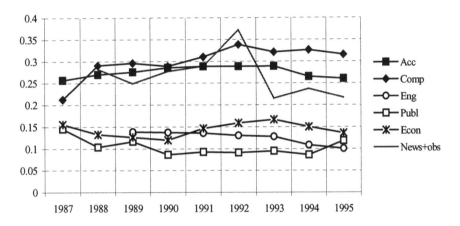

Figure 3. Concentration Rates in Dutch Business Services, 1987-1995

However, there are problems with using concentration rates as a measure of competition. First, if entrants in business services operate in a niche, they do not compete directly against incumbents. In that case the market concentration rate based on a rather broadly defined industry classification, is not a suitable indicator of the pressure that new firms can generate on incumbents. Over the years, the business services market may have become more segmented. Entrants probably pursue a strategy of seeking new segments and products, whereas incumbents stick to the regular customers. Second, the business services market may not yet be in equilibrium. New firms, either viable or incompetent, are attracted to the market. Then a relation between a price-cost margin and concentration rate will only be apparent in the long-run. In fact, as noted by Boone (1999), a rise in competition may well increase the market share and profits of the most efficient firms in the market. In other words a rise in concentration rates may incur a reduction in competition (an increase in barriers to entry) or an increase in competition (a switch from Cournot competition to Bertrand competition).

Table 11. Standard Deviation, Productivity, and Entry/Exit Rates

	acc	comp	eng	publ	Econ	news+ obs
1995						
Standard deviation productivity level[a]	1.05	1.13	0.88	1.29	1.09	1.14
1988-1995		Total percentage change				
Productivity growth	8	-11	0	4	-30	15
Standard deviation productivity level	7	-16	2	-16	-6	0
Net entry/exit rates[b]	%					
Unweighted	44	39	47	112	253	77
Weighted	38	133	59	75	155	100

[a] Productivity is in logs, assuming that the distribution of this variable is approximately lognormal.
[b] Net entry/exit rates are defined as (weighted) entry minus (weighted) exit divided by the (weighted) geometric mean of total firms in 1987 and 1995.

Another rough competition indicator is the *standard deviation of the log of productivity*. In general productivity differences between firms will be smaller in markets with stronger competition. Due to learning effects and market selection over time The indicator lies between 0.88 and 1.29. The dispersion in productivity is relatively high in "publicity" and is relatively low in "engineering." Hence we ask whether competition is in the latter tougher than in the former? To give a straightforward answer is not easy. Extensive competitive pressure makes firms exposed to each others' action. Inefficiencies cannot be tolerated and firms must compete or exit. Based on both measures, *i.e.* market concentration rate and standard deviation, competition in engineering seems to be tougher than in other industries. These results cannot be compared with other Dutch industries. Furthermore, a comparison between industries is limited due to the fact that industries differ in other ways which could account for the differences in productivity.

With regard to the *net entry rates*, there is again wide variation by industries. Net entry rates in "economic consultancy" are much higher than in other services industries. Nevertheless net entry rates in Dutch business services are relatively high compared to those in other sectors of the Dutch economy. The high entry and exit rates in business services therefore point to low entry barriers and suggest a high degree of competition. Yet these high turnover rates have not raised labour productivity growth rates.

Relatively high net entry rates by industry generally coincide with reductions in the productivity distribution over time. Probably differences in productivity have declined over time due to the entry and exit of firms. However, a clearly positive relation between entry rates and productivity growth seems to be lacking.

Table 12. Investments, Price-cost Margin and Sales Costs of Incumbents, Entrants and Exits[a]

	Investments rate		Sales costs[b]		Price-cost margin[c]	
	1987	1995	1987	1994	1987	1995
			% of gross output			
Acc						
Incumbents	3½	2¼	10	9	31	35
Entrants	3¾	2	13	10	21	29
Exits	3¾	4¼	10	10	37	42
Comp						
Incumbent	4½	3½	11	10	34	35
Entrant	12¾	4¾	14	13	30	35
Exits	1½	2	12	10	25	30
Publ						
Incumbent	1¼	2	6	6	12	27
Entrant	36¼	2¾	10	7	.	26
Exits	1¼	1	6	6	13	18
Eco						
Incumbent	2¾	2¾	16	17	27	35
Entrant	4¾	2¼	22	19	36	27
Exits	6¼	6¾	12	15	15	24

[a] 1994.
[b] Sales costs include *e.g.* advertising and expenses of office. No figures available for 1995.
[c] Price-cost margins are defined as the value of output minus input and labour costs divided by the value of gross output.

Theoretical models of industry dynamics emphasise the importance of sunk costs as *entry/exit barriers* (see Section 3). Moreover, low entry costs such as investments and advertising may promote entry and exert pressure on inefficient firms to exit, thus speeding up the reallocation of resources from inefficient to more efficient firms.

The extent of the investment levels and sales costs does not point to entry barriers in business services. To start a firm in business services does not initially require much capital. A personal computer, a telephone and a room or small office might suffice. Table 12 shows that, in most branches, entrants invest relatively more when they start their operations than do incumbents. In the course of time entrants' investments activities fall back to normal levels in succeeding years.

New firms incur additional costs in the form of advertising campaigns to make their product known announced and price cuts in order to achieve sufficient market shares. However, except for "economic consulting agencies" (the industry which has the highest entry/exit rates) the differences in sales costs between continuing, exiting and entering firms are remarkably small (see Table 12). Therefore sales costs are probably not a severe barrier to entering firms.

The final competition indicator considered here is the *price-cost margin*. Monopoly power is reflected in higher price-cost margins because dominant positions of firms on a market yield higher mark-ups. A more transparent market offers clients the opportunity to buy products at a low price. Price-cost margins tend to rise in most industries over time in spite of the increasing number of firms. Based on this indicator competition pressure in business services seems to be mild.

In a nutshell the extent of market competition in business services seems to be still insufficient to boost productivity in business services. Although high entry rates and low entry barriers suggest tough competition, other indicators suggest the opposite.

4.2   Productivity Performance of Continuing Firms

Section 3 concluded that between 1987 and 1995 incumbents' productivity on average hardly increased mainly because of a decline in productivity in "computer services" and "economic consulting agencies." Compared to Dutch manufacturing fewer continuing firms could enhance their productivity levels in business services.

I will therefore now focus on the performance of the four types of continuing firms in more detail. Several questions will be addressed. What drives some survivors more productive than other survivors? Did productive firms tend to move ahead or did weak firms catch up? Why is there such a huge variety in growth rates between the four types of survivors? I will argue that it is difficult to draw conclusions due to the wide variety in productivity and heterogeneity within and between those four groups of incumbents. However, some similarities can be observed across industries.

Successful incumbents showed yearly productivity growth rates of 3-5 percent, while unsuccessful incumbents' productivity fell by 3-5 percent per year. Regression analysis suggests that productivity growth is fastest in initially low productive firms. This so-called "regression to the mean" is significant in all industries within business services. Therefore differences in productivity between firms at any moment in time seem to be due to transitory factors. Yesterday's losers could be today's winners. In 16 out of 24 cases (*i.e.* six industries and four different types of firms) the dispersion of log productivity slightly decreased over time.

Other indicators hint at a finely tuned story. Productivity differences might be more permanent than originally thought. According to the ranking of most productive firms per industry, today's champions are in many cases the same as yesterday's. Many survivors, who were at the top twenty ranking of best practices in 1987, were still well-ranked almost ten years later. Moreover, the correlation coefficients between firms' productivity in the last year and first year of the sample are less than 1 in most industries, but they are still considerable high.

Table 13 presents several variables that could help in finding causes for productivity performance differences among the four groups of incumbents. It illustrates that some similarities in ranking or general trends can be observed among the four groups. Similarities in ranking emerge for labour productivity, in the extent of capital intensity, and as a consequence, in the extent of total factor productivity (TFP). The TFP level is a residual which is measured as the difference in the level of output and the weighted input-levels. The TFP level reflects, for instance, the effective use of inputs. Firms classified as successful down-sizers or unsuccessful down-sizers are relatively more capital intensive than the other two groups. The differences in capital intensity among the four groups are great, even wider than the variety in labour productivity.[6]

The TFP levels were the highest in successful up-sizers and the lowest in unsuccessful down-sizers in all industries. The TFP-levels suggest that the latter are inefficient firms. They persistently use more inputs per unit of output.

Finally, unsuccessful firms have initially higher productivity levels than successful down-sizers. These findings correspond to those of Bartelsman *et al.* (1995). There appear to be opportunities for successful down-sizers to catch up. However, this offers no explanation for the decline in productivity by unsuccessful down-sizers.

Besides similarities in absolute levels there are also common trends among the four groups of incumbents. First, the labour productivity growth rates of each group are of comparable magnitude within the selected industries. Second, a positive relation between labour productivity growth (levels) and wage growth rates (levels) can be distinguished. Firms that significantly increased labour productivity also had a high wage growth rate. Similarly, firms with high (low) productivity levels have on average high (low) wage levels as well. For example, successful down-sizers in publicity had the lowest productivity ranking as well as the lowest wage level ranking. But this type of firm attained the strongest growth rates in labour

---

[6]   Differences in capital intensity between the four groups are presumably not due to variations in firm size, because the difference in allocation of firm size is negligible.

productivity and in wage rate. Regression analysis does not reject these findings.

Table 13. Some Main Indicators for Incumbents

	Acc	comp	publ	eco
Number of firms (in %)				
Successful up-sizers	39	23	31	9
Successful down-sizers	21	19	17	28
Unsuccessful down-sizers	6	23	44	25
Unsuccessful up-sizers	34	36	8	38
Capital intensity: level/growth				
Successful up-sizers	4/neg	3/neg	3/neg	3/neg
Successful down-sizers	1/pos	2/pos	2/pos	2/pos
Unsuccessful down-sizers	2/pos	1/pos	1/pos	1/pos
Unsuccessful up-sizers	3/neg	4/neg	4/neg	4/neg
TFP: level/growth				
Successful up-sizers	1/pos	1/pos	1/pos	1/pos
Successful down-sizers	2/pos	2/neg	3/neg	2/pos
Unsuccessful down-sizers	4/neg	4/neg	4/neg	4/neg
Unsuccessful up-sizers	2/pos	3/neg	2/neg	2/pos
Productivity growth/wage growth				
Successful up-sizers	+ / + +	+ / + +	+ + / +	+ + / + + +
Successful down-sizers	+ + / + +	+ + / + +	+ + + / + + + +	+ + + / + + +
Unsuccessful down-sizers	- / +	- - / +	- - / + +	- - / =
Unsuccessful up-sizers	- / +	- - - / -	- - / +	- / + +
Ranking productivity level/ wage level [b]				
Successful up-sizers	2 / 2	2 / 1	1 / 2	2 / 3
Successful down-sizers	2 / 4	4 / 2	4 / 4	4 / 2
Unsuccessful down-sizers	2 / 2	2 / 4	2 / 1	1 / 1
Unsuccessful up-sizers	1 / 1	1 / 2	3 / 3	3 / 2

[a] Growth rates: = 0% ; + < 2½%; 2½ %< + + < 5%; 5% < + + + < 10 %, + + + + > 10% (vice versa negative growth rates/negative signs)
[b] Ranking according to 1987; 1= highest level, 4= lowest level.

The latter finding is also found by Baily *et al.* (1996). A first interpretation of this relation between wages and productivity is that some of the wage changes observed are determined by changes in labour quality, where wage differentials are assumed to reflect productivity differentials. However, many factors other than labour productivity affect wages. Another interpretation of this relation refers to rent sharing. Workers might benefit from increases in productivity if part of that increase benefits them. The third and final interpretation refers to capital/labour substitution. High wage pressure could fortify the incentives of firms to invest in new and relatively cheaper capital. Thus wage pressure can intensify capital deepening and, consequently, productivity growth. It is therefore striking that developments in capital intensity in business services suggest an opposite trend. All successful up-sizers became less capital-intensive over time while wages grew relatively rapidly among this group. Conversely, unsuccessful down-sizers became more capital-intensive despite their lower wage increases.[7] Strikingly, successful down-sizers adopted a different strategy as they intensified their capital-labour ratio.

Further common trends found in Table 13 include the developments of TFP by successful up-sizers and unsuccessful down-sizers. The first group increases its leading position whereas the latter lost ground.

Finally, the developments in profits are the same for each group across the selected industries. Profits of successful up-sizers increased in the period 1987-1995 whereas profits of unsuccessful firms declined. Although developments in output and employment were the same for successful up-sizers and unsuccessful down-sizers, *i.e.* both output and employment increased, developments in profits were the opposite. The discrepancy could be explained by assuming that unsuccessful up-sizers are becoming inflexible firms in utilising their fixed inputs. These firms are reluctant to change their organisation and management while their environment is rapidly changing. As the firms were successful in the past, *i.e.* they had relatively high productivity levels, they have a tendency to become rigid leading to a decline in profitability (see for example Baaij, 1996).

Despite the similarities between groups of firms, no clear-cut explanations for the relatively high percentage of unsuccessful continuing firms in Dutch business services are available at the moment. What (other) factors could determine the relatively skewed distribution of firms in business services? In this regard, as already noted at the top of this section, a plausible explanation seems to be that firms in business services are subject to less competitive pressure than are firms in manufacturing. Hitherto unsuccessful firms in business services could easily maintain their positions in a booming market by making supernormal profits because unimpeded competition in services is probably lacking or has become eminent only in recent years. In this context it must be noted that the profitability of unsuccessful firms deteriorated through the years (see Table 13). So the prospects for these firms are insecure in the longer run if competition becomes more fierce.

Labour productivity growth in Dutch business services could also be hampered due to a light labour market. In business services labour demand exceeds labour supply whereas in most manufacturing industries it is the other way round. Based on the developments of the average wage level, in some indistinct way, some firms are more hampered than other firms.

---

[7] However, in contrast, CPB-research suggests that wage moderation can have a significant role in boosting employment as well as productivity (see e.g. Bartelsman, 1997).

Unsuccessful up-sizers probably attracted more inexperienced or lower qualified workers for their new jobs than did successful up-sizers, leading to negative productivity growth between 1987 and 1995. However, these former firms could also have been aimed at a long term strategy in which new workers receive their training on-the-job.

While productivity growth was modest in most industries within business services, it was actually negative for *economic consultancy agency* and for *computer services*. The productivity decline of incumbents in both industries is especially due to the high share of unsuccessful firms, in particular up-sizers, and their relatively low productivity level. Almost 65 percent of the continuing firms within economic consultancy agencies failed to increase their productivity level.

Both unsuccessful industries have at least, one thing in common. The growth rates in aggregate output were the highest among business services' industries. The output growth of the continuing firms, however, was considerably lower than that of the overall output growth, and was actually negative in economic consulting agencies. These remarkable differences suggest that the products supplied by these types of continuing firms are in their mature phase of the product-life-cycle. Demand substitutes towards new products (*e.g.* one-stop-shopping service concept). Moreover, customers have become more discerning in selecting their suppliers and do not automatically return to the firm from which they previously bought their services.

4.3   Productivity Performance of Entering and Exiting Firms

Obviously one of the most salient features of business services is the high rate of entry and exit. However, hitherto entry and exit have not raised productivity growth in the short-term because the average productivity level of entrants was lower than that of exiting firms in most of the branches. This contrasts with the findings of Bartelsman *et al.* (1995) for the Dutch manufacturing industry. Using Israeli (manufacturing) data, Griliches and Regev (1992) also found that entering firms typically have higher productivity levels than exiting firms.

Apparently this observation suggests that productivity in business services is a rather minor factor affecting the likelihood of survival. Success and failure seem to depend on factors other than labour productivity. In the period considered booming demand attracted many new firms. It is likely that these new firms filled the gap in demand because incumbents did not extend their activities beyond some scale. The poor overall performance of entrants could be due to a lack of experience or to the fact that new firms which will fail in the future, are still active. It is also possible that these new entrants do not compete directly with incumbents because they operate in a niche.

This section looks in more detail at the productivity performance of entrants vis-à-vis that of exiting firms and incumbents. How many entrants have survived and why? Do they catch-up? Conversely, why do firms have to exit and after how many years?

Low survival of entrants in business services

The lifetime of new firms in business services as a whole is shown in Table 14. In general some 15 to 25 percent of these entrants had already disappeared by the end of their first year. After five years not more than 25 to 40 percent were still in operation. Table 14 also provides information about the average length of life of exiting firms. The mean lifespan is rather low especially in economic consulting agencies. According to EIM (1997), the mean lifespan of exiting firms in other Dutch services industries, which are relatively young industries as well, are significantly higher.

These cohort data suggest that entry in business services is easy, but that survival is not. According to Geroski (1991) there are at least two characterisations of this entry process. First, entrants are essentially "hit-and-run starters." High profitability, growing demand, low entry barriers and new niches in the market attract new firms. However, the opportunities represented by these factors can change or cease to exist very easily in the short run.

Second, this entry process is primarily a selection process not unlike the evolution of animals, namely survival of the fittest. Entry is a type of passive learning. Jovanic (1982) constructed a dynamic model in which heterogeneous producers continually learn about their relative costs through market participation. New firms are relatively small, heterogeneous and less cost-efficient on average than incumbents. As these new firms acquire experience, they eventually choose to expand and to improve productivity or they are forced to exit.

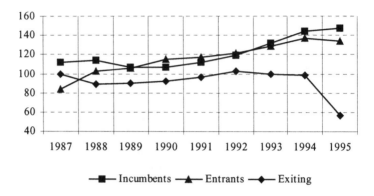

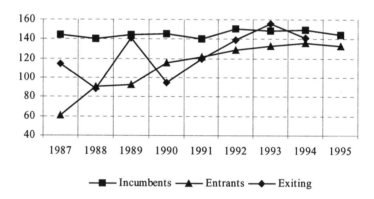

Figure 4. Labour Productivity Levels of Incumbents, Entering and Exiting Firms, 1987-1995

Table 14. Lifetime of Entering Firms and Average Mean Life of Exiting Firms[a]

	year 1	year 2	year3	Year 4	year 5	Year 6
Cohort	%					
1987	84	67	60	52	42	36
1988	74	65	56	42	34	20
1989	84	70	52	41	25	22
1990	82	60	46	28	24	
	acc	Comp	Eng	publ	econ	News+obs
Average mean life of exiting firms	8	5	8	6	4	5

[a] Average mean life of exiting firms is based on cohort data from 1993-1995.

Productivity levels of entrants: a rapid temporary catch up[8]

Labour productivity level of new firms at their "time of birth" is notably lower than that of incumbents (see Figure 4). However, the differentials in productivity level between the branches are large. For example, the productivity gap between incumbents and entrants in economic consulting agencies is more than 50 percent. The gap in accountancy, however, was approximately no more than 25 per cent.

The low labour productivity level of entrants may be due to their inexperience. Small firms have a lower productivity level than medium and large firms have (see Table 8). As new firms mature their productivity level rises rapidly. In some branches productivity level of new firms became comparable to that of incumbents within approximately five years.[9]

This pattern suggests that learning-by-doing effects are present and are probably essential in order for a firm to survive the selection process. In this regard the catch-up process in business services appears to be remarkably quick compared to findings in manufacturing. New firms in the Canadian manufacturing industry, for instance, attained a comparable level after roughly ten years, post-entry (see Baldwin, 1995).

After 1992 the productivity gap in some of the branches widened between entering and continuing firms. One tentative hypothesis is that, relative to incumbents, entering firms are more cyclical in output and labour productivity because entering firms cannot easily adjust the number of employees. Therefore, labour productivity growth of entering firms will lag behind that of incumbents during an economic downswing. On average

[8] These results are based on the cohort 1987. Entering firms are those firms that started in 1987, exiting firms are those firms that actually vanished in 1995. Finally, incumbents are those firms that already existed in 1987 and are still active after 1995.
[9] However, the profitability of new firms does not catch-up that quickly.

entrants are smaller and probably face less overhead (low-skilled) personnel, which renders them less flexible in adjusting the number of employees. When output levels fall incumbents find it easier to lay off relatively low-skilled workers that are not needed for current production, while entrants cannot fire themselves or their single employee. An indication of this difference in employment structure is the persistent lower average wage level of incumbents.[10] In addition, incumbents probably notice a more sustained demand because they have more regular customers and produce more (noncyclical) product varieties.

Why do firms exit?

The general notion is that poorly performing firms are the ones who fail and exit. If productivity levels are the benchmark, the overall result confirms this notion. In all branches except in publicity, productivity of exiting firms lagged behind that of continuing firms.

Figure 4 also supports this view. The cohort 1987 is followed over time. The productivity level of exiting firms is generally below that of incumbents. Note that around 1992 the productivity level of the exiting firms (in accountancy) deteriorated and the "shadow-of-death" effect emerges (see Griliches and Regev, 1992). The shadow-of-death effect implies that these firms are in a downward spiral, and they might well get worse if they hang around any longer. What is the driving force behind this breakdown ending in a (compulsory?) exit? Is it a lack of profits or expectations or does it come down to wrong expectations about future market conditions. Or is it something else entirely? At this stage of research, I can only point towards some trends and put forward some conjectures.

First and foremost neither the profitability level nor the price-cost margins of the exiting firms appear to explain the decision to exit.[11] Both financial indicators were not noticeably lagging behind that of incumbents or did not deteriorate dramatically. These findings coincide with Geroski (1998) who states that profitability is not a very useful summary measure of corporate performance.[12]

Second, the phase of the market probably contributed to the breakdown and ultimately the exodus of these firms. Most exiting firms were hit by contracting demand around 1992. This decline coincided with a cyclical

[10] Alternatively, the higher wage level of entering firms could point to a fierce labour market competition. Entering firms may have to pay a mark-up to attract employees.

[11] The profitability level is based on the profits before tax as a percentage of total sales. There are no considerable differences in profits among continuing, entering and exiting firms of the cohort 1987 over time.

[12] According to Geroski, profitability is statistically incongruent with many other performance measures.

downturn in the economy. The breakdown probably occurred because recessions can have highly selective effects on a firm's performance. Yet it is amazing that the average wage level of exiting firms hardly increased between 1987 and 1995. What does this mean? Did high-skilled employees leave these firms?

Finally, the quality of services (*e.g.* advice) may be insufficient to survive in a changing environment. Because preferences of customers change rapidly, *i.e.* requiring more specific and differentiated services, firms have to decide which customers they want to serve. Perhaps, after all, exiting firms realised that they could not provide these new products. By way of illustration, traditionally sales of accountancy came from auditing. Meanwhile growth in auditing has been slipping, whereas growth in management advice (*e.g.* IT advice, change management and re-engineering) has been soaring. Consequently firms in accountancy should in some way transform their organisation, tasks and product variety to be confident of maintaining their activities.

I conclude this section by summarising the main findings of possible causes for the sluggish productivity growth. Entry in business services looks easy. More than 75 percent of all firms active in 1995 did not exist in 1987. However, less than 30 percent of all entrants in 1987 kept their businesses going for more than eight years. Some of them noticeably raised labour productivity within a short period. Exiting firms, on the other hand, with initially medium productivity levels, were confronted within a short period with a remarkable decline in output and in productivity. These patterns suggest that demand opportunities are changing rapidly. In addition the findings on incumbents suggest that a lack of or insufficient competitive pressure, including insufficient managerial effort, and a shift in demand towards new products are possible causes for the poor productivity performance of incumbents in business services. Again, these hypotheses need further research before conclusions can be drawn.

5. CONCLUSIONS AND PLANS FOR ADDITIONAL RESEARCH

Using internationally unique firm-level data of the Dutch business services for the period 1987 to 1995, this paper documents the link between productivity performance and firm turnover in order to shed some light on the poor productivity performance of the services industries. These micro level data are primarily exploited to examine the relationship between microeconomic productivity dynamics and aggregate productivity growth in business services, which has grown into one of the most important industries of the Dutch economy. Special attention is given to the contribution of entrants and exits to productivity growth. This paper also contains a first attempt to determine the factors underlying the sluggish productivity growth.

The main findings of this paper are summarised as follows. First, productivity growth rates of business services were apparently sluggish in the period 1987-1995. Thus firm-level data of the business services confirm the overall picture of a poor productivity performance of Dutch market services. Moreover incumbents' average productivity hardly changed over time. Nonetheless some incumbents considerably enhanced their productivity in the period investigated. It proves that not all firms in business services face a productivity problem.

Second, tremendous within-industry heterogeneity exists in business services. The extent of productivity dispersion across firms within business services is very wide in any year. Some firms are substantially more productive than other firms. In addition large differentials occur in the rates of productivity growth among firms within the same industry. Successful up-sizers and successful down-sizers in business services expanded their labour productivity by 3-5 percent annually. By contrast, labour productivity of unsuccessful firms diminished by 3-4 percent per year. This wide diversity among firms is also noticeable in variables like profits, costs and capital-labour intensities. The sources of this heterogeneity and diversity, however, are less evident.

Third, entering firms are less productive than incumbents. During the period 1987-1995 many entrants penetrated the market, while their productivity levels were initially low. Consequently the high entry rates have hampered productivity growth so far. The weak performance of entrants is probably due to inexperience or to the fact that firms that will fail in future are still active. When entrants do survive, their productivity level is raised within approximately five years to a level comparable to that of incumbents.

Exiting firms are on average equally as productive as entrants and therefore less productive than incumbents. However, exiting firms are initially quite productive compared to entrants in some industries. A factor that could explain the exit of these firms is probably a lack of sufficient demands, combined with quality of services (*e.g.* advice). As the preferences of customers were changing rapidly some firms were not able to provide the expanded range of expertise required.

Entry in business services looks easy. More than 75 percent of all firms active in 1995 did not exist in 1987. However, only a fraction of all entrants in 1987 kept their businesses going after more than eight years. The high entry and exit rates in business services suggest that the role of firm turnover is very important in this industry. Booming demand and relatively low entry barriers have persuaded many new entrepreneurs to start up a firm of their own. It could be that these entrepreneurs filled the gap in demand because incumbents did not extend their firm beyond some scale. On the other hand it is also possible that new entrants do not compete directly with incumbents because they operate in a niche. If profits are abundant in both situations, then productivity improvements are not necessary in the short-term, especially, if competition is not fierce. However, it can be expected that in the longer run, if competition becomes more fierce and demand grows at a moderate pace, more firms will be forced to enhance efficiency or will be forced to exit.

Finally, this study confirms findings of other recent micro-level studies that there is a tremendous reallocation of across firms, especially in services. However, the huge reallocation in Dutch business services has hampered aggregate productivity growth so far. The latter result contrasts with the findings for Dutch manufacturing, in which firm turnover appeared to account for one-third of the productivity growth.

The purpose of this paper has been mainly descriptive. In some ways it is still in preliminary form. Much work remains to be done on evaluating the results. Further research is clearly needed to examine the determinants of dynamics and the causes of the poor productivity growth. There are many open issues that deserve further attention. The open issues to be addressed include the following: what is the impact of competition, and entry rates on the growth rate of labour productivity in business services? Why do firms leave the market? What exact role did the business cycle play? Why do firms try to penetrate the market of business services, as the chances of survival are so meagre – not to mention the chances of success?

A LIST OF BRANCHES OF INDUSTRY IN BUSINESS SERVICES

This paper uses a sample of the Dutch business services for the period 1987-1995. This sample is based on a yearly survey by Statistics Netherlands (CBS) that is held among enterprises with their main activity in business services (SBI 84). At the outset neither legal service (84.1) nor securities (SBI 84.96) were included in this survey. A full list of the branches included in business services compared to our sample is presented in Table A. Although temporary employment agencies are present in the survey, this branch has been left aside.

Recently a new and quite different Standard Industrial Classification called SBI 1993 (in Dutch: Standaard BedrijfsIndeling) was introduced, and this one replaced the SBI 1974. Starting at the statistical year 1993 all industrial statistics, including the Census of Production, have been produced on the new basis. As a result, some branches, *e.g.* press and news agencies, are no longer classified in the SBI 1993 as a branch of industry within the business services. On the other hand, some branches were added as new types of business services. In this paper, I still employ the SBI 1974 classification. Although the consequences of the new industrial classification for the business service are limited, to create a consistent sample of firms some firms had to be reclassified. However, this could easily be done, due to the fact that each firm has a unique firm classification code.

Table A. Branches of Industry in Business Services According to SBI 1974[a]

	Branch	Sub-branch	SBI 93	Sample
84.1	Legal services			No
	84.11	Lawyers offices		
	84.12	Legal advice agencies		
	84.13	Notary's offices		
	84.14	Sheriffs' offices (?)		
	84.15	Patent offices		
84.2	Auditors, accountancy, and tax-experts.			Yes
	84.21	Auditor offices		
	84.22	Accountancy		
	84.23	Tax-consultancy		
84.3	Computer services		72	Yes
84.4	Engineers, architects and other technical designing and consulting agencies			after 1988
	84.41	Engineer services		
	84.42	Architects		
	84.43	Designing and consulting agencies		
	84.44	Expertise- and appraisal offices	672/703	
	84.49	other technical designing n.e.c.		
84.5	Publicity & Advertising			yes
84.6	Economic consulting agencies			yes
84.7	Press- and news agencies		924	
	84.71	Press- and news agencies		
	84.72	Self-employed journalists		
84.8	Temporary employment agencies			yes
84.9	Other business services			
	84.91	Collecting agencies		yes
	84.92	Translation offices		yes
	84.93	Copy agencies	222	no
	84.94	Phototype	222	no
	84.95	Exhibition and congress		yes
	84.96	Security services		no
	84.97	Auction		yes
	84.99	Other business services n.e.c.	140/911/913	no

[a] Only (sub)branches, which, after the introduction of SBI 1993, no longer belong to the business services do have a SBI 1993 code.

B   MEASUREMENT ISSUES

The productivity growth rates of the sample aggregated by branch do not necessarily have to correspond fully with the growth rates of the National Accounts. In fact the National Accounts use different sources of data on income and expenditure and try to present a consistent overall result for the whole economy.

Table B. Output, Employment and Labour Productivity Growth of Business Services[a], 1988-1995

	Volume gross output		Employment		Labour productivity	
	NA	Production Census	NA	Production Census	NA	Production Census
	annual percentage changes					
Acc	5	4½	2¾	3½	2¼	1
Comp	9¾	8¾	3	10½	6½	-1½
Publ	5¾	6¼	4½	5	1¼	0
Econ	10¼	9¼	5¼	14½	4¾	-4½
News+obs	10	7¾	16	6	-5¼	1¾
Business services[b]	6¾	7	7¾	7	-1	0

[a] Employment in full time equivalents for National Accounts (NA).
[b] Including acc, comp, publ, econ, and news+obs.
Source: National Account: Additional information CBS National Accounts.

According to the National Accounts the scanty labour productivity performance of the business services does not relate to the entire business services. The only branch of the business services to lag behind the average productivity growth was the news agencies and other business services, where productivity contracted by 5 percent. In all other branches productivity grew by 1 percent or more. In particular economic consulting agencies and computer services considerably improved their productivity level. Surprisingly this is completely in contrast with the findings in this paper. However, it is hard to imagine that the growth of employment in news agencies was the highest among business services.

The differences between the results of the National Account and the Census of Production suggest some weaknesses in official statistics. The differences in employment growth are especially remarkable at a lower level of aggregation. Although the National Account and the Census of Production apply different employment concepts, *i.e.* full time equivalents (National Accounts) versus number of people employed (Census of Production), this does not distort the comparison between the two sources on an aggregated level.

REFERENCES

Baaij, M. (1996), *Evolutionary Strategic Management: Firms and Environment, Performance over Time*, Dissertation, Eburon-Nijenrode University Press.

Baldwin, J.R. (1995), *The Dynamics of Industrial Competition; A North American perspective*, Cambridge: Cambridge University Press.

Baily, M.N., E.J. Bartelsman and J. Haltiwanger (1996), *Labour Productivity: Structural change and Cyclical Dynamics*, National Bureau of Economic Research, Working Paper 5503.

Baily, M.N., E.J. Bartelsman and J. Haltiwanger (1995), "Downsizing and Productivity Growth: Myth or Reality," in David G. Mayes (ed.), *Sources of Productivity Growth in the 1980s*, Cambridge: Cambridge University Press.

Bais, J.S., K.L. Bangma and W.H.J. Verhoeven (1997), Creation and Loss of Jobs in the Netherlands, EIM, Zoetermeer.

Bartelsman, E.J., G. van Leeuwen and H.R. Nieuwenhuijsen (1995), "De industrie: banenschepper of banenvernietiger?," *Economische Statistische Berichten*, pp. 504-508.

Bartelsman, E.J. (1997), "Productivity and Specificity in Factor Inputs," in S. Biffignadi (ed.), *Micro and Macrodata of Firms; Statistical Analysis and International Comparison*, Heidelberg: Physica-Verlag.

Biema, M. van and B. Greenwald (1997), "Managing Our Way to Higher Services Sector Productivity," *Harvard Business Review*, July-August.

Boone, J. (1999), *"Measuring Product Market Competition"*, internal mimeo.

CBS (1994), *Zakelijke dienstverlening; Samenvattend overzicht 1992*, Voorburg.

CPB (1998), Recent trends in Dutch Labour Productivity: the Role of Changes in the Composition of Employment, Working Paper No 98, The Hague.

Creusen, H.P.W.A. (1997), An Analytical Framework of Industrial Organisation for Policy Analysis, Research Memorandum no 138, The Hague.

EIM (1997), Het belang van bedrijfstypen voor de werkgelegenheid, Zoetermeer.

Foster, L., J.C. Haltiwanger and C.J. Krizian (1998), *"Aggregate Productivity Growth: Lessons from Microeconomic Evidence,"* NBER Working Paper No. 6803, November.

Geroski, P.A. (1991), *Market Dynamics and Entry*, Oxford: Basil Blackwell.

Geroski, P.A. (1998), "An Applied Econometrician's View of Large Company Performance," *Review of Industrial Organisation* 13, pp. 271-293.

Griliches, Z. and H. Regev (1992), Productivity and firm turnover in Israeli Industry, NBER Working Paper 4059, National Bureau for Economic Research, Cambridge, Mass.

Hopenhayn, H. (1992), "Entry, Exit, and Firm Dynamics in Long-run Equilibrium," *Econometrica* 60, pp. 1127-1150.

Jovanic, B. (1982), "Selection and Evolution of Industry," *Econometrica* 50, pp. 649-670.

Maclean, D. (1997), Lagging Productivity Growth in the Service Sector: Mismeasurement, Mismanagement or Misinformation, Bank of Canada, working paper 97-6.

O'Mahony, M. (1999), Britain's Productivity Performance 1950-1996. An international perspective, National Institute of Economic and Social Research, London.

Wiel, H.P. van der (1998), "Productivity Slowdown in Commercial Services," *CPB-report 1998/1*, pp. 41-44.

Wiel, H.P. van der (1999), "Productivity in Dutch Business Services: the Role of Entry and Exit," *CPB-report 1999/2*, pp. 36-41.

Chapter 8

Productivity and Specificity in Factor Inputs

Eric J. Bartelsman

Economic and Social Institute, Free University of Amsterdam

Key words: Productivity growth, Vintage capital, Wage bargaining, Specificity

Abstract: This paper considers the effect on productivity growth of the wage moderation policy embarked upon in the Netherlands starting in 1982. The paper describes how the effect depends on the macroeconomic importance of the hold-up problem that results from specificity in factor markets. The analysis is based on a vintage model of capital with embodied technology. In a traditional vintage model, a decline in wages relative to cost of capital will delay scrapping and postpone new investment, thus reducing productivity growth in the medium term. In a recent version of the vintage model, where the specific production relationship between capital and labour gives rise to problems associated with appropriability of rents, institutionalised wage moderation will increase new investment and improve productivity. A preliminary analysis of micro-level data of industrial firms does not yet lead one to reject the important role of specificity.

1. INTRODUCTION

This paper provides an empirical evaluation of the macroeconomic importance of specificity in factor markets. The paper compares the model of specificity with a base model by considering the different short- and medium-term effects on productivity growth of wage moderation that took place in the Netherlands after 1982. An analysis is also made of differential behaviour under the two models of a collection of indicators on investment, employment, and capital stocks in individual industrial firms in the Netherlands. In particular, observed behaviour of capital investment at the

227

micro level allows one to distinguish between the two competing hypotheses.

The first model is based on a production structure with technology embodied in vintage capital. In this model, wage moderation leads to a transitional reduction in productivity growth. The mechanism is that reduced wage pressure reduces incentives for firms to invest in new capital, and delays scrapping of old capital, thus allowing a decline in the capital-labour ratio. The second model has a similar vintage production structure, but posits the existence of a rent-appropriation, or hold-up, problem associated with specificity of labour and capital in the production relationship (see Caballero and Hammour, 1998). In this model, wage moderation via consensus acts as a fortuitous institutional advance that reduces the appropriability problem. In the model, reductions in specificity curb opportunism and pull resources into production, thus increasing productivity. In this paper, the empirical distinction between the two models is not based on estimation of a structural model of firm dynamics. Instead analysis of carefully selected indicators provides support for the macro-economic importance of specificity as described by Caballero and Hammour, and points towards a significant role of wage moderation in boosting employment as well as productivity.

Although the paper is primarily concerned with evaluating the relevance of specificity problems in macroeconomics, it does so by considering the effects of wage moderation. A short digression on the institutional setting of wage moderation and on the manner in which wage moderation can be modelled is thus in order. Wage moderation has been credited with the extraordinary growth in hours worked in the Dutch economy since 1983. During the first "Lubbers administration" wage bargaining between social partners was replaced with consensus building over common policy goals. The social partners (confederation of unions and employers organisation) provided qualitative recommendations on specific issues, while sectoral trade unions took into account sector specific conditions that allowed variation within the central guidelines. Wage moderation affects more than 80 percent of workers who were directly covered through collective agreements or through mandatory extension (see CPB, 1997). Following the "Agreement of Wassenaar" of 1982, the common policy goal became employment creation, and the common vehicle wage moderation.

The operational definition of wage moderation to use in a model is intertwined with the type of economic interaction which determines wage setting. The wage itself is an endogenous variable in most economic models. In a neo-classical labour market with perfectly elastic labour supply, wages are determined by workers' reservation wage. Wage moderation could be achieved by lowering workers' outside options, for example through reductions in unemployment benefits. With perfectly inelastic labour supply, wages depend on the state of labour demand and the level of labour supply. A helicopter drop of highly educated workers would lower wages, all else equal. In a model with wage bargaining, wage moderation could denote any action that weakens the position of labour in bargaining, such as helicopter drops of workers, reductions in benefits, posting of employment bonds by workers, reduction in workers' share of negotiable surplus. In order to compare the effects of wage moderation in the two models, we need to find a description of wage moderation that can be applied in both. A reduction in benefits, such as occurred when policy makers decoupled benefit levels from minimum wages is an exogenous event to both models.

The policy debate surrounding wage moderation that took place in Dutch economics journals in the early and mid-1980s is summarised nicely by Bovenberg (1997). According to the arguments, three main channels exist through which lower wages led to employment growth. First, profitability of firms improved, creating the financial room and incentives to invest. Next, the competitive position of firms improved on world markets, raising exports. Finally, production became more labour intensive. While the effects on employment are clear, the effects on total factor productivity (TFP) are not. In a vintage capital model with embodied technology, the first channel leads to more new capital, thus to higher TFP. The second channel is ambiguous because it is not clear which firms raise output to meet export demand. If existing firms with old technology increase utilisation and output or delay scrapping, TFP will be held back. If firms with new capital gain market share, TFP will improve. The third channel lowers labour productivity, and may retard TFP growth if increased demand is met by adding labour to existing capital (with old embodied technology).

The combined effect on productivity (TFP) of wage moderation through the three channels above is ambiguous. The analysis is clouded because two different models underlie the descriptions of employment and capital growth following wage moderation. For example, the first channel only makes sense in a model with a production surplus, where the share going to labour through bargaining decreases with wage moderation.[1] The second channel, the competitive effect, is only operative in an open economy and will depend on the size and time-structure of the export demand elasticity. We will argue that the direction of TFP growth following wage moderation can be used to distinguish between the two stylised models and can test whether specificity plays an important role. We will look at the macro, sectoral, and micro-level implications of wage moderation under the two competing models. We will show why sectoral data cannot be used to

---

[1] This channel could work in a neo-classical setting if we assume that firms are credit constrained, and need cash-flow to invest.

disentangle the effects of wage moderation on productivity. Instead we will assess whether findings from the micro data are consistent with the implications of one of the two hypotheses.

The organisation of the paper is as follows. First, the two models are presented. Next, a macro- and sectoral overview is presented of wage moderation and its implications under the competing hypotheses, followed by implications at the micro level. The empirical section starts with a discussion of the macro- and sectoral evidence, or lack thereof. Finally, summary statistics on investment behaviour and age of the capital stock, and some indicators of TFP and capital growth are shown which are consistent with the model of specificity. A final section concludes and sketches an outline for a structural model that nests the two hypotheses.

2. PRODUCTIVITY AND FACTOR INPUTS: TWO MODELS

What are the determinants of technological change? For both models, the growth rate of available technology is assumed to be exogenous. We further assume that available technology is embodied in capital, and that all investment is in new capital that embodies the best available technology. Once capital is in place, it cannot be shifted costlessly to another use. In other words, a proportion of the investment is sunk. The vintage structure of capital, the embodied nature of technology, and the sunk costs are common to both models. In both models, wage moderation is taken to mean an exogenous increase in effective labour supply elasticity, for example through reductions in unemployment benefits.

First, the model of Caballero and Hammour (1998), hereafter CH, will be introduced. This model highlights the role of specific investments made by capital and labour in order to produce jointly, the effect of the sunkness of these investments on the bargaining which takes place ex-post, and the macroeconomic consequences of decisions made by factor inputs. Next, a more traditional vintage model will be introduced and the differences with the CH model will be noted.

2.1 The CH model: Specificity in input markets

In a production relationship, capital and labour join forces to produce more output than they could generate independently. The production function, with its associated properties of scale and substitution elasticities and diminishing marginal returns has been well described in the literature. More recently, another aspect of joint production has come to the forefront in (macro)economics, namely the temporary nature of the production relationship. Jobs are created and destroyed, firms come and go, capital is put in place and scrapped.[2] Each discrete decision has irreversible elements because investments in the relationship are sunk. Besides obvious reasons why a portion of capital investment may be sunk, for example underground cables, specificity may arise from hiring (and firing) costs, and investment in training. Specificity for labour may arise from search costs and from acquisition of firm-specific knowledge. Net specificity combines the outside options and potential losses from separation, and points to the factor that is subject to appropriation, or opportunism, by the other factor.

The costs incurred in the specific relationship need to be recouped during the lifetime of the joint effort. When the relationship is broken, a remainder is lost. The economic problem is that it is difficult to form ex-ante contracts to cover the division of the flow of rents which are generated to cover the fixed costs. In words of Caballero and Hammour (1998), the "...specific quasi-rents may not be divided *ex post* according to the parties' *ex ante* terms of trade." This problem, known in the literature as the "hold-up" problem occurs when one party to a transaction can appropriate a portion of the quasi-rents associated with the relationship.[3]

In a particular market, the hold-up problem leads to an undercommitment of resources, because the factor is concerned that future quasi-rents may be appropriated by others. An introduction of a new technology which is profitable given factor prices, may not lead to adoption if the benefits cannot be shielded from future opportunism of other contracting parties. Institutional arrangements are thought to evolve in order to compensate for the hold-up problem although they are generally acknowledged not to solve the problem completely.[4] In the empirical section of this paper, we examine whether wage moderation in the Netherlands in the years after 1982 can be seen as an institutional change that reduced the hold-up problem in the eyes of the market participants.

In the model of Caballero and Hammour the hold-up problem plays a central role in the functioning of the macro-economy. In particular, "...a highly inefficient macro "solution" to the unresolved microeconomic contracting problems" results as the problem of deciding on investments and sharing the benefits on an individual level spreads throughout the economy. The basic macro implications are that the market for the appropriating factor is segmented and that the productive structure is sclerotic. In other words, if

---

[2] See Dunne *et al.* (1988), Davis *et al.* (1996), and Caballero *et al.* (1995) for examples of plant dynamics, employment gross flows, and micro capital behaviour.

[3] An overview of the problem as related to labour markets is presented by Malcomson (1997).

[4] See CPB (1997), chapter 2.

workers attempt to get more than what was predicated on their ex-ante terms of trade, involuntary unemployment will occur and too many low productivity units will be kept in operation.

The ingredients of the CH model, taken nearly directly from Caballero and Hammour (1998), are presented in Appendix A, together with some of the main results. Below a verbal description of the model is given. Because no formal testing of the models takes place in this paper, a verbal description of the predictions of both models following wage moderation should suffice in order to evaluate the empirical evidence.

In the CH model of the economy there are two factors of production that can either produce in autarky or commit to joint production relationships with partly irreversible fixed costs. The ex-ante terms of trade are derived from their autarky options and determine the factor supply curve; when operating jointly the factors are complementary and cannot be given payments based on marginal products. The quasi-rents arising from a specific relationship consist of the difference between the value of the joint product and the sum of the autarky products. The hold-up problem occurs because a party can threaten to break the relationship, leaving the other with a loss. In the equilibrium outcome, division of rents and allocation of factors to joint production is such that no party has an incentive to deviate from its choices, given the choices of others. In the general framework of CH, the factors labour and capital are symmetrical. They differ only in the proportion of investment that is sunk and the supply elasticity derived from the value of the outside option (autarky). These differences, together with a parameter of bargaining strength, determine net-specificity or which factor receives more in joint production than in autarky. An interpretation of the autarky option may be unemployment with benefits for workers, and flight to international assets for capital.

The CH model is further akin to the vintage model described below, with a distribution of productivity among the existing production units, a lower bound on productivity below which the unit is scrapped, and a free entry condition for creating new units with the best available technology. However, in the vintage model (VM) labour does not sink any resources in joint production and is not able to bargain away any portion of the production surplus. These assumptions require that two of the parameters of the CH model, φ_l, and β, be set to zero.

If the interplay between outside options and sunk costs are such that specificity in factors is not balanced (net specificity points to one factor) an inefficient equilibrium with the following properties will result. First, there will be underemployment (positive allocation of resources to autarky) and market segmentation (the appropriated factor will always receive its autarky marginal product, while the appropriating factor will earn less in autarky).

This latter effect can be thought of as involuntary unemployment for the appropriating factor. The number of joint production jobs is limited by the low allocation of the appropriated factor to the joint sector, which is their response to the appropriability problem. Secondly, with unbalanced specificity the scrapping margin is at a lower level of productivity than would occur if specificity were balanced or if complete enforceable contracts could be made. This happens because resources freed up by scrapping the marginal unit would not receive the benefits from the new technology with certainty, but would have a probability of earning less in autarky. Finally, the model shows that in equilibrium creation will be insufficient and destruction excessive. The latter occurs because the social opportunity cost of labour (return in autarky) is lower than the wage in joint production.

So far the model does not say much about the capital-labour ratio. The model posits fixed proportions in the short run. In the long run the model allows for technological choices from a range of proportions, with perfect substitutability. In equilibrium the appropriated factor chooses the technology. The direction of the capital-labour ratio following a change in specificity depends on the extent to which net specificity itself varies with the capital-labour ratio. For example, if specificity is caused by severance pay, a higher capital-labour ratio for a given level of output reduces the magnitude of the problem. In this case an exogenous increase in specificity of capital leads to lower employment and a higher capital labour ratio for new vintages. If on the other hand specificity does not depend on the capital-labour ratio, the earlier described mechanism of withdrawing capital to autarky will dominate after an exogenous increase in capital specificity, reducing the capital-labour ratio of new vintages. In either case the capital-labour ratio is sub-optimal, given outside factor prices.

2.2 Traditional Vintage Model

The vintage model (VM) used in this paper is a variant of the dynamic general equilibrium model of Broer (1996) where firms make capital investment, hiring, and vintage scrapping decisions in order to maximise a stream of future expected profits. Some of the assumptions of the Broer model are changed in order to be consistent with the CH model, and in order to better fit a small open economy. First, labour supply is not perfectly elastic. Instead the labour supply elasticity is assumed to decrease as unemployment benefits rise. Next, product markets are not imperfectly competitive. Instead the world output price is taken as fixed. These two changes in assumptions are complementary in the sense that they cause level of output in equilibrium to be bounded, albeit in different ways. In Broer, the product demand curve limits the amount of elastically supplied labour that can be put to work at the reservation wage, while in VM the increasing wages needed to supply more labour restrict the amount of output that can be produced at competitive prices.

In the VM, wage moderation, as modelled by an increase in labour supply elasticity, has a clear transitional effect on the actions of the representative firm. First, the age at which old vintages cease to be profitable, at the margin, increases. Second, all the existing vintages will be used in production with a higher level of associated labour. Output can thus increase somewhat without adding newer vintages of capital with their embodied technology. The lull in new capital spending may be longer or shorter, depending on the speed with which the economy proceeds to the new equilibrium, where output and employment are higher than prior to wage moderation.

3.   IMPLICATIONS OF WAGE MODERATION

This paper attempts to assess which of the two models better fits the Dutch economy. The method is to find an economic event that generates a different response under the two models, and to analyse which set of predictions best fit the actual data. The following sections show that the two models predict different outcomes for a few indicators following wage moderation. However, two obstacles cloud the ability to distinguish between the two models. First, what is the nature of the wage reduction? Is it an exogenous occurrence, for example caused by a helicopter drop of highly educated workers. Or is it caused by an institutional change in the way in which wages are negotiated? If so, is the implication that the specificity of labour was reduced? One path for implementing wage moderation is in the lowering of the value of the outside option, which increases the supply elasticity of labour. This would bring net specificity closer to zero in the CH model, but could be interpreted as an effective increase in labour supply, thus resulting in more moderate wages, under VM. Another path is more direct through the belief of market parties that the consensus agreement will be honoured, and that opportunistic behaviour will be limited. In the CH model, this is brought about by exogenously changing the bargaining parameter, thereby moving towards balanced specificity. However, in the VM this path has no operational meaning. The choice made in this paper is to study predictions of the models following wage moderation brought about through the lowering of the outside option.

The second obstacle is the level at which the models generate differences in outcomes. Possibly a difficulty could exist in isolating the theoretical differences in outcomes of indicators from observed differences at the sectoral level. At the micro-level such problems of interpretation may be less severe.

The importance of micro-level data in distinguishing between sources of changes in aggregates lies at the heart of the above problem. As an example, the evolution of aggregate TFP is broken down into its micro-components. Aggregate or sectoral productivity (TFP) growth is the result of both the development of productivity at each production unit and of the allocation, usually through market mechanisms, of sectoral or aggregate output across firms. Aggregate TFP is thus a weighted average of the productivity associated with technology embodied in each unit of capital, with the weight being equal to the share of output produced by that unit of capital (together with associated labour). Firm level TFP can only change with a change in the age structure of its capital, either through the introduction of new units of capital or the scrapping of old units. Aggregate TFP can increase without changes in productivity at the firm level, for example if highly productive firms gain market share, new firms enter the industry, or less productive firms exit the industry. We will see below how knowledge of micro-level developments in indicators indeed can aid in understanding the channels through which effects occur in the two models.

3.1 Aggregate and Sectoral Indicators

Table 1 shows the short- and medium-term effect on a selection of macro (or sectoral) variables following wage moderation under the two models, the traditional vintage model (VM) and the model of specificity (CH). The first line shows the effect on output. In the CH model, output grows because of the increase in resources drawn into joint production. Labour increases in VM, through an increase in labour intensity, while employment grows in CH because of a reduction in market segmentation. The effect on the capital-labour ratio in the CH model is ambiguous because, even though capital is drawn into joint production, the choice of technique might favour labour if the degree of specificity depends on factor intensity. Labour productivity is depressed in VM because of the higher labour intensity and because of the postponement of purchases of new vintages. In the CH model, labour productivity may decline if the effects of new vintage purchases are offset by the possible decline in capital intensity.

Table 1. Aggregate and Sectoral Indicators

Indicator	VM	CH
Output	+	+
Employment	+	+
Capital-labour ratio	−	±
Labour productivity	−	±
Labour share of income	−	−
Investment	−	+
TFP	−	+

The next line shows labour share of income, which is related to the cause, wage moderation, as well as to the effects, output and employment. The fall in labour share resulting from the increase in the labour supply elasticity can partly be offset by the fall in labour productivity under VM, but could be strengthened by an increase in labour productivity under CH.[5] The first five rows of the table do not provide indicators that can be used to distinguish the two models.

The models do have distinct effects on investment spending and TFP. Investment clearly goes through a lull in VM as the stock sits around waiting until the new, increased, obsolescence age is reached.[6] In the CH model, sclerosis is reduced and new vintages are purchased as capital is drawn into joint production. Unfortunately the very cyclical nature of investment makes it hard to determine whether the movements in investment over time are the results of the change in the labour environment, or because of other (international) macroeconomic disturbances.

Similarly the different prediction for TFP, a decline under VM and an improvement under CH, may be hard to distinguish in practice because one does not know what the direction of TFP would have been in the absence of wage moderation. Of course a structural model with appropriate instruments for other effects could be used, but in practice such instruments are difficult to find. Nonetheless we will briefly describe the aggregate and sectoral indicators in the Section 4.

---

[5] The institutional setting of wage moderation in the Netherlands ensured that labour share of income would fall. This occurs because product wage increases are negotiated within boundaries of the "wage-space," namely some proportion of labour productivity growth, and agreement was reached to reduce the share going to labour. This story has no meaning under the wage setting setup under the VM model.

[6] In the earlier discussion of the analysis of Bovenberg (1997) on the employment effects of wage moderation, the first channel was an increase in investment. This channel is important when firms are credit constrained and need cash-flow for investment. The other explanation for increased investment, namely improvements in expected profits, are related to the CH model.

3.2   Micro-level Indicators

The richness of micro-level data provides dimensions that aid in distinguishing between the two models. Individual firms vary significantly from each other in many ways, whether size, age, technology, profitability, productivity, cyclicality, *etc.*. This heterogeneity seems to be the one constant found by analysts looking at longitudinal micro datasets, *i.e.* datasets that cover a large sample of all firms or establishments over time, and that form the basis for the official sectoral and aggregate statistics.[7]

Some of the stylised facts from analysis of longitudinal micro datasets (LMDs) in various countries fit the theoretical constructs in the CH model quite nicely. Table 2 shows the direction of certain measurable quantities from the micro data following wage moderation under the two models. Before discussing the table, it is helpful to introduce terminology that has become standard in the analysis of LMDs. First, measurements can take place along the "within" or "between" dimension. "Within" productivity growth, for example, shows a weighted average of firm level productivity with initial input shares as weights. "Between" productivity growth shows how much aggregate productivity changes through a shift in output shares, given initial productivity levels. Next, a cross-term shows the contribution to the aggregate of the covariance between changes in productivity and changes in shares. Finally, entry and exit affect aggregate productivity.

Table 2. Micro-level Indicators

Indicators	VM	CH
Model features		
Factor substitution		
short-run	Yes	No
long-run	Yes	Yes
Lumpy investment	Yes	Yes
TFP growth		
Within	after spike	After spike
between, entry, exit	Yes	Yes
Wage moderation		
Firms with spike	–	+
Average age of capital	+	–
DD estimate of effect		
TFP growth	–	+
Capital growth	–	+

---

[7] For surveys of the burgeoning literature, see for example McGuckin (1995) and Bartelsman and Doms (2000).

Another term to be used is a difference-in-differences estimator (DD). This method looks at differences in outcomes of a group which is influenced by an effect before and after the effect occurred, with differences before and after in a group which is not influenced. For example, if wage moderation only can have influence on a firm's technology choice if they are at the vintage stage where they are ready to implement a new technology, we can compare outcomes of firms which do major re-tooling before and after wage moderation, with outcomes of firms which are not at the re-tooling stage. This technique can be argued to provide a "control group" to filter out influences of other factors.

Returning to Table 2, we review some general features of the data, and what they would look like under the two models. The degree of factor substitutability depends on the dimension along which it is measured. Substitution occurs "within" micro-units, takes place over time as older units are replaced (entry-exit) or cross-sectionally through reallocation of output shares across micro-units with different factor intensities ("between"). For capital-energy substitution in the U.S. industrial sector it is well-documented (see Doms, 1993) that the "within" dimension shows little action. This fact also fits the modern views in energy modelling (see Koopmans, 1997). Little "within" substitutability of capital and labour at a particular firm in the short-run, and possibly even complementarity, would fit the CH model nicely. In the long run both the VM and CH models exhibit substitutability between capital and labour.

Next, investment behaviour is analysed by counting the number of firms that experience a "major investment project" in a particular year, where "major investment project" is defined as investment expenditures that make up a significant portion of total investment spending of the firm over a long horizon (see for example, Doms and Dunne, 1993; or Cooper *et al.* (1994)). Both models should show significant lumpiness in investment, because in a vintage model a period of inaction follows after a new unit of capital has been put in place.

Productivity (TFP) growth changes only in the within dimension following an investment spike of a firm, under both models. Between effects, and entry and exit contributions also play a role in both models.

The next rows of the table show the effects of wage moderation on certain indicators. The first effect is the number of investment spikes in the years following moderation, which should go up under CH as expected realisable profits increase and scrapping age decreases, and decline under VM as more firms will find themselves in the range of inaction. Next, the within measure of the age of the capital stock should decline under CH and increase under VM. The lowering of opportunistic behaviour of labour creates an incentive for investments in new highly productive capital.

Further the scrapping age decreases leaving many firms with capital that can be scrapped immediately.

An investment spike of a firm gives the econometrician a nice tool to see what choices a firm has made for capital investment and for the implementation of new technology. The last two rows of the table show the expected difference-in-differences estimates for the effect of wage moderation on changes in capital and on TFP growth.

The capital stock clearly is boosted following a spike in investment at the firm. Changes in the capital stock in firms in years where no major investment project takes place could be positive if investment is larger than the amount of scrapping, or could be negative, but in any case is smaller than for firms with spikes. Capital stock growth following wage moderation will be different under the two models, and will depend on whether spikes occur. More spikes are expected under CH, but even under VM spikes will occur with a positive probability. Conditional on a spike occurring, the growth in capital will be lower following moderation under VM, all else equal, because desired capital stock is reduced. Under VM capital growth for firms without a spike will be higher than before, all else equal, because the scrapping margin is extended. Under CH growth at firms without spikes will decline, because more scrapping takes place, and growth at firms with spikes will increase because firms desire to draw more capital into joint production. Thus under CH the relative growth of spike to non-spike firms increases following wage moderation while it declines under VM. The difference in differences estimate helps in the "all else equal" clause because external influences, such as an exogenous increase in the cost of capital, will affect aggregate investment and the probability of the spike, but will have no, or less, effect on the relative change of spike to non-spike firms.

For TFP we look at the contribution to total TFP growth of the firms with a spike compared with firms without a spike, before and after wage moderation. Although we thereby implicitly take into account the number of firms which have a spike, we are able to correct for underlying differences in technological opportunity because we use the control group of firms without a spike. The expectation is that the relative contribution to TFP of firms with a spike increases following wage moderation under CH and decreases under VM.

4.   EMPIRICAL EVIDENCE

4.1   Aggregate and Sectoral Data

The empirical section starts with a cursory glance at aggregate and sectoral data. Sources and definitions of the data are provided in appendix B. Chart 1 shows four panels with the developments in the industrial sector in the Netherlands between 1975 and 1995. The top left panel shows labour share of income on the left scale and the minimum wage (deflated with product prices) on the right scale. These indicators show the policy shift following the agreement of Wassenaar in 1982. The top right panel shows the development of output – the solid line –, hours worked – the declining dotted line – and investment. A clear shift takes place in the trend of hours worked, starting in 1985, although an increase in investment is far more prominent. Bottom left, we see the developments of wages and user cost of capital, both relative to the output deflator. The turning point in the trend of product wages takes place in 1985. Wages relative to user cost of capital actually are increasing until around 1985. Disinflation and reductions in nominal interest rates suppress the cost of capital significantly throughout the decade.

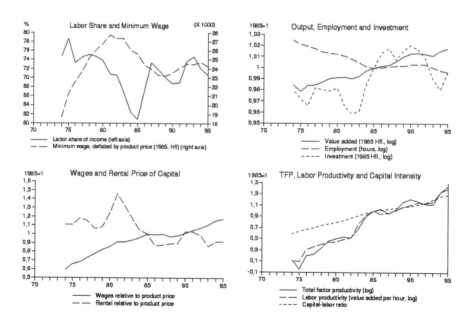

Figure 1. The Developments in the Industrial Sector in the Netherlands between 1975 and 1995

Finally, the bottom right chart shows the developments in (log) of TFP, (log) of labour productivity, and the capital-labour ratio. TFP shows a noticeable upturn after 1983, although cyclical factors are notorious in bouncing around measured TFP.

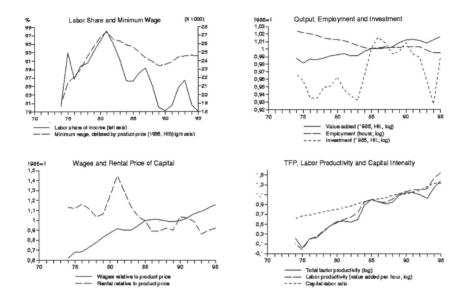

Figure 2. Indicators for Metal and Electronics in the Netherlands (ME)

Figures 2 and 3 show the same indicators for the selected industries, Metal and electronics (ME), and Food, alcohol, and tobacco (VG). The layout of the charts is the same. It should be noted that the minimum wage is deflated with the relevant output prices deflator, thereby exhibiting a different pattern in each chart. The metal sector shows an earlier turnaround in labour income share than aggregate industry, and also an earlier recovery in investment.

Overall, the data do not provide evidence to support one model over the other. The movement in TFP and investment would have provided evidence, if one had information on their development in the absence of wage moderation. Of course instrumental variable techniques could provide an empirical means for filtering out unwanted effects, such as exogenous shifts in export demand, consumer confidence, state of the business cycle, and others. While instrumental variables techniques are quite standard in many econometric analyses, direct access to micro-data can provide more robust identification.

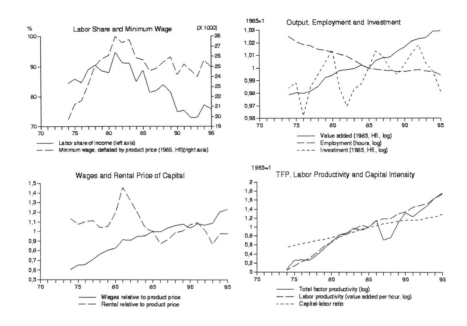

Figure 3. Indicators for Food, Alcohol, and Tobacco (VG*)*

4.2   Micro-level Data

The simplicity of the empirical tests applied to the micro-data belies the considerable amount of data manipulation needed to construct the relevant measures. Table 3 shows the number of firms with an investment spike in each year. The table is constructed from investment data from a balanced panel of firms, namely firms that occur in all available survey years of the investment statistics database. Next, for each firm a sum is created for real (deflated) investment in transport vehicles and in equipment. A spike occurs if real investment of a firm in a given year on the relevant asset type is more than 25 percent of sum real investment on that asset type by that firm over time.

It should not be surprising to those who have followed the recent literature on investment that such spikes occur with the frequency they do (see for example a survey by Caballero, 1997). In fact, in the Netherlands half the firms spend more than 25 percent of their total investment in transport vehicles over a 16-year span in one year. For equipment investment, the size of the median spike is 20 percent. These figures are roughly the same as for U.S. manufacturing firms, where the median spike is 25 percent (see Dunne and Doms, 1993). It is surprising that firm-level data show similar lumpiness to establishment level observations in the U.S, because firms are able to smooth the necessary lumpiness in plant investment by shifting resources across plants over time, if they want to.

A spike indicator, S_{it}, shows if firm i had a spike in year t:

$$S_{it} = \begin{cases} 1, & \text{if } I_{it} / \sum_t I_{it} > .25 \\ 0, & \text{if } I_{it} / \sum_t I_{it} \le .25 \end{cases} \tag{1}$$

where I_{it} measures deflated investment. The Spikes column in the table below is defined as:

$$Spike_t = \sum_i S_{it} \tag{2}$$

Table 3. Investment Indicators, the Netherlands

Year	Transport vehicles		Equipment	
	Spikes[a]	Investment[b]	Spikes	Investment
1980	37	101	20	1215
1981	20	90	17	1093
1982	25	84	10	1103
1983	21	86	12	1260
1984	22	90	18	1876
1985	49	112	26	1947
1986	40	99	31	1947
1987	39	97	32	1613
1988	37	106	29	1535
1989	48	117	33	1880
1990	53	115	55	1955
1991	58	110	40	1954

Source: Authors's calculation at CeReM, panel of 1351 firms.
a: Number of firms with > 25% of 16 years of Inv in a year
b: Inv.; total investment for firms in panel, 1985 guilders.

The data in Table 3 indeed show a significant increase in the number of firms that have a spike in 1985. This is the same year that aggregate hours increased, and lags the Wassenaar agreement by three years. The increase in spikes goes against the VM model and is not contradictory to the CH model.

Next, Table 4 shows the average age of the stock of transport vehicles and equipment over time. The construction of the age variable is described in Appendix B. After increasing through 1983, the average age starts declining. The fact that age falls reflects both an increase in investment as well as a reduction of the scrapping age under CH. In the previous table we saw that investment does not pick up until 1985. The margin of rejuvenation therefore initially took place through scrapping. It should be noted that aggregate industrial investment picked up sooner than investment in the balanced panel of firms, reflecting the fact that many smaller firms and entrants boosted their investment at an earlier stage.

Table 4. Average of Capital Stock

Year	Transport Vehicles	Equipment
1978	7.9	8.6
1979	8.3	8.9
1980	8.6	9.1
1981	8.7	9.2
1982	8.6	9.2
1983	8.3	9.2
1984	8.2	9.1
1985	8.2	8.8
1986	7.0	8.6
1987	7.6	8.1
1988	7.3	7.6
1989	7.0	7.4
1990	6.6	7.3
1991	6.3	6.9

Source: Author's calculation at CeReM, 1435 firms.

Finally, Table 5 shows the difference in differences estimates of the effects of wage moderation on TFP growth and capital growth. Consistent with the CH model, it is seen that the contribution to aggregate TFP growth of firms in the years surrounding an investment spike minus the contribution of the firms which had no spike in that year increased following wage moderation. Spikes are considered in the years 1979, 1980 and 1981 for before moderation, and in 1983 1984 and 1985 following moderation. Firm level TFP growth (computed from Solow residual) is calculated from the year prior to the spike to two years following the spike.

The row relative TFP change contains the following computations:

$$\hat{\tau}_{s0} - \hat{\tau}_{\neg s0} \text{ and } \hat{\tau}_{s1} - \hat{\tau}_{\neg s1} \tag{3}$$

Where ^ denotes productivity growth of firms, the set S includes firms with spikes in the relevant year, and $\neg S$ firms with no spike. Period 0 refers to any of the years 1979, 1980 and 1981, and period 1 refers to years 1983, 1984 and 1985.

$$\hat{\tau}_{s1} = \sum_{i \in \{I | S_{it} = 1, t \in (83,84,85)\}} \omega_{it} \hat{\tau}_{it} \tag{4}$$

Where ω is an appropriate weight for aggregating TFP changes, such as net output share.

The difference in differences growth of capital also exhibits the pattern expected under CH. In this case the figures are based on average growth rates of firms in the appropriate set rather than on contributions to aggregate growth used, as was for TFP. In other words, they reflect the within behaviour of capital stock growth for firms with a spike versus firms without. It is seen that changes in growth rates for firms with a spike relative to those without, increased following wage moderation, reflecting both a reduction in scrapping age, and an improvement in profitability outlook for investments as expected under CH.

Table 5. Effects of Wage Moderation

Difference-in-differences estimates		
Indicator	Before moderation	After moderation
Relative change in TFP[a]	.13	.42
Relative change in K^b	8.1	16.0

Source: Author's calculation at CeReM, 1350 firms.
a: Average TFP growth of firms with spike in year *t* minus TFP growth firms with no spike.
b: Average *K* growth of firms with spike in year *t*, minus *K* growth firms with no spike. Growth rate differences in percentage points.

5. CONCLUSIONS AND SUGGESTIONS FOR FURTHER RESEARCH

In this paper some preliminary results are presented of an empirical test of the relevance of specificity in macroeconomics. The very elegant theory of Caballero and Hammour, of course, is based partly on empirical observation, but as yet no rigorous empirical testing has taken place. The preliminary results presented here do not meet standards of rigour, but are suggestive that future research will be fruitful.

The methodology used in the paper to assess whether specificity plays a role in macroeconomics is to see how wage moderation in the Netherlands has affected productivity (TFP) growth. Using a vintage model (VM) as the null hypothesis and a vintage model with appropriability of quasi-rents (CH) as a description of the world with specificity, we see whether the development of certain indicators leads us to reject the CH model.

The paper discusses why it is difficult to make assessment concerning the role of specificity with aggregate and sectoral data. Further a preview is given of the possibilities to distinguish the models using micro-level data. Especially the ability to make non-standard aggregations and make special queries allows one to tailor series to conform to indicators which are expected to differ between both models on theoretical grounds. The number of firms which show an unusually large investment in a particular year is such a statistic. The figure would not have been generated through the traditional process of statistical offices, but requires retrospective analysis of the micro data.

This paper is still in a very preliminary form. Much work remains to be done to assess the robustness of the indicator on capital age to changes in methodological assumptions, selection of firms, changes in aggregation of asset categories, *etc.*. Further work remains to be done on evaluating the short-term substitutability of capital and labour. Finally, the paper still requires some general statistics on the behaviour of the chosen sample compared with the behaviour of the universe of industrial firms, let alone the rest of the economy.

Beyond the preliminary nature of this paper, one can think of extensions which would make a more rigorous test of the two models possible. The VM model can be thought of as a special case of CH, namely the case where specificity between the factors is perfectly balanced so that no appropriation takes place. The hypothesis would then be that net specificity of capital in the economy was reduced following wage moderation. An open question would be whether institutional arrangements in the Netherlands have resulted in balanced specificity, thus solving the macroeconomic problems flagged by Caballero and Hammour.

A   THE CH MODEL

The material presented here follows very closely the description given in Caballero and Hammour (1996). In the model, there are two factors of production, 1 and 2, and one consumption good, which acts as numeraire. Decision for allocation of the factors are made by optimising agents who derive utility from consumption. Production can take place either in autarky of in joint production, or both. U_i is autarky use of factor i, and E_i is allocation of i in joint production.

Production of output in a joint production unit is given by

$$\widetilde{y} = Min(x_1, x_2),$$

where x_1, $x_2 > 0$, and $\tilde{y}$ are given by existing technologies. It is possible to generalise model such that factor substitution is allowed in long-run, or even in short run, under certain conditions. The analysis of CH is forward looking, but collapses the future into one future period. E^0 pre-existing production units are already in place, and U_1^0 and U_2^0 of autarky factors also are given. Total supply of each factor is normalised to unity.

The production structure has a vintage nature, with new production units producing y^0 and pre-existing units having heterogeneous production from a distribution which depends on the history of technology adoption and shocks. In the model, the endogenous scrapping boundary, below which units will not operate, is denoted by y^0.

The specificity of the factors is given by the fact that if a *new* production unit is created a share φ_i of each factor is no longer usable if the factors separate, only $(1-\varphi_i)x_i$ of a factor committed to joint production can be used elsewhere.

The factors receive a reward in autarky given by:

$$\pi_i = F_i'(U_i)$$

A specific functional form can be assumed for the autarky production function:

$$F_i(U_i) = \frac{1}{1+1/\eta_i}\left[1 - (1-U_i)^{1+1/\eta_i}\right], \ \eta_i > 0$$

so that we get a constant supply elasticity η_i for factor i into joint production: $E_i = p_i^{\eta_i}$. A lowering of factor rewards in autarky for each given level of U_i is then equivalent to an increase in that factor's supply elasticity.

In an efficient equilibrium, that is one where there are efficient contracts so that factors receive ex-post payments in joint production equal to there *ex-ante* marginal product in autarky, the following holds for the wage:

$$w_i^* = p_i^*$$

In the incomplete-contract equilibrium, *i.e.* where the parties can bargain *ex-post*, their ex-post opportunity cost is given by $(1-\varphi_i)p_i$. The rents which can be bargained for in such an economy is given by:

$$s'' = y'' - (1-\varphi_1)p_1 x_1 - (1-\varphi_2)p_2 x_2$$

With Nash bargaining, each factor then receives a compensation:

$$w_i'' x_i = (1-\varphi_i)p_i x_i + \beta_i s''$$

where β_i is the bargaining power of factor i with $\beta_1 + \beta_2 = 1$.
The model further has free entry and exit. Factors will join together if

$$y^n \geq p_1 x_1 + p_2 x_2 + \Delta,$$

where Δ denotes the degree of net specificity. If factors are balanced with each other in terms of what they have to lose, then $\Delta=0$, and we have *balanced specificity*. The hurdle for entry will be higher if there is an appropriating and an appropriated factor.

Balanced specificity, $\Delta=0$, occurs when $\varphi_1 p_1 x_1 = \varphi_2 p_2 x_2$, which happens if, and only if,

$$\frac{1}{x_1}\left(\frac{\varphi_2}{\frac{\beta_2}{\beta_1}\varphi_1 + \varphi_2}\frac{y^n}{x_1}\right)^{\eta_1} = \frac{1}{x_2}\left(\frac{\varphi_1}{\frac{\beta_1}{\beta_2}\varphi_2 + \varphi_1}\frac{y^n}{x_2}\right)^{\eta_2}$$

All else equal, the appropriating factor will be the factor with i) the highest β, ii) the lowest specific investment φx, and iii) the factor with the lowest supply elasticity, η.

In the model, the following macro outcomes occur when specificity is not balanced:

- Underemployment, $E_i < E_i^*$, i = 1,2
- Market segmentation; appropriated factor (*i*) gets outside option, appropriating factor ($\neg i$) in involuntary unemployment: $w_i^n = p_i$ and $w^n_{\neg i} > p_{\neg i}$.
- Sclerosis: $y^0 < y^{0*}$, scrapping margin is lower than in efficient equilibrium.

B   DATA

Aggregate and sectoral data
The aggregate and sectoral data are sourced from the sectoral timeseries database of CPB, and are based on efforts to put National Income Accounts data from Statistics Netherlands on a common basis over time. The capital stock data are created using timeseries on investment by type and sector from 1950 through 1995, using the perpetual inventory method. Initial stocks (1948) are provided by Statistics Netherlands, along with information on mean service life. The PIM method using a stochastic mean service life, with a truncated normal distribution centred about the mean life, with a variance of one quarter the mean life, and truncation at 50 percent above and below the mean. Further, a beta-decay function using $\vartheta = .90$ is applied to the remaining stock to reflect efficiency loss. Capital stock by type are aggregated to the sectoral level using expenditure shares, in order to created a measure of capital service inputs, following the methodology of Jorgenson *et al.* (1987). The user-cost of capital needed to compute capital service flows is based on average long-bond and equity returns, tax rate information from the CPB macro model FKSEC (1992), and sectoral information on tax deductibility, accelerated depreciation allowances, and investment tax credits.

Micro-level data
The micro-level datasets are available on-site at CeReM, Statistics Netherlands for authorised research projects. The data used in the study come from three sets of surveys, the production

statistics (PS), the investment statistics (IS) and the capital stock survey (CS). The PS are an annual census of large manufacturing firms, and a survey of small firms (10 employees). Firms are queried about employment (in workers), sales, production, inventories, materials and energy use. Each year, on the order of 10000 firms are in the dataset. A balanced panel of firms from 1978 through 1993 can be made with about 6000 firms.[8]

The investment statistics, available from 1980 through 1993 provide information on investment spending by asset type by firm. The survey is smaller, with an integral count of the largest firms (>500). A balanced panel containing observations of a firm for all years results in a selection of about 1400 firms.

The CS survey is a small sample of very large firms, with information on capital stocks, by asset type and by vintage. The sample is drawn from a rotating selection of industries (SBIs) and contains between 150 and 400 firms per year, from 1983 through 1995. Owing to the sample selection method, only roughly 600 firms are sample more than once throughout the period, usually with a 5 year span in between observations.

Deflators for output, and materials are available at a 3-digit level, from Statistics Netherlands. Investment deflators by asset type also are from Statistics Netherlands.

Construction of timeseries of the capital stock for as large a group as possible occurs in steps. The reader should be warned that the methodology contains many untested assumptions. Results have not been tested as extensively for robustness to assumptions as I would like.

The first step was to use all firms that were observed twice over time to estimate the parameters for a mean stochastic service life PIM methodology. This can be done by using information on the quantity of capital in firm i of type j and vintage τ observed in year t_0 and comparing it to the quantity observed in t_1. This can be done for all i, j, τ observed in t_0. Stacking the observations over survey pairs, allowing for differences in time-span between observation, allow one to run a non-linear regression to fit the chosen functional form (Truncated Normal).

The next step is to extend an observed vintage/type capital structure backwards in time for each firm by blowing up observed values with the estimated scrapping function. Then, a beta-decay is applied to vintage structure to create an annual stock for each firm for all years prior- and up to the survey year. The average age of the stock of a firm in each year is a (post-decay) stock weighted average of the age of each vintage. For years following the survey date, the scrapping function is applied to earlier vintages, and the investment data from IS is used for the lastest vintage. All vintage values are than summed, after applying beta-decay. Age is a (post-decay) stock weighted average of age in each vintage. The above process is applied to to aggregates of asset type, namely transport vehicles which is a sum of vehicles for internal and external use, and equipment.

TFP is constructed as a Solow residual, using cost-shares rather than expenditure shares as weights for factor inputs. Output is measured as value added, and factors of production are labour, transport vehicle stock and equipment stock.

---

[8]   See Abbring and Gautier (1997) for some notes on panel linking.

REFERENCES

Abbring, J.H. and P.A. Gautier (1997), "Gross Job Flow in Netherlands Manufacturing: A Panel Data Analysis," mimeo.

Bartelsman, E. J. and M. E. Doms (2000), "Understanding Productivity: Lesson from Longitudinal Microdata, " *Journal of Economic Literature*, forthcoming.

Bartelsman, E.J. , G. van Leeuwen and H. Nieuwenhuijsen (1998), "Adoption of Advanced Manufacturing Technology in the Netherlands," *Economics of Innovation and New Technology* 6, pp. 291-312.

Bovenberg, L. A. (1997), "Dutch Employment Growth: An Analysis," CPB-report 2 (2), 16-24.

Broer, D.P. (1996) On The Theory of Investment in Vintage Capital Models, Tinbergen Institute Discussion Paper 96-92/4, Tinbergen Institute.

Caballero, R.J. (1997), "Aggregate Investment, A 90's View," May, mimeo.

Caballero, R.J. and M.L. Hammour (1996), "The Macroeconomics of Specificity", NBER Working Paper Series 5757, September.

Caballero, R.J., E.M. Engel and J.C. Haltiwanger (1995), "Plant-level Adjustment and Aggregate Investment Dynamics," in *Brookings Papers on Economic Activity* Washington, D.C., pp. 1350-1368.

Cooper, R., J. Haltiwanger and L. Power (1994), "Machine Replacement and the Business Cycle: Lumps and Bumps," mimeo.

CPB (1992), *FKSEC: A Macro-econometric Model of the Netherlands*, Nijmegen: Stenfert-Kroese.

CPB (1997), *Challenging Neighbours*, Berlin: Springer Verlag.

Davis, S., J. Haltiwanger and S. Schuh (1996), *Job Creation and Job Destruction*, Cambridge, MA: MIT Press.

Doms, M. E. (1993), "Inter Fuel Substitution and Energy Technology Heterogeneity in U.A. Manufacturing,"discussion paper CES 93-5, U.S. Bureau of Census, Center for Economic Studies, March.

Dunne, T. and M. Doms (1993), "An Investigation into Capital and Labour Adjustment at the Plant Level," mimeo, Center for Economic Studies.

Dunne, T., M. Roberts and L. Samuelson (1988), "Patterns of Firm Entry and Exit in U.S. Manufacturing Industries," *RAND Journal of Economics* 19, pp. 495-515.

Fare, R. (1994), "Productivity Growth, Technical Progress, and Efficiency Change in Industrialized Countries," *American Economic Review* 84, pp. 66-83.

Jorgenson, D., F. Gollop and B. Fraumeni (1987), *Productivity and U.S. Economic Growth*, Cambridge: Harvard University Press.

Kleinknecht, A.H. (1994), "Heeft Nederland een loongolf nodig?," *Economisch Statistische Berichten*, January, pp. 5-24.

Koopmans, C., (1997), "NEMO: CPB's new energy model," *CPB-report*, vol. 2 (2), pp. 34-38.

Malcomson, J.M. (1997), "Contracts, Hold-up and Labour Markets," *Journal of Economic Literature* 35, pp. 1916-57.

McGuckin, R.H. (1995), "Establishment Microdata for Economic Research and Policy Analysis: Looking beyond the Aggregates," *Journal of Business and Economic Statistics* 13, pp. 121-26.

PART III

TECHNOLOGY DIFFUSION AND GROWTH

Chapter 9

Knowledge, Technology, and Economic Growth during the Industrial Revolution

Joel Mokyr

Departments of Economics and History, Northwestern University, Evanston, Ill.

Key words: Technological change, Economic history, Industrial revolution, Economic growth

Abstract: This paper takes a look at the events leading to the British Industrial Revolution and renews the argument that a theory of useful knowledge is required to fully understand the timing of the event as well as the reasons why it did not peter out after a few decades the way previous waves of technological progress had done. It develops such a theory in some detail, distinguishing between Useful Knowledge and Techniques. It is argued that in the century before 1760, fundamental developments associated with the enlightenment and the Scientific Revolution took place that made the Industrial Revolution possible.

"It is clear from the preceding that every "art" [technique] has its speculative and its practical side. Its speculation is the theoretical knowledge of the principles of the technique; its practice is but the habitual and instinctive application of these principles. It is difficult if not impossible to make much progress in the application without theory; conversely, it is difficult to understand the theory without knowledge of the technique. In all techniques, there are specific circumstances relating to the material, instruments and their manipulation which only experience teaches."

Denis Diderot, article on "Arts" in the *Encyclopédie*

1.   INTRODUCTION

Can we "explain" the Industrial Revolution? Recent attempts by leading economists (Lucas, 1998; Hansen and Prescott, 1998; Acemoglu and Zilibotti, 1997) focus more on the issue of timing ("why did it happen in the eighteenth century") than the issue of place ("why Western Europe?"). Both questions are equally valid, but they demand different types of answers. In what follows, I will answer the first question only, although the ideas used here can readily be extended to the second. The answer for the timing question is to link the Industrial Revolution to a prior or simultaneous event that clearly was not caused by it. Rather than focus on political or economic change that prepared the ground for the events of the Industrial Revolution, I submit that the Industrial Revolution's timing was determined by intellectual developments, and that the true key to the timing of the Industrial Revolution has to be sought in the scientific revolution of the seventeenth century and the enlightenment movement of the eighteenth century. The key to the Industrial Revolution was technology, and technology is knowledge.

The idea that changes in human knowledge are a crucial ingredient in economic growth seems so self-evident as to leave elaboration unnecessary, were it not that with some notable exceptions – especially the work of the Stanford school embodied by the work of Nathan Rosenberg and Paul David – economists actually rarely have dealt with it explicitly. Even the "New Growth Theory," which explicitly tries to incorporate technology as one of the variables driven by human and physical capital does not try to model the concept of knowledge and its change over time explicitly. Yet nobody would seriously dispute the proposition that living standards today are higher than in the eleventh century primarily because we know more than medieval peasants. We do not say that we are smarter (there is little evidence that we are) and we cannot even be sure that it is because we are better educated (though of course we are). The central phenomenon of the modern age is that as an aggregate we know more. But who is "we"? What is meant by "know" and what kind of knowledge really matters?

In what follows I will sketch a rough outline of what a theory of knowledge of interest to economic historians should look like and then apply it to the issues around the sources of the Industrial Revolution in Britain. The central conclusion from the analysis is that economic historians should re-examine the epistemic roots of the Industrial Revolution, in addition to the more standard economic theories explaining it that focus on institutions, markets, geography and so on. In particular, the interconnections between the Industrial Revolution and those parts of the Enlightenment movement that sought to rationalise and spread knowledge may have played a more important role than recent writings (*e.g.* the essays in Mokyr, 1998c) have given it credit for. This would explain the timing of the Industrial Revolution following the enlightenment and – equally importantly – why it did not fizzle out like similar bursts of macroinventions in earlier times. It might also help explain why the Industrial Revolution took place in Western Europe (although not why it took place in Britain and not in France or the Netherlands).

2.   A THEORY OF USEFUL KNOWLEDGE

To start with, we need to define *useful* knowledge. The term "useful knowledge" originates with Kuznets (1965, pp. 85-87) and I will use it here to describe knowledge (that is to say, beliefs) about *natural* phenomena.[1] The essence of production technology is the manipulation of nature for our material purposes. Hence useful knowledge deals with natural phenomena that *potentially* lend themselves to manipulation such as materials, energy, and living beings.[2] There is some arbitrariness in this, of course, since it leaves somewhat ambiguous whether psychological, anthropological, or sociological knowledge, which presumably lends itself to the manipulation of people by other people, should be included. It could also be argued that *economic* knowledge (*e.g.* about prices or rates of return on assets) should be included since it is necessary for efficient production and distribution. For

---

[1]   Kuznets confined his set to "tested" knowledge that is potentially useful in economic production. In what follows below, this definition is far too restrictive. There exists of course no universally accepted definition of what "testing" means; any testing procedure is a social convention at the time of convention. Instead I am relying below on a more relativistic concept of "tightness" of knowledge.

[2]   "Production" should be taken to include household activities such as cooking, cleaning, childcare and so forth, which equally require the manipulation of natural phenomena and regularities.

the present purposes I will largely depend on a narrower definition including *natural* phenomena only, so as to concentrate on technological issues.

Knowledge resides either in people's minds or in storage devices from which it can be retrieved. From the point of view of a single agent, another's mind is a storage device as well. The total useful knowledge in a society can then be defined simply as *the union of all the pieces of useful knowledge contained in living persons' minds or storage devices*. I will call this set Ω. A discovery then is simply the addition of a piece of knowledge hitherto not in that set. Learning or diffusion would be defined as the transmission of existing knowledge from one individual or device to another.[3]

Useful knowledge takes two forms. One is the observation, classification, measurement, and cataloguing of natural phenomena. The other is the establishment of regularities, principles, and "natural laws" that govern these phenomena and allow us to make sense of them. Such a definition includes mathematics insofar as mathematics is used to describe and analyse the regularities and orderliness of nature.[4] This distinction, too, is not sharp, since many empirical regularities and statistical observations could be classified as "laws" by some and "phenomena" by others. Useful knowledge includes "scientific" knowledge as a subset, but it involves a great deal more: practical informal knowledge about nature such as geography; the properties of materials, heat, plants, and animals; intuitive understanding of basic mechanics such as levers, pulleys, and cranks; regularities of ocean currents and the weather; and folk wisdoms in the "an-apple-a-day-keeps-the-doctor-away" tradition. It also includes engineering knowledge, more formal than folk wisdom and the pragmatic knowledge of the artisan, but less than science, what Edwin Layton (1974) has termed "technological science" or "engineering science" and Walter Vincenti (1990) has termed "engineering knowledge."[5] This part of Ω concern not so much the general

---

[3] Formally, if Ω is the union of all the individual sets of knowledge contained in either minds or storage devices, diffusion and learning would concern the *intersection* of these sets. The larger the number of units in all intersections, the larger the *density* of Ω.

[4] As Crosby (1997, p. 109) notes, "measurement is numbers and the manipulation of numbers means mathematics." The great mathematician David Hilbert is reputed to have remarked that there is nothing more useful than a good mathematical theory (cited in Casti, 1990, p. 33).

[5] A good example is the knowledge of the properties of materials, one of the cornerstones of all techniques. By the early nineteenth century, this part of material science was being analysed by scientists who learned to distinguish between elastic strength and rupture strength. But until then, this entire Ω was controlled by old-fashioned engineers and carpenters who "limited themselves to instinctively measuring the influence of the differences in buildings which appear to serve a similar function" (Guillerme, 1988, p. 242). This informal, intuitive and instinctive knowledge of natural regularities and of what could and could not be done is what most of Ω consisted of before modern science formalised substantial portions of it.

"laws of nature" as much as the formulation of quantitative empirical relations between measurable properties and variables, and imagining abstract structures that make sense only in an engineering context, such as the friction-reducing properties of lubricants or thermodynamic cycle of an internal combustion engine (Ferguson, 1992, p. 11). It seems pointless, on the other hand, to argue about whether components of Ω are "correct" or not. Theories and observations about nature may have been of enormous practical influence and yet regarded today as "incorrect."

Evolutionary epistemology views knowledge as an entity subject to "selection" by agents. Selection has two dimensions: first, given the huge size of Ω, selectors have to decide which knowledge they choose to acquire themselves since they cannot acquire it all. Second, knowing is not believing. What is interesting, in addition to its practical importance, is to what extent knowledge is "tight" that is, to what extent the rhetorical conventions accepted in society persuade people that something is "true" or at least "tested." Tightness determines the confidence that people have in the knowledge and – what counts most for my purposes – thus their willingness to act upon it. Such rhetorical conventions vary from "Aristotle said" to "the experiment demonstrates" to "the estimated coefficient is 2.3 times its standard error." The rhetorical rules are pure social constructs, but they are not independent of how and why knowledge, including "useful" knowledge, grows over time. The actual structure of Ω is self-referential. A great deal of knowledge consists of knowing that something is known and knowing how to find out in case of need.

The role that useful knowledge can play in a society's technological development depends on three elements: how large is Ω (that is, *what* is known); how diffuse is this knowledge (*who* and *how many* know what is known); and the marginal access costs (*how much does it cost* me to find out what I do not know). A lot will depend on the efficiency and cost of access to knowledge. Although knowledge is a public good in the sense that the consumption of one does not reduce that of others, the private costs of acquiring it are not negligible in terms of time and often real resources as well. When the access costs become very large, in the limit it could be said that knowledge has disappeared.[6] Access costs depend on the technology of

---

[6]   This cost function determines how costly it is for an individual to access information from a storage device or from another individual. The *average* access cost would be the average cost paid by all individuals who wish to acquire the knowledge. More relevant for most useful questions is the *marginal* access cost, that is, the *minimum* cost for an individual who does not yet have this information. A moment reflection will make clear why this is so: it is very expensive for the average member of a society to have access to the Schrödinger wave equations, yet it is "accessible" for advanced students of quantum mechanics at low cost. If the rest of society "needs" to know something it will clearly go to someone for whom this cost is as low as possible to find out. Such people would then be

access, the trustworthiness of the sources, as well as on the total size of Ω; the larger it is, the more specialisation and division of knowledge is required. Experts and special sources dispensing useful information will emerge providing access. Information Technology is exactly about that. The much heralded IT revolution of our own age is not just about the fact that we *know* more (and different) things, but that the flows of information in and out of agents' minds are much more rapid. The continuous interchange of useful knowledge between the minds of agents and between those of other agents and storage devices has been greatly speeded up and become enormously cheaper in the past ten years. Access costs also depend on the *culture* of knowledge. If those who possess it regard it as a source of wealth, power, or privilege, they will tend to guard it more jealously. Secrecy and exclusionary practices are, of course, artificial ways to increase access costs. To be sure, language, notation, and jargon were also barriers to access (as they are today) but "popularised" versions of scientific books became necessary if scientists were to reach their paying audiences and patrons.

For the historian, the dynamic questions about Ω are the most interesting. An evolutionary approach can help us clarify our thinking about it, although analogies with biology and genetics have to be pursued with caution (Mokyr, 1998a, 1998b). Much like DNA, useful knowledge does not exist by itself, it has to be "carried" by people or in storage devices. Unlike DNA, however, carriers can acquire and shed knowledge so that the selection process is quite different. Clearly this raises question of how it is transmitted over time, and whether it can actually shrink as well as expand. All carriers have finite lives and thus need to reproduce themselves in some fashion. The existence of non-living carriers does expedite this transmission, but it is also clear that some crucial components cannot be codified or stored in devices that require codification. This "tacit" knowledge cannot be stored and therefore dies with its live carrier. In principle there is nothing to stop knowledge from being lost altogether or becoming so expensive to access that for all practical purposes it might as well be. Much of the likelihood of knowledge being transmitted depends on the social organisation of knowledge, storage technology, and who controls access to it. If useful knowledge is controlled by an Imperial bureaucracy, as was the case in China, or a small aristocratic elite, as was the case in classical civilisation, much of it can be lost or made inaccessible. These social conditions also determine how likely it is that Ω will expand, that is, that new discoveries and knowledge will be added.

---

defined as experts, and much of the way knowledge has been used has relied on such experts. The cost of finding these experts and retrieving knowledge from them thus determines marginal access costs. Equally important, as we shall see, is the technology that provides access to storage devices.

In addition to useful knowledge about the natural world, there is a second form of knowledge which I call techniques. Techniques are essentially sets of instructions or recipes on how to manipulate nature. These instructions, like all knowledge, either reside in people's brains or in storage devices. It consists of designs and instructions on how to adapt means to a well-defined end, much like a piece of software or a cookbook recipe. They are usually the end product of some knowledge in Ω so they have an *epistemic base* in Ω. I will refer to this set as λ. If Ω is *episteme*, λ is *techne*. Elements of λ consist of "do loops" replete with "if-then" statements instructing one on how to carry out certain activities that broadly constitute what we call "production." They all can be taught, imitated, and improved upon. A "how to" manual is a codified set of techniques. Not all techniques are explicit, codified, or even verbalised. Thus riding bicycles or playing a musical instrument consist of neuro-muscular movements that cannot be made entirely explicit.[7] Others consist of "tacit" knowledge that could be made explicit but never is. Much like elements of Ω, the elements of λ require carriers to be expressed (that is, used) and transmitted over time and across space. Each society has some feasible metaset of all techniques available to it, a monstrous compilation of blueprints and instruction "manuals" that describe what this society *can* do. These are often hard to pin down.[8] All the same, they must have existed. From that set, economic decision-makers be they households, small producers, or large corporations, select techniques. This choice is the technological analogue of natural selection and since Nelson and Winter first enunciated it in 1982, it has remained the best way to describe and analyse technological change.

Naturally, only a small subset of λ is in use at each point of time. How society "selects" these techniques and rejects others is an important question, but not one I will address here (see Mokyr, 1998a). Techniques, too, need to be passed on from generation to generation because of wear and tear to their carriers and can be taught without necessarily including the entire body of Ω that serves as their base. A plumber can be trained to fix leaking pipes without burdening him with the hydraulics and material science underlying his skill - though in general the more of the underlying knowledge passed on, the better the skills. To be sure, an invention in plumbing *could* be made

---

[7] Many techniques have elements and refinements that can only be stored in people's minds and transmitted, if at all, by personal contact. Some of them are "knacks" that are uncodifiable and defy any formalisation, and if valuable enough, yield large rents to their carrier. Thus the skills of basketball- or violin-playing can be codified and taught, but the techniques applied by Michael Jordan or Itzhak Perlman clearly are not wholly transmissible.

[8] Hall (1978, p. 96) points out that the historian finds it very difficult to identify λ from early records, because in the past shipwrights, toolmakers, and so on left few records of their "instructions" and inferring these from the end-products can be misleading.

through pure luck or inspiration by someone totally ignorant of these areas, but the probability of this happening quickly declines not only with the complexity of the problem but also with the number of previous serendipitous inventions.

Is the distinction between Ω and λ meaningful? Both reflect some form of knowledge and thus are subject to the same kind of difficulties that economics of knowledge and technology encounters. But the knowledge set is partitioned by *kinds* of knowledge. Michael Polanyi (1962, p. 175) points out that the difference boils down to observing that Ω can be "right or wrong" whereas "action can only be successful or unsuccessful." He also notes that the distinction is recognised by patent law which will patent inventions (additions to λ) but not discoveries (additions to Ω). Yet Polanyi fails to recognise the important historical implications of the two kinds of knowledge and maintains that "up to [1846] natural science had made no major contribution to technology. The Industrial Revolution had been achieved without scientific aid" (p. 182). Yet the implicit definition he uses for Ω implies a much larger entity than formal science.[9] The distinction between Ω and λ parallels the distinction made famous half a century ago by Gilbert Ryle (1949), who distinguished between knowledge "how" and knowledge "what." Ryle rejected the notion that one can meaningfully distinguish *within a single individual* knowledge of a set of parameters about a problem and an environment from a set of instructions derived from this knowledge that directs an individual to take a certain action. Yet what may not be true for an individual is true for society as a whole: for a technique to exist, it normally has an epistemic base in Ω. In other words, somebody needs to know enough about a natural principle or phenomenon on which a technique is based to make it possible.[10] How much "enough" is, depends on the complexity of the technique and many other factors. It is not necessary, moreover, that the same person carrying out the technique have access to this knowledge. I typed these lines on a computer even though I have only rudimentary knowledge of the physical and mathematical rules that make my computer work. But at some time in the past, somewhere, somebody had this knowledge. The probability that a laptop computer would be made by a group of people with no knowledge of computer science, advanced electronics, materials science, and whatever else is involved is nil. Layton

---

[9]   In addition to "pure science", he includes an intermediate set of enquiries that are "systematic technology" and "technically justified science." Yet he must mean even less formal elements when he points out that "technology always involves the application of some empirical knowledge... our contriving always makes use of some anterior observing" (Polanyi, 1962, p. 174).

[10] Strictly speaking, even if Ω is the null set, some elements in λ *could* exist. A beaver's technique of building dams or bees' ability to construct hives are techniques that have no demonstrable basis in anything we could define as useful knowledge.

(1974, p. 40) remarks that " "knowing" and "doing" reflect the fundamentally different goals of communities of science and technology." But most of what is in Ω has nothing to do with understanding the universe but with mundane, prosaic properties of materials, motion, temperature, mechanisms, and living beings: simple natural regularities that imply certain actions and rule out others. It should also be kept in mind that Ω contains such elements as "technique λ_i exists and works satisfactorily" and hence the diffusion of techniques in λ depends on the characteristics of Ω. Different elements in λ may be involved in constructing artefacts and using them, writing down the instructions and interpreting them, and so on. Useful knowledge is a social good, and as long as it exists *somewhere* and others have access to it, it can result in improved techniques, that is, lead to technological progress.[11]

The set Ω maps into λ and thus imposes a constraint on it. Certain societies, including our own, do not have access to some techniques because they lack a needed base in Ω. Medieval Europe could not design a technique describing the ocean route to Australia or how to produce antibiotics against the Black Death. Our own societies have been unable to tame nuclear fusion and make effective anti-virus agents because we do not know enough about high-energy physics and virology. Nonetheless, we cannot be sure that such knowledge will never exist; all that matters is that *we* do not have it. I have argued elsewhere that the relationship between Ω and λ is in some ways akin to the relationship between genotype and phenotype in evolutionary biology in that not every gene ends up coding for a protein, but for any phenotype to emerge, some basis for it has to exist in the genome. Of course, the existence of some piece of knowledge does not guarantee that any mapping will occur. Hellenistic civilisation created Ptolemaic astronomy but never used it, apparently, for navigational purposes. The Chinese under the Song had excellent knowledge of clockmaking but never used it for anything but ornamental devices, nor did their understanding of optics translate into the making of telescope or spectacles. What matters, clearly, is the incentive and penalty structure for people who suggest new techniques. New techniques can emerge from pure novelty much like mutations, or from recombining existing elements in Ω in novel ways. On the way they encounter all kinds of technological and political resistance, and only the smallest fraction of novelties ever find their way to usage.

There are thus interesting parallels and important differences between technological and biological evolution.[12] Yet it could be misleading to think

---

[11] The distinction I am making here is somewhat different from the one that formed the basis of a debate between Layton (1974) and Hall (1978) about the validity of a distinction between "knowledge" and "knowledge how."

[12] For more details on this line of thinking, see Mokyr (1998a, 1998b).

of the mapping from Ω to λ as equivalent to the mapping from genotype to phenotype. In technology, unlike in biology, the epistemic base on which a technique rests is not wholly determinate. Moreover, unlike what happens in biology, λ can produce a feedback into Ω. As we shall see, this feedback is of pivotal historical importance.

The mapping function remains one of the more elusive historical phenomena and is the key to explanations of "invention" and "technological creativity." What has not been sufficiently stressed, however, is that changes in the size and internal structure of Ω can themselves affect the chances that it will be mapped and the nature of the techniques that will emerge. Above all, the boundaries of Ω at any moment limit what *can* be mapped.

As noted, the epistemic base of techniques can be narrow or wide. The narrower the base in Ω of a particular technique, the less likely it is to keep growing and expanding after its first emergence. In the absence of a good understanding of why and how a technique operates, further improvements ran quickly into diminishing returns. In the limiting case, the base of a particular technique is so narrow that *all* that is known (and is thus contained in Ω) is the trivial element that "technique i works." These techniques, which might be called "singleton techniques" (since their domain is a singleton), usually emerged as the result of serendipitous discoveries. Much technological progress before the Industrial Revolution was of that nature. While new techniques appeared, they rarely if ever led to continued and sustained further improvements and never attained the cumulative momentum that provides most of the economic benefits of innovation. While at times they had enormous practical significance, they were usually dead ends. Such techniques are also less flexible and adaptable to changing circumstances, a problem that is particularly acute in medicine (Mokyr, 1998d).[13] Thus Jenner's 1796 discovery of the vaccination process, one of the most successful singleton techniques in history, led to no further vaccinations until the triumph of the germ theory, and smallpox flare-ups due to ignorance and improper usage were common till the end of the nineteenth century. The correct use of fertiliser in agriculture in ancient times improved but slowly until the development of organic chemistry by von Liebig and his followers and the systematic experimentation of John Benet Lawes at Rothamsted after 1840. The more complex a technology, the less likely that a singleton technique will be discovered. All the same, pharmaceutical research still has room for serendipity and contains an element of "try every bottle on the shelf." When a compound is discovered that works for a particular purpose, the fine details of its *modus operandi*

---

[13] Hall (1978, p. 97) points out that a shipwright who knows "how" to build a ship without having any knowledge of the underlying rules would not be able to build a whole series of different ships.

often emerge much later.[14] Alternative medicine, to pick another example, is full of narrow-based or singleton techniques that have little basis in Ω.[15] Techniques that have narrow or negligible bases in Ω tend also to be "untight" and their inventors encounter more difficulty persuading the public to use them if only because something might be more believable if it is known not only that it seems to work but also *why*. This tightness depends on other factors as well: if the technique is demonstrably superior, its base in Ω may have little effect on its acceptability (as was surely the case with Jenner).[16]

The dynamics of information differ in crucial ways from that of DNA: there is a feedback loop going back from λ to Ω in which knowledge about "how" feeds back into knowledge about "what." The simplest case occurs when a technique is discovered serendipitously and the fact that it works is translated into the realm of Ω. But changes in techniques also open up new scientific questions and technical developments in instruments and laboratory methods make new research possible. Positive feedback from Ω and λ and back can lead to virtuous cycles much more powerful than can be explained by technological progress or scientific progress separately. The self-sustained nature of the process occurs because the two types of knowledge are complementary in the technical sense that a growth in one increases the marginal product of the other (Milgrom, Qian, and Roberts, 1991). If there is sufficient complementarity between an upstream process (Ω) and a downstream process (λ) in the system, persistent, self-reinforcing economic change can occur even without increasing returns. It could also be thought that there are feedback mechanisms from λ onto itself, in that new technology leads directly to further new technology. Historically, of course, this was precisely the nature of technological change, but a proper definition

---

[14] As *The Economist* wrote in its Millennium Special Issue, before Djerassi drugs were developed it in a "suck it and see" fashion: either their mode of action remained unknown, or it was elucidated after their discovery. *The Economist,* Jan 1, 2000, p. 102.

[15] Thus magnetic pain therapy, in which magnets are used to relieve pain – by now a multibillion industry in the United States – is agnostic on its base in Ω. Nobody who believes that this technique is effective (still a small minority) seems to have any serious idea or care very much about *how* it is supposed to work.

[16] Yet clearly this is not invariably the case. An example is the conquest of scurvy. The importance of fresh fruit in the prevention of scurvy had been realised even before James Lind published his *Treatise on Scurvy* in 1746. The Dutch East India Company kept citrus trees on the Cape of Good Hope in the middle of the seventeenth century, yet despite the obvious effectiveness of the remedy, the idea obviously did not catch on and the idea "kept on being rediscovered and lost" (Porter, 1995, p. 228). In any event, apart from the fact that there was an apparent connection between the consumption of fresh fruit and vegetable and the occurrence of scurvy, nothing was added to Ω until a century and a half later.

of Ω (which includes the "master catalog" of all elements in λ) would keep the formal mechanics straight.

One of the interesting characteristics of these evolutionary models of knowledge is that they imply that the tightness of Ω and λ are mutually reinforcing. Knowledge in Ω will become tighter if it maps into techniques that actually can be shown to work. Thus once biologists discovered that insects could be the vectors of pathogenic microparasites, insect-fighting techniques gained wide acceptance. The success of these techniques in eradicating yellow fever and malaria was the best confirmation of the hypotheses about the transmission mechanisms of the disease and helped gain them wide support. Another example is the relationship between aeronautics and the techniques of building machines that would actually fly.[17] To put it crudely, the way we are persuaded that science is true is that its recommendations work visibly: chemistry works – it makes nylon tights and polyethylene sheets (Cohen and Stewart, 1994, p. 54). Strictly speaking, this is not a correct inference, because a functional technique could be mapped from knowledge that turns out to be false. At the same time, techniques may be "selected" because they are implied by a set of knowledge that is gaining acceptance.[18] The chronological order of this mutual reinforcement between Ω and λ differs from case to case, but at least since the middle of the nineteenth century there is a gradual if incomplete shift toward a priority of Ω. That is to say, in the twentieth century more and more techniques require some prior scientific breakthrough before they become feasible although almost invariably the technique feeds back into the science.

---

[17] The fundamentals were laid out early by George Cayley in the early nineteenth century. Much of the knowledge in this branch of engineering was experimental rather than theoretical, namely, attempts to tabulate coefficients of lift and drag for each wing shape at each angle. The Wright brothers relied on the published work (especially of Otto Lilienthal) at the time to work out their own formulas, but they also ended up working closely with the leading aeronautical engineer of the time, Octave Chanute, who supplied them with advice right up to Kitty Hawk (Crouch, 1989). It is clear, however, that the Wright brothers were avid consumers of engineering science and that their greatness lies precisely in the mapping function.

[18] For an example of the give and take between Ω and λ in the case of household technology and bacteriology in late nineteenth century, see Mokyr and Stein (1997) and Mokyr (1997, 1998d).

3.   KNOWLEDGE, SCIENCE, AND TECHNOLOGY DURING THE INDUSTRIAL REVOLUTION

The Industrial Revolution was not the beginning of economic growth. There is by now considerable evidence that on the eve of the Industrial Revolution Britain and other parts of Western Europe had gone through long periods of economic growth, perhaps not as sustained and rapid as modern economic growth, but growth all the same (Mokyr, 1998c, pp. 34-36 and sources cited there). It remains to be seen how much of this growth can be attributed to increases in technological knowledge about production and how much to other factors, such as gains from trade or more efficient allocations. Much of the analysis of growth in history, of course, does not lend itself to such neat decompositions: the geographical discoveries after 1450 and improvements in shipping and navigational technology were in and of themselves a pure growth in Ω, mapping into improved techniques, but they led to increased trade as well. The Industrial Revolution, however, constitutes a stage in which the weight of the knowledge-induced component of economic growth experienced a marked increase. It did not start from zero, nor did it go to unity. All the same, the period 1760-1815 was one in which continuous political disruptions must have reduced the importance of "Smithian growth." Britain was able to sustain a rapidly rising population without a sharp decline in income, which may be regarded as a signal for a new "type" of growth.

It has become a consensus view that economic growth as properly defined was very slow during the Industrial Revolution, and that living standards barely nudged upward until the mid 1840s (Mokyr, 1998c). There have even been some voices calling for abandoning the term altogether. Yet it is by now recognised that there are considerable time lags in the adoption and macroeconomic effects of major technological breakthroughs and so-called General Purpose Technologies and that growth traditionally measured even during the difficult 1760-1815 years was, in fact, respectable once we take into account the negative political and demographic shocks of the period. In the longer run, the macroeconomic effects of the technological breakthroughs that constituted the Industrial Revolution have not seriously been questioned. The growth of *scientific* knowledge was part of this knowledge, but a relatively small part. Most practical useful knowledge in the eighteenth century was uncodified, unsystematic, and informal, passed on from master to apprentice or horizontally between agents. Yet formal and informal knowledge were strict complements in the development of new techniques, and the technology of knowledge transmission itself played a major role.[19]

The true question of the Industrial Revolution is not why it "took place" at all but why it was sustained beyond, say, 1820. There had been earlier clusters of macroinventions, most notably in the fifteenth century with the emergence of movable type, the casting of iron, and advances in shipping and navigation technology. Yet in the earlier cases these mini-industrial revolutions had always petered out before their effects could launch the economies into sustainable economic growth. Before the Industrial Revolution, the economy was characterised by negative feedback; each episode of growth in the end ran into an obstruction or resistance of some sort that put an end to it.[20] The best-known of these negative feedbacks mechanisms are Malthusian traps, a prime example of negative feedback, and technological resistance in which entrenched interests were able to stop technological progress using non-market mechanisms (Mokyr, 1994a, 1994b, 1998e). What was different in the eighteenth century is that the Scientific Revolution and the Enlightenment changed the structure of Ω to the point where useful knowledge could increase abruptly by continuously feeding on itself whereas previously it always was suppressed by economic and social factors.[21] Negative feedback was thus replaced by positive feedback, which eventually became so powerful that it became self-

---

[19] Margaret Jacob (1997), whose work has inspired much of what is to follow, summarises the developments in eighteenth century Europe as follows: "Knowledge has consequences. It can empower; if absent, it can impoverish and circumstances can be harder to understand or control" (p. 132). Yet her statement that "people cannot do that which they cannot understand, and mechanisation required a particular understanding of nature that came out of the sources of scientific knowledge" (p. 131) goes too far. Depending on what one means by "understand," it is obvious that people *can* do things they do not understand, such as build machines and design techniques on the basis of principles and laws that are poorly or misunderstood at the time.

[20] An early use of the idea of such feedbacks is found in Needham's description of the dynamics of Imperial China, which he describes as a "civilisation that had held a steady course through every weather, as if equipped with an automatic pilot, a set of feedback mechanisms, restoring the status quo [even] after fundamental inventions and discoveries" (Needham, 1969, pp. 119-20). Needham may overstate the degree of technological instability in pre-1750 Europe, but his intuition about the difference between the two societies being in the dynamic conditions of stability is sound.

[21] An explanation of this phenomenon has been proposed recently by David (1998). He envisages the community of "scientists" to consist of local networks or "invisible colleges" in the business of communicating with each other. Such transmission between connected units can be modelled using percolation models in which information is diffused through a network with a certain level of connectivity. David notes that these models imply that there is a minimum level of persistently communicative behaviour that a network must maintain for knowledge to diffuse through and that once this level is achieved the system becomes self-sustaining.

sustaining. Such positive feedback effects between Ω and λ resulted in a self-reinforcing spiral of knowledge augmentation that was impossible in earlier days of engineering without mechanics, iron-making without metallurgy, farming without organic chemistry, and medical practice without microbiology.[22] "Growth" in Ω meant not only an increase in the *size* of Ω (through discovery) but also in its *density* (through diffusion). All in all, the widening of the epistemic base of technology meant that the techniques that came into use after 1750 relied on a broader and broader base in Ω. This made a gradual stream of improvements and microinventions possible. In short, the Industrial Revolution should be understood in the context of changes in useful knowledge and its applications.

How much of the changes in Ω in Britain before and during the Industrial Revolution could be attributed to what we would call today "science"? The notion that Britain was the first to undergo an Industrial Revolution because somehow British technological success was due to Britain's having more "advanced" science is unsupportable. The premise itself is in dispute (Kuhn, 1977, p. 43), but even if it were true, the consensus is that techniques developed during the British Industrial Revolution owed little directly to "scientific knowledge" as we would define it today. Unlike the technologies that developed in Europe and the United States in the second half of the nineteenth century, science, by conventional wisdom, had little direct guidance to offer to the Industrial Revolution (Hall, 1978, p. 151). Gillispie (1957) points out that the majority of scientific endeavours of the time concerned subjects of limited technological use: astronomy, botany, crystallography and early exploration of magnetism, refraction of light, and combustion. Eventually many of those discoveries found economic applications, but these took place, with few exceptions, after 1830.

If science played a role in the Industrial Revolution, it was first and foremost through the incidental spillovers from the scientific endeavour on the properties of Ω. These spillovers affected the way in which *new* knowledge was generated, but equally important they affected the technology and culture of access to information. We may distinguish among three closely interrelated phenomena: scientific method, scientific mentality, and scientific culture. The penetration of scientific *method* into technological research meant accurate measurement, controlled experiment, and an insistence on reproducibility. William Eamon (1990), and more recently Paul David (1997) have pointed to the Scientific Revolution of the seventeenth century as the period in which "open science" emerged, when knowledge

---

[22] As Cohen and Stewart (1994, pp. 420-21) point out, because Ω and λ have a different "geography," their attractors do not match up nicely and "the feedback between the spaces has a creative effect... the interactions create a new, combined geography that in no sensible way can be thought of as a mixture of the two separate geographies."

about the natural world became increasingly non-proprietary and scientific advances and discoveries were freely shared with the public at large. Thus scientific knowledge became a public good, communicated freely rather than confined to a secretive exclusive few as had been the custom in medieval Europe. This sharing of knowledge within "open science" required systematic reporting of methods and materials using a common vocabulary and consensus standards. Scientific "method" here also should be taken to include the changes in the rhetorical conventions that emerged in the seventeenth century, during which persuasive weight continued to shift away from pure "authority" towards empirics, but which also increasingly set the rules by which empirical knowledge was to be tested so that useful knowledge could be not only accessed but trusted.[23] Margaret Jacob (1997, p. 115) has indeed argued that by 1750 British engineers and entrepreneurs had a "shared technical vocabulary" that could "objectify the physical world" and that this communication changed the Western world forever. These shared languages and vocabularies are precisely the stuff of which reduced access costs are made of.

Even more important, perhaps, was scientific *mentality*, which imbued engineers and inventors with a faith in the orderliness, rationality, and predictability of natural phenomena – even if the actual laws underlying chemistry and physics were not fully understood (Parker, 1984, pp. 27-28). Because technology at base involves the manipulation of nature and the physical environment, the metaphysical assumptions under which people engaged in production operate are ultimately of crucial importance. The growing belief in the rationality of nature and the existence of knowable natural laws that govern the universe, the archetypal enlightenment belief, led to a growing use of mathematics in pure science as well as in engineering and technology. In this new mode, more and more people rebelled against the idea that knowledge of nature was "forbidden" or better kept secret (Eamon, 1990). Scientific mentality also implied an open mind, a willingness to abandon conventional doctrine when confronted with new evidence, and a growing persuasion that no natural phenomenon was beyond systematic investigation and that deductive hypotheses could not be held to be true until tested. Yet, as Heilbron (1990) and his colleagues have argued,

---

[23] Shapin (1994) has outlined the changes in trust and expertise in Britain during the seventeenth century associating expertise, for better or for worse, with social class and locality. While the approach to science was ostensibly based on a "question authority" principle [the Royal Academy's motto was *nullius in verba* – on no one's word –] in fact no system of useful or any kind of knowledge can exist without some mechanism that generates trust. The apparent scepticism with which scientists treated the knowledge created by others increased the trust that others had in the findings, since outsiders could then assume – as is still true today – that these findings had been scrutinised and checked by other "experts."

in the second half of the eighteenth century "truth" became less a concern than an "instrumentalist" approach to scientific issues, in which quantifying physicists and chemists surrendered claims to "absolute truth" for the sake of a more pragmatic approach and gained ease of calculation and application of the regularities and phenomena discovered.

Finally, scientific *culture*, the culmination of Baconian ideology, placed applied science at the service of commercial and manufacturing interests (Jacob, 1997). Science in the seventeenth century became increasingly permeated by the Baconian motive of material progress and constant improvement, attained by the accumulation of knowledge.[24] Scientific culture led to the gradual emergence of engineering science and the continuous accumulation of orderly quantitative knowledge about potentially useful natural phenomena in "all matters mineral, animal, and vegetable."[25] Although such relations are impossible to quantify, it stands to reason that in that regard science laid the intellectual foundations of the Industrial Revolution by providing the tacit and implicit assumptions on which technological creativity depended.

Returning to the framework laid out earlier, these developments changed the internal structure of Ω during the eighteenth century and early nineteenth

---

[24] Robert K. Merton (1970 [1938], pp. ix, 87) asked rhetorically how "a cultural emphasis upon social utility as a prime, let alone an exclusive criterion for scientific work affects the rate and direction of advance in science" and noted that "science was to be fostered and nurtured as leading to the improvement of man's lot by facilitating technological invention." He might have added that non-epistemic goals for useful knowledge and science, that is to say, goals that transcend knowledge for its own sake and look for some application, affected not only the rate of growth of the knowledge set but even more the chances that existing knowledge will be translated into techniques that actually increase economic capabilities and welfare.

[25] The paradigmatic figure in the growth of the subset of Ω we now think of as "engineering" knowledge was John Smeaton (1724-1792). Smeaton's approach was pragmatic and empirical, although he was well versed in theoretical work. He limited himself to ask questions about "how much" and "under which conditions" without bothering too much about the "why." Yet his approach presupposed an orderliness and regularity in nature exemplifying the scientific mentality. Vincenti (1990, pp. 138-140) and Cardwell (1994, p. 195) attribute to him the development of the method of parameter variation through experimentation, which is a systematic way of gradual improvements in λ. It establishes regularities in the relationships between relevant variables and then extrapolates outside the known relations to establish optimal performance. At the same time, Smeaton possessed a great deal of the non-scientific component of useful knowledge: in the little workshop he used as a teenager, he taught himself to work in metals, wood and ivory and could handle tools with the expertise of a regular blacksmith or joiner (Smiles, 1891). It may well be, as Cardwell notes, that this type of progress did not lead to new macroinventions, but the essence of progress is the interplay between "door-opening" and "gap-filling" inventions. Setting up this systematic component in the mapping from Ω to λ, in addition to his own wide-ranging contributions to engineering, stamp Smeaton without question as one of the "Vital Few" of the Industrial Revolution.

century. They created "a community" of knowledge, within which much of the knowledge resided. It matters less what one individual knows than what the community "knows" – that is, the size of Ω. Yet the significance of communal knowledge matters for economic history only if it can be accessed, believed, and used. Useful knowledge, as Shapin points out, is always communal. No individual can know everything. Western societies experienced both an increase in the size of Ω and an ever-growing ability to map this useful knowledge into new and improved techniques, as access costs declined and new principles of authority, expertise, and verifiability were set up.

Some developments in the cost of access are well known and documented. The Royal Society, of course, was the very embodiment of the ideal of the free dissemination of useful knowledge.[26] In eighteenth and early nineteenth century Britain, popular lectures on scientific and technical subjects by recognised experts drew eager audiences. Some of these were given at scientific society meeting places, such as the famous Birmingham Lunar Society whereas others were given in less famous societies in provincial towns such as Hull, Bradford, and Liverpool. Still others were freelance and ad hoc, given in coffee-houses and masonic lodges. Audiences breathlessly watched experimental demonstrations illustrating the application of scientific principles to pumps, pulleys, and pendulums (Inkster, 1980). Yet, as Robert Schofield (1972) has argued, the formal meetings were secondary to the networking and informal exchange of technical information among members. Scientific culture reinforced the entrepreneurial interests of science's audience by demonstrating how applied mechanics could save costs and enhance efficiency and thus profits. Outside England, formal technical education played a larger role in fulfilling these functions. In France, artillery schools opened in the 1720s; in the late 1740s the *École des Ponts et Chausées* and the *École du génie* for military officers were opened, to be followed famously by the *Polytechnique* in 1794. Other countries on the Continent followed suit, with mining schools founded in Saxony and Hungary, among others. England, where the public sector rarely intervened in such matters, lagged behind in formal education, but its system of public lectures, informal scientific societies, and technical apprenticeship sufficed – for the time being. Yet what was there in natural knowledge that the mechanics and engineers felt they needed?

---

[26] The idea of reducing access costs encountered the kind of problem that is typical in "markets" for technological knowledge, namely how best to secure some form of appropriability for a public good. The Royal Society's project on the history and description of trades (i.e. manufacturing) ran into the resistance of craftsmen reluctant to reveal their trade secrets (Eamon, 1990, p. 355).

Despite its apparent shortcomings, eighteenth century scientific knowledge did provide implicit theoretical underpinnings to what empirically minded technicians did, even if the epistemic base was still narrow compared to what it would become later. Without certain elements in Ω, many of the new techniques would not have come into existence at all or not worked as well. Thus the steam engine depended both on the understanding of atmospheric pressure, discovered by Continental scientists such as Evangelista Torricelli and Otto von Guericke, and the early seventeenth century notion that steam was evaporated water and its condensation created a vacuum.[27] This discovery led to the idea that this pressure could be used for moving a piston in a cylinder, which could then be made to do work. The proto-idea of an engine filtered down to Newcomen despite the fact that his world was the local blacksmith's rather than the cosmopolitan academic scientist's. Improvements in mathematics, especially the calculus invented by Leibniz and Newton, became increasingly important to improvements in the design and perfection of certain types of machinery although in many areas its importance did not become apparent until much later. The advances in waterpower in the eighteenth century depended increasingly on a scientific base of hydraulic theory and experimentation despite a number of errors, disputes, and confusions (Reynolds, 1983).[28] The importance of waterpower in the Industrial Revolution is still not given its due recognition because steam was more spectacular and in some sense more revolutionary.[29] The technique of

---

[27] Usher (1954, p. 342) attributes this finding to Solomon De Caus, a French engineer and architect in a 1615 book. Uncharacteristically, Usher is inaccurate here: in 1601, Giambattista Della Porta already described a device based on the same idea, and both were apparently inspired by the appearance in 1575 of a translation of Hero of Alexandria's *Pneumatics* which, while not grasping either the notion of an atmospheric engine nor that of a condensation-induced vacuum, focused the attention on steam as a controllable substance. It is hard to imagine anyone reading Hero without realising that steam was evaporated water and that upon condensation "the vapour returns to its original condition."

[28] The input of formal mathematics into technical engineering problems was most remarkable in hydraulics and the design of better water wheels in the eighteenth century. Theoreticians such as the Eulers and Charles Borda made major contributions towards the understanding of the relative efficiency of various designs. It should be added however that experimental work remained central here and at times had to set the theorists straight. Calculus also found its way into mechanical issues in construction such as the theory of beams, especially Charles Coulomb in his celebrated 1773 paper applying calculus to "Statical Problems with Relevance to Architecture."

[29] John Smeaton was well-versed in the theoretical writings of French hydraulic scientists such as Antoine de Parcieux. In the 1750s, Smeaton carried out experiments showing that the efficiency of overshot wheels tended to be around 2/3, while that of undershot wheels was about 1/3. In 1759 he announced his results firmly establishing the superiority of the gravity wheel. At that point, Smeaton realised the vast potentialities of the breast wheel: it was a gravity wheel, but one that could be constructed in most sites previously suitable

chlorine bleaching depended on the prior discovery of chlorine by the Swedish chemist Carl Wilhelm Scheele in 1774. Phlogiston theory, the ruling physical paradigm of the eighteenth century, was eventually rejected in favour of the new chemistry of Lavoisier but some of its insights (*e.g.*, the Swede Tobern Bergman's contributions to metallurgy) were valuable, even if their scientific basis seems flawed and their terminology quaint to modern readers. Cardwell (1972, pp. 41-43) has shown that the idea of a measurable quantity of "work" or "energy" derived directly from Galileo's work on mechanics and played a major role in the theories and lectures of engineers such as Desaguliers. Harrison's great marine chronometer was only conceivable in the context in which Ω already contained the observation that longitude could be determined by comparing local time with time at some fixed point. Often, of course, bogus science produced bogus results, as in Jethro Tull's insistence that air was the best fertiliser and the amazingly eccentric theories still rampant in late eighteenth century medicine.[30]

In the "development" stage of basic inventions – in which engineers and technicians on the shopfloor improved, modified, and debugged the revolutionary insights of inventors such as Arkwright, Cartwright, Trevithick, and Roberts to turn them into successful business propositions – pure science played only a modest role. The mechanical inventions that constituted the Industrial Revolution involved little formal science, yet they still required a great deal of the pragmatic and informal knowledge of how certain materials respond to physical stimuli and heat, how the selective breeding of animals can be accomplished, how motion can be transmitted through pulleys and shafts, how and where to lubricate moving parts to reduce friction, and similar components of Ω. What is clear is that Britain was a society that provided both the incentives and the opportunities to apply useful knowledge to technology.

---

only for undershot wheels. Once fitted with the tightly fitting casing, it combined the advantages of the gravity and the impulse wheels. The breast wheel turned out to be one of the most useful and effective improvements to energy generation of the time. See especially Reynolds (1983).

[30] A Scottish physician by the name of John Brown (1735-88) revolutionised the medicine of his age with Brownianism, a system that postulated that all diseases were the result of over- or under-excitement of the neuromuscular system by the environment. Brown was no enthusiast for bleeding, and treated all his patients instead with mixtures of opium, alcohol, and highly seasoned foods. His popularity was understandably international: Benjamin Rush brought his system to America, and in 1802 his controversial views elicited a riot among medical students in Göttingen, requiring troops to quell it. Brown was asserted to have killed more people than the French Revolution and the Napoleonic Wars combined (cited by McGrew, 1985, p. 36).

An example of how such partial knowledge could lead to a new technique was the much-hailed Cort puddling and rolling technique.[31] The technique depended a great deal on prior knowledge about natural phenomena, even if the epistemic basis of the technique in terms of the physics and chemistry of metallurgy was still in the future. Cort realised full-well the importance of turning pig iron into wrought or bar iron by removing what contemporaries thought of as "plumbago" [a term taken from phlogiston theory and equivalent to a substance we would call today carbon]. The problem was to generate enough heat to keep the molten iron liquid and to prevent it from crystallising before all the carbon had been removed. Cort knew that reverberating furnaces using coke generated higher temperatures. Cort also realised that by rolling the hot metal using grooved rollers, its composition would be much more homogenous. How and why he mapped this prior knowledge into his famous invention is not exactly known, but the fact that so many other ironmasters were following similar tracks indicates that they were all drawing from a common pool.[32] All the same, it should be kept in mind that in coal and iron above all, craft-based tacit skills were of unusual importance in the finer details of the jobs, and that codifiable knowledge more than anywhere else would be insufficient in these industries unless accompanied by these informal skills (Harris, 1976).

Another example, not normally part of the history of the Industrial Revolution, is that most paradigmatic of all macroinventions, ballooning, which for the first time in history broke the tyranny of gravity. Speculation over how the idea first emerged is widespread, but Bagley's (1990, p. 609) verdict that "there is no apparent reason why this technology could not have appeared centuries earlier" is contradicted by the fact that British scientists had only discovered gases lighter than air – specifically "inflammable air" (hydrogen) isolated by Cavendish – and the knowledge that hot air expands and thus becomes lighter, in 1766. This knowledge was communicated to Joseph Montgolfier by his cousin, a medical student at Montpelier. Needless to say, the scientific basis of ballooning was not yet altogether clear, and contemporaries did not see for instance, that there was a fundamental difference between physically (hot air) and chemically (hydrogen) filled

---

[31] Hall (1978, p. 101) points to the puddling process as an example of a technique in which "useful knowledge" did not matter: a man either knows how to do it or he does not. Clearly this refers to the person actually carrying out the technique, not the technique itself.

[32] Reverberatory furnaces had been used in glassmaking and were first applied to iron by the Cranage brothers in Coalbrookdale. Puddling had been experimented with by the Cranage brothers as well, as well as by Richard Jesson and Peter Onions (who both took out similar patents two years before Cort's success). Grooved rolling had been pioneered by the great Swedish engineer Christopher Polhem. None of those attempts seems to have had much success: recombining obviously must be done in some specific way and not others.

balloons (Gillispie, 1983, p. 16). But *some* knowledge was necessary, and the timing seems better explained this way.

To summarise, then, the changes in technological knowledge in the century after 1750 involved three different types of processes. First, there were pure additions to Ω that occurred as part of an autonomous system of discovery about nature unrelated to economic needs and conditions. The great discoveries of Cavendish and Lavoisier establishing modern chemistry were clearly in this category. Such expansions in useful knowledge led to new mappings and eventually became one of the driving forces behind technological advances. Second, there were changes in some of the properties of Ω and λ, which became denser (more people shared the knowledge) and more accessible (better organised and easier to communicate). These changes yielded new mappings into λ, that is inventions, drawing both on the new and a pre-existing pool of knowledge. At first glance it may be hard to see, for instance, what there was in the original spinning jennies that could not have been conceived a century before.[33] Yet once such techniques are discovered, the knowledge that they are possible becomes part of Ω, and subsequent inventors can then draw upon it. Crompton's mule was a standard example of recombining two existing techniques into a novel one. Explaining the exact timing of such mappings is impossible, but the changing structure of Ω in terms of density and access costs was of central importance. In other words, changes in the overall size of Ω (what was known) may have been less important in the Industrial Revolution than the *access to* that knowledge. Moreover, the process was highly sensitive to outside stimuli and incentives. The social and institutional environment has always been credited with a central role in economic history. All I would argue is that the set-up proposed here sheds some light on *how* this mechanism worked.[34] In that respect the evolution of technology again resembles biological evolution. Changes in the environment (including changes in the availability of complements and substitutes) may trigger the activation of existing knowledge or select those techniques that happen to "express" information adapted to a new environment.

---

[33] Acemoglu and Zilibotti (1997, p. 716) attribute with apparent approval to E.J. Hobsbawm the absurd statement that there was "nothing new in the technology of the British Industrial Revolution and the new productive methods could have been developed 150 years before." In fact Hobsbawm's statement (1968, p. 37) is that the Scientific Revolution cannot explain the Industrial Revolution because at the end of seventeenth century European "scientific technology" (sic) was potentially quite adequate for the sort of industrialisation which developed eventually. It is still quite wrong, yet pointing this out does not deny that venture capital scarcity of the type emphasised by Acemoglu and Zilibotti and changes in its supply were of importance as well in determining the timing of the Industrial Revolution.

[34] For some attempts in this direction, see Mokyr (1998c, pp. 39-58).

Third, there was feedback from techniques to knowledge. A great number of major and minor scientific revolutions were driven not just by conceptual innovation but by new tools and techniques.[35] Famous examples are the steam engine, which led to the formulation of the laws of thermodynamics, and the microscope improved by Joseph J. Lister (father of the famous physician), which made bacteriology possible.[36] Such a feedback phenomenon is what makes the evolution of technology "Lamarckian."[37] It is this Lamarckian property that changed the dynamic nature of technological change during the Industrial Revolution and allowed for economic change to become the sustainable norm rather than the ephemeral exception.

4.   A KNOWLEDGE REVOLUTION

More or less contemporaneous with the Industrial Revolution was a revolution in what we would call today information technology.[38] The knowledge revolution affected the nature of Ω and through it the techniques mapped from it. Some of these changes were directly related to scientific breakthroughs, but from what I argued above it follows that what matters here is the advances in the organisation, storability, accessibility, and communicability of information in Ω, as well as the methods employed in expanding it. The blossoming of open science and the emergence of informal "scholarly communities," spanning different countries in which scholars and scientists kept close and detailed correspondences with each other in the seventeenth century compounded the discoveries

As a consequence, the amount of useful knowledge on which techniques in actual use could draw increased. In other words, the manipulation of

---

[35] This is emphasised in Dyson (1997), pp. 49-50. The telescope drove the Galilean revolution just as X-ray diffraction to determine the structure of big molecules drove the DNA revolution.

[36] It is interesting to note that Carnot's now famous *Reflexions sur la puissance motrice du feu* (1824) was wholly ignored in France, and found its way second hand and through translation into England, where there was considerably more interest in his work because of the growing demand for this kind of insight on the part of the builders of gigantic steam engines such as William Fairbairn in Manchester and Robert Napier in Glasgow (Crosbie Smith, 1990, p. 329).

[37] The impact of technology on natural knowledge is stressed by Nathan Rosenberg (1982), though Rosenberg confines his essay to "science." Yet many elements in Ω are made possible through better techniques that we would not think of as "science" including for example the European discoveries of the fifteenth century, made possible by better ship-building and navigational techniques.

[38] This revolution is the subject of a new and exciting book by Professor Daniel Headrick (2000). I am grateful to Professor Headrick for allowing me to see his unpublished ms. on which much of the following is based.

natural processes and regularities in farming, engineering, chemistry, medicine and so on came to depend on increasingly complex natural knowledge. Even within a single firm the subset of Ω necessary to form the basis for the techniques used became so large that no single individual could carry them all. Thus the division of labour, much as Adam Smith thought, played a pivotal role in technological change, but it was not so much "limited by the extent of the market" as much as necessitated by the extent of the knowledge involved and the limitations of the human mind (Becker and Murphy, 1992). The growth of useful knowledge led to the rise of specialisation in useful knowledge and the emergence of experts, consulting engineers, accountants, and thousands of other occupations controlling a particular subset of Ω. This meant that co-ordination between the activities of these specialists became increasingly necessary, and hence we have one more explanation of the rise of the factory system, the hallmark of the Industrial Revolution.

One aspect that is often overlooked is the speed and efficiency with which knowledge travelled. As Harris (1976, p. 173) has argued, much of the tacit, crafts-based knowledge spread through the continuous movement of skilled workers from one area to another. It is natural to think that the great discontinuity here occurred *after* the Industrial Revolution: the railroads in the early 1830s, the telegraph about a decade later. Yet as Rick Szostak (1991) has shown, the cost of moving about in Britain started to decline in the eighteenth century with the improved road system, ever more reliable stagecoach service, coastal shipping, and canals.[39] Moreover, it is by now recognised that the cost of and speed of the transmission of certain types of information was already declining before the telegraph. The Chappe semaphore telegraph, operating through France as well as in other parts of Western Europe, was a first step in this direction.[40] The Chappe system was a government monopoly and did not serve as a means of transmission of private information, yet it testifies to the age's increasingly rational and innovative approach to the transmission and dissemination of knowledge. The same is true for postal services: cross-posts (bypassing London) came into being after 1720, and by 1764 most of England and Wales received

---

[39] Merton (1970 [1938], pp. 216 ff.) points out that by the end of seventeenth century a system of stagecoaches and postal service was already in operation, and argues that social interaction and the exchange of information were crucial to the development of science in this period.

[40] Under optimal conditions the semaphore system could transmit a bit of information from Paris to Toulon in 12 minutes in contrast with the two full days it would take a messenger on horseback. A 100-signal telegram from Paris to Bordeaux in 1820 took 95 minutes; in 1840 it took half as long. Given that a "signal" was picked from a code book with tens of thousands options, this was a huge amount of information. The optical telegraph at its peak covered 5,000 miles and included 530 relay stations.

mail daily. Although the rates were high and their structure complex until Rowland Hill's postal revolution, which established the inland penny postage in 1840, postal services in England long before that were providing easy and reliable access to knowledge generated elsewhere. In the United States, as Richard John (1995) has shown, the postal service was a truly revolutionary agent. In 1790 each post office served 43,000 people, by 1840 each post office served only about 1,100 persons and for many years the postal service was by far the largest branch of the Federal government. Much of the post delivered consisted of newspapers.

Equally important is the standardisation of information. For communication between individuals to occur, a common terminology is essential. Language is the ultimate General Purpose Technology, to use Bresnahan and Trajtenberg's (1995) well-known term. It provides the technology that creates others. Language is one way in which culture can affect the pathway from knowledge to technology and thus economic performance in the long run. It is a standard of efficient communication, necessary if people are to draw knowledge from storage devices and from each other. How important is language as a component of the kind of culture that eventually brings about economic development?

The seventeenth and eighteenth centuries in Europe were the period in which technical and scientific writings switched from Latin to the various vernacular languages; thus even those without a classical education were given access. Of course, this reflects demand as much as cultural change. Either way, it marks the growing trend toward lower access costs that characterised Western European culture in the century before the Industrial Revolution.[41] To be sure, language and its use can adapt to changing circumstances, and Chinese writing today is quite different from the traditional *wen yen* or "written words."[42]

---

[41] The importance of language as a communication tool and the need for a language designed along rational precepts modelled after mathematics, with exact correspondences between words and things was particularly stressed by Etienne Bonnot the Condillac (1715-1780), a central figure of the French enlightenment See for instance Rider (1990).

[42] All the same, one of the most eminent Sinologists of our time, Derk Bodde, has made a startling argument in which he points to language as an impediment to the emergence and diffusion of scientific and technological knowledge. Bodde (1991) points out the inherent weaknesses of the Chinese language as a mode of transmitting precise information and its built-in conservative mechanisms. To summarise his views, Chinese language placed three obstacles in the way of the growth of useful knowledge in China. One was the large gap between literary Chinese and spoken Chinese. This made written documents far less accessible for people without considerable training and thus made it less easy for artisans and technicians to draw upon the useful knowledge accumulated by scholars and scientists. Second, the absence of inflection and punctuation created considerable ambiguity over what texts exactly meant. While Bodde's critics are right to point out that much of this ambiguity could be resolved if one knew the context, the point is that efficient commun-

The language that came to dominate technical communications and thus "access costs" increasingly became the language of mathematics, a widely noted consequence of the scientific revolution. It was associated more than anyone else with Galileo, who famously wrote that the book of the Universe was written in the "language of mathematics, without which it is impossible to understand a single word of it." Yet what counted is not just better and more useful mathematics, but also its accessibility to the people who might use it, engineers, instrument makers, designers, chemists, artillery officers, and so on.[43] In chemistry, such as it was, the scientific revolution created a movement in the direction of better comprehensibility and smoother communication, reducing access costs (Golinski, 1990) and its increasing quantification of the methods and language of chemistry in the eighteenth century made it increasingly accessible to potential users (Lundgren, 1990). In Sweden, around 1700, Christopher Polhem was the first to try to construct a mechanical "alphabet."

Another important component of such a system of communication is an accepted set of standards for weights and measures. During the eighteenth century technology gradually became more systematic about its reliance on quantitative measures (Lindqvist, 1990), and such a standardisation became essential. Useful knowledge, much more than other kinds of knowledge, requires a strict and precise "I-see-what-you-see" condition to be communicated and transmitted. Mathematics was one such language, quantitative measures and standards another. The introduction of the metric system on the Continent during the French Revolution and the Napoleonic period, established a common code that despite some serious resistance eventually became universally accepted.[44] The United States and Britain chose to stick to their own system: in the eighteenth century most people

---

ication must be able to provide as much information as possible with little context. Finally, Bodde points out that written Chinese was a formidably conservative force: it created a cultural uniformity over time and space that was the reverse of the dynamic diversity we observe in Europe. The way a nineteenth century official would describe Western barbarians was very similar in metaphor and illustration to the way this would be done by a Han statesman two millennia earlier (Bodde, 1991, p. 31). Of course, this third point is not entirely consistent with the second.

[43] Arithmetics, of course, was an international language that could be understood by all. But more complex mathematics was changing the world as well. For instance, Mahoney (1990) points out that in the seventeenth century the mechanical view of the world and the formal science of motion changed dramatically because of the ability of mathematicians to represent it as differential equations of one form or another. This involved a dramatic change in the way mathematics was understood, yet once it was accepted it clearly represented a vastly superior way of representing relations between physical objects.

[44] After some backtracking from the pure metric system as passed in 1799, the French government brought it back in full force in 1837; after 1840 it became the only legal system in France. See Alder (1995).

used accepted measures of the pound, and the standard yard was made in 1758-60 and deposited in the House of Commons (Headrick, 1998, ch. 2). In 1824, Britain enacted the Imperial System of Weights and Measures codifying much of the existing system.[45] Such standardisations had been attempted many times before, but they required the coercive powers and co-ordination capabilities of the modern state.

Metrology was thus of considerable importance. The uniform organisation of measurement and standards is a critical property of Ω if marginal access costs are to be kept low.[46] Many systems of codifying technical knowledge and providing standards were devised or improved during the Enlightenment. Headrick mentions two of the most important ones: the Linnaean system of classifying and taxonomising living species, and the new chemical nomenclature designed by John Dalton and simplified and improved into its current form by Berzelius in 1813-14.[47] But other useful concepts were also standardised: In 1784 James Watt set the horsepower as the amount of energy necessary to raise 33,000 pounds one foot in one minute. Less well-known but equally important is the work of Thomas Young (1773-1829) whose modulus of elasticity (1807) measured the resistance of materials under stress in terms of the pull in pounds that it would take to stretch a bar to double its original length.[48] There were even some attempts to quantify precisely the amount of physical work one man could be expected to do in a day (Ferguson, 1971; Lindqvist, 1990).

Of great importance to the streamlining of access to knowledge were what Ferguson (1992) has called "Tools of Visualisation." The art of mechanical illustration was an early phenomenon and well established in the second half of the sixteenth century. Yet the great books of technical

---

[45] Witold Kula (1986, pp. 117-19) has drawn a link between the enlightenment and the eighteenth century attempts to standardise measures, arguing that "disorder" of the kind caused by their proliferation could not be tolerated. While the reforms clearly had political and fiscal reasons, they led – perhaps as a largely unintended by-product – to a rationalisation in knowledge-transmission.

[46] Latour (1990, p. 57) states with some exaggeration that "the universality of science and technology is a cliché of epistemology but metrology is the practical achievement of this mystical universality."

[47] Although the periodic table of elements was not finalised by Mendeleev till 1869, earlier attempts to represent the elements in an orderly and organised manner go back to Lavoisier himself. In 1817 a German chemist, Johann Döbereiner showed how the elements known at that time could be arranged by triads, encouraging others to search for further patterns. See Scerri (1998).

[48] Young's work was complex and poorly written and might have been forgotten in an earlier age. The Industrial Revolution era, however, had ways of disseminating important knowledge and his work found its way to the engineering community through the textbooks of Thomas Tredgold (widely read by engineers at the time), and articles in the Encyclopedia Britannica.

illustrations published at that time by Besson (1578) and Ramelli (1588) do not describe real existing machines as much as idealised concepts, and were lacking in visual perspective. Only the illustrations accompanying the *Encyclopédie* and the 80 volumes of the *Description des arts et métiers* (1761-1788) approached technical mastery. Ferguson (1992, p. 135) thinks that the impact of these volumes on stimulating technological change was "probably slight" and he is more inclined to attribute radical changes to the systematic works describing possible rather than actual mechanical movements such as Jacob Leupold's *Theatrum Machinarum* (1724-39). Ferguson thus underestimates the importance of access to knowledge of *existing* techniques as a key to their improvement and their recombination into novel "hybrids." In any case, the eighteenth century witnessed a great deal of progress in "technical representation," and by the middle of the eighteenth century technical draughtsmanship had begun to be taught systematically (Daumas and Garanger, 1969, p. 249).[49] In addition, descriptive geometry was developed by the French mathematician Gaspard Monge between 1768 and 1780 (Alder, 1997, pp. 136-146) which made graphical presentations of buildings and machine design mathematically rigorous.[50] In Alder's words (p. 140), "it marks a first step toward understanding how the way things are made has been transformed by the way they are represented." The impact of Monge's sophisticated diagrams on the actual practice of engineering was probably modest at first, and technical drawings and orthographic projections were used by other engineers independently and long before Monge's work. My argument is simply that "the way things are represented" is a way of organising Ω and that the visual organisation of technical knowledge made enormous progress in the age of Enlightenment.[51] No doubt, Alder is right in pointing out that all such ways are "social constructions" and "cultural conventions," yet it is

---

[49] Alder (1998, p. 513) distinguishes between three levels of mechanical drawing in pre-Revolutionary France: the thousands of workshops where experienced artisans taught free-hand drawing to their apprentices; state-sponsored schools in which drawing teachers taught basic geometry; and the advanced engineering schools in which mechanical drawing was taught by mathematicians.

[50] Monge's technique essentially solved the problem of reducing three dimensional entities to two dimensions while at the same time depicting the relationships between the parts constituting the shape and configuration of the entity.

[51] In an interesting and iconoclastic paper, Latour (1990) attributes the emergence of modern science and technology to the representation of information in two-dimensional space where it can be manipulated and processed. He calls these representations "inscriptions" and points out that the role of the mind has been exaggerated, and that the mind's ability to process knowledge depends entirely on whether it has to deal with the real world or with these representations. At a less lofty but more sensible level, Alder (1998) argues that graphical representation was a mechanism to make "thick" (complex) reality into something "thin" (that is, comprehensible).

hard to deny that some social constructions lend themselves better to access and diffusion of knowledge than others. To be sure, no device can be reproduced from a drawing alone, and that when French engineers tried to assemble a Watt steam engine from a drawing prepared by him, the pieces did not always fit (Alder, 1997, p. 146). Yet such drawings clearly told people what could and had been done, and the mechanical principles on which it was based. No amount of dexterity and instinctive technical sense could make much progress without access to such knowledge. Moreover, Alder points out that these precise representations made standardisation and interchangeability possible, and thus led eventually to the modularization characteristic of the second Industrial Revolution.

If the access costs are to be affordable so that production can draw on accumulated useful knowledge, there has to be social contact between "knowers" and "doers." There is too much tacit and uncodeable knowledge in technology for the written word and the graphical representation to do it all. Any society in which a social chasm exists between the workers, the artisans and the engineers on one side, and the natural philosophers and "scientists" (the word does not exist till the 1830s) will have difficulty mapping continuously from useful knowledge onto the set of recipes and techniques that increase economic welfare. If the *savans* do not deign to address practical problems where their knowledge could help resolve difficulties and do not make an effort to communicate with engineers and entrepreneurs, the *fabricans* will have difficulty accessing Ω. Within Europe, the depth of this chasm varied a lot (though nowhere was it totally absent).[52] Yet compared to China or classical antiquity it appears to be shallow. Above all, Britain was the country in which it may have been already the shallowest by 1700, and furthermore it was becoming shallower over the eighteenth century.[53] The point is not whether engineers and artisans "inspired" the Scientific Revolution nor, conversely, whether the Industrial Revolution was "caused" by science. It is the strong complementarity, the continuous feedback between the two types of knowledge that set the system on a new course.

---

[52] Interestingly enough, the bridging of the social gap between the sphere of the learned scientist and that of the artisan was used by sociologists such as Zilsel to explain the origins of modern science, but with few exceptions has not played a similar role in explanations of the Industrial Revolution (see for instance Eamon, 1990, pp. 345-46; Cohen, 1994, pp. 336ff).

[53] Even the champions of Chinese science and technology have to concede that Chinese artisans were remarkably good at carrying out empirical procedures of which they had no scientific understanding. The real work in engineering was "always done by illiterate or semi-literate artisans and master craftsmen who could never rise across that sharp gap which separated them from the 'white collar literati'" (Needham, 1969, p. 27).

Personal and informal contact was naturally of primary importance in the eighteenth century. I have already referred to the scientific societies, academies, masonic lodges, coffee-house lectures and other meetings. Some of those had the purpose of smoothing the path of knowledge between scientists and engineers on the one side and those who carried out the instructions and used the techniques on the other side. The circulation and diffusion of knowledge within Ω was equally important, and hence the importance of such bodies as the Royal Society and the Society of Civil Engineers founded by Smeaton in 1771. By the middle of the nineteenth century, there were 1,020 associations for technical and scientific knowledge in Britain with a membership that Inkster estimates conservatively at 200,000 (Inkster, 1991, pp. 73, 78-79).

Access to useful information also was determined by literacy and the availability of reading material. At least for Britain it is now widely agreed that increases in literacy were relatively modest during the Industrial Revolution (Mitch, 1998). Yet literacy is not all that useful unless people actually read, and for the purposes of technological change, it also mattered *how much* and *what* people read. At least two well-known inventions of the Industrial Revolution made the availability of reading material more widespread, the Robert method of producing continuous paper (applied in Britain by Brian Donkin around 1807) and the improvements in printing due to the introduction of cylindrical printing and inking using steam power invented by the German immigrant Friedrich Koenig in 1812. There is some evidence that with the development of lending libraries and the decline in the price of books, reading materials became more available.[54] Newspapers increased steadily in numbers and circulation, although the period of the Industrial Revolution was one of steady progress rather than quantum leaps forward (Black, 1994). I am not suggesting, needless to say, that people actually found technical descriptions in newspapers. The self-referential structure of Ω implies that before one can try to access knowledge, it is necessary to know that it actually exists or that a technique is used somewhere so that a search can be initiated. Here newspapers, magazines, and even "popular encyclopaedias" played an important role. A part of the improvement in access technology resulted from an ability to ask better questions that were based on shards of knowledge. Without these shards, producers might not know what to look for. Asking the correct question and knowing whom to ask is more than half the way to getting to the answer.

Moreover, relevant and useful knowledge became more easy to access even for non-specialists. A major contributor to this was the growth of general purpose encyclopaedias which had material arranged alphabetically

---

[54] An example is the gradual replacement of leather with cloth binding, making books "less aristocratic , less forbidding, less grand" (Manguel, 1996, p. 140).

or (in a minority of cases) thematically. Encyclopaedias had been an old idea, and in 1254 Vincent of Beauvais completed his vast *Speculum*. By the time of the scientific revolution, the idea had caught on that existing knowledge could only be tapped if this knowledge was sorted and arranged systematically. Not surprisingly, the most eloquent call for such a project came from Francis Bacon himself.[55] The alphabetical organisation of the material was first attempted in Louis Moréri's *Grand dictionaire historique* (1674). Fifteen years later Antoine Furetière published his issue of *Dictionnaire universel des arts et sciences* (1690), which placed the kind of emphasis on arts and sciences that Bacon had called for. The first encyclopaedia of what I termed "useful knowledge" in English appeared in 1704, John Harris's *Lexicon Technicum*, dealing with a host of technical issues. Its most prominent successor in English was Ephraim Chambers's *Cyclopedia*, first published in 1728, which went through many editions. Harris's book was perhaps the prototype of a device meant to organise useful knowledge efficiently: it was weak on history and biography, strong on brewing, candle-making, dyeing. It, too, contained hundreds of engravings, cross references and an index. It was, in Headrick's words, "a handy and efficient reference tool." The best example is Diderot's justly famous *Encyclopédie*, the epitome of enlightenment literature, with its thousands of very detailed technical essays and plates.[56] As Headrick points out, the editors of the *Encyclopédie* covered the useful arts in painstaking detail, visiting workshops, interviewing the most skilled craftsmen they could find. The approximately 72,000 entries included long ones on mundane topics such as masonry (33 pages), glassmaking (44 pages), and mills (25 pages). These essays were accompanied by many clear engravings. The *encyclopédie*, moreover, was a best-seller. The original version sold four thousand copies, but the total may have reached twenty five thousand copies if the many pirated and translated versions are counted, at an average of 30

---

[55] Bacon in his famous *Novum Organum* called for an organisation of knowledge according to Platonic notions, much like his contemporary Mathias Martini (1606). His inspiration was acknowledged by the *encyclopédistes*: d'Alembert [1751], 1995, acknowledged "the immortal chancellor of England" as "the great man we acknowledge as our master" even if he and Diderot eventually chose a somewhat different way of organising the knowledge (pp. 74-76).

[56] In the *Encyclopédie*, in his article on "arts", Diderot himself made a strong case for the "open-ness" of technological knowledge, condemning secrecy and confusing terminology, and pleading for easier access to useful knowledge as a key to sustained progress." He called for a "language of [mechanical] arts" to facilitate communication and to fix the meaning of such vague terms as "light" "large", "middling" to enhance the accuracy of information in technological descriptions. The *Encyclopédie*, inevitably perhaps, only fulfilled these lofty goals very partially and the articles on technology differed immensely in detail and emphasis. For a recent summary of the work as a set of technological representations, see Pannabecker, 1998.

volumes per set.[57] Diderot and d'Alembert's masterwork was widely imitated. The *Encyclopaedia Britannica*, the most famous of these products in the English language, first appeared in 1771 as a fairly small project (3 volumes in 3 years) written by one person, William Smellie. It too focused on the sciences, useful arts, medicine, business and mathematics. Much larger editions soon expanded the range. German equivalents followed as well, culminating in the formidable *Brockhaus*, whose encyclopaedia began appearing in 1809.[58] It remains to be seen if the encyclopaedias and compilations were more than an expensive device by which a nouveau riche bourgeoisie demonstrated its intellectual imprimaturs for whom, in Headrick's words the technical essays constituted "intellectual voyeurism." At times, the knowledge contained in these compilations was already obsolete at the time of publication or became so soon after. In other cases, books about the useful arts were written by scholars to whom the esteem of the scholarly world was of first concern, and who were more inclined to cite past authorities than to examine with some care what was happening at the shopfloor (Harris, 1976, p. 169). Of course I do not argue that one could learn a craft just from reading an encyclopaedia article (though some of the articles in the *encyclopédie* read much like cookbook entries). But they informed the reader of the dimensions and limits of Ω underlying λ and once the reader knew what was known, he or she could look for details elsewhere.[59] The order of articles was organised in a form designed to minimise access costs: while alphabetisation was not new, the idea of organising useful information that way was quite radical.[60] This system, with its logical extension, the alphabetical index, must be regarded as the first search engine, though by the time of the Industrial Revolution it was far from perfect as those consulting original editions of *The Wealth of Nations* can verify. It might be added that Chinese characters do not lend themselves to something akin to alphabetisation and that the organisation of useful knowledge in Chinese encyclopaedias and compilations was awkward.

[57] Interestingly, the *encyclopédistes*, no more than Adam Smith, had any inkling of the imminent Industrial Revolution. The author of the article on *Industrie*, Louis Chevalier de Jaucourt, noted that Industry appears to have entered a stage in which changes are much more mild and the shocks far less than violent than before (Lough, 1971, p. 360).

[58] Johann Beckmann, whose *Anleitung zur Technologie* (1777) was one of the first works to actually use the term, became Professor of Technology in Göttingen in the 1770s.

[59] Thomas Blanchard in his 1820 application for a patent on his lathe, attributed the cammotion that created irregular shapes to Diderot's *Encyclopédie* as well as to a depiction in the *Edinburgh Encyclopedia* (M.R. Smith, 1977, p. 125).

[60] While not all encyclopaedias or compendia followed this format, when they did not they became series of unrelated textbooks, less efficient for some purposes but still crammed full of relatively accessible knowledge. An example is Charles-Joseph Panckoucke's *Encyclopédie méthodique*, a huge work conceived in the 1780s which over half a century published 166 volumes of text alone and many more of maps, plates, engravings.

Other ways of cataloguing useful knowledge also emerged, especially in France. Encyclopaedias were supplemented by a variety of textbooks, manuals, and compilations of techniques and devices that were somewhere in use. An early example was Joseph Moxon's 1683 *Doctrine of Handyworks*; the biggest one was probably the massive *Description des arts et métiers* produced by the French Académie des Sciences. Following the theoretical work of Monge and Lazare Carnot, the polytechniciens developed kinematics, a method of classifying mechanical movements by function, resulting in Jean Hachette's *Traité élémentaire des machines* (1808) and similar compendia. By the middle of the nineteenth century, reference books such as Henry T. Brown's *Five Hundred and Seven Mechanical Movements* (1868) had become quite exhaustive .

Of particular interest is the rise of statistics as a way of interpreting information about the physical world. The Newtonian view of the world was strictly deterministic rather than stochastic, and natural scientists were uneasy about the uncertainty it implied. It was readily realised, however, that a probabilistic approach was necessary for the formalisation of empirical regularities in natural phenomena, the mechanisms of which were not fully understood or for which not all the information necessary was available.[61] The notion that empirical inferences could be made this way and that knowledge from large samples trumped personal experience no matter how detailed is another product of the enlightenment. Demography, medicine, crime and public health were obvious applications of statistics, but eventually they were applied to other areas in which they would prove useful, such as agriculture.[62] After 1815, statistics flourished, with statistical societies founded everywhere, and government all over the Western starting to collect more or less orderly statistical censuses and other types of information. It is this kind of empirical methodology that led to important breakthroughs in practical medicine, such as the reaction against bloodletting therapy spearheaded by the statistical researches of C-A Louis and the discoveries that cholera and typhus are transmitted through water. These increments in Ω obviously mapped into some transparantly useful techniques.

Did all this organisation of useful knowledge matter? It is beyond question that the technological leaders of the Industrial Revolution, men like

---

[61] The insight that only an omniscient Supreme Being could dispense with probability because it had infinite knowledge but that human ignorance required some knowledge of the error term was first fully formulated by Laplace in the 3-volume *Théorie analytique des probabilités* (1812-20). See Porter (1986), pp. 71-73.

[62] One of the great private data collection projects of the time was Arthur Young's work in which he collected hundreds of observations on farm practice in Britain and the Continent - although at times his conclusions were contrary to what his own data indicated. See Allen and Ó Gráda (1988).

Smeaton, Watt, Trevithick, Roebuck, Wilkinson, Maudslay, and Roberts, were well-read in technical matters. So, by all accounts, were scores of lesser lights whose contribution, cumulatively, made all the difference. Moreover, in Britain many literate people, including entrepreneurs and peers in the House of Lords, possessed in Jacob's words "significant technical competence." How this familiarity with "science" and more widely with technical and useful knowledge precisely affected Britain's inventiveness remains a matter of some controversy. All codified knowledge surely needed to be complemented by tacit and implicit skills such as dexterity, a sense of "what worked" and so on.[63] But often such skills are directed and focused by knowledge acquired from others or from reading. For certain technical devices the knowledge that it worked *at all* or a very rough outline of how it did so sufficed for skilled engineers, physicians, chemists, or farmers. They could fill in the details.[64] The exact mapping from useful knowledge to technique took complex forms, and it is striking that France seems to have led Britain in terms of technical education, engineering textbooks, encyclopaedias, and other access-cost-reducing developments.[65] Yet this observation does not refute the argument I made here. Britain's success in the Industrial Revolution was to a remarkable extent based on French inventions. From chlorine bleaching to gaslighting to Jacquard looms, Britain greedily looked to France for inspiration. To oversimplify to the point of absurdity, one could say that France's strength was in Ω, Britain's in λ, and that the mapping function bridged the Channel.[66] Perhaps the crucial difference between the two was in the way the political structures affected the mapping function. In France, engineering knowledge was mostly

---

[63] The importance of such tacit knowledge has been re-emphasised by Ferguson (1992), relying on the work of John R. Harris. The French had figured out that, as one mid eighteenth century French author put it, "eye and practice alone can train men in these activities." Yet tacit knowledge and formal visual or verbal knowledge should not be thought of as substitutes but as complements.

[64] Two cases of difficult access to *existing* stored knowledge are often cited. One is the existence of a copy of Vittorio Zonca's *Nuovo Teatro di Machine et Edificii* (pub. in 1620) in the open shelves of the Bodleian, unbeknownst to John Lombe who spent two years travelling in Italy to secure knowledge on the silk-throwing machine described therein he could have found closer to home. The other is the existence of a copy of Euclid's *elements* – translated into Chinese – in the Imperial library in the thirteenth century (Needham, 1959, p. 105), yet which apparently never noticed by the Chinese astronomers. The Zonca anecdote is usually cited as support for the importance of hands-on experience and personal observation, yet it is still unresolved whether a detailed prior knowledge of what the machine looked like and how it worked would not have greatly facilitated the Lombe's adoption.

[65] J.R. Harris (1976, p. 171) points out that there is more to be learned about coalmining – even British coalmining – from French sources than from English ones.

[66] For more details on the different scientific and technological trajectories of France and Britain, see Mokyr (1998c).

regarded as inspired by and in the service of national interests and political objectives, both on the part of those in control of the state and on the part of those wishing to undermine it. In Britain, overall, the subsets of λ of interest to the engineers and scientists of the time were far more industrial and commercial. At the same time, the French government became aware very soon of its backwardness and took various measures to reverse what Jean-Antoine Chaptal called this "inversion of natural order" (cited by Jacob, 1998, p. 78). Chaptal, who was Minister of the Interior under Napoleon, was convinced that British industrial success was due to its superior "mechanical knowledge" and the close ties between the *savans* and the *fabricans* (Jacob, 1997, pp. 182-183). France's innovation in this regard, in addition to engineering schools, was the organisation of industrial expositions, in which technical knowledge was diffused in an efficient and concentrated manner. These are merely differences of degree and timing, minor if we compare the West to Eastern Europe or the Middle East, but perhaps enough to explain much of the differences within Western Europe.

To repeat: the knowledge revolution of the Industrial Revolution was not just the emergence of *new* knowledge, it was better access to knowledge that made the difference. In some instances scholars have tended to overstate how much novelty had occurred in the centuries before the Industrial Revolution, minimising its technological achievements.[67] To be sure, engineering knowledge during the age of the baroque had achieved some remarkable successes, and beside Leonardo a number of brilliant engineers and inventors are known to have proposed precocious devices: one thinks of Cornelis Drebbel, Simon Stevin, Giambattista Della Porta, Robert Hooke, Blaise Pascal, Gottfried Wilhelm Leibniz – among many others. Yet their knowledge remained very difficult for subsequent rank-and-file engineers and mechanics to access, often presented to a selected audience or never published at all. The Enlightenment began a process that dramatically lowered these access costs. To return to the evolutionary framework, the knowledge revolution of the eighteenth century, that is, the changes in the structure of Ω, made the process of evolution more *efficient* in the sense that techniques that were superior spread faster because the ways they became known and could be tested improved. It is worth pointing out that such an increase in efficiency is *not* meaningful in a biological context, because there is no easy way to define "superior" independent of fitness (that is, the probability of being selected).

---

[67] Thus Ferguson (1992, pp. 63-64) states that a modern automobile engine contains mostly components that were known when Leonardo was alive, leaving electrical components and microprocessors aside. Yet the concept of the engine itself, transforming heat into work by burning fossil fuels was clearly absent in Leonardo's day.

Moreover, we should keep in mind that a substantial portion of invention consists of *recombination*, the application of a number of rather remote and disjoint sections of Ω together to form something novel. This is probably equally true today, and it is one of the chief reasons why access functions are so important in triggering the new mapping of techniques from Ω to λ. If taken to an extreme, such recombination can lead to dazzling rates of invention, because the rate of invention will be combinatorical, which is faster than exponential (Weitzman, 1996). Both Cort's puddling and rolling process and Crompton's mule were recombinations, but less famous examples are not hard to come by.[68] It may be an exaggeration to say with François Jacob that "to create is to recombine" (Jacob, 1977, p. 1163), as some elements were truly novel, but it surely is true that much of technological innovation consists of precisely such activities. Hence the extreme importance of efficient and accessible sources of useful knowledge in which one could check what was known about a particular natural phenomenon or process, or about techniques in actual use, and transfer them to novel applications.

5.   CONCLUSION

I am suggesting that any historical account of economic progress, and above all accounts of the Industrial Revolution and its aftermath, need to incorporate *knowledge* explicitly. The much discussed "Information Technology" of our own age is one in which marginal access costs have been lowered enormously, and in many areas have been reduced to practically zero. The hardwired Internet II, which will be implemented in the next decade, will make current technology look archaic by comparison. This may be regarded as opening the floodgates to further technological progress in our age. The differences between the two episodes are at least as instructive as the similarities, and not too much should be made of such historical analogies. Perhaps the most striking conclusion to be drawn from it is that it is enormously difficult for contemporaries to realise how drastically their world is changing, what the important elements are, and how all this will work out in the future. The great economic minds of the age, from Smith to Ricardo, had only the faintest notion of the pending changes.[69]

---

[68] Thus Richard Roberts' multiple spindle machine used a Jacquard-type control mechanism for the drilling of rivet holes in the wrought iron plates used in the Britannia tubular bridge (Rosenberg and Vincenti, 1978, p. 39).

[69] This is much less true for other writers of the time. For more details on the issue to what extent contemporary writers were unaware of the Industrial Revolution see Mokyr (1994c and 1998c).

In a world of positive feedbacks, self-sustaining and self-reinforcing changes, and non-linear dynamics, in the words of Stuart Kauffman, "all bets are off."

REFERENCES

Acemoglu, D. and F. Zilibotti (1997), "Was Prometheus Unbound by Chance: Risk, Diversification and Growth," *Journal of Political Economy* 105, pp. 709-751.

Alder, K. (1995), "A Revolution to Measure: The Political Economy of the Metric System in France," in: M. Norton Wise (ed.), *The Values of Precision*, Princeton: Princeton University Press.

Alder, K. (1997), *Engineering the Revolution: Arms, Enlightenment, and the Making of Modern France*, Princeton: Princeton University Press.

Alder, K. (1998), "Making Things the Same: Representation, Tolerance and the End of the *Ancien Régime* in France," *Social Studies of Science* 28, pp. 499-545.

d'Alembert, J. Le Rond. [1751], (1995), *Preliminary Discourse to the Encyclopaedia of Diderot*, translated by R. N. Schwab, Chicago: University of Chicago Press.

Allen, R.C., and C. Ó Gráda (1988), "On the Road Again with Arthur Young: English, Irish, and French Agriculture During the Industrial Revolution," *Journal of Economic History* 38, pp. 93-116.

Bagley, J.A. (1990), "Aeronautics," in I. MacNeil (ed.), *An Encyclopaedia of the History of Technology*, London: Routledge.

Becker, G. S. and K. M. Murphy (1992), "The Division of Labour, Co-ordination Costs, and Knowledge," *Quarterly Journal of Economics*, 107, pp. 1137-1161.

Black, J. (1994), "Continuity and Change in the British Press, 1750-1833," *Publishing History*, vol. XXXVI, pp. 39-85.

Bodde, D. (1991), *Chinese Thought, Society, and Science*, Honolulu: University of Hawaii Press.

Bresnahan, T. F. and M. Trajtenberg (1995), "General Purpose Technologies: 'Engines of Growth'? ," *Journal of Econometrics* 65, pp. 83-108.

Cardwell, D.S.L (1972), *Turning Points in Western Technology*, New York: Neale Watson Science History Publication.

Cardwell, D.S.L. (1994), *The Fontana History of Technology*, London: Fontana Press.

Casti, J. (1990), *Searching for Certainty: What Scientists can Know about the Future*, New York: William Morrow.

Cohen, H. F. (1994), *The Scientific Revolution: a Historiographical Inquiry*, Chicago: University of Chicago Press.

Cohen, J. and I. Stewart (1994), *The Collapse of Chaos: Discovering Simplicity in a Complex World*, Harmondsworth: Penguin.

Crosby, Alfred B. (1997), *The Measure of Reality: Quantification and Western Society, 1250-1600*, Cambridge: Cambridge University Press.

Crouch, Tom (1989), *The Bisho's Boys: A Life of Wilbur and Orville Wright*, New York: Norton.

Daumas, M. and A. Garanger (1969), "Industrial Mechanization," in Maurice Daumas (ed.), *A History of Technology and Invention*, Vol. II, New York: Crown.

David, P. A. (1997), "Reputation and Agency in the Historical Emergence of the Institutions of 'Open' Science," Unpublished manuscript., Oxford University.

David, P. A. (1998), "The Collective Cognitive Performance of 'Invisible Colleges'."
    Presented to the Santa Fe Institute Workshop on "The Evolution of Science."

Dyson, F. (1997), *Imagined Worlds*, Cambridge: Harvard University Press.

Eamon, W. (1990), "From the Secrets of Nature to Public Knowledge," in D. C. Lindberg and
    R. S. Westman (eds.), *Reappraisals of the Scientific Revolution*. Cambridge: Cambridge
    University Press, pp. 333-365.

Ferguson, E. (1971), "The Measurement of the 'man-day'," *Scientific American* 225, pp. 96-
    103.

Ferguson, E. (1992), *Engineering and the Mind's Eye,* Cambridge: MIT Press.

Gillispie, C. (1957), "The Natural History of Industry," *Isis* 48, pp. 398-407.

Gillispie, C. (1983), *The Montgolfier Brothers and the Invention of Aviation*, Princeton NJ:
    Princeton University Press.

Golinski, J. (1990), "Chemistry in the Scientific Revolution: Problems of Language and
    Communication," in D.C. Lindberg and R. S. Westman (eds.), *Reappraisals of the
    Scientific Revolution*, Cambridge: Cambridge University Press, pp. 367-396.

Guillerme, A. (1988), "Wood *vs.* Iron: The Strength of Materials in early 19th Century
    France," *History and Technology* 6, pp. 239-252.

Hall, A. R. (1978), "On Knowing and Knowing How To ...," *History of Technology* 3, pp. 91-
    104.

Hansen, G. D. and E.C. Prescott (1998), "Malthus to Solow," Unpublished ms, presented to
    the Minneapolis Federal Reserve Bank Conference on Economic growth and Productivity,
    Oct. 1998.

Harris, J.R. (1976), "Skills, Coal and British Industry in the Eighteenth century," *History* 61,
    pp. 167-182.

Headrick, Daniel (2000), *When Information Came of Age: Technologies of Knowledge in the
    Age of Reason and Revolution, 1700-1850*, New York: Oxford University Press,
    forthcoming.

Heilbron, J.L (1990), "Introductory Essay," in T. Frängsmyr, J.L. Heilbron, and R. E. Rider
    (eds.), *The Quantifying Spirit in the 18th Century*, Berkeley: University of California Press,
    pp. 1-23.

Hobsbawm, E. J. (1968), *Industry and Empire*, Harmonsworth: Penguin Books.

Inkster, I. (1980), "The Public Lecture as an Instrument of Science Education for Adults - the
    Case of Great Britain, c. 1750-1850," *Paedagogica Historica* 20, pp. 80-107.

Inkster, I. (1991), *Science and Technology in History: An Approach to Industrial
    Development*, New Brunswick: Rutgers University Press.

Jacob, F. (1977), "Evolution and Tinkering," *Science* 196, no. 4295, pp. 1161-66.

Jacob, M. (1997), *Scientific Culture and the Making of the Industrial West*, New York:
    Oxford University Press.

Jacob, M. (1998), "The Cultural Foundations of Early Industrialization," in: M. Berg and K.
    Bruland (eds.), *Technological Revolutions in Europe*, Cheltenham: Edward Elgar, pp. 67-
    85.

John, R. (1995), *Spreading the News: the American Postal System from Franklin to Morse*,
    Cambridge, Mass.: Harvard University Press.

Kuhn, T. S. (1977), *The Essential Tension: Selected Studies in Scientific Tradition and
    Change*, Chicago: University of Chicago Press.

Kula, W. (1986), *Measures and Men*, Princeton: Princeton University Press.

Kuznets, S. (1965), *Economic Growth and Structure*, New York: W.W. Norton.

Latour, B. (1990), "Drawing Things Together," in M. Lynch and S. Woolgar (eds.),
    Representation in Scientific Practice, Cambridge, MA: MIT Press.

Layton, E. T. (1974), "Technology as Knowledge," *Technology and Culture* 15, pp. 31-41.

Lindqvist, S. (1990), "Labs in the Woods: The Quantification of Technology During the late Enlightenment," in T. Frängsmyr, J.L. Heilbron, and R. E. Rider (eds.), *The Quantifying Spirit in the 18th Century*, Berkeley: University of California Press, pp. 291-314.

Lough, J. (1971), *The Encyclopédie*, New York: David McKay.

Lucas, R.E., *The Industrial Revolution: Past and Future*, Unpublished manuscript.

Lundgren, A. (1990), "The Changing Role of Numbers in 18th Century Chemistry," in T. Frängsmyr, J.L. Heilbron, and R. E. Rider (eds.), *The Quantifying Spirit in the 18th Century*, Berkeley: University of California Press, pp. 245-66.

Mahoney, M. S. (1990), "Infinitesimals and Transcendent Relations: the Mathematics of Motion in the late Seventeenth Century," in D.C. Lindberg and R.S. Westman (eds.), *Reappraisals of the Scientific Revolution*, Cambridge: Cambridge University Press.

Manguel, A. (1996), *A History of Reading*, New York: Viking.

McGrew, R.E. (1985), *Encyclopedia of Medical History*, London: McMillan.

Merton, R.K (1970) [1938], *Science, Technology, and Society in Seventeenth century England*, 2nd Edition, New York: Fertig.

Milgrom, P., Y. Qian and J. Roberts (1991), "Complementarities, Momentum, and the Evolution of Modern Manufacturing," *American Economic Review* 81, pp. 84-88.

Mitch, D. (1998), "The Role of Education and Skill in the British Industrial Revolution," in J. Mokyr (ed.), *The British Industrial Revolution: an Economic Perspective*, 2nd ed., Boulder: Westview Press.

Mokyr, J. (1994a), 'Progress and Inertia in Technological Change," in J. James and M. Thomas (eds.), *Capitalism in Context: Essays in honor of R.M. Hartwell*, Chicago: University of Chicago Press.

Mokyr, J. (1994b), "Cardwell's Law and the Political Economy of Technological Progress," *Research Policy* 23, pp. 561-74.

Mokyr, J. (1994c), "That Which We Call an Industrial Revolution," *Contention* 4, pp. 189-206.

Mokyr, J. (1997), "Why Was There More Work for Mother? Technological Change and the Household, 1880-1930," Presented at the Economic History Association annual meeting, New Brunswick, September.

Mokyr, J. (1998a), "Innovation and Selection in Evolutionary Models of Technology: Some Definitional Issues," in J. Ziman (ed.), *Technological Innovation as an Evolutionary Process*, Cambridge: Cambridge University Press, forthcoming.

Mokyr, J. (1998b), "Science, Technology, and Knowledge: What Historians can learn from an Evolutionary Approach," Unpublished paper, Max Planck Institute for Research in Economic Systems, Papers on Economics and Evolution, pp. 98-03.

Mokyr, J. (1998c), "Editor's Introduction: The New Economic History and the Industrial Revolution," in J. Mokyr (ed.), *The British Industrial Revolution: an Economic Perspective*, 2nd ed., Boulder: Westview Press.

Mokyr, J. (1998d), "Induced Technical Innovation and Medical History: an Evolutionary Approach," *Journal of Evolutionary Economics* 8, pp. 119-137.

Mokyr, J. (1998e), "The Political Economy of Technological Change: Resistance and Innovation in Economic History", in M. Berg and K. Bruland (eds.), *Technological Revolutions in Europe*, Cheltenham: Edward Elgar, pp. 39-64.

Mokyr, J. and R. Stein (1997), "Science, Health and Household Technology: the Effect of the Pasteur Revolution on Consumer Demand," in R. J. Gordon and T. Bresnahan (eds.), *The Economics of New Goods*, Chicago: University of Chicago Press and NBER, pp. 143-205.

Needham, J. (1969), *The Grand Titration*, Toronto: University of Toronto Press.

Needham, J. (1959), *Mathematics and the Sciences of Heaven*, in J. Needham (ed.), *Science and Civilisation in China* 3, Cambridge: Cambridge University Press.

Pannabecker, J.R. (1998), "Representing Mechanical Arts in Diderot's *Encyclopédie*," *Technology and Culture* 39, 33-73.

Parker, W.N. (1979) (1984), *Europe, America, and the Wider World*, Cambridge: Cambridge University Press.

Polanyi, M. (1962), *Personal Knowledge: Towards a Post-Critical Philosophy*, Chicago: Chicago University Press.

Porter, R. (1995), "The Eighteenth Century," in L. Konrad *et al.* (eds.), *The Western Medical Tradition, 800 BC to AD 1800*, Cambridge: Cambridge University Press.

Porter, T. (1986), *The Rise of Statistical Thinking, 1820-1900*, Princeton: Princeton University Press.

Reynolds, T.S. (1983), *Stronger than a Hundred Men: A History of the Vertical Water Wheel*, Baltimore: Johns Hopkins University Press.

Rider, Robin E. (1990), "Measure of Ideas, Rule of Language: Mathematics and Language in the eighteenth Century," in T. Frängsmyr, J.L. Heilbron and R. E. Rider (eds.), *The Quantifying Spirit in the 18th Century*, Berkeley: University of California Press, pp. 113-140.

Rosenberg, N. (1982), "How Exogenous is Science?," in *Inside the Black Box: Technology and Economics*, Cambridge: Cambridge University Press.

Rosenberg, N. and W. G. Vincenti (1978), *The Britannia Bridge: The Generation and Diffusion of Technological Knowledge*, Cambridge, MA: M.I.T. Press.

Ryle, G. (1949), *The Concept of Mind*, Chicago: University of Chicago Press.

Scerri, E. R. (1998), "The Evolution of the Periodic System," *Scientific American*, Sept., pp. 78-83.

Schofield, R. (1972), "The Industrial Orientation of Science in the Lunar Society of Birmingham," in A.E. Musson (ed.), *Science, Technology and Economic Growth in the Eighteenth Century*, London: Methuen.

Shapin, S. (1994), *The Social History of Truth*, Chicago: University of Chicago.

Smiles, S. (1891), *Lives of the Engineers*, London: Clowes and Sons.

Smith, C. (1990), "Energy," in R.C. Olby *et al.* (eds.), *Companion to the History of Science*, London: Routledge.

Smith, M. R. (1977), *Harper's Ferry Armory and the New Technology*, Ithaca: Cornell University Press.

Szostak, R. (1991), *The Role of Transportation in the Industrial Revolution*, Montreal: McGill's-Queen's University Press.

Usher, A.P. (1954), *A History of Mechanical Inventions*, Cambridge, MA: Harvard University Press.

Vincenti, W. (1990), *What Engineers Know and How They Know It*, Baltimore: Johns Hopkins Press.

Weitzman, M. (1996), "Hybridizing Growth Theory," *American Economic Review* 86, pp. 207-13.

Chapter 10

Human Capital, R&D, Productivity Growth and Assimilation of Technologies in the Netherlands

Bas Jacobs, Richard Nahuis, and Paul J.G. Tang
University of Amsterdam, Tinbergen Institute and NWO "Scholar," Tilburg University and CentER, CPB Netherlands Bureau of Economic Policy Analysis

Key words: Human capital, R&D, Spillovers, Productivity growth, Assimilation

Abstract: This paper analyses technological change in the Dutch economy at a sectoral level. Total factor productivity is explained by human capital, R&D accumulation (knowledge) and spillovers of R&D in other sectors and other countries. First, we find no evidence that human capital explains TFP growth. Second, R&D and spillovers from R&D, both from domestic and foreign R&D sources, are important. The TFP-elasticity of R&D is about 0.35, domestic spillovers from R&D have a TFP-elasticity of about .14, and foreign spillovers have a TFP-elasticity of .03. Third, we look at the role of human capital in the process of assimilation and diffusion of technologies. Also here, we cannot find evidence that human capital is important for the assimilation of technologies. Empirical evidence favours innovation driven economic growth, rather than human capital based growth.

1.   INTRODUCTION

The theory of endogenous growth can be divided crudely into theories where growth is driven by R&D and those where growth is driven by human capital accumulation.[1] R&D based models originate from the work of Romer

---

[1]   Of course there are other approaches based on learning by doing for example, see Young (1991), or public capital, see for example Barro (1990). Nevertheless, most recent work builds on human capital and R&D based models.

(1990a), Grossman and Helpman (1991) and Aghion and Howitt (1992). In all these models economic growth is the result of technological change that derives from purposive R&D activities by firms. Patents and blueprints are non-rival goods that can be accumulated without bounds, so that diminishing returns of capital accumulation can be avoided and growth continues.

Human capital based growth models, deriving from the work by Lucas (1988), place accumulation of human capital at the heart of the growth process. By accumulating both physical and human capital, constant returns to a broad concept of capital apply so that economic growth does not diminish. Although the R&D based models do not exclude a potential role of human capital (Romer, 1990a), the human capital based theories do not incorporate R&D activities. The empirical question which of the two classes of models is the most relevant is far from being settled.

The first contribution of this paper is therefore to analyse whether human capital and R&D are important determinants in explaining TFP growth for the Netherlands. In Jacobs, Nahuis, and Tang (1999) (JNT) it is found that R&D is a robust variable in explaining TFP growth. A TFP-elasticity of R&D roughly equal to .33 is found in the Netherlands. Here, we extend our previous analysis by explicitly incorporating human capital as a determinant of TFP growth.

The second point of this paper relates to a policy oriented question. Recently, the Netherlands is redesigning its technology policy. For long, policy has been nothing more than providing generic subsidies to R&D projects and subsidising R&D-intensive firms in general. Gradually policy has shifted towards stimulating the assimilation and diffusion of knowledge (see Wijers *et al.,* 1997). The question is whether this policy shift has been sensible. In a small open economy one could doubt whether stimulating R&D is an effective policy, since the benefits of this policy might leak to foreign countries, rather than speeding up domestic productivity growth. This could be the case in the Netherlands where multinational firms have a significant share in R&D activities. Additionally, there can be large informational difficulties in judging the effectiveness of stimulating R&D. Consequently, stimulating R&D is a difficult policy to implement.

However, an emphasis in policy on assimilation and diffusion of knowledge critically hinges on the question whether there *are* knowledge spillovers from research, and if so, *how* these could be assimilated. In JNT the first question is examined. Substantial spillovers associated with R&D are found. This holds for both domestic spillovers and foreign spillovers of R&D. Notwithstanding that the latter are relatively modest in size. One of the reasons is that we assume that knowledge is embodied in traded goods. Trade within the Netherlands is far more important than trade between the Netherlands and the rest of the world.

The finding that foreign spillovers are dominated by domestic spillovers can give rise to two distinct conclusions. The first conclusion is that the policy shift has not been a sensible one. Hence the most important market failure, the fact that domestic firms do not take into account the full return of their R&D expenditures for society, should be resolved by means of an R&D subsidy. A second conclusion, however, could be that a policy increasing the effects of foreign spillovers is desirable.

Both human capital and R&D can serve as "assimilation devices" for knowledge spillovers. Cohen and Levinthal (1989) show that doing R&D is beneficial for assimilating knowledge developed by others. Also, JNT present some weak evidence that R&D itself improves the assimilation and diffusion of spillovers. Not only R&D but potentially also human capital can be important in the process of technology diffusion. Benhabib and Spiegel (1994) present empirical evidence in favour of this conjecture.

The second contribution of this paper is thus to investigate whether human capital can serve the function of an assimilation device in the Netherlands. Thus we investigate whether a large stock of human capital is beneficial in order to internalise spillovers from research, from both domestic and foreign sources.

We use panel data of eleven sectors for the Netherlands over the period 1973-92. Our method is similar to the one employed by Coe and Helpman (1995). The first question, whether human capital is an important determinant of TFP growth, cannot be supported by our empirical findings. The second question whether human capital is beneficial for assimilating technology spillovers does not receive empirical support either. Disaggregating the sample in manufacturing and services sectors reveals that the absence of human capital effects remains for both the services and manufacturing sectors.

The remainder of the chapter is organised as follows. The next section outlines briefly the theory and reviews some of the empirical research carried out so far. Section 3 explains the construction of the explanatory variables and discusses several econometric issues. Section 4 gives an overview of the data and characterises the sectors under consideration. The main empirical findings are presented in Section 5. The last section concludes.

2.   HUMAN CAPITAL, R&D, AND TECHNOLOGICAL CHANGE

The introduction raised several questions to assess the possibility to base technology policy on assimilation and diffusion of knowledge. First, what is the relative relevance of human capital versus R&D as an engine of growth? Second, how important are foreign spillovers? Third, does human capital help to internalise spillovers from R&D?

The first question can be tackled directly and indirectly. In the overview, which is not exhaustive, both lines will be followed. An indirect approach to examine the relevance of the two growth engines is to provide surveys of the literature examining *one* of the growth engines. This is well beyond the scope of this chapter but it is well established that a robust positive effect of R&D on productivity exists. For overviews see Griliches (1992), Los (1997a) and Mohnen (1996).

The research on the effects of human capital is less abundant. Further, the influence of human capital on economic growth is found to be not that robust. Following the contribution by Lucas (1988), many authors have found an effect of (initial) *levels* of human capital on economic growth generally based on cross sections of countries, including Romer (1990b), Barro (1991), Mankiw, Romer and Weil (1992), and Barro and Sala-i-Marin (1995). However, this result does not seem to be very robust when human capital variables are taken in *changes*. Benhabib and Spiegel (1994) find that there does not seem to be a connection between output growth and human capital growth for various human capital measures – based on the Kyriacou (1991), or Barro and Lee (1994) data sets. These results are confirmed in Hamilton and Monteagudo (1998).

Human capital measures might also be heavily correlated with country specific effects as Islam (1995) has shown. Islam (1995) re-estimates the Mankiw, Romer and Weil (1992) specification on the basis of a panel data. Islam finds that the Mankiw, Romer and Weil results are flawed: estimated coefficients loose their statistical significance and switch in sign occasionally when country specific effects are included.

These results may be due to the lack of good quality data on human capital. Krueger and Lindahl (1999) show that measurement error in human capital variables is substantial. After corrections for measurement error, they find estimates of the effect of human capital on output that are consistent with the micro-economic literature. This implies however that large externalities at the macro level are probably absent. Krueger and Lindahl also find that the initial level of human capital does *not* explain cross-sectional differences in growth rates. This is caused by too narrow restrictions on the estimates in regression equations used so far.

Griliches (1996) gives another explanation. Most of the human capital growth has been achieved in the public and services sectors. However, there are great problems in the measurement of real output and productivity growth in these sectors. Quality improvements need not be reflected in the data. Therefore, the role of human capital is probably underestimated on the basis of current data.

A third argument is that the growth regressions are based on a misspecified regression equation. Jones (1996) argues that the *log(income) - log(human capital)* specification is not consistent with the robust findings in the micro-economic literature where human capital variables enter in *levels*, and not *log(levels)*, in a regression equation with *log(income)* as the explained variable. On the basis of the Barro and Lee (1994) data set, Jones resolves the levels *vs.* differences puzzle. Regressions in levels and first-differences produce estimates that are similar and comparable to conventional micro-economic estimates. This finding also reflects that it is unlikely that there are positive externalities of human capital.

Only a few studies compare R&D and human capital directly by looking simultaneously at the role of human capital and R&D in the process of economic growth. Nonneman and Vanhoudt (1996) estimate the Mankiw, Romer and Weil (1992) specification with the inclusion of R&D intensities to control for increases in the stock of "know how." They find that the influence of human capital on income growth is seriously reduced, and the estimated coefficients on human capital loose their statistical significance, whereas R&D variables appear significantly.

Klenow (1998) compares directly both human capital based and innovation based growth models in a panel of industry data for the US. Klenow (1998) finds that R&D based models do a considerably better job in explaining US productivity growth. The reason is that if the human capital based growth models are true, then growth in human capital intensive sectors should be higher, other things being equal. The reverse holds, *ceteris paribus*, for the innovation based growth models: sectors with large shares of capital or use of intermediate goods should display higher growth rates.

Research on the second question, the relevance of international spillovers, is initiated by the seminal paper of Coe and Helpman (1995, *further* CH). They analyse international spillovers at a country level.[2] CH find substantial technological spillovers between OECD countries. The elasticity of total factor productivity with respect to foreign R&D, embodied in traded goods, is about 0.06.

Keller (1997) carries out a similar exercise as CH for all OECD countries using sectoral data. Domestic and foreign R&D stocks are a weighed sum of R&D expenditures in other sectors, where the weights have been constructed

---

[2]   Lichtenberg and Pottelsberghe de la Potterie (1996) re-examine the estimated equations and the construction of foreign R&D stocks and examine a different transmission channel, namely FDI. Coe, Helpman and Hoffmaister (1997) focus on global North-South knowledge spillovers.

from input-output data and a technological distance matrix. Foreign R&D turns out to be a perfect substitute for domestic R&D. In contrast to Keller, Verspagen (1997) estimates production functions and constructs the foreign R&D spillover stock somewhat differently. He finds roughly equal effects for foreign and domestic spillovers.

Some studies elaborate on the third question, whether a role exists for human capital in assimilating and diffusing R&D spillovers. Engelbrecht (1997) tests the robustness of the results of Coe and Helpman (1995) by introducing a human capital variable and a catch-up factor. The qualitative results of CH turn out to be insensitive for the introduction of these additional explanatory variables. The level of human capital has a significant and positive influence on total factor productivity. An important finding of Engelbrecht is the robustness of the results to the estimation method. Estimations in log differences yield similar (and significant) results as those obtained by estimating cointegrated relations. Engelbrecht reports to have estimated equations where an interaction term of human capital and the TFP catch-up factor and an interaction term between human capital and the foreign R&D stock were included. These variables "had large standard errors relative to their coefficient estimates" (p.1481). Hence, he rejects the hybrid models.

Benhabib and Spiegel (1994) cast doubt on the impact of human capital as a separate production factor based on the estimation of Cobb-Douglas production functions. Their alternative model is a hybrid model where the level of human capital has a positive effect on the assimilation of external or advanced knowledge, see also Nelson and Phelps (1966). This mechanism whereby human capital drives assimilation of foreign technology turns out to be a powerful one empirically.

A related approach is explored in Romer (1993). He examines the interaction between imports of technologically advanced goods (machinery and equipment) and the level of human capital in a cross-country growth regression. This interaction term is significantly positive. Hence, a country benefits from interacting with the rest of the world in proportion to the level of human capital. This can be interpreted as evidence for the technology-assimilation enhancing effect of human capital that we are going to explore (for the Netherlands) in the next section.

3.   CONSTRUCTION OF DATA AND ESTIMATION METHOD

In this section we derive our regression model from the following production function:

$$Y_i = A_i(R_i, R_j, R_{kj}, H)F(Q, L), i, j \in \{1, ..., N\}, k \in \{1, ...K\} \qquad (1)$$

where Y, Q, L denote value added, capital and labour, respectively. N is the number of industries whereas K is the number of countries. The total factor productivity (TFP) level denoted by A is a function of the "own" R&D stock (R), R&D stocks of other sectors in the domestic economy, R&D stocks in foreign countries and the human capital stock in the industry.[3] Van der Wiel (1997) constructs TFP (T) indices by correcting changes in value added for the weighted labour and capital inputs applying the Jorgenson growth accounting approach.

Before proceeding a remark should be made. R&D expenditures are accounted for in the growth accounting approach. Essentially the same holds for human capital. The reason is that in the growth accounting approach the labour services have been adjusted for quality (for details, see the Appendix). When incorporating R&D or human capital variables as an explanatory variable in a TFP regression, one measures essentially an "excess return." It is the return in excess (or in short) of the returns attributed to either R&D or human capital in the growth accounting procedure.[4]

With respect to R&D, large returns are typically found, in the order of 30 percent or more, see for example Nadiri (1993). This implies that the actual return is a lot higher than the "return" that is presumably used in the growth accounting approach – for instance, the user cost of capital. It are therefore the excess "excess returns" that end up in the TFP figures.

Adjustments for changes in quality of labour are usually made on the basis of wage differentials. This has the implication that returns of human capital are controlled for in the growth accounting approach, and that, consequently only true positive externalities of human capital at the macroeconomic level end up in the TFP figures.

To limit the number of coefficients to be estimated, it is necessary to construct spillover stocks that are a weighted average of domestic and foreign R&D stocks respectively. Weighting R&D stocks of different sectors can be done in several ways. For domestic R&D spillovers Input-Output related weights are most common alongside technology flow approaches. Los (1997b) compares different weighting schemes and finds that results are reasonably robust to different weighting schemes. As the qualitative results do not seem to hinge on the weighting schemes and it is beyond the scope of this paper to enter the discussion on weighting matrices, we simply follow common practice and use IO weights. Hence the stock of domestic R&D

---

[3] Stocks are constructed out of R&D flows by a perpetual inventory method. See the Appendix for details.

[4] The authors thank Eric Bartelsman for making this point.

spillovers is constructed as follows. The growth rates of R&D stocks of other Dutch sectors ($j{\neq}i$) are weighted with the intermediate deliveries by these sectors to create a sector-specific domestic R&D stock (R^d_i),

$$\frac{R^d_{i,t} - R^d_{i,t-1}}{R^d_{i,t-1}} = \sum_{j=1,j\neq i}^{N} c_{ji,t} \frac{R_{i,t} - R_{i,t-1}}{R_{i,t-1}} \tag{2}$$

c_{ji} is the share intermediate inputs purchased from sector j in total production of sector i. From this constructed growth rate on the left-hand side of equation above we construct an index that, after taking logs, is our independent variable.

Also with respect to international spillovers a similar discussion on the appropriateness of different weighting schemes is going on, see for example Verspagen (1997), Lichtenberg and Pottelsberghe de la Potterie (1996) and Branstetter (1996). The construction of the foreign stock R^f_i is similar to the domestic R&D stock:

$$\frac{R^f_{i,t} - R^f_{i,t-1}}{R^f_{i,t-1}} = \sum_{k=1}^{K} \sum_{j=1,j\neq i}^{N} c_{ji,t} b_{kj,t} \frac{R_{kj,t} - R_{kj,t-1}}{R_{kj,t-1}} \tag{3}$$

where b_{kj} is the share of country k in total Dutch imports of goods produced by sector j. Note that this is an approximation. The reason is that data for bilateral trade do not distinguish between intermediate and final goods. Further, imports of goods are not distinguished by industry of use.

The construction of indirect R&D stocks based on weighted growth rates deserves some elaboration. Weighting levels of the various R&D stocks is *not* appropriate for the following reasons. First, by directly weighting the stocks, the changes in the weights also matter. Therefore, a shift towards inputs from a R&D-intensive sector or from a sector in a large country would then raise total factor productivity. This implication is implausible.

Second, a weighting procedure based on levels of R&D stocks suffers from a serious aggregation bias. In our approach this bias is absent if some restrictions apply. Lichtenberg and van Pottelsberghe de la Potterie (1996) point at the aggregation bias in the work of CH. Their solution to eliminate the bias is only insensitive to aggregation under strong restrictions. Both solutions, however, share the feature that the aggregation bias is only marginal compared to that in the approach of CH.

We have sectoral data on the number of workers with a particular educational attainment. Seven levels of education are distinguished: primary education (Basisonderwijs), secondary education, which is split up in four types: lower vocational education (LBO), higher vocational education

(MBO), lower general education (MAVO), higher general education (HAVO and VWO) and higher education, which is split up between workers with a professional or academic education (HBO and WO) and students who are working.

The sectoral total human capital stock is constructed by multiplying employment of workers with a certain educational attainment with the number of years it approximately takes to achieve that level of education for every sector. The resulting sum is total years of education per sector (H_i):

$$H_i = \sum_{s=1}^{S} \omega_s L_{is} \tag{4}$$

where ω_s is the total years of schooling to reach education level s, and L_{is} is total employment of workers with education level s in sector i. For the stocks of human capital an index (1973=1) is used in the estimations in accordance with the procedure to construct the R&D stocks.

A system of equations relating TFP to the different stocks and interactions is estimated. On basis of the discussion so far we can formulate the regression model in a formal way as:

$$
\begin{aligned}
T_{1t} &= \alpha_1 + \beta_{1,D} D_{1t} + \beta_{1,I} I_{1t} + \beta_{1,F} F_{1t} + \beta_{1,H} H_{1t} + \beta_{1,X} X_{1t}^p + \varepsilon_{1t} \\
T_{2t} &= \alpha_2 + \beta_{2,D} D_{2t} + \beta_{2,I} I_{2t} + \beta_{2,F} F_{2t} + \beta_{2,H} H_{2t} + \beta_{2,X} X_{2t}^p + \varepsilon_{2t} \\
&\vdots \\
T_{it} &= \alpha_i + \beta_{i,D} D_{it} + \beta_{i,I} I_{it} + \beta_{i,F} F_{it} + \beta_{i,H} H_{it} + \beta_{i,X} X_{it}^p + \varepsilon_{it}
\end{aligned}
\tag{5}
$$

where T, D, I, and F stand for log levels of total factor productivity, the direct stock of R&D, the indirect stock of domestic R&D, and the indirect foreign stock of R&D in sector i respectively. The human capital stock H is taken in levels instead of log-levels in conformity with the Mincerian wage equations. X^p is an interaction term that can be an element p of the following set of cross-products: $\{H*D, H*I, H*F\}$. ε denotes an error term. A constant α_i is added to capture sector specific effects. $\beta_{i,D}$, $\beta_{i,I}$, $\beta_{i,F}$, $\beta_{i,H}$, and $\beta_{i,X}$ are the parameters to be estimated.

4. CHARACTERISATION OF SECTORS AND DATA

We examine 11 Dutch industries, of which four are services sectors and seven manufacturing sectors. For these industries we construct direct R&D stocks, indirect domestic R&D stocks using input-output data, and indirect foreign R&D stocks combining input-output data with bilateral trade data. This section discusses briefly our data sources and characterises the eleven sectors.

4.1   Data Sources

The data set used in this study contains four main components: TFP growth rates, R&D data, the weights to link these two, and human capital data.

TFP figures are constructed by van der Wiel (1997) on the basis of the growth accounting approach: TFP growth is constructed as value added corrected for weighted labour services (contract hours) and capital services.

The OECD (ANBERD) data set contains R&D data for manufacturing (and for some service industries). The ANBERD data are supplemented with R&D data from Statistics Netherlands (CBS) for the services sectors in the Netherlands. Business enterprise R&D expenditures are available for 15 countries and 26 manufacturing industries.

We use Dutch input-output data from the CPB Netherlands Bureau for Economic Policy Analysis according to a Dutch sectoral classification (SBI) for the construction of the weights. These IO tables are aggregated from the National Accounts 80x80 IO data from Statistics Netherlands (CBS).

To construct weights for the foreign stocks, we use bilateral trade data for manufacturing on a sectoral level (STAN Bilateral Trade Database) provided by the OECD. For non-manufacturing industries trade data are not available. Moreover, sectoral import shares cannot be computed for Construction, Communication and Utility, since data for these services are lacking or consist of zeros. We therefore set the foreign R&D stocks for service sectors equal to zero.

The data on human capital are collected by van der Wiel (1997) and comprise the data from the so called "Arbeidskrachtentellingen" and "Enquete Beroepsbevolking" from the CBS (Statistics Netherlands) and OSA (Organisation for Strategic Labour Market Research). Data for missing years have been replaced by taking weighted averages of the years before and after.

4.2   Industry Characterisation

A more extensive overview of the data is provided in the Appendix. Here we highlight only some features of the data for the eleven industries. The eleven industries are subdivided as services and manufacturing sectors. The latter are:
–   Food, beverages and tobacco (Food);
–   Textile, wearing apparel and leather (Textile);

- Wood, furniture and building material (Wood);
- Paper, paper products and printing (Paper);
- Petroleum refineries and miscellaneous products of petroleum and coal (Petroleum);
- Chemical and rubber products (Chemicals);
- Metal industries (Metal).

The latter two industries contain most of the so called "high-tech" industries (see Kusters and Minne, 1992).

In the service industries we distinguish:
- Electricity, gas and water (Public utilities);
- Construction (Construction);
- Communication services, sea, air and other transport and storage (Communication);
- Real estate exploitation, trade, banking, insurance and engineering, commercial, social and health services (Other services).

4.3   Description of Data

During the period 1973-1992 all industries, except Petroleum as a consequence of the oil crises, show positive TFP-growth. Table 1 shows the level in 1992 relative to the level in 1973 for TFP, the human capital stocks, and the R&D stocks. The sector Communication, the sectors Food, Textile and Paper, and the "high-tech" industries Metal and Chemical experienced (cumulative) TFP growth rates above the unweighted average (14 percent).

The sector Other services accounts for over 40 percent of value added in 1992, whereas the others each hardly account for 5 percent. The shares do not sum up to unity as agriculture, mining and the public sector are excluded.

The index of human capital displays the fastest growth for the sector Other Services: the stock has increased more than 2.5 times in last two decades. As this sector accounts for 42 percent of value added, the bulk of human capital growth has been in this sector while TFP growth has been relatively low. Chemicals, and Communication also show high human capital growth. Textile, Petroleum, Wood and Construction have experienced a decrease in the stock of human capital. Although the average level of education has been increasing, lower levels of human capital in these sectors are due to lower employment levels.

Between 1973 and 1992 the "own" R&D stock increased in all industries. In Chemicals, Communication and Other services it increased by a factor five or even six. It is, however, important to note that even in 1992 the R&D intensity of the last two sectors, Communication and Other services, is very small (less than 1 percent of value added). In the other industries the stock at least doubled.

We have also derived the sectoral R&D intensities as measured by the share of R&D expenditures in value added. The highest R&D intensity is found in the Chemical industry: 12.4 percent in 1992. Other industries with substantial R&D activity are Metal with almost 5 percent and Petroleum and Food with almost 2 percent.

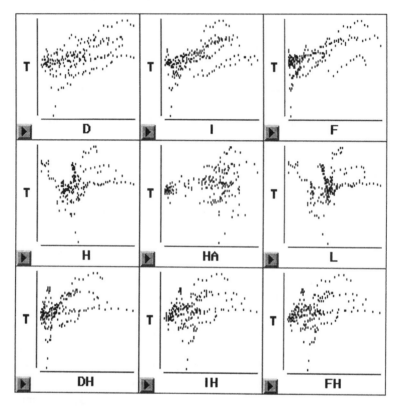

HA denotes average human capital per worker
L denotes employment

Figure 1. Scatter Plot of R&D and Human Capital Variables against TFP

Overall changes in the indirect domestic R&D stock are less dramatic. Increases vary from only 8 percent in Petroleum to somewhat more than 50 percent in Construction. The more moderate development here compared to "own" R&D can traced back to the fact that intermediate use as a share of gross production is usually less than 50 percent (see the last column in Table

1).[5] The fastest expansion in the indirect domestic R&D stock in Construction is explained by, first, the fact that this sector uses a lot of intermediate inputs and therefore potentially benefits a lot from others sectors' R&D. Secondly, the composition of the intermediate inputs is important. For example, Construction uses a large fraction of total inputs from the Metal industry compared to other industries. Metals is an industry that experienced a fivefold increase in the "own" R&D stock. Moreover, the use of supplies from Chemicals in Construction is also above average.

Table 1. Sectoral Statistics in 1992 (1973=1.0)[a]

	T	H	R	I	F	Va	Int	Imp	Interm
Chemicals	1.54	1.69	6.19	1.34	1.64	2.5	12.4	30.9	38.6
Metal	1.33	1.13	5.00	1.36	1.54	5.7	4.9	28.0	34.9
Petroleum	.89	.83	2.00	1.08	1.03	1.3	1.9	51.6	13.6
Food	1.34	1.22	3.86	1.29	1.29	2.7	1.8	24.2	54.3
Textile	1.24	.85	3.13	1.41	1.79	.5	.8	37.4	29.9
Communication	1.24	1.79	5.04	1.31	–	5.6	.7	13.7	28.0
Wood	1.01	.87	2.33	1.49	1.63	1.0	.4	27.0	34.2
Public utilities	1.03	1.36	4.09	1.10	–	1.4	.1	7.0	54.8
Other services	1.08	2.51	6.28	1.23	–	41.8	.1	5.0	29.7
Paper	1.26	2.11	3.80	1.35	1.43	1.8	.1	23.1	36.4
Construction	1.06	.91	2.38	1.53	–	4.4	.1	12.2	52.5
Average	1.14	1.35	4.01	1.32	1.48		2.1	23.6	37.0

[a] where *T* = TFP, *H* = Human capital, *R* = "Own" R&D, *I* = Domestic R&D spillover, *F* = Foreign R&D spillover, Va = Value added[b], Int = R&D Intensity[c], Imp = Imports[d], and Interm = Intermediate inputs[d]
[b] % of GDP, percentages do not sum to hundred since agriculture, mining and public sector are excluded.
[c] As a percentage of value added.
[d] As a percentage of industries' gross production.
Sources: R&D data are from ANBERD. The other data are provided by CPB The Netherlands Bureau for Economic Policy Analysis.

Changes over time in foreign indirect R&D stocks are somewhat more pronounced again. R&D-intensive industries, such as Metal and Chemicals, and the Textile industry face increases in foreign R&D stocks over 50 percent.

In Figure 1 we plotted the scatter diagrams of the log index of TFP (*T*) against the logs of R&D and the human capital indices used in the estimations. It is clear from these figures that all plain R&D variables show positive correlation with TFP. Human capital and the interaction variables with human capital show a less clear pattern.

---

[5] Here, intra-industry deliveries are included as well as deliveries by the sectors Mining and Agriculture.

5.   EMPIRICAL FINDINGS

The major findings are presented in this section. However, before turning to the results some econometric issues are addressed. We estimated a fixed effects regression model, to capture the sector-specific effects. This procedure is equivalent to a pooled estimation where sector-specific constants are added. Furthermore, we added time-dummies to capture time-specific effects. One may regard the model as a "two-way" fixed effects model. Capacity utilisation rates are included to correct for the business cycle. We note that the basic estimations results here slightly differ from those in JNT (1999).[6]

We report that we did some diagnostic checks on unit roots and the order of cointegration. The so called *t-bar* panel unit-root tests developed by Im, Pesaran and Shin (1997) has been applied and it was found that most variables are I(1).[7] We also tested for cointegration by applying the *t-bar* statistic to the residuals of the regression equations. Most of the panel statistics turned out to remain inconclusive about the order of cointegration due to the short time series used here.

5.1   The Aggregate Model

In the aggregate estimations we restrict all parameters to be the same across all sectors. Table 2 presents the estimations. Column (I) gives the base run estimation. Here the sectoral R&D and human capital stocks are included as well as the two measures for indirect domestic and foreign R&D. The elasticity of own R&D (D) is about .33. This elasticity is also the elasticity of output with respect to R&D. The domestic (I) and foreign (F) spillover terms are positive and significant. Remember that the foreign R&D stock is relevant for manufacturing sectors only.

The weights to construct indirect R&D stocks must be used to find TFP-elasticities of these stocks, see also JNT (1999). We then find that the TFP elasticity associated with the domestic spillover is .14. Consequently, we find a substantial effect from domestic spillovers on TFP. For OECD countries Keller (1997) finds a coefficient of .21, whereas Verspagen (1997) finds an elasticity of .1. Our result is in between these findings.

With respect to the foreign effect we find that the TFP elasticity is .03 for the total economy. The reason for this relatively low figure is that services

---

[6]   In previous estimations we used time-trends instead of time-dummies and used sectoral specific capacity utilisation rates. Furthermore, the standard errors have been computed differently.

[7]   The *t-bar* statistic is the average of the sectoral ADF statistics, see Im, Pesaran, and Shin (1997).

sectors have a low share in international trade – in our sample these shares were set to zero – and a high share in domestic output. Computing the implied TFP elasticity for manufacturing sectors separately, we find an TFP elasticity of .14. As such, foreign R&D spillovers are roughly equally important as domestic spillovers for manufacturing. This figure is comparable to the findings by Coe and Helpman (1995).

Table 2. OLS-estimation Results Aggregate Model. Dependent Variable is *ln* (TFP)[a]

Variable	(I)	(II)	(III)	(IV)
D	.329***	.316***	.329***	.326***
	(.047)	(.060)	(.042)	(.043)
I	.901***	.902***	.907***	.907***
	(.18)	(.18)	(.18)	(.18)
F	.698***	.692***	.709***	.707***
	(.10)	(.099)	(.099)	(.099)
H	.0341	–	–	–
	(.034)	–	–	–
D*H	–	.0185	–	–
	–	(.020)	–	–
I*H	–	–	.00395	–
	–	–	(.0030)	–
F*H	–	–	–	.000825
	–	–	–	(.00065)
R^2	.64	.64	.64	.64
N	220	220	220	220
$F_{(24,185)}$	25.36	25.34	25.49	25.47

[a] Sample period is 1973-1992, 11 sectors. Sector specific constants, time-dummies and capacity utilisation rates are included. Standard errors are given in parentheses under the estimates. *, ** and *** denote statistical significance at the 10% level, the 5% level, and the 1% level, respectively.

The human capital variable produces an insignificant but positive estimate. Therefore, we cannot confirm positive externalities of human capital at an economy-wide level. A reason could be that a lot of growth in human capital has been in the services sectors, as mentioned by Griliches (1996). This would not imply that this growth has not led to increases in productivity. Problems in measuring quality changes are especially relevant for the services sectors. So there might have been changes in productivity growth as a consequence of a larger human capital stock, but these changes are not recorded in the TFP figures.

The result that human capital is not able to explain TFP growth confirms findings by Islam (1995), Jones (1996), Nonneman and Vanhoudt (1996),

Hamilton and Monteagudo (1998), and Krueger and Lindahl (1999). In all these studies it is concluded that human capital variables are either not robust in explaining economic growth or there is no evidence of externalities from human capital accumulation.

We have to be aware that the human capital variable might also pick up scale effects. Sectors that have a larger size, measured by employment, might also be growing faster. However, sectors that have larger levels of employment, also have larger human capital stocks. To separate the effects from human capital accumulation, and from employment shifts, one would rather use average human capital per worker instead. This turned out, however, to produce problems with multicollinearity as the correlations of average human capital per worker and the R&D variables are rather high, see also Table 5 in the appendix. The estimate of the average human capital per worker was -.068 (.15), and the coefficient on own R&D increased about 3 percentage points to .362 (.032).

To get an idea to which extent scale effects are important, we have also done a regression where employment is included as a variable, besides R&D variables. This produced an estimate of .031 (.041). Given that the estimated coefficient of employment is almost the same as the coefficient on human capital in the estimations in Table 3, we cannot exclude the possibility that a scale effect is driving the positive estimate on human capital. We note, however, that none of the coefficients is statistically significant at standard confidence levels.

Although there might not be a robust direct role of human capital, it can be crucial for the assimilation of technologies as the innovation driven growth theories pointed out. We test whether human capital improves the capacity to absorb ideas and technologies by incorporating an interaction term of human capital and indirect domestic or foreign R&D.

Since the idea is concerned with pure knowledge spillovers, we take the unweighted sum of stocks as a measure for indirect domestic and foreign R&D. This has the additional advantage that we are now able to construct a cross-term for the service sectors as well, though import data are lacking. As a "by-product" of the empirical analysis we can test whether human capital and R&D are in fact complementary by including the product of human capital and the R&D stocks in a sector. To avoid multicollinearity in the estimations we include only one interaction term at a time.

Column (II) gives the estimations to investigate the possible complementarity of human capital and R&D. We cannot find robust evidence for the complementarity of human capital and "own" R&D. Although the estimated coefficient is positive, it is not significantly different from zero. In column (III) we interact human capital with the "indirect" domestic stock of R&D. Also, this coefficient is insignificantly positive. As such we cannot find robust evidence that human capital serves as an assimilation device. The interaction of human capital in column (IV) with the foreign R&D stock also gives an insignificant finding so that we cannot conclude that foreign spillovers can be assimilated by means of human capital.

Overall we cannot conclude nor reject that human capital serves as an assimilation device. The results do not confirm the findings of Benhabib and Spiegel (1994). However, we support the finding by Engelbrecht (1997) that the interaction of human capital with foreign R&D variables is unimportant.

5.2   The Disaggregated Model

In Table 3 we present estimations where a distinction between manufacturing and services sectors is made. It could be that the estimated parameters differ for manufacturing and services. A subscript *m* denotes a coefficient for manufacturing, and a subscript *s* stands for services.

Column (I) presents the base run. The coefficients on R&D for manufacturing are in the same range as in the aggregate estimations. Coefficients for services however change considerably. First, we find that the effect of "own" R&D falls and becomes weakly insignificant. Second, the indirect effect in services is far more important than in aggregate estimations: about three times as high. This is not surprising in light of the low R&D intensities in services sectors and the fact that services sectors are mainly sheltered sectors. In columns (I), (II), (III), and (IV), human capital variables are small and remain to enter insignificantly in all estimations. These effects are consistent with the aggregate estimations.

Table 3. OLS-estimation Results Manufacturing versus Services. Dependent variable is *ln* (TFP)[a]

Variable	(I)	(II)	(III)	(IV)
D_m	.338***	.337***	.317***	.316***
	(.047)	(.059)	(.046)	(.047)
I_m	.810***	.794***	.787***	.790***
	(.19)	(.19)	(.11)	(.18)
F_m	.679***	.655***	.700***	.697***
	(.12)	(.11)	(.11)	(.11)
H_m	.0379	–	–	–
	(.044)	–	–	–
$D_m{*}H_m$	–	.0114	–	–
	–	(.022)	–	–
$I_m{*}H_m$	–	–	.00575	–
	–	–	(.0038)	–
$F_m{*}H_m$	–	–	–	.0117
	–	–	–	(.00081)
D_s	.105	.0803	.168	.163
	(.097)	(.11)	(.11)	(.11)
I_s	3.02***	3.05***	2.96***	2.97***
	(.29)	(.28)	(.29	(.29)
H_s	.0010	–	–	–
	(.040)	–	–	–
$D_s{*}H_s$	–	.0113	–	–
	–	(.030)	–	–
$I_s{*}H_s$	–	–	-.0017	–
	–	–	(.0039)	–
$F_s{*}H_s$	–	–	–	-.000354
	–	–	–	(.00085)
R^2	.66	.68	.67	.67
N	220	220	220	220
$F(27,182)$	26.03	25.97	26.34	26.30

[a] Sample period is 1973-1992, 11 sectors. Sector specific constants, time-dummies and capacity utilisation rates are included. Standard errors are given in parentheses under the estimates. *, ** and *** denote statistical significance at the 10% level, the 5% level, and the 1% level, respectively.

6. CONCLUSION

First, we find evidence for the relevance of domestic and foreign R&D spillovers for productivity growth, both when considering the entire Dutch economy and when distinguishing between services and manufacturing. We find that R&D and spillovers from R&D are important in explaining TFP growth. An elasticity of TFP to R&D at a sectoral level is found to equal 0.33. Furthermore, a TFP-elasticity of domestic spillovers from R&D is found to be about .14. For foreign spillovers the TFP-elasticity is approximately .03.

Second, in this chapter we made an attempt to unravel two potential roles of human capital in the process of technological change. First, is human capital, besides R&D, a determinant of TFP growth in the Netherlands? Second, is human capital an "assimilation device" for R&D spillovers? We find no evidence for positive external effects of human capital in the Netherlands. Further, we attempt to unravel whether the assimilation of both domestic as foreign technologies is facilitated by human capital. Again, no positive role for the absorption of domestic and foreign technologies by human capital is found in both the aggregate and disaggregated estimations.

In this study we find that R&D variables systematically have positive effects on productivity increases whereas human capital variables do not seem to influence TFP growth. These results indicate that the innovation driven growth theories are perhaps better vehicles to describe the growth process than human capital based growth models.

One might wonder whether the policy shift towards increasing the assimilation of technologies has been sensible. Clearly, spillovers from domestic research are found. This would provide a rationale for subsidies on R&D as the social rate of return falls below the private rate of return. We cannot, however, find that these spillovers can be assimilated easily with the aid of human capital. In our previous paper (JNT, 1999) we find some weak evidence that assimilation of spillovers can be enhanced by means of R&D, but the question "how to assimilate spillovers" remains. Further research is therefore needed.

A DATA

Van der Wiel (1997) constructed the TFP figures. The Jorgenson growth accounting approach is used: TFP growth is constructed as value added corrected for weighted labour services and capital services. Weights are average (Divisia) nominal income shares. Labour services are (contract) hours worked. Labour services are adjusted for quality by weighting changes in the composition of characteristics of workers. Characteristics of workers are related to quality by estimating an equation with wages (as a proxy for quality) as dependent variable on worker characteristics.

R&D data are from the OECD (ANBERD), supplemented with data from Statistics Netherlands (CBS) for the Communication industry in the Netherlands. The maximum time period covered is 1973 to 1995 (we use: 1973-1992). Business enterprise R&D expenditures are available for 15 Countries and 26 manufacturing industries and five service sector industries. CBS data have been downloaded from (http:// statline.cbs.nl /witch /etc /scratch /531924634 /6376r_d00.html) on 25-6-97. Statistics Netherlands data for 1988 have been interpolated as huge outliers were found for some industries. Statistics Netherlands (CBS) data available as expenditure in guilders have been transformed in constant dollars using the GDP PPP indicator from STAN bilateral trade data. CBS data turn out to correspond very well with available ANBERD data using the imperfect PPP measure.

R&D stocks (R) are constructed as a perpetual inventory of the flow of R&D investments (RD). The first data point constructed as,

$$R_{t=0} = \frac{RD_{t=0}}{\delta + g}$$

where g is the average growth rate of the R&D investments and δ is the depreciation rate. Subsequent stocks are constructed as follows,

$$R_t = \sum_{t=1}^{\tau} RD_t - \delta R_{t-1}$$

Nadiri and Prucha (1993) estimate the depreciation rate to be 0.12. Pakes and Schankerman (1984) find a rate of 0.25. The depreciation rate we apply equals 15 percent, and is the same as in Coe and Helpman (1995) appendix B, Branstetter (1996) and Los and Verspagen (1996).

Dutch input-output data are from the CPB Netherlands Bureau for Economic Policy Analysis in the SBI (used for the Athena model). The data are without structural changes in definitions. IO tables are aggregated from the National Accounts 80x80 IO data from Statistics Netherlands (CBS).

Bilateral trade data for manufacturing on a sectoral level from OECD (STAN) Bilateral Trade Database are available for Australia, Canada, Denmark, Finland, France, Federal Republic of Germany, Ireland, Italy, Japan, The Netherlands, New Zealand, Norway, Portugal, Spain, Sweden, The United Kingdom and The United States. The available length of the time series is 1970 to 1992 (we use: 1973-1992). Data for Ireland, New Zealand, Portugal are not used.

To aggregate the ANBERD data, STAN Bilateral Trade Database, CPB IO data, a concordance is used, which is available upon request from the authors.

Human capital stocks are constructed from data on sectoral employment of different education levels, provided by van der Wiel (1997). Seven categories are distinguished: primary education (H_p), secondary education, which is splitted up in four types: lower vocational education (H_{slv}), higher vocational education (H_{shv}), lower general education (H_{slg}), higher general education (H_{shg}), students enrolled in tertiary education (H_{ts}) and, higher education (H_h), which comprises both professional and academic education (HBO and WO). The human capital stock is constructed as follows:

$$H = 6H_p + 10H_{slv} + 15H_{shv} + 10H_{slg} + 12H_{shg} + 14H_{ts} + 17H_h$$

where the coefficients reflect approximately the total number of years

Data on educational attainment were only available for the years 1973, 1975, 1977, 1979, 1981, 1983, 1985, 1990, 1991, and 1992. We have constructed the stocks for missing years by taking the weighted average of the observations before and after a miss.

Table 4 gives the means and standard deviations of the variables used in the estimations.

Table 4. Means and Standard Deviations of Variables

Variable	N	Mean	S.D.	Min	Max
P	220	.08	.15	-.57	.49
D	220	.68	.48	0	1.84
I	220	.14	.10	0	.43
F	220	.15	.15	0	.58
H	220	12.09	.36	.45	2.51
H^a	220	12.08	.12	1.00	1.46
D*H	220	.93	.90	0	4.61
I*H	220	67.16	5.13	0	25.09
F*H	220	310.16	24.23	0	120.30

H^a = average human capital

Table 5 gives the partial correlations between all variables.

Table 5. Correlation Matrix

	P	D	I	F	H	H^a	D*H	I*H	F*H
P	1.00	.55	.55	.67	.18	.27	.44	.35	.36
D	.55	1.00	.63	.48	.60	.76	.92	.89	.90
I	.55	.63	1.00	.83	.08	.70	.45	.59	.58
F	.67	.48	.83	1.00	.15	.58	.24	.34	.34
H	.18	.60	.08	.15	1.00	.24	.85	.74	.75
H^a	.27	.76	.70	.58	.24	1.00	.57	.72	.71
D*H	.44	.92	.45	.24	.85	.57	1.00	.93	.94
I*H	.35	.89	.59	.34	.74	.72	.93	1.00	1.00
F*H	.36	.90	.58	.34	.75	.71	.94	1.00	1.00

H^a = average human capital

REFERENCES

Aghion, P. and P. Howitt (1992), "A Model of Growth through Creative Destruction," *Econometrica* 51, pp. 675-692.

Barro, R.J. (1990), "Government Spending in a Simple Model of Endogenous Growth," *Journal of Political Economy* 98, pp. 103-125.

Barro, R.J. (1991), "Economic Growth in a Cross-section of Countries", *Quarterly Journal of Economics* 106, pp. 407-443.

Barro, R.J. and J.W. Lee (1994), "International Comparisons of Educational Attainment," *Journal of Monetary Economics* 32, pp. 363-394.

Barro, R.J. and X. Sala-i-Martin (1995), *Economic Growth*, New York: McGraw-Hill.

Benhabib, J. and M.M. Spiegel (1994), "The Role of Human Capital in Economic Development. Evidence from Aggregate Cross-country Data," *Journal of Monetary Economics* 34, pp. 143-173.

Branstetter, L. (1996), "Are Knowledge Spillovers International or Intranational in Scope? Microeconometric Evidence from the U.S and Japan," *NBER Working Paper*, 5800.

Coe, D. T. and E. Helpman (1995), "International R&D Spillovers", *European Economic Review* 39, pp. 859-887.

Coe, D. T., E. Helpman and A.W. Hoffmaister (1997), "North-South R&D Spillovers", *Economic Journal* 107, pp. 134-149.

Cohen, W.M. and D.A. Levinthal (1989), "Innovation and learning: the two faces of R&D," *Economic Journal* 99, pp. 569-597.

CPB - Netherlands Bureau for Economic Policy Analysis (1997), IO-data (used in the Athena model).

Engelbrecht, H.J. (1997), "International R&D Spillovers, Human Capital and Productivity in OECD Economies: An Empirical Investigation," *European Economic Review* 41, pp. 1479-1488.

Griliches, Z. (1992), "The Search for R&D Spillovers," *Scandinavian Journal of Economics* 94, pp. 29-47.

Griliches, Z. (1996), "Education, Human Capital and Growth: A Personal Perspective," NBER Working Paper, 5426.

Grossman, G.M. and E. Helpman (1991), *Innovation and Growth in the Global Economy*, Cambridge-MA: MIT Press.

Hamilton, J.D. and J. Monteagudo (1998), "The augmented Solow-model and the Productivity Slowdown," *Journal of Monetary Economics* 42, pp. 495-509.

Islam, N. (1995), "Growth empirics: A Panel Data Approach", *Quarterly Journal of Economics* 110, pp. 1127-1170.

Im, K.S., M.H. Pesaran and Y. Shin (1997), "Testing for Unit Roots in Heterogenous Panels," Mimeo, University of Cambridge.

Jacobs, B., R. Nahuis and P.J.G. Tang (1999), "Sectoral Productivity Growth and R&D Spillovers in the Netherlands," CPB Research Memorandum, No 149. Appeared also as: CentER Discussion Paper, 9915.

Jones, C.I. (1996), "Human capital, ideas, and economic growth," Paper prepared for the VIII Villa Mondragone International Economic Seminar on Finance, Education, and Growth in Rome on June 25-27.

Keller, W. (1997), "Trade and the Transmission of Technology," NBER Working Paper, 6113.

Klenow, P.J. (1998), "Ideas *vs.* Rival Human Capital: Industry Evidence on Growth Models," *Journal of Monetary Economics* 42, pp. 3-24.

Kusters, A. and B. Minne (1992), "Technologie, marktstruktuur en internationalisatie: de ontwikkeling van de industrie," CPB Onderzoeksmemorandum, 99.

Krueger, A.B. and M. Lindahl (1999), "Education for Growth in Sweden and the World," NBER Working Paper, 7190.

Kyriacou, G. (1991), "Level and Growth Effects of Human Capital," Working Paper 91-26, C.V. Starr Center, New York.

Lichtenberg, F. and B. van Pottelsberghe de la Potterie (1998), "International R&D Spillovers: A Comment," *European Economic Review* 42, pp. 1483-1491.

Los, B., (1997a), "A Review of Interindustry Technology Spillover Measurement Methods," Mimeo, University of Twente.

Los, B. (1997b), "The Empirical Performance of a New Interindustry Technology Spillover Measurement Measure," Mimeo, Maastricht University.

Los, B. and B. Verspagen (1996), "R&D Spillovers and Productivity: Evidence from U.S. Manufacturing Microdata," Merit Research Memorandum, 2/96-007.

Lucas, R.E., jr. (1988), "On the Mechanics of Economic Development," *Journal of Monetary Economics* 22, pp. 3-42.

Mankiw, N.G., D. Romer and D.N. Weil (1992), "A Contribution to the Empirics of Economic Growth," *Quarterly Journal of Economics* 107, pp. 407-437.

Mohnen, P. (1996), "R&D Externalities and Productivity Growth," *STI-Review OECD*, pp. 39-66.

Nadiri, M.I. (1993), "Innovations and Technological Spillovers," NBER Working Paper, 4423.

Nadiri, M.I. and I.R. Prucha (1993), "Estimation of the Depreciation Rate of Physical and R&D Capital in the U.S. Total Manufacturing Sector," NBER Working Paper, 4423.

Nelson, R. and E. Phelps (1966), "Investment in Humans, Technological Diffusion and Economic Growth", *AER Papers and Proceedings* 61, pp. 69-75.

Nonneman, W. and P. Vanhoudt (1996), "A Further Augmentation of the Solow model and the Empirics of Economic Growth for OECD Countries," *Quarterly Journal of Economics* 111, pp. 943-953.

Organisation for Economic Development and Cooperation (1997), DSTI(ANBERD), 1997, Paris.

Organisation for Economic Development and Cooperation (1997), DSTI(STAN), 1997, Paris.

Pakes, A. and M. Schankerman (1984), "The Rate of Obsolescence of Patents, Research Gestation Lags, and the Private Rate of Return to Research Resources", in Z. Griliches (ed.), *R&D, Patents and Productivity*, Chicago: Chicago University Press.

Romer, P.M. (1990a), "Endogenous Technological Change," *Journal of Political Economy* 98, pp. S71-S103.

Romer, P.M. (1990b), "Human Capital and Growth: Theory and Evidence," *Carnegie-Rochester Conference Series on Economic Policy* 32, pp. 251-286.

Romer, P.M., (1993), "Idea Gaps and Object Gaps in Economic Development," *Journal of Monetary Economics* 32, pp. 543-573.

Statistics Netherlands (CBS) (1997), R&D data downloaded on May 25 1997 on: http://statline.cbs.nl /witch /etc /scratch /531924634 /637r_d00.html

Verspagen, B. (1997), "Estimating International Technology Spillovers Using Technology Flow Matrices," *Weltwirtschaftliches Archiv* 133, pp. 226-248.

Wiel, H. van der (1997), "Sectorale productiviteitsgroei in Nederland 1960-1995," Mimeo, CPB Dutch Bureau for Economic Policy Analysis.

Wijers, G.J., Th.J.A. Roelandt and Y.L.C.H. Volman (1997), "Clusters en innovatiebeleid," *Economisch Statistische Berichten*, pp. 942-946.

Young, A., (1991), "Learning by Doing and the Dynamic Effect of International Trade," *Quarterly Journal of Economics* 106, pp. 369-405.

Chapter 11

The Effect of Pharmaceutical Utilisation and Innovation on Hospitalisation and Mortality

Frank Lichtenberg
Columbia Business School

Key words: Pharmaceuticals, Innovation, Economic growth, Mortality, Health care, Hospitals, Surgery, Technology, New products, Longevity, Productivity, R&D

Abstract: This paper presents an econometric analysis of the effect of changes in the quantity and type of pharmaceuticals prescribed by physicians in outpatient visits on rates of hospitalisation, surgical procedure, mortality, and related variables. It examines the statistical relationship across diseases between changes in outpatient pharmaceutical utilisation and changes in inpatient care utilisation and mortality during the period 1980-92.

1.   INTRODUCTION

The explanation of long-run growth in the value of per capita output is a central issue in economics. In recent years, economists have increasingly recognised that traditional, official measures of growth in real per capita output significantly understate true economic growth. One reason is that the price indices that are used to deflate nominal output tend to overestimate inflation, by approximately 1-1.5 percentage points per year (Advisory Commission to Study the Consumer Price Index, 1995).

A second reason is that GDP does not fully account for several important, highly-valued "commodities," such as leisure, health, and longevity. The average person born in 1995 expects to live 22 years (41 percent) longer than the average person born in 1920. Although the rate of increase of longevity appears to be declining, between 1970 and 1991 mean age at death still increased 5.4 years. In a recent paper, Nordhaus (2000) argues that the

317

underestimation of economic growth resulting from failure to account for increased longevity is substantial. He estimates that, "to a first approximation, the economic value of increases in longevity over the twentieth century is about as large as the value of measured growth in non-health goods and services." In other words, economic growth adjusted for longevity increase is twice as large as unadjusted economic growth.

The Solow model, which is perhaps the most widely-accepted theory of economic growth, implies that technological progress is the fundamental source of growth in per capita income. While early models of growth treated the rate of technological progress as an exogenous variable, more recent ("endogenous growth") models recognise that technological progress depends on investment in research and development (R&D) and on the creation of new products and processes. There is abundant empirical evidence that supports the hypothesis that the growth in conventionally-defined per capita output (or total-factor productivity) is positively related to previous investments in research and development. Griliches and Lichtenberg (1984), for example, found that the most R&D intensive manufacturing industries tend to have the highest rates of growth of output per worker.

Aggregate data indicate that in 1991, people were seeing a doctor and consuming medicines about as often as they were in 1980, but they were living longer and spending less time in hospitals. Since ambulatory care, pharmaceuticals, and inpatient care are the three major health inputs, and increased longevity is presumably a desired outcome (or output) of health care, one might interpret this as an indication of productivity growth in the health care sector. The objective of this paper is to investigate the hypothesis that pharmaceutical innovation (reflected in changes in the distribution of drugs prescribed to patients) contributes to productivity growth. It reduces the demand for hospitalisation (which accounts for almost half of U.S. health care expenditure) without reducing (and perhaps even increasing) life expectancy.[1]

---

[1] To assess the impact of (non-pharmaceutical) innovation on economic outcomes (*e.g.*, productivity growth) in other sectors of the economy (*e.g.* manufacturing), economists sometimes use a cross-industry research design: they compare the productivity growth of sectors experiencing rapid technological progress with those experiencing slow technological progress. (For example, Griliches and Lichtenberg (1984) examined the relationship between R&D-intensity and productivity growth at the industry level.) Our analysis fits within this framework: diseases correspond to different "bads," just as industries correspond to different "goods", and bads are equivalent to negative goods. The hypothesis that innovation has a positive impact on the growth of output of goods (conditional on input growth), also implies that it should have a negative impact on the growth of output of bads.

Bresnahan and Gordon (1997) claim that, in general, "new goods are at the heart of economic progress." Unfortunately, econometric investigations of the impact of technological change are often hampered by lack of reliable data on the introduction and utilisation of new goods. But thanks to government regulation of the pharmaceutical industry and the Freedom of Information Act, we are able to reconstruct the precise history of innovation in the pharmaceutical industry – one of the most R&D intensive sectors of the economy – during the last almost 60 years. In particular, we can identify, date, and classify every major and minor innovation since 1939. We obtained from the Food and Drug Administration a computerised list of all New Drug Approvals (NDAs) and Abbreviated New Drug Approvals (ANDAs) since 1939. The list includes the NDA or ANDA number, the approval date, the generic and trade names of the drug, the dosage form, route of administration, strength, applicant name, "therapeutic potential" (priority or standard), and "chemical type" (new molecular entity, new formulation, new manufacturer, *etc.*). We also measure the consumption (utilisation) of about 900 distinct drugs (molecules) since 1980, using data from National Ambulatory Medical Care Surveys (NAMCS), which survey doctor-office visits, and (more recently), from the National Hospital Ambulatory Medical Care Survey (NHAMCS), which surveys visits to hospital outpatient departments and emergency departments.[2] These surveys enable us to estimate the number of drug "mentions" (prescriptions), by molecule, in 1980 and subsequent years.

We will perform an econometric analysis of the effect of changes in the quantity and type of pharmaceuticals prescribed by all kinds of physicians, to all kinds of patients throughout the U.S., on rates of hospitalisation, surgical procedure, mortality, and related variables. This is done by constructing and analysing data on *changes* in medical inputs and outcomes in a cross-section of 2-digit International Classification of Diseases (ICD9) diseases. This methodology controls for "fixed (diagnosis) effects" and for the effects of any general economic and social trends (such as changes in wealth, nutrition, or insurance coverage) that affect *average* hospitalisation and mortality rates.

Case studies of a number of specific drugs have shown that these drugs reduced the demand for hospital care, and, in some cases, mortality. Other case studies have indicated that government-imposed rationing of pharmaceuticals led to increased use of hospital care. While these studies are valuable, the extent to which their findings apply to pharmaceutical use in general is unclear. Moreover, these studies have yielded mixed results about

---

[2] The National Center for Health Statistics first administered the NHAMCS in 1992. Unfortunately, there are no publicly-available data on pharmaceutical utilisation in an inpatient setting.

(or have not addressed) the issue of whether the reduction in hospital cost was outweighed by the increase in pharmaceutical cost.

In the next section we summarise evidence provided by some of the previous research on this topic. We begin to discuss our own research design in the third section , which describes the data on utilisation of specific drugs, by patient diagnosis and year. These data enable us to construct an index of pharmaceutical innovation, hence to determine the impacts of such innovation – changes in the distribution of chemical substances prescribed by physicians to treat diseases. (We also examine the impact of innovations in surgical techniques.) Linkage of the drug data to data on inpatient and outpatient care utilisation and mortality, and summary statistics for all variables, are discussed in the fourth section. Issues of econometric specification are treated in the fifth section. The empirical results are presented in the sixth section, and the final section contains a summary and conclusions.

2.   EVIDENCE FORM PREVIOUS STUDIES

A report by the Boston Consulting Group (1993) provided anecdotal evidence about several major drugs. The following are three of the report's main conclusions. (1) Operations for peptic ulcers decreased from 97,000 in 1977, when H2 antagonists were introduced, to 19,000 in 1977 – a reduction of 80 percent. This saved $224 million in annual medical costs. (2) Before antibiotics, the typical [tuberculosis] patient spent three to four years in a sanatorium, and had a 30 to 50 percent chance of dying. Today, treated with antibiotics, he or she is highly likely to recover in six to 12 months. Antibiotics have saved over $10 billion since 1947. (3) Until the late 1950s, schizophrenia accounted for the vast majority of patients in mental hospitals, and two out of three schizophrenic patients spent the major portion of their lives under sedation in these institutions. By the late 1980s, 95 percent of patients were being treated on an outpatient basis. With the introduction of Clozapine in the late 1980s, many schizophrenic patients were able to return to work or undertake productive work for the first time. Drug treatments have saved the cost of keeping about 400,000 patients in mental institutions: about $25 billion annually.

There have probably been many controlled studies of the impact of specific drugs. One recent study was the Scandinavian Simvastatin Survival Study of 4,444 volunteers. The study indicated that "giving the drug simvastatin to heart patients reduced their hospital admissions by a third during five years of treatment. It also reduced the number of days that they had to spend in the hospital when they were admitted, and reduced the need for bypass surgery and angioplasty" (New York Times (1995a). But treatment with the \$2/day pill that lowered cholesterol did not actually save money: hospital costs were \$8 million lower among the 2221 volunteers who got the drug, but the medicine itself cost \$11 million. The total number of days patients had to spend in the hospital for heart problems was reduced 34 percent.

Another recent study was the West of Scotland Coronary Prevention Study of 6,595 ostensibly healthy men aged 45 through 64. The results indicated that the cholesterol-lowering drug "pravastatin reduces the risk of heart attack and death in a broad range of people, not just those with established heart disease, but also among those who are at risk for their first heart attack" (New York Times (1995b). "Over five years, those [healthy individuals] treated with the cholesterol-lowering drug pravastatin suffered 31 percent fewer nonfatal heart attacks and at least 28 percent fewer deaths from heart disease than a comparable group of men who received a placebo." "In previous studies, pravastatin had been shown to reduce the risk of heart attack by 62 percent in patients with high cholesterol who already heart disease." But the medication is expensive: it costs about \$800 a year to treat each person.

Soumerai *et al.* (1991) analysed the effect of limits imposed by the New Hampshire Medicaid program on the number of reimbursable medications that a patient can receive on rates of admission to nursing homes and hospitals. Imposition of the reimbursement cap resulted in a 35 percent decline in drug use and an approximate doubling of the rate of nursing home admissions among chronically ill elderly patients. There was also a small, but statistically insignificant, increase in the hospitalisation rate during the period of the cap.

Soumerai *et al.* (1994) examined the effects of a three-prescription monthly payment limit (cap) on the use of psychotropic drugs and acute mental health care by non-institutionalised patients with schizophrenia. The cap resulted in immediate 15-49 percent reductions in the use of antipsychotic drugs, antidepressants and lithium, and anxiolytic and hypnotic drugs. It also resulted in coincident (43-57 percent) increases of 1 to 2 visits per patient per month to community mental health centres, sharp increases in the use of emergency mental health services and partial hospitalisation, but no change in the frequency of hospital admissions. The estimated average increase in mental health care costs per patient during the cap (\$1,530) exceeded the savings in drug costs to Medicaid by a factor of 17.

Although the studies surveyed above have shown that the consumption of certain specific drugs on an outpatient basis have reduced the demand for inpatient care (hospitalisation and surgery), or that limitations on access to some drugs increased the demand for inpatient care, these studies may not reveal the effect of pharmaceuticals *in general* on the demand for inpatient care, since the drugs used (or to which access was denied) are not necessarily a random sample of all pharmaceuticals. It is possible, for example, that the distribution of benefits of pharmaceuticals (including reduced need for hospitalisation and surgery) is highly skewed to the right – a few drugs confer enormous benefits, but the majority confer modest benefits[3] – and that the specific drugs enumerated above tend to be concentrated in the upper tail of the benefit distribution.

3.   DATA ON UTILISATION OF SPECIFIC DRUGS, BY PATIENT DIAGNOSIS AND YEAR

Our objective is to determine the "aggregate or average" effect of changes in the quantity and type of drugs prescribed by physicians in outpatient visits on the frequency of hospitalisation, performance of surgical procedures, and mortality. Our strategy is to examine the statistical relationship across diseases between changes in outpatient pharmaceutical utilisation and changes in inpatient care utilisation and mortality during the period 1980-92.

To perform the analysis, we require data at the disease level at at least two (reasonably distant) points in time on the distribution of drugs prescribed to treat that disease, the number of hospital stays and surgical procedures associated with (or due to) that disease, and mortality data by disease. We obtained data on drugs prescribed by physicians in outpatient visits, by disease, from the 1980 and 1991 National Ambulatory Medical Care Survey (NAMCS) Drug Mentions files produced by the National Center for Health Statistics (NCHS). NAMCS is a random sample of approximately 30 to 50 thousand outpatient visits that provides information about patient diagnoses, drugs prescribed by the physician during the visit, and other information about both the patient and the doctor; government estimates of the aggregate number of patient visits (by diagnosis, doctor specialty, *etc.*) and drug mentions are based on these surveys. The Drug Mentions files provide detailed data on the drugs prescribed in the (roughly 60 percent of) office visits in which at least one drug is prescribed. (Unfortunately, although NCHS has conducted the NAMCS survey since at least the early 1970s, 1980 is the first year in which it produced a Drug Mentions file containing the data coded in the way that we require.)

---

[3]   The pharmaceutical industry is among the most R&D intensive industries, and it is well known that the returns to R&D are highly skewed. Of course, even the set of all drugs ever taken by patients is a highly non-random sample of all drugs ever pursued in R&D by pharmaceutical companies, since the former must be approved by the FDA (*i.e.*, they must be found to be "safe and effective.")

Each record in the Drug Mentions file includes a code for the specific drug prescribed, codes for up to three diagnoses (4-digit codes from the International Classification of Diseases, 9th revision, clinical modification), and a "drug weight": a weight for computing population estimates of drug mentions from the survey data. If the drug is a combination drug (about 20 percent of the drugs are), the record specifies codes for up to five individual substances comprising the combination drug. We treated a prescription for a combination drug consisting of, for example, three substances, as three prescriptions, one for each substance. Because there can be multiple diagnoses cited in a given record, we sometimes confront the problem of "allocating" the mention of a drug across diagnoses. We adopted the simple, feasible, approach of *equal* allocation of the drug mention across the several diagnoses. For example, if two diagnoses were cited and the drug weight was 10,000, we replaced the mention of that drug by two mentions of the same drug, one for each diagnosis, each with a drug weight of 5,000; this procedure does not change the population estimates of drug mentions, by drug type.

Having dealt with the issues of combination drugs and multiple diagnoses in these ways, we constructed population (weighted) estimates of the number of drug mentions, by diagnosis and specific drug. In order to have a reasonably large average number of drug mentions per diagnosis[4], we use the *two-digit* disease classification. (Examples of 2-digit disease categories are "hypertensive disease" and "pneumonia and influenza".) Let N_{ijt} represent the population estimate of the number of mentions of molecular entity (drug) i associated with 2-digit diagnosis j in year t (t=1980, 1991). Data on N_{ijt} enable us to construct (noisy) indicators of the change during 1980-91 in the *quantity and composition* of drugs prescribed, by diagnosis. Let $N_{jt} = \sum_i N_{ijt}$ denote the total number of mentions of all drugs associated with diagnosis j in year t, and $n_{ijt} = N_{ijt} / N_{jt}$ denote drug I's share in total drugs prescribed for diagnosis j in year t. Then $QUANTITY = (N_{j,91} / N_{j,80})$ represents the ratio of total quantity of drugs prescribed for diagnosis j in 1991 to the corresponding quantity in 1980.

The data enable us to characterise the degree of similarity (or dissimilarity) of disease j's 1980 and 1991 distributions of drug mentions, by molecule. We seek to measure "how different" the mix of drugs prescribed in different years to patients with a given diagnosis was. We constructed the following index of the degree of dissimilarity of drugs prescribed in 1980 and 1991, or "novelty" of drugs prescribed in 1991, relative to those described in 1980:

---

[4]   As discussed in greater detail below, the larger a population estimate is, the greater its relative precision (the lower its relative standard error).

$$NOVELTY_i = 1 - \frac{\sum_i n_{ij,80} n_{ij,91}}{\sqrt{\sum_i n_{ij,80}^2 \sum_i n_{ij,91}^2}} \tag{1}$$

This index is one minus the cosine of the percentage distributions of diagnosis j's 1980 and 1991 drug mentions, by molecule.[5] It is bounded between zero and one; a value of zero indicates no novelty, *i.e.* perfect similarity of the two distributions, and a value of one indicates complete novelty, *i.e.* zero similarity.[6]

Percentage distributions of 1980 and 1991 drug mentions for all diagnoses, by specific drug, for the top 20 drugs[7] (ranked by total number of mentions), are shown in Table 1. In 1980, the most frequently prescribed drug was hydrochlorothiaside, which received an estimated 3.54 percent of the 743 million drug mentions. By 1991, this drug's share of total mentions had declined by half, to 1.75 percent. Amoxicillin was the most frequently prescribed drug in 1991. Its share of total mentions was 3.71 percent, having risen from 1.50 percent in 1980.

---

[5]   Jaffe (1986) used the cosine of firms' distributions of patents by patent class to measure their technological proximity.

[6]   We also explored two other indexes of drug novelty at the disease level. The first was a chi-square statistic for testing the null hypothesis of independence of the 1980 and 1991 distributions of drug mentions, by molecule. This turned out not to be very informative, however: its magnitude was almost always very large – indicating rejection of the null hypothesis of identical distributions – and was extremely highly correlated with sample size (the total number of mentions in the two years). The second index was the fraction of 1991 drug mentions that were for drugs that had been approved by the Food and Drug Administration after a given year (*e.g.*, 1975 or 1980); drugs approved in 1982, for example, could not have been prescribed by doctors in 1980. This index was constructed by matching the 1991 Drug Mentions file to a list of FDA drug approvals obtained from the FDA. Unfortunately, we were unable to determine the FDA approval dates for about half of the drugs cited in the Drug Mentions file. Moreover, since there may be long and variable lags in the diffusion of drugs to patients after their approval by the FDA, it is not clear which approval date cut-off one should choose in constructing this index.

[7]   Overall, there were 754 distinct drugs cited in the 1980 NAMCS file, and 787 drugs in the 1991 file.

Table 1. Frequency of 1980 and 1991 Drug Mentions for All Diagnoses, by Specific Drug: Top 20 Drugs

	YEAR	
	1991	1980
Total Mentions	891 M.	743 M.
% of Total Mentions in Year:		
AMOXICILLIN	3.71	1.50
ACETAMINOPHEN	3.18	2.00
HYDROCHLOROTHIAZIDE	1.75	3.54
ASPIRIN	1.48	2.78
ERYTHROMYCIN	1.80	2.11
PHENYLPROPANOLAM	1.30	2.23
PHENYLEPHRINE	1.44	2.07
CODEINE	1.42	1.75
ALCOHOL	0.91	2.23
DIGOXIN	1.17	1.61
FUROSEMIDE	1.14	1.34
PENICILLIN	0.34	2.28
PSEUDOEPHEDRINE	0.82	1.65
IBUPROFEN	1.49	0.78
GUAIFENESIN	1.14	1.19
CHLORPHENIRAMINE	0.70	1.60
TETRACYCLINE	0.49	1.74
HYDROCORTISONE	0.89	1.17
NEOMYCIN	0.72	1.31
PROPRANOLOL	0.59	1.39

Of course, the distribution of drugs prescribed in a given year (and changes in the distribution between years) varies considerably across diagnoses – this is precisely the variation we wish to exploit to analyse the effects of pharmaceutical innovation. To illustrate this heterogeneity, Table 2 shows the 1980 and 1991 distributions of the top 20 drugs prescribed to patients with a specific (and relatively common) diagnosis: ischemic heart disease and diseases of pulmonary circulation (ICD9 code 41). Two out of the top 3 drugs on this list (nitroglycerin and isosorbide) do not appear in the list of top 20 drugs for all patients. Four drugs (diltiazem, nifedipine, lovastatin, and atenolol) that were not prescribed at all in 1980 – in some cases because they had not been approved by the FDA by that year – together accounted for over 14 percent of 1991 drug mentions for patients with this diagnosis. But the fact that aspirin's share of drug mentions increased 164 percent, from 2.55 percent to 6.72 percent, indicates that "old" drugs may also experience sharp increases in market share.

Table 2. Frequency of 1980 and 1991 Drug Mentions for ICD9 Code 41 (Ischemic Heart Disease and Diseases of Pulmonary Circulation), by Specific Drug: Top 20 Drugs

	YEAR	
	1980	1991
Total Mentions	25 M.	23 M.
% of Total Mentions in Year:		
NITROGLYCERIN	9.78	9.16
DIGOXIN	9.74	5.52
ISOSORBIDE	8.79	3.20
PROPRANOLOL	9.70	1.95
ASPIRIN	2.55	6.72
HYDROCHLOROTHIAZIDE	5.84	2.59
FUROSEMIDE	4.53	3.81
DILTIAZEM	0.00	6.39
POTASSIUM REPLACEMENT	2.43	2.14
NIFEDIPINE	0.00	4.60
TRIAMTERENE	2.52	1.22
DIPYRIDAMOLE	0.88	2.29
WARFARIN	1.69	1.19
INSULIN	1.09	1.68
LOVASTATIN	0.00	2.63
ATENOLOL	0.00	2.45
QUINIDINE	1.63	0.56
METOPROLOL	0.69	1.57
DIAZEPAM	1.49	0.39
METHYLDOPA	1.59	0.20

As *eq.* (1) indicates, *NOVELTY* is calculated from estimated proportions of patients with a given diagnosis in a given year taking each specific drug. These proportions are subject to sampling error: for example, the standard error of $n_{ij,80}$ is proportional to $[(n_{ij,80} (1 - n_{ij,80})) / N_{j,80}]^{1/2}$. The standard error of the proportion is inversely related to the size of the denominator of the proportion. This suggests that the *expected value* of *NOVELTY* under the null hypothesis of no change in the distribution of drugs is inversely related to the (average) number of drug mentions for the diagnosis. In other words, relatively uncommon diagnoses are likely to have higher values of *NOVELTY* than common diagnoses. To see why, suppose that there are only two drugs, A and B, and that the true (population) probability of taking drug A is 50 percent in both years: zero novelty in the population. If we draw samples of size N in a given year, the proportion of the sample taking drug A may differ from 50 percent; the smaller the sample, the greater the likelihood of observing a sample proportion less than 40 percent or greater than 60 percent, for example. Consequently even if the population distribution has not changed, the 1980 and 1991 sample proportions are likely to be more dissimilar, and the *NOVELTY* index higher, the smaller the sample. This inverse relationship is quite evident in our data. The correlation coefficient across diagnoses between the log of the *NOVELTY* index and the log of the average of the number of drug mentions in 1980 and 1991 (denoted *AVG_MENT*) is -.61, which is highly significant. To make accurate inferences about the effect of pharmaceutical innovation from the *NOVELTY* index, it will therefore be essential to control for sample (diagnosis) size. We do this by defining an "adjusted novelty" index *ADJ_NOV* as the *residual* from the regression of log(*NOVELTY*) on log(*AVG_MENT*). The coefficient on *ADJ_NOV* will then capture the effect of *deviations* of *NOVELTY* from the value implied (or predicted) by the diagnosis size.

4.   LINKING DRUG DATA TO DATA ON INPATIENT AND OUTPATIENT CARE UTILISATION AND MORTALITY

To analyse the relationship between changes in the pattern of drug utilisation and changes in the utilisation of other medical inputs and mortality, we computed disease-level aggregate statistics from six additional NCHS data sets: the NAMCS 1980 and 1991 patient files, the 1980 and 1992 National Hospital Discharge Survey (NHDS) files, and the 1980 and 1991 Vital Statistics-Mortality Detail files.

The NAMCS patient files provide estimates of the number of outpatient visits, by disease, as well as the frequency of ambulatory surgical procedures and the frequency of referrals.

The NHDS is a survey of discharge records in a random sample of short-stay hospitals. Each wave of the NHDS contains about 250,000 records, which is roughly a 1/2 - 1 percent sample of the 30-40 million annual hospital discharges. Each discharge record indicates: (1) up to seven patient diagnoses[8]; (2) the number of nights the patient spent in the hospital; (3) the number of surgical procedures performed; and (4) discharge status (in particular, whether the patient was discharged dead). Hence, we can estimate the number of hospital stays (discharges), nights (or days), inpatient surgical procedures, and hospital deaths, by diagnosis,[9] in both 1980 and 1992.

Just as the Drug Mentions files report the specific drugs prescribed by physicians during office visits, the NHDS files disclose the specific surgical procedures performed in the course of hospital stays. Hence it is possible to construct, and we have constructed, measures of the novelty of *surgical procedures* analogous to the measures of drug novelty described above. Thus

---

[8]   The percentage distribution of non-newborn patients, by number of diagnoses, is as follows:
No. of diagnoses Percent (1) 15.7; (2) 21.2; (3) 16.6; (4) 13.6; (5) 12.6; (6) 6.7; (7) 13.6.

[9]   In the absence of a better alternative, we allocated these variables equally across listed diagnoses in a manner similar to the one used for allocating drug mentions.

we can investigate the behaviour of two types of medical innovation: pharmaceutical innovation and surgical innovation. We expect that these two types of innovation would have opposite effects on the demand for hospitalisation and surgery: the adoption of new surgical procedures is likely to stimulate hospital admissions, whereas the adoption of new drugs is likely to reduce them.[10]

The last two files we use are the 1980 and 1991 Vital Statistics-Mortality Detail files. Unlike the other datasets we use, these are complete *censuses* as opposed to surveys: they include records (from death certificates) of each of the approximately 2 million U.S. deaths per year. (Apparently slightly less than half of deaths occur in hospitals.) Each record indicates the underlying cause of death (diagnosis), and the age at death, so that we can obtain (sampling-error-free) data on the number of deaths and mean age at death, by disease.

In principle, it is possible to extend this database on health inputs and outputs, by disease and year, in several ways. The National Medical Expenditure Survey (and its predecessors) provides detailed data on pharmaceutical and inpatient and outpatient care expenditure, and the National Health Interview Survey provides data on various health indicators (work-loss days, restricted activity days, self-reported health status). But these are household surveys believed to be subject to far greater reporting error (particularly with regard to diagnosis) than the provider surveys described above. Full investigation of these data is a task for future research.

Summary statistics from the ambulatory care survey, hospital discharge survey, and mortality detail files are presented in Table 3. The number of doctor office visits increased at roughly the same rate as the U.S. population, so that per capita office visits remained essentially constant at about 2.6. Drug mentions per office visit decreased from 1.78 to 1.63.[11] The reported number of referrals by physicians to other physicians increased more than twice as fast as the number of office visits; the "propensity to refer" patients increased from 2.6 percent to 3.3 percent. The number of ambulatory

[10] In principle, one would expect the surgical novelty index to be negatively correlated across diagnoses with the average number of surgical procedures, for the same reason that the drug novelty index is negatively correlated with the average number of drug mentions. This is not evident in our data, however: the correlation between the logs of the two surgery variables is essentially zero (.04). In subsequent analysis we therefore don't control for the average number of surgical procedures.

[11] Only about 63 percent of office visits are "drug visits" – visits in which at least one drug is prescribed. However two or more drugs are prescribed in almost half of drug visits. Moreover, about 17 percent of these drugs are combination drugs; we follow the NCHS practice of treating the mention of a combination drug as mentions of each of its ingredients.

surgical procedures performed fell slightly, so that procedures per visit declined about 20 percent.

Table 3. Summary Statistics

I. Aggregates from NAMCS Patient files

	1980	1991
Office visits (millions)	463.3	551.9
Drug mentions (millions)	822.9	898.9
Referrals (millions)	13.4	19.6
Ambul. surg. procs. (millions)	32.5	36.8
Number of records in file	46,081	33,795

II. Aggregates from NHDS files

	1980	1992
Hospital stays (millions)	34.7	28.5
Hospital days (millions)	258.8	179.5
Inpatient surg. procs. (millions)	28.2	38.1
Hospital deaths (millions)	0.95	0.79
Number of records in file	223,785	274,273

III. Aggregates from Vital Statistics-Mortality Detail files

	1980	1991
Total deaths (millions)	1.99	2.17
Mean age at death (years)	67.74	69.96

Data from the hospital discharge surveys indicate a 20 percent decline in the number of hospital admissions. The aggregate number of hospital bed-days fell almost twice as much as the number of hospital admissions, indicating a decline in average length of stay from 7.5 days to 6.3 days. The number of inpatient surgical procedures performed, however, increased by almost a third: average number of procedures per stay increased from 0.81 to 1.34. In both years, about 2.4 percent of hospital stays ended with the death of the patient.

The mortality detail statistics indicate that the fraction of deaths occurring in hospitals fell from about 50 percent in 1980 to 38 percent in 1991. The crude mortality rate declined: the population increased more than the number of deaths. Mean age at death (mean completed duration of life) increased more than 2 years (3.3 percent) over the 11-year period, from 67.7 years to 70.0 years.

5.   ECONOMETRIC SPECIFICATION

Our primary objective is to examine the effect of changes (from 1980 to 1991) in the quantity and distribution of drugs prescribed on changes in the utilisation of other medical inputs (especially inpatient care), and changes in mortality. We will use the adjusted drug novelty index *ADJ_NOV* to measure the change in the percentage distribution of drug mentions, by molecule. We will also account for the change in the percentage distribution of surgical procedures, by type, by including the surgical novelty index *SURG_NOV* in our regression equations.

When examining the relationship between changes in drug utilisation and changes in inpatient care utilisation and mortality, it is essential to attempt to control for changes in the incidence of diseases in the population. If the number of people suffering from a particular disease is increasing especially rapidly, we would expect both the number of drug mentions and the number of hospital stays associated with that disease to rise faster than average. Exogenous changes in disease incidence are likely to induce a positive correlation between drug growth and hospital admissions growth. We attempt to control for changes in disease incidence by including as a regressor the growth rate in the number of patients diagnosed with the disease by physicians in outpatient visits (calculated from the NAMCS patient files). Because drugs are prescribed in about 60 percent of office visits, the correlation across diagnoses between the growth of patients (or visits) and the growth rate of drug mentions is very high – about .80. When the growth in visits is included in the regression, the coefficient on the growth in drug mentions essentially reveals the effect of changes in the number of drug mentions *per person visiting the doctor with that diagnosis* on the number of hospital admissions per person visiting the doctor with that diagnosis. To the extent that the growth in outpatient visits is an imperfect indicator of true changes in disease incidence, the coefficient on changes in drug quantity is likely to be biased upwards. We are less likely to observe a negative association between this variable and the growth in hospital stays, even if one really exists. In this respect, our test of the hypothesis that increases in pharmaceutical quantity (and perhaps novelty) reduce the demand for hospitalisation would be a "strong test."

The type of model we will estimate is of the form

$$
\begin{aligned}
\ln Y_{j,91} - \ln Y_{j,80} = \beta_0 &+ \beta_1 \ln QUANTITY_j + \beta_2 \ln ADJ\_NOV_j \\
&+ \beta_3 \ln SURG\_NOV_j + \beta_4 \ln VISITS_j + \varepsilon_j
\end{aligned}
\tag{2}
$$

where Y is a variable indicated in Table 3, such as the number of hospital stays or mean age at death; j denotes the 2-digit ICD9 diagnosis; *QUANTITY* is the ratio of 1991 to 1980 drug mentions; *ADJ_NOV* is the adjusted index of drug dissimilarity described above; *SURG_NOV* is the index of surgical procedure dissimilarity; *VISITS* is the ratio of 1980 and 1991 outpatient visits; and ε is a disturbance. If *Y* is defined as the number of hospital stays, then the hypothesis that, ceteris paribus, higher pharmaceutical utilisation and innovation reduced growth in the demand for hospital stays implies that $\beta_1 < 0$ and $\beta_2 < 0$. It is perhaps worth noting that when we estimate this equation, we are analysing the relationship between *deviations from means*: we are determining whether diagnoses with above-average pharmaceutical innovation tended to exhibit above-average declines in hospital stays. Factors other than pharmaceutical innovation (*e.g.*, changes in government and private health insurance reimbursement policies) may have affected the average or aggregate incidence of hospitalisation. If these unmeasured determinants of hospitalisation did not vary much across diagnoses (or, if they did, were uncorrelated with *ADJ_NOV*), we will obtain unbiased estimates of the parameters of *eq.*(2).

There is very good reason to expect the disturbances of *eq.*(2) to be heteroskedastic. As reported in the NHDS documentation, the relative standard error (RSE) of an estimated *Y* value – the ratio of the standard error (SE) of the estimate to the (point) estimate (*Y*) itself – is inversely related to Y; in particular, RSE $(Y) = $ SE $(Y) / Y = [a + (b / Y)]^{1/2}$, where *a* and *b* are constants. This is also a reasonable approximation for SE(ln *Y*), so that var(ln *Y*) $= [a + (b / Y)]$. Under the reasonable assumption that sampling errors in the two years are independent, var(ln $Y_{j,91}$ – ln $Y_{j,80}$) $= [2a + b \{(1 / Y_{j,80}) + (1 / Y_{j,91})\}]$: the variance of the growth rate is inversely related to the size of the estimates in both years. The reliability of estimates of the growth rate of hospital stays and related variables is greater for common diagnoses than for uncommon ones.[12]

One would therefore expect the estimated growth rates for less common diagnoses to be further away from the mean growth rate (in both directions). We investigated this by calculating the correlations between squared deviations from mean growth rates and variables of the form $\{(1 / S_{j,80}) + (1 / S_{j,91})\}$, where *S* is one of several alternative measures of diagnosis size (total number of deaths, surgical procedures, or hospital bed-days). Define $y_j = $ (ln $Y_{j,91}$ - ln $Y_{j,80}$), $\underline{y} = $ mean(y_j), $y_j' = (y_j - \underline{y})^2$, and $s_j = \{(1 / S_{j,80}) + (1 / S_{j,91})\}$. Correlations between y_j' and s_j for different definitions of *Y* and *S* are shown in Table 4.

---

[12] The size distribution of 2-digit ICD9 diagnoses is essentially lognormal: the majority of cases are accounted for by a relatively small number of diagnoses.

Table 4. Correlations between *y'* and *s* for Different Definitions of *Y* and *S*

		Y					
		STAYS	*DAYS*	*NSURG*	*HDEATH*	*DEATHS*	*AGE*
	M	0.72994	0.82797	0.10908	0.09452	0.01933	0.53581
		0.0001	0.0001	0.2800	0.3649	0.8486	0.0001
S	S	0.51375	0.50927	0.03345	-0.02436	-0.01066	0.29631
		0.0001	0.0001	0.7287	0.8070	0.9162	0.0028
	D	0.59387	0.58516	0.06099	-0.01200	-0.02325	0.35240
		0.0001	0.0001	0.5268	0.9042	0.8184	0.0003

M = total number of deaths
S = number of hospital stays (discharges)
D = number of hospital days

Several of the variables – *STAYS*, *DAYS*, and *AGE* – clearly exhibit heteroskedasticity: their squared deviations from mean growth rates are strongly positively correlated with all three inverse measures of diagnosis size. For all of the variables, the measure of diagnosis size whose inverse has the largest correlation with the squared deviation (an indicator of variance) is the number of deaths. Presumably this is partly due to the fact that the number of deaths is based on a complete census (it is not subject to sampling error), whereas the number of hospital stays and days is based on a random sample of less than 1 percent of hospitalisations. Moreover, a single diagnosis is cited in the mortality records, whereas up to seven diagnoses are cited in the hospital discharge survey; our procedure of allocating stays, days, *etc.*, equally across diagnoses undoubtedly results in errors of measurement in the frequency of these variables, by diagnosis.

Because the dependent variables of *eq.*(2) exhibit marked heteroskedasticity, and their variance is most strongly inversely related to the number of deaths reported in the mortality detail files, we will estimate *eq.* (2) using weighted least squares, with weights equal to $\{(1 / DEATHS_{j,80}) + (1 / DEATHS_{j,91})\}^{-1}$. Diagnoses that are reported to have caused a larger number of deaths will receive greater weight in analysing the relationship, across diagnoses, between pharmaceutical utilisation and innovation and changes in hospitalisation and mortality.

6.   EMPIRICAL RESULTS

Weighted least-squares estimates of *eq.*(2) are presented in Table 5. In column (1) the dependent variable is the growth in hospital stays. The estimates indicate that there is a strong inverse relationship between the growth in hospital stays and both the index of pharmaceutical innovation and the growth in total drug mentions. *The number of hospital stays declined most rapidly for those diagnoses with the greatest increase in the total number of drugs prescribed and the greatest change in the distribution of drugs*. The growth in stays is *positively* (and significantly) related to the extent of surgical innovation: the more dissimilar the 1980 and 1991 distributions of surgical procedures – presumably because of the adoption of new surgical techniques – the greater the increase in hospital admissions. About one-fourth of the cross-diagnosis variation in the growth of hospital stays is explained by the regressors.

The second column of Table 5 reports estimates of the regression of growth of total hospital bed-days on the same set of variables. The estimates are qualitatively similar to those in column (1), but the magnitudes of the coefficients on ln *QUANTITY* and *ADJ_NOV* are about 60 percent larger. The growth rate of the average length of a hospital stay is equal to the growth rate of total hospital days minus the growth rate of the number of stays; the regression of this variable is shown in column (3). These estimates suggest that *greater quantity and novelty of pharmaceuticals had a negative impact on average length of stay in hospitals, as well as on the number of hospital stays*. While diagnoses with high rates of surgical innovation had below-average declines in the number of hospital admissions, they had essentially average declines in average length of stay.

The dependent variable in column (4) is the growth in the number of inpatient surgical procedures performed. As in the total bed-days regression in column (2), the coefficients of both of the pharmaceutical variables are negative and highly significant, and the magnitude of the *QUANTITY* coefficient (as well as R^2) is about 1/3 higher in column 4. *Increases in the quantity of pharmaceuticals prescribed appear to have a somewhat more negative impact on the growth of surgical procedures than they do on the growth of hospital stays and total bed-days*. This implies, of course, that the *average* number of procedures performed per stay increased more slowly for diagnoses with higher growth in drug quantity and novelty. The coefficient on *SURG_NOV* implies that diagnoses with greater surgical innovation exhibited higher growth in the average number of procedures per stay, as well as in the number of stays, which is not surprising.

Table 5. Weighted Least-Squares Estimates of eq. (2) (t-statistics in parentheses)

Dep. var. Regressor Column	(1) STAYS	(2) DAYS	(3) ALOS	(4) NSURG	(5) HDEATH	(6) DEATHS	(7) AGE	(8) AMBUL	(9) REFER
ln *QUANTITY*	-.403	-.641	-.239	-.872	-.640	-.343	-.017	.021	-1.04
	(2.91)	(4.17)	(3.53)	(3.82)	(2.91)	(3.35)	(0.53)	(0.04)	(2.72)
ADJ_NOV	-.215	-.337	-.122	-.417	-.423	-.083	-.005	-.041	-.137
	(2.77)	(3.92)	(3.24)	(3.26)	(3.44)	(1.46)	(0.28)	(0.17)	(0.82)
ln *SURG_NOV*	.269	.280	.010	.553	.143	.107	.016	.069	-.940
	(3.40)	(3.18)	(0.27)	(4.24)	(1.14)	(1.83)	(0.83)	(0.25)	(5.07)
ln *VISITS*	.238	.541	.303	.274	.598	.818	.056	.421	.535
	(1.30)	(2.67)	(3.39)	(0.91)	(2.06)	(6.07)	(1.28)	(0.64)	(1.20)
Intercept	.076	-.252	-.327	1.19	-.374	.148	.049	1.04	-.420
	(1.07)	(3.22)	(9.52)	(10.3)	(3.35)	(2.84)	(2.91)	(4.51)	(2.67)
R^2	.274	.332	.187	.436	.187	.384	.040	.023	.317
N	93	93	93	93	93	93	93	74	74

Columns (5) through (7) present regressions of three different indicators of mortality: the number of deaths in hospitals, the total number of deaths, and mean age at death (for all deaths). The coefficients on drug quantity and novelty in the hospital deaths equation are similar to those in the *DAYS* equation, and larger than those in the *STAYS* equation. This implies that increases in these variables are associated with reductions in deaths per hospital stay (but not per hospital bed-day). The fact that the coefficient on the surgical innovation variable is much smaller in col. (5) than it is in col. (4) indicates that more rapid surgical innovation is associated with a decline in deaths per procedure. In the total deaths equation in col. (6), the coefficient on *ln QUANTITY* is again negative and significant – consistent with the hypothesis that increased pharmaceutical consumption reduces mortality rates – but it is only about half as large as its counterpart in col. (5), which implies that the non-hospital mortality rate is much less sensitive to pharmaceutical consumption than the hospital rate. The drug novelty variable has only a marginally significant negative effect on the increase in total deaths. The estimates in col. (7) reveal that none of the regressors have a significant impact on the change in completed life expectancy.

The first four regressions suggest that increases in drug consumption and novelty reduce the utilisation of inpatient care; the next three regressions suggest that this does not come at the expense of higher mortality, and there is even some evidence that mortality is also reduced.

The last two regressions in Table 5 examine the behaviour of two aspects of *outpatient* resource allocation, namely the number of ambulatory surgical procedures performed and the number of referrals to other physicians. In principle, it is possible that the reduction in inpatient surgical procedures associated with greater pharmaceutical utilisation and novelty could be offset (partially or completely) by an increase in outpatient procedures; perhaps only the *locus* of performance of procedures changed (from hospital to doctor's office). The estimates in col. (8) do not support this conjecture. The change in ambulatory procedures appears to be unrelated to all of the regressors.

Estimates of the last equation reveal a significant negative correlation between the increase in the number of referrals (conditional on the number of office visits) and the increase in drug mentions (as well as the surgical novelty index). The greater the increase in the probability that the visited doctor prescribes a drug (or the expected number of drugs prescribed), the lower the increase in the probability that he or she refers the patient to another physician.

So far our discussion of empirical results has been concerned with hypothesis testing, *i.e.* with the signs and statistical significance of the parameter estimates reported in Table 5. We now consider the *magnitudes* of the implied "marginal effects" of changes in the number of drug mentions on the dependent variables. In particular, we calculate the effect of an increase of 100 prescriptions on a variable Y by multiplying the estimate of the elasticity β_1 by the ratio of aggregate Y to aggregate drug mentions M: $dY / dM = \beta_1 (Y_A / M_A)$, where the A subscript denotes (average of 1980 and either 1991 or 1992) aggregate values.[13]

Dependent variable	β_1	Y_A	Effect of 100-prescrip. increase on Y: $dY / dM = \beta_1 (Y_A / 8.61)$
STAYS	-.403	31.6	-1.48
DAYS	-.641	219	-16.3
NSURG	-.872	33.2	-3.36
HDEATH	-.640	871	-0.065
DEATHS	-.343	2.08	-0.083
REFER	1.04	16.5	-1.99

The estimates imply that, holding constant the novelty of drugs and surgical procedures and the number of outpatient visits, an increase of 100 prescriptions is associated with 1.48 fewer hospital admissions, 16.3 fewer hospital days, 3.36 fewer inpatient surgical procedures and 1.99 fewer outpatient referrals; there would be 83 fewer deaths (65 fewer hospital deaths) per 100,000 increase in prescriptions.

Using the following data on aggregate U.S. health expenditure in 1991 contained in the OECD Health Database, we can also attempt to estimate the effect of changes in pharmaceutical expenditure on inpatient care (and total health) expenditure:

Pharmaceutical expenditure:	$ 60.7 b.
Hospital care expenditure:	346.5 b.
Ambulatory care expenditure:	224.7 b.
-- physicians' services expenditure	142.0 b.

The parameter estimates imply that a 10 percent increase in drug mentions is associated with a 4.0 percent reduction in hospital stays and a 6.4 percent reduction in hospital bed-days. We therefore think that it is reasonable to suppose that a 10 percent increase in pharmaceutical *expenditure* is associated with a 6.4 percent reduction in hospital care *expenditure*.[14] (This estimate may be conservative because the surgery elasticity is larger in magnitude than the bed-days elasticity, and cost per bed-day is likely to increase with procedures per bed-day.) Since total

---

[13] Y_A is measured in millions. The mean of 1980 and 1991 aggregate drug mentions is 861 million.

[14] Total expenditure on hospital care presumably depends much more on the number of days than on the number of stays.

expenditure on hospital care is 5.7 times as large as total pharmaceutical expenditure, this implies that *a $1 increase in pharmaceutical expenditure is associated with a $3.65 reduction in hospital care expenditure*. This estimate implies that, if changes in pharmaceutical utilisation had no other effects on health care costs, a $1 increase in pharmaceutical expenditure would reduce total health care expenditure by $2.65. But there are at least two reasons to believe that changes in pharmaceutical utilisation *would* affect other costs, in both directions.

An increase in pharmaceutical utilisation may necessitate an increase in ambulatory care utilisation: a physician is required to prescribe the drugs. The slope coefficient from the (weighted) regression of the growth in office visits on the growth in drug mentions is .656: a 10 percent increase in drug mentions is associated with a 6.6 percent increase in office visits. If a 10 percent increase in drug expenditure would increase "expenditure on physicians' services" by 6.6 percent,[15] a $1 increase in drug expenditure would be associated with a $1.54 increase in expenditure on physicians' services. This would offset 42 percent of the estimated reduction in inpatient expenditure.[16]

On the other hand, "hospital care expenditure" measures only the *direct* costs of hospitalisation; it does not reflect the value of the patient's lost work and leisure time that presumably often accompanies hospitalisation and surgery. If the indirect cost of hospitalisation is, say, 25 percent as large as the direct cost, then the reduction in the "social" (direct plus indirect) hospitalisation cost per dollar of increased pharmaceutical expenditure is 20 percent larger than the $3.65 figure calculated above.

We conclude this section with a brief discussion of the magnitude of the coefficients on the pharmaceutical novelty index *ADJ_NOV*. The .25 and .75 quantiles of the *ADJ_NOV* distribution are -.113 and .288, respectively. Thus the difference between the .75 and .25 quantile values is .402, which is similar to the (unweighted) standard deviation of *ADJ_NOV* (.433). Below we calculate the predicted response of several dependent variables to a .402 increase in *ADJ_NOV* – a movement from the first to the third quartile of the adjusted novelty distribution:

---

[15] "Ambulatory care expenditure," as defined by OECD, also includes expenditure on dentists' services and on laboratory and diagnostic tests, which presumably need not increase with an increase in pharmaceutical utilisation.

[16] The fact that the probability of referral to another physician is inversely related to drug utilisation suggests that these figures slightly overstate the increase in physicians' services associated with higher drug utilisation.

	predicted log change from .402 increase in *ADJ_NOV*	actual log change in aggregate value
Variable		
STAYS	-.086	-.197
DAYS	-.135	-.369
SURG	-.168	+.301
HDEATH	-.170	-.182

The rate of growth of hospital stays of a diagnosis at the .75 percentile of the *ADJ_NOV* distribution is estimated to be 8.6 percentage points lower than that of a diagnosis at the .25 percentile.

By performing calculations similar to those made above with the *QUANTITY* coefficients, we could calculate the *benefits* (in the form of hospital cost reductions) of pharmaceutical novelty, *i.e.* of changes in the distribution of prescriptions, by drug. It is more difficult, however, to assess the *cost* of changing the distribution of drugs. R&D expenditures by pharmaceutical firms represent a substantial part of these costs. According to the National Science Foundation, in 1991 these firms spent $6.1 billion on R&D. This is a very substantial amount, but it is only 1.8 percent of national expenditure on hospital care in that year. Thus *pharmaceutical R&D spending would reduce total health expenditure (including pharmaceutical R&D) if it reduced hospital expenditure by as little as about 2* percent. Our estimates indicate that changes in the distribution of pharmaceuticals are associated with significant hospital cost reductions. We hypothesise that the extent of changes in the pharmaceutical distribution are positively correlated across diagnoses with (lagged) R&D expenditure, but since we lack data on R&D spending by diagnosis[17], we cannot examine the relationship between pharmaceutical R&D and hospital costs directly.

7.   SUMMARY AND CONCLUSION

Case studies of a number of specific drugs have shown that these drugs reduced the demand for hospital care, and, in some cases, mortality. Other case studies have indicated that government-imposed rationing of pharmaceuticals led to increased use of hospital care. While these studies are valuable, the extent to which their findings apply to pharmaceutical use *in general* is unclear. Moreover, these studies have yielded mixed results about (or have not addressed) the issue of whether the reduction in hospital cost was outweighed by the increase in pharmaceutical cost.

---

[17] Cockburn and Henderson (1996) have compiled data on pharmaceutical R&D at the "program" (and even the project) level. In principle, it might be possible to calculate R&D expenditure by diagnosis from their data, but unfortunately they are proprietary.

In this paper we have examined the effect of changes in the quantity and type of pharmaceuticals prescribed by all kinds of physicians, to all kinds of patients throughout the U.S., on rates of hospitalisation, surgical procedure, mortality, and related variables. Our unit of analysis was a (ICD9 2-digit) disease or diagnosis, which we argued is analogous to a product (or industry) in industrial organisation economics. We controlled for the presence of "fixed (diagnosis) effects" by analysing *growth rates* of the variables. To perform the analysis, we first constructed a database on diagnosis-level inputs and outcomes at two points in time (1980 and 1991 or 1992). This entailed the linkage of eight large files produced by the National Center for Health Statistics. Each file contained between 30 thousand and 2 million records.

The limitations of the available data posed a number of statistical problems. The diagnosis-level data on drug utilisation, ambulatory care, and hospitalisation that we constructed are based on surveys, and are subject to sampling error. Moreover, these errors are heteroskedastic; we therefore estimated models using weighted least squares. Also, due to the presence of sampling error, the expected value of the drug novelty index is inversely related to sample size; we corrected for this by using an adjusted novelty index. Exogenous changes in disease incidence are likely to induce a ("spurious") correlation between drug growth and hospital admissions growth, although both theory and evidence suggest that this will bias the correlation upward, making our hypothesis tests "strong tests." We attempted to control for changes in disease incidence by including as a regressor the growth rate in the number of patients diagnosed with the disease by physicians in outpatient visits. An additional problem was posed by multiple diagnoses sometimes being cited in connection with a single drug mention, office visit, or hospital stay; lacking any alternative, we simply allocated the "event" equally across listed diagnoses.

Our principal findings may be summarised as follows. (1) The number of hospital stays, bed-days, and surgical procedures declined most rapidly for those diagnoses with the greatest increase in the total number of drugs prescribed and the greatest change in the distribution of drugs. The estimates imply that an increase of 100 prescriptions is associated with 1.48 fewer hospital admissions, 16.3 fewer hospital days, and 3.36 fewer inpatient surgical procedures. (2) Greater quantity and novelty of pharmaceuticals had a negative impact on average length of stay in hospitals, as well as on the number of hospital stays. (3) The average number of inpatient procedures performed per stay increased more slowly for diagnoses with higher growth in drug quantity and novelty. (4) Increases in drug quantity and novelty are associated with reductions in both the number of hospital deaths and deaths per hospital stay; they have much weaker effects on non-hospital mortality, and are unrelated to changes in mean age at death. (5) The greater the increase in the probability that a doctor prescribes a drug, the lower the increase in the probability that he or she refers the patient to another physician. (6) Changes in the number of ambulatory surgical procedures appear to be unrelated to changes in drug utilisation. (7) A $1 increase in pharmaceutical expenditure is associated with a $3.65 reduction in hospital care expenditure (ignoring any indirect cost of hospitalisation), but it is also associated with a $1.54 increase in expenditure on ambulatory care. (8) Diagnoses subject to higher rates of *surgical* innovation exhibited larger increases (or smaller declines) in hospitalisation, and marginally significantly larger increases in mortality.

A   DATA

1.   **Variable names and labels**

Variable	Sum	Mean	N	Label
NOVELTY	47.6755835	0.4966207	96	Drug novelty index
TOT80	822918535	8312308.43	99	Total no. of drug mentions, 1980
TOT91	898905305	9079851.57	99	Total no. of drug mentions, 1991
STAYS80	34690497.00	346904.97	100	Hospital stays, 1980
STAYS92	28527116.00	285271.16	100	Hospital stays, 1992
DAYS80	258751963	2587519.63	100	Hospital bed-days, 1980
DAYS92	179455208	1794552.08	100	Hospital bed-days, 1992
NSURG80	28173303.00	281733.03	100	No. of hosp. surgical procedures, 1980
NSURG92	38136335.00	381363.35	100	No. of hosp. surgical procedures, 1992
SNOVELTY	52.4893114	0.5248931	100	Surgical novelty index
HDEATH80	949645.00	9790.15	97	Hospital deaths, 1980
HDEATH92	792184.00	8251.92	96	Hospital deaths, 1992
DEATHS80	1993137.00	19931.37	100	Total deaths, 1980
DEATHS91	2173060.00	21730.60	100	Total deaths, 1991
AGE80	5666.97	56.6696937	100	(Unweighted) mean age at death, 1980
AGE91	5891.28	58.9127568	100	(Unweighted) mean age at death, 1991
VISITS80	463344593	4633445.93	100	No. of outpatient visits, 1980
VISITS91	551902184	5631654.94	98	No. of outpatient visits, 1991
AMBUL80	32548288.00	325482.88	100	No. of ambulatory surgical procedures, 1980
AMBUL91	36831295.00	375829.54	98	No. of ambulatory surgical procedures, 1991
REFER80	13428846.00	134288.46	100	No. of outpatient referrals, 1980
REFER91	19581978.00	199816.10	98	No. of outpatient referrals, 1991

2. List of 2-digit ICD9 diagnosis codes*and diagnosis names

00 Intestinal infectious diseases (001-009)

01 Tuberculosis (010-018)

02 Zoonotic bacterial diseases (020-027)

03 Other bacterial diseases (030-041)

04 Poliomyelitis and other non-arthropod-borne viral diseases of central nervous system (045-049)

05 Viral diseases accompanied by exanthem (050-057)

06 Arthropod-borne viral diseases (060-066)

07 Other diseases due to viruses and Chlamydiae (070-079)

08 Rickettsioses and other arthropod-borne diseases (080-088)

09 Syphilis and other venereal diseases (090-099)

10 Other spirochetal diseases (100-104)

11 Mycoses (110-118)

12 Helminthiases (120-129)

13 Other infectious and parasitic diseases Late effects of infectious and parasitic diseases (130-139)

14 Malignant neoplasm of lip, oral cavity, and pharynx (140-149)

15 Malignant neoplasm of digestive organs and peritoneum (150-159)

16 Malignant neoplasm of respiratory and intrathoracic organs (160-165)

17 Malignant neoplasm of bone, connective tissue, skin, and breast (170-175)

18 Malignant neoplasm of genitourinary organs (179-189)

19 Malignant neoplasm of other and unspecified sites (190-199)

20 Malignant neoplasm of lymphatic and hematopoietic tissue (200-208)

21 Benign neoplasms (210-229)

22 Benign neoplasms (210-229)

23 Carcinoma in situ Neoplasms of uncertain behaviour Neoplasms of   unspecified nature (230-239)

24 Disorders of thyroid gland (240-246)

25 Diseases of other endocrine glands (250-259)

26 Nutritional deficiencies (260-269)

27 Other metabolic disorders and immunity disorders (270-279)

28 DISEASES OF BLOOD AND BLOOD-FORMING ORGANS (280-289)

29 Organic psychotic conditions (290-294) Other psychoses (295-299)

30 Neurotic disorders, personality disorders, and other nonpsychotic mental disorders (300-316)

31 Mental retardation (317-319)

32 Inflammatory diseases of the central nervous system (320-326)

33 Hereditary and degenerative diseases of the central nervous system (330-337)

34 Other disorders of the central nervous system (340-349)

35 Disorders of the peripheral nervous system (350-359)

36 Disorders of the eye and adnexa (360-379)

37 Disorders of the eye and adnexa (360-379)

38 Diseases of the ear and mastoid process (380-389)

39 Acute rheumatic fever (390-392) Chronic rheumatic heart disease   (393-398)

40 Hypertensive disease (401-405)

41 Ischemic heart disease (410-414) Diseases of pulmonary circulation (415-417)

42 Other forms of heart disease (420-429)

43 Cerebrovascular disease (430-438)

44 Diseases of arteries, arterioles, and capillaries (440-448)

45 Diseases of veins and lymphatics, and other diseases of circulatory system (451-459)

46 Acute respiratory infections (460-466)

47 Other diseases of upper respiratory tract (470-478)

48 Pneumonia and influenza (480-487)

49 Chronic obstructive pulmonary disease and allied conditions (490-496)

50 Pneumoconioses and other lung diseases due to external agents (500-508)

51 Other diseases of respiratory system (510-519)

52 Diseases of oral cavity, salivary glands, and jaws (520-529)

53 Diseases of esophagus, stomach, and duodenum (530-537)

54 Appendicitis (540-543)

55 Hernia of abdominal cavity (550-553) Noninfective enteritis and colitis (555-558)

56 Other diseases of intestines and peritoneum (560-569)

57 Other diseases of digestive system (570-579)

58 Nephritis, nephrotic syndrome, and nephrosis (580-589)

59 Other diseases of urinary system (590-599)

60 Diseases of male genital organs (600-608)

61 Disorders of breast (610-611) Inflammatory disease of female pelvic organs (614-616)

62 Other disorders of female genital tract (617-629)

63 Ectopic and molar pregnancy and other pregnancy with abortive outcome (630-639)

64 Complications mainly related to pregnancy (640-648)

65 Normal delivery, and other indications for care in pregnancy, labor, and delivery (650-659)

66 Complications occurring mainly in the course of labor and delivery (660-669)

67 Complications of the puerperium (670-676)

68 Infections of skin and subcutaneous tissue (680-686)

69 Other inflammatory conditions of skin and subcutaneous tissue (690-698)

70 Other diseases of skin and subcutaneous tissue (700-709)

71 Arthropathies and related disorders (710-719)

72 Dorsopathies (720-724) Rheumatism, excluding the back (725-729)

73 Osteopathies, chondropathies, and acquired musculoskeletal deformities (730-739)

74 CONGENITAL ANOMALIES (740-759)

75 CONGENITAL ANOMALIES (740-759)

76 Maternal causes of perinatal morbidity and mortality (760-763)

77 Other conditions originating in the perinatal period (764-779)

78 Symptoms (780-789)

79 Nonspecific abnormal findings Ill-defined and unknown causes of morbidity and mortality (790-799)

80 Fracture of skull (800-804) Fracture of spine and trunk (805-809)

81 Fracture of upper limb (810-819)

82 Fracture of lower limb (820-829)

83 Dislocation (830-839)

84 Sprains and strains of joints and adjacent muscles (840-848)

85 Intracranial injury, excluding those with skull fracture (850-854)

86 Internal injury of chest, abdomen, and pelvis (860-869)

87 Open wound of head, neck, and trunk (870-879)

88 Open wound of upper limb (880-887)

89 Open wound of lower limb (890-897)

90 Injury to blood vessels Late effects of injuries, poisonings, toxic effects, *etc.*(900-909)

91 Superficial injury (910-919)

92 Contusion with intact skin surface (920-924) Crushing injury (925-929)

93 Effects of foreign body entering through orifice (930-939)

94 Burns (940-949)

95 Injury to nerves and spinal cord Certain traumatic complications and unspecified injuries (950-959)

96 Poisoning by drugs, medicinals and biological substances (960-979)

97 Poisoning by drugs, medicinals and biological substances (960-979)

98 Toxic effects of substances chiefly nonmedicinal as to source (980-989)

99 Other and unspec. effects of external causes Complications of surgical and medical care, nec (990-999)

REFERENCES

Advisory Commission to Study the Consumer Price Index (1995), "Toward a More Accurate Measure of the Cost of Living," Interim Report to the Senate Finance Committee, Sept. 15.

Boston Consulting Group, Inc. (1993), "The Contribution of Pharmaceutical Companies: What's at Stake for America, Executive Summary," September.

Bresnahan, T., and R. Gordon (1997), *The Economics of New Goods,* Chicago: University of Chicago Press, 1997.

Cockburn, I. and R. Henderson (1996), "Scale, Scope, and Spillovers: The Determinants of Research Productivity in Drug Discovery," *Rand Journal of Economics* 27, pp. 32-59.

Griliches, Z. and F. Lichtenberg (1984), "R&D and Productivity at the Industry Level: Is There Still a Relationship?," in Z. Griliches, (ed.), *R&D, Patents, and Productivity*, Chicago: Univ. of Chicago Press.

Jaffe, A. (1986), "Technological Opportunity and Spillovers of R&D: Evidence from Firms' Patents, Profits, and Market Value," *The American Economic Review* 76, pp. 984-1001.

New York Times (1995a), "Cholesterol Pill Linked to Lower Hospital Bills," March, p. A11.

New York Times (1995b), "Benefit to Healthy Men is Seen from Cholesterol-cutting Drug,"
    p. A1.
Nordhaus, W. (2000), "Incorporating the Health of Nations in the Wealth of Nations: The
    Contribution of Improved Longevity to National Income," in K. Murphy and R. Topel
    (eds.), *The Value of Medical Research*, Chicago: University of Chicago Press,
    forthcoming.
Soumerai, S., D. Ross-Degnan, J. Avorn, T. McLaughlin, and I. Choodnovskiy (1991).
    "Effects of Medicaid Drug-payment Limits on Admission to Hospitals and Nursing
    Homes," *New England Journal of Medicine* 325, No. 15, pp. 1072-7.
Soumerai, S., T. McLaughlin, D. Ross-Degnan, C. Casteris, and P. Bollini (1994). "Effects of
    a Limit on Medicaid Drug-reimbursement Benefits on the Use of Psychotropic Agents and
    Acute Mental Health Services by Patients with Schizophrenia," *New England Journal of
    Medicine* 331, No. 10, pp. 650-5.

Chapter 12

Productivity, R&D Spillovers and Trade

Jan Fagerberg and Bart Verspagen
University of Oslo, TIK and ECIS, Eindhoven University of Technology & MERIT, Maastricht University

Key words: Innovation, Diffusion, R&D, Trade

Abstract: That innovation and diffusion of technology drives long run productivity growth is by now commonly accepted. The crucial question is: how? For instance, what is the role of own R&D in the firm, industry or country, as opposed to technology developed through R&D efforts elsewhere, whether embodied in goods or services or not. This is the question we address in this paper. We do this in two steps. First, we consider the different theoretical approaches, the empirical relationships they entail, and the related evidence. Then we present a comprehensive data set, consisting of 1974-1992 annual data for 14 countries and 22 manufacturing industries, which we use in attempt to discriminate between some of the most popular arguments in this area. The results indicate that own R&D is very important for productivity, both in its own right, and in interaction with other variables that take part in the growth process and that there are several, complementary channels of technology diffusion, of which R&D embodied in goods and services is only one (and not a major one).

1.   INTRODUCTION

That innovation and diffusion of technology drives long run productivity growth is by now commonly accepted. The crucial question is: how? For instance, what is the role of own R&D in the firm, industry or country, as opposed to R&D done elsewhere? Is the former a precondition for rapid productivity growth, or is it possible to prosper by exclusively relying on

345

imported technology? These are questions of high theoretical and practical importance. But the answers are not so clear yet. In fact, as we will show in the next section, the existing evidence points in very different directions. Can this conflicting evidence be reconciled to give a consistent picture? This is the question we address in this paper. We do this in two steps. First, we consider the different theoretical approaches, the empirical relationships they entail, and the related evidence. Then we present a comprehensive data set, consisting of 1974 – 1992 annual data for 14 countries and 22 manufacturing industries, which we use in an attempt to discriminate between some of the most popular arguments in this area, and to explore the reasons behind some of the conflicting evidence presented in the existing empirical literature. We discuss the findings and implications in the concluding section.

2.   THEORY AND EVIDENCE

There are basically three streams of thought in this area worth mentioning (see Fagerberg, 1994, for an overview). The first is the old neo-classical theory, which focuses solely on the public good aspects of technology. Second, there is a less "orthodox," and more empirically based, tradition, often called the "technology-gap" theory of economic growth (Fagerberg, 1987), characterised by a more comprehensive analysis of the different aspects of technology, and the interaction between technology and other variables that take part in the growth process. Third, and more recent, there is the so-called new growth theory, which combines insights from the two other streams.

Of these three approaches, the first is clearly the least relevant. If technology is a completely public good, freely available to anyone, it cannot be used as an explanatory factor behind differences in productivity growth (although it may have an impact on world-wide growth). Hence for technology to explain growth differences, diffusion of technology must require efforts and/or capabilities that cannot be taken for granted. It is such a perspective that forms the basis for the "technology-gap theory" of economic growth. The starting point was the observation that for countries lagging behind the world best-practice technology level, innovations do not arise so much from original research, as from imitation of technologically more advanced countries. This inspired Gerschenkron (1962) to introduce the term "advantage of backwardness," *i.e.,* the possibility that countries lagging behind the technology frontier can grow by using a backlog of knowledge created elsewhere. However, he also pointed out that exploiting this backlog is not an easy process, but requires a lot of investments, infrastructures and institution building. Abramovitz (1979), arguing along the same lines, used the concept "absorptive capacity" to denote the domestic capability to assimilate foreign spillovers. Thus, instead of technology as a free good, a picture emerges in which imitation of more advanced foreign technology is a costly activity, that requires investment in indigenous capabilities, capital equipment, infrastructure, *etc.*. Without a sufficient level of such investments, a country is unlikely to benefit from backwardness, and risk of falling behind relative to the technology leaders, rather than catching up (Verspagen, 1991).

New growth theory combines a traditional neo-classical framework with a richer description of technology that allows for proprietary aspects as well as spillovers. However, these theoretical advances have not yet produced many new insights on diffusion. Typically, very stylised assumptions are adopted: either spillovers are completely global in scope, or completely national, at the level of the country or industry (see, for example Grossman and Helpman, 1991). If spillovers are global, we are more or less back to the traditional neo-classical model, at least as far as diffusion is concerned. With national spillovers, market size matters, and hence we should expect higher returns to R&D in larger economies. Apart from this, there are relatively few testable predictions that have been derived from this framework, and it is seems fair to say that the advent of new growth theory has not – or at least not until very recently – led to much new applied work on diffusion.[1]

Apart from descriptive analyses, empirical work based on these perspectives usually consists of cross-country regressions with the growth rate of labour productivity as the dependent variable, and the level of initial labour productivity, used as an indicator of initial backwardness, and variables reflecting absorptive capacity (and other relevant factors) as independent variables. The latter include investment in fixed capital and human capital, R&D expenditures, openness to international trade, etc. Studies of this type (see Fagerberg, 1994) for an overview) have generally arrived at positive signs for many of the latter, while the level of initial GDP per capita usually turns up negatively. The latter may be seen as a confirmation of the potential advantages of international technology diffusion for countries behind the technology frontier.

It may be argued, however, that the gap in productivity relative to the frontier is a very broad measure of the potential for diffusion, open to rival interpretations,[2] and that more precise measures would be desirable. In fact,

---

[1] Arguably, the recent contributions by Coe and Helpman (1995), Coe, Helpman and Hoffmaister (1997) and Eaton and Kortum (1997) may be exceptions to this rule. We discuss these below.

[2] For instance, following the traditional neo-classical perspective, the negative impact of a relatively high initial productivity level may be explained by decreasing returns to capital-labour substitution.

new technology may diffuse in many different ways: embodied in goods or services that make use of new technology, through foreign direct investments by multinational firms or by imitative activities by domestic firms, drawing on a multitude of sources, as well as (necessary) complementary assets/capabilities. Ideally, one would have wished to take all of these into account, but this has generally not been possible due to lack of relevant data. For instance, data on technology flows by multinationals are almost non-existent.[3]

One option that has been followed with some success is to weight R&D in other countries with imports to arrive at a measure of foreign R&D acquired through imports of goods and services. For instance, one study based on this methodology (Coe and Helpman, 1995) reports that the impact of foreign R&D acquired in this way on productivity is positive and significant, and comparable to that of domestic R&D.[4] They also found that the returns to domestic R&D are higher in large countries, consistent with some of the predictions from new growth theories. This implies that for most small and medium-sized countries, foreign R&D is a more important source of productivity growth than domestic R&D (since domestic R&D is likely to be small compared to total foreign R&D). However, others, using essentially the same type of indicator of imported R&D, fail to reproduce these results (Verspagen, 1994; Gittleman and Wolff, 1995). In fact, the latter do not find any significant impacts of foreign R&D embodied in imports of goods and services on productivity. This calls for some caution in interpreting the existing evidence.

The reasons for this state of affairs are not clear. One possible explanation could be weaknesses in methodology. For instance, in these studies, R&D in other countries is weighted by the shares of these countries in the total imports of the country in question. Hence, it matters for the estimate of imported R&D whether a country imports fruit from, say, high-R&D US or low-R&D Spain. Furthermore, since these studies focus on the country as a whole, there is no distinction between direct R&D in the industry and R&D done in other industries in the same country. However, a much more elaborate study by Papaconstantinou *et al.* (1995), using a detailed sector breakdown, did not find any significant impact of imported R&D either. Another possibility might be that what causes these different results is not so much how variables are measured, but rather what kind of statistical/econometric framework is adopted. The problem here is the conventional one in empirical studies of technology: time series are short,

---

[3] One possibility is to use patents applied for or granted by foreigners as a measure of foreign technology flows. See Eaton and Kortum (1997).

[4] Lichtenberg and van Pottelberghe (1996) apply a similar model, but use FDI flows between countries to weight R&D.

and one is left with either doing a cross-section or pooling time-series and cross-sectional data (*i.e.*, a panel). This may give rise to conflicting evidence depending on which empirical approach is adopted. In fact, the exercises that do not find any significant impact of imported R&D are all cross-sectional in nature, while the one that finds such effects uses a panel. Verspagen (1997b), who has presented an elaborate test, using sector-level data for a number of OECD countries (and different weighting schemes reflecting different assumptions on how technology flows are embodied), found that the impact of foreign R&D is much more significant when a panel is used than in a traditional cross-sectional test. Commenting on this finding, he suggested that one possible reason is that the former, in contrast to the latter, usually contain country dummies, that are likely to pick up differences in time- and sector-invariant factors such as, for instance, absorptive capacity across countries. Hence, following this interpretation, the positive impact of imported R&D found in some studies (panel data) is strongly conditional on differences in absorptive capacity and other factors. Thus, achieving high productivity growth through imports of, say, high-tech machinery, may not be as easy as some existing studies, taken at face value, might lead us to believe.

A weakness of many studies in this category is that only one measure of technology diffusion is allowed for, such as R&D embodied in goods and services (or FDI). Other types of technology flows, that may be equally or more relevant, are usually not considered. This may easily lead to biased estimates. Ideally, one would like to include other types of technology flows as well, but as mentioned relevant data from which indicators could be constructed are not easily forthcoming. It also makes sense to distinguish, as has been done much in the literature on catching-up and/or convergence (Abramovitz, 1979), between the potential for rapid productivity growth through adopting best-practice technologies, and the actual realisation of this potential, which may depend on the presence of other (complementary) factors as well. The initial GDP per capita (or productivity) variable, for instance, used in many earlier and contemporary studies of productivity growth, is mainly a measure of the potential for productivity advance, while imports of technologically sophisticated goods and services could be seen as one among several factors that contribute to the exploitation of this potential. Since we are short of data when it comes to these additional factors, we will use a dummy-variable approach to correct for the possible bias to our estimates from failing to take these factors properly into account.

3.   EXPLORING THE IMPACT OF INNOVATION
AND DIFFUSION ON PRODUCTIVITY GROWTH

In order to perform a test of the impact of knowledge flows on productivity, we will use data from the OECD STAN, ANBERD and BITRA databases (with two exceptions noted below). Our dependent variable is growth of labour productivity. The explanatory variables are the potential for catching up in productivity (proxied with the level of labour productivity lagged one year), growth of capital intensity, growth in the own R&D stock, growth of embodied R&D spillovers (domestic and foreign) and a set of country and sector dummies introduced to correct for the exclusion of other relevant country- and/or sector specific factors. The data set consists of annual data for 14 countries and 22 manufacturing industries between 1974 and 1992. With respect to the definition of variables,[5] labour productivity is defined as value added in constant prices in US dollars, divided by labour input. The capital stock is constructed by applying a perpetual inventory method to the time series for investment (constant prices).[6] The same approach is used to construct so-called knowledge stocks, using investments in R&D instead of investment in physical capital.[7]

We use several R&D stocks, the first of which is so-called own R&D, defined as sectoral R&D expenditures. For the domestic indirect knowledge stock, *IRD*, this is done as follows:

$$IRD_{ik} = \sum_{j} \omega_{jk} RD_{ij} (1 - m_{ij}),$$

(1)

where *m* denotes the share of imports on the domestic market, ω_{jk} is the share of inventions made in sector *j* spilling over to sector *k* (see below), RD_{ij} denotes R&D expenditures in country *i* and sector *j*. For the indirect international knowledge stock, *IRF*, the definition is:

---

[5] Source where no other information is given is the OECD STAN Data Base. This data base contains sectoral producer price indices, which were used to convert data in current prices to constant prices. Labour input is measured as the number of persons employed since data on hours worked were not available.

[6] The time series was converted to US dollars using the PPP for investment (source: Penn World Tables). An exogenous deprecation rate of 15% per year was assumed. The initial capital stock (at time *t*) is calculated as investment at *t*+1 times 5, consistent with an initial growth rate of the stock of 5%. In the estimations, the two first observations for the knowledge and capital stocks were omitted, in order to avoid problems related to the initialisation of these stocks.

[7] In this case, a specific deflator is not available, and the PPP for GDP (source: Penn World Tables) is used to convert to a common currency.

$$IRF_{ik} = \sum_{h} \sum_{j} \omega_{jk} RD_{hj} s_{ihj} m_{ij},$$ (2)

where s_{ihj} is the share of country h in imports of goods j into country i. Thus, indirect R&D is both weighted by both imports and sectoral technology flows.

The weights for the sectoral technology flows are based on information contained in patents from the European Patent Office (EPO), and are taken from Verspagen (1997a).[8] We follow earlier contributions such as Verspagen (1997a) and van Meijl (1995) in setting the diagonal of the spillover matrix to zero ($\omega_{jj} = 0$) when calculating domestic spillovers. The reason for doing so is that if the diagonals are relatively important, "own" (direct) R&D and (domestic) spillovers will be correlated due to double counting, leading to multicollinearity. Setting $\omega_{jj} = 0$ avoids double counting by internalising intra-sectoral spillovers into the elasticity of "direct" (own) R&D. For foreign spillovers, there is no double counting, so there is no direct danger for multicollinearity (nor is it possible to "internalise" spillovers similarly to the domestic case). Thus, the diagonal is not set to zero for foreign R&D spillovers.

Our basic regressions are documented in Table 1. The first two columns report estimates using OLS on the complete panel, i.e., cross-country, cross-sector and time series dimensions are taken into account. In these regressions, no attempt has been made to take into account country- or sector specific factors by including dummy variables. Also, we do not take into account any short-run variables, for example related to business cycles. This is an obvious shortcoming of the analysis, and is likely to influence the proportion of explained variance in a negative way. We envisage to solve this problem in future work.

---

[8] Verspagen (1997 a, b) discusses several possible weighting schemes. We employ only one of these schemes here (Verspagen's EPO1 measure), although we carried out all regressions with three different schemes. For the estimates here, the differences between the schemes turn out to be relatively minor. Estimations with alternative schemes are therefore not documented explicitly, but are available from the authors on request.

Table 1. Estimation Results for Models of Productivity Growth with Indirect and Direct R&D, with and without Dummy Variables (*p*-values between brackets)

	(1)	(2)	(3)	(4)	(5)
Capital-labour ratio	0.180 (0.000)	0.182 (0.000)	0.181 (0.000)	0.167 (0.002)	0.239 (0.000)
Own R&D	0.083 (0.000)	0.078 (0.000)	0.082 (0.000)	-0.003 (0.899)	-0.006 (0.805)
Domestic indirect R&D	0.025 (0.007)	0.023 (0.012)	0.019 (0.032)	0.059 (0.024)	0.073 (0.014)
Foreign indirect R&D	0.030 (0.004)	0.029 (0.006)	0.025 (0.015)	0.095 (0.029)	0.081 (0.132)
Initial labour productivity		-0.019 (0.000)	-0.045 (0.000)	-0.007 (0.045)	-0.020 (0.000)
Constant	0.014 (0.000)	0.206 (0.000)	0.467 (0.000)	0.084 (0.018)	0.206 (0.000)
Country Dummies					
Australia			-0.021 (0.010)		-0.011 (0.173)
Canada			-0.009 (0.227)		-0.002 (0.826)
Germany			-0.019 (0.018)		-0.004 (0.624)
Denmark			-0.036 (0.000)		-0.019 (0.037)
Spain			-0.023 (0.092)		-0.016 (0.155)
Finland			-0.011 (0.175)		0.009 (0.289)
France			-0.007 (0.372)		-0.002 (0.842)
United Kingdom			-0.003 (0.700)		0.014 (0.067)
Italy			-0.005 (0.593)		0.011 (0.199)
Japan			0.009 (0.251)		0.023 (0.007)
Netherlands			-0.011 (0.275)		0.018 (0.050)
Norway			-0.036 (0.000)		-0.019 (0.029)
Sweden			-0.023 (0.014)		-0.007 (0.463)
Sector Dummies					
Food etc.			-0.006 (0.641)		-0.024 (0.041)
Textiles etc.			0.052 (0.000)		0.034 (0.003)
Wood etc.			0.059 (0.000)		0.042 (0.000)
Paper & printing			0.076 (0.000)		0.032 (0.015)
Chemicals			0.026 (0.033)		0.015 (0.141)
Pharmaceuticals			0.010 (0.425)		0.003 (0.749)
Refined Oil			0.021 (0.095)		0.014 (0.201)
Rubber & plastic			0.003 (0.785)		-0.002 (0.849)
Glass etc.			0.037 (0.003)		0.025 (0.022)
Ferrous metals			0.017 (0.155)		0.005 (0.640)
Non-ferrous metals			0.011 (0.381)		0.008 (0.426)
Metal products			-0.008 (0.523)		-0.007 (0.472)
Computers & office machines			0.005 (0.678)		0.005 (0.594)
Machinery			0.025 (0.039)		0.018 (0.088)
Electronics			0.031 (0.010)		0.023 (0.031)
Electrical machinery			0.013 (0.272)		0.003 (0.735)
Transport equipment nec			0.005 (0.688)		0.001 (0.902)
Ships and boats			0.013 (0.280)		0.002 (0.878)
Automobiles			-0.005 (0.656)		0.002 (0.830)
Aerospace			0.030 (0.013)		0.020 (0.051)
Instruments			0.001 (0.875)		-0.005 (0.655)
Adj. *R*2	0.05	0.06	0.08	0.09	0.36
N	3722	3722	3722	268	268
F-tests for Null					
All dummies = 0			4.46 (0.000)		4.36 (0.000)
All country dummies = 0			4.37 (0.000)		6.03 (0.000)
All sector dummies = 0			4.98 (0.000)		3.49 (0.000)

(1), (2), (3): OLS on panel, no dummies

(4), (5): OLS on time series means (BETWEEN)

In Table 1 all variables have the expected sign and are highly significant. The first column documents a specification without the potential for catch-up in productivity, whereas the second column includes this variable. Including initial productivity increases the explanatory power of the regression, without changing the estimates of the other variables much (apart form the constant term). Initial productivity itself is also highly significant. These results confirm that both the potential for catch-up and foreign R&D acquired through imports of goods and services are important for productivity growth.

Column (3) introduces country- and sector-dummies into the model, to take into account differences in technological opportunity across sectors, and differences between countries with respect to absorptive capacity and other factors. The dummies are specified as intercepts, and are set up in such a way that the benchmark case is the sector "other manufacturing" in the United States. *F*-tests for the inclusion of dummies point out that both types are highly significant. In terms of explanatory power, they add 2%-points to the R^2.

In terms of the coefficients obtained for our explanatory variables, the main effect of the inclusion of dummies is to increase the importance of the potential for catch-up, as measured by initial productivity. Our interpretation of this result is as follows. One of the effects picked up by the dummy variables will be related to the capability to absorb spillovers. Thus, any distortion due to mis-specification will be less than in the model without dummies. The result, *i.e.*, that the potential for catch-up doubles when dummies are introduced, accords with the hypothesis – central to the technology-gap theory – that the potential for technology diffusion across countries is only partly realised (due to differences in absorptive capacities across countries). Interestingly, the estimated effects of embodied R&D spillovers (whether "imported" from abroad or stemming from domestic sources) are less influenced by the inclusion of dummies than the potential for catch-up (as captured by the initial productivity level). This might indicate that there is relatively little interaction between the potential for productivity advance and "embodied R&D, " *i.e.*, the importance of the latter for successful catch-up may be limited.

With regard to the sector dummies, a number of sectors which are usually considered as "low-tech" have relatively large estimates for the dummy variables. This includes textiles, wood, paper & printing, and non-metallic minerals (glass *etc.*). These are sectors which spend relatively little on R&D. We interpret this result as showing that for these sectors, significant productivity gains may be realised without formal R&D.

In the country dimension, all dummy variables, except the one for Japan, turn out to be negative, which indicates a general tendency for the United

States (the benchmark country) and Japan to grow relatively rapidly compared to the others. The G7 member countries (Canada, Japan, Italy, France and UK, with the exception of Germany) show values close to, and not significantly different from, zero. Many of the smaller countries in the European periphery (Denmark, Spain, Norway and Sweden) perform relatively bad, with strongly negative dummies (Finland is the main exception to this trend). Arguably, there seems to be a "large country effect" at work here, since most G7 countries grow fast compared to the others.

To compare these results with previous work we also report (Column (4) and (5), Table 1) two purely cross-sectional regressions (*i.e.*, excluding the part of the total variance that relate to the time-series dimension). This is done by taking the means of all individual time series, yielding only 268 observations, and estimating the model on these. Column (4) does not include any dummies, whereas Column (5) includes both country- and sector dummies as before. In both cases own R&D totally loses its significance, and the potential for catch-up also becomes much less important (compared to the corresponding models on time-series data, Column (2) and (3), Table 1). In contrast, the estimated impact of embodied R&D spillovers is actually higher than when estimated on the full data set, but less significant, *i.e.*, estimated with less precision. In fact, when dummies are included, foreign indirect R&D loses its significance altogether, consistent with the results from previous tests on cross-sectional data.

This shows that the method of estimation matters for the results, as argued previously. The most likely reason for this is that when the time series information is left out the analysis, it becomes more difficult to distinguish between the various sources of productivity growth such as, for instance, the potential for catch-up compared to what is actually realised due differences in absorptive capacity and other factors. Moreover, multicollinearity problems multiply. Hence, we put more reliance in the estimates on the full data set, including the time-series dimension, and allowing for differences in sectoral and country specific trends (Column 3).

As is evident from Table 1, the explanatory power of the regression is rather limited. In an attempt to increase the explanatory power of the model, and test various hypotheses that may be found in the literature, we experimented with a number of additional variables that might be deemed relevant, including so-called interaction effects. These results are documented in Table 2. We used the functional form specified in Column (3) in Table 1 (*i.e.*, OLS on complete panel with country and sector dummies), but we no longer document the dummies.

Table 2. Introducing Additional Variables and Interaction Effects into the Basic Regressions Explaining Productivity Growth

	(1)	(2)	(3)	(4)	(5)
Capital-labour ratio	0.172 (0.000)	0.177 (0.000)	0.173 (0.000)	0.181 (0.000)	0.186 (0.000)
Own R&D	0.093 (0.000)	0.083 (0.000)	0.089 (0.000)	0.081 (0.000)	0.064 (0.000)
Domestic indirect R&D	0.019 (0.033)	0.019 (0.036)	0.019 (0.036)	0.019 (0.033)	0.018 (0.042)
Foreign indirect R&D	0.025 (0.016)	0.025 (0.017)	0.025 (0.017)	0.025 (0.016)	0.025 (0.017)
Initial labour productivity	-0.049(0.000)	-0.046 (0.000)	-0.048 (0.000)	-0.045 (0.000)	-0.047 (0.000)
Additional Variables:					
- Openness				-0.005 (0.598)	
- Scale					-0.008 (0.017)
Interaction of own R&D with:					
- Initial labour productivity	0.108 (0.008)		0.063 (0.162)		
- Capital-labour ratio		0.098 (0.002)	0.077 (0.024)		
- Openness				0.042 (0.513)	
- Scale					-0.027 (0.006)
N	3722	3722	3722	3722	3722
R2	0.09	0.09	0.09	0.09	0.09

Note: OLS on complete panel, constant and country and sector dummies included, but not documented, *p*-values between brackets

The first column of Table 2 introduces an interaction term between own R&D and initial labour productivity (relative to the sector mean).[9] This interaction term turns up as positive and highly significant. Other variables in the regression, including own R&D and initial labour productivity are not affected to any significant extent (compare Column (3) in Table 1). A possible interpretation of this result is that (direct) R&D is more productive in countries with high levels of productivity. The second column of Table 2 introduces a similar interaction term, but now between own R&D and the capital-labour ratio (again relative to the sector mean). This interaction term

---

[9] I.e., we specified the interaction term as the product of the own R&D variable as used before and a new variable, which is defined as the natural log of initial labour productivity minus the mean for the sector of that variable.

is also positive and significant, while the other variables are again relatively unaffected. Our interpretation of this result is that R&D and capital are strongly complementary: high capital intensity enhances the efficiency of R&D, and R&D enhances the efficiency of capital. The third column of Table 2 shows that when both interaction effects are introduced simultaneously, both of them loose in terms of significance (particularly the one between own R&D and labour productivity).

In Column (4), an interaction term between own R&D and openness is introduced. We include this variable in order to test the commonly found hypothesis that exposing a sector to foreign competition has a beneficial effect on productivity. Openness is in this case defined as the share of imports in total sectoral consumption (*i.e.*, production plus imports minus exports), again calculated by subtracting the sector mean. Our results do not yield any support for this hypothesis, however, because neither the openness variable nor the related interaction term turn up significantly.

Column (5) tests for the effects of scale economies. We define scale as the number of employees (again, relative to the sector mean), but we obtained similar results to the ones documented here using output as an indicator of scale. Somewhat surprisingly, perhaps, the result indicates that there are significant diseconomies of scale, *i.e.*, R&D is more efficient in small countries. However, as pointed out previously, large countries tend to have higher trend growth rates, so we cannot rule out scale effects altogether. But they do not seem to reside in R&D.

Table 3. Rates of Return (excluding spillover effect) of R&D and Fixed Capital, Based on Sample Means and Coefficients in Tables 1 and 2

Rate of return on:			
- fixed capital	0.146		
- own R&D	0.232		
Rates of return including		Efficiency of R&D at:	
interaction effects:	Mean	Mean + 1 std	Mean – 1 std
- Initial productivity	0.263	0.388	0.137
- Capital-labour ratio	0.234	0.369	0.100
- Scale	0.181	0.072	0.289

The results using the interaction terms indicate that the efficiency of R&D is greatly influenced by a number of variables. Table 3 documents the extent of this impact in terms of rates of return to R&D and fixed capital. The first part of the table documents the rates of return on fixed capital investment and R&D.[10] The results indicate that the rate of return on R&D is higher than the one for capital (0.23 vs. 0.15). This may be due to a risk

---

[10] These are calculated by dividing the elasticities of Column 3 in Table 1 by the sample means for the capital / output and R&D / output ratio.

premium on R&D, but may also to some extent reflect differences in social and private returns to R&D.[11] The second part of Table 3 compares the "total" rate of return on R&D at various levels of productivity, capital intensity and scale, on the basis of the estimations with interaction terms in Table 2.[12] In the case of interaction between R&D and labour productivity, the estimated rates of return of R&D vary between 14% (low productivity) and 39% (high productivity). A similar finding results for interaction between R&D and capital intensity, with estimated returns on R&D between 10% (low capital intensity) and 37% (high capital intensity). These differences are rather large, and show that the returns to R&D are higher in technologically and economically more advanced settings. In the case of scale, for which our results were somewhat counter-intuitive, the estimated returns to R&D range between 7% (high scale) and 29% (low scale).

Table 4. The Sources of Productivity Growth, According to Different Specifications of the Model, in Percentual Shares of the "average" Sector/country

Source	Equation 2, Table 1	Equation 3, Table 1
Capital-labour ratio	21	18
Own R&D	19	16
Domestic R&D spillovers	4	3
Foreign R&D spillovers	9	6
net catch-up	47[1]	57[2]
of which:		
- Potential catch-up[3]		100
- Absorptive capacity/country-dummies [4]		-43

[1] Sum of contributions of initial labour productivity and constant.
[2] Sum of the two lines below.
[3] Sum of contributions of initial labour productivity, constant and sector dummies.
[4] Sum of contributions of country dummies.

Finally, we carry out a decomposition of the growth rate of labour productivity, as predicted by our basic model, into the various components corresponding to the variables. These results are documented in Table 4. The first column of this table gives results based on Equation 2 in Table 1, i.e., the estimations without dummy variables. We define "net catch-up" as the sum of the effect related to initial labour productivity and the constant term.

[11] Note that the estimate of own R&D reported here is likely to capture effects of intra-sectoral R&D spillovers.
[12] This is done by multiplying a value for initial productivity, the capital-labour ratio, and scale with the coefficient obtained on the interaction term, and then adding this to the coefficient obtained on own R&D. We used the sample means (zero by definition for the interaction terms), and the sample means plus/minus one standard deviation as values for the variables.

Net catch-up defined in this way accounts for about half of total growth of labour productivity of the average country/sector.[13] Investments in physical capital is responsible for about one fifth, as is investments in own R&D. Embodied R&D spillovers account for only about 13% of total productivity growth, with foreign spillovers taking the largest part of this (about two thirds). Thus, overall, embodied R&D spillovers seem to be of relatively modest importance compared to other sources of growth.

The second column of Table 4 reports a similar decomposition, but this time based on the estimation with dummy variables (Equation 3 in Table 1). Much in the same way as before, "net catch up" is defined as the sum of the contribution of initial labour productivity, the constant term and the means of the sector- and country dummies. However, the contribution of "net catch up" is larger than in the previous case (without dummies). The introduction of dummies may allow us to make a rough distinction between potential catch-up and the effect of differences across countries in absorptive capacity and other (country-specific) factors.[14] The results indicate that the potential for catch-up is substantial, about twice the level of what is actually realised, consistent with the finding that the estimated "catch-up coefficient" doubles in size when dummies are introduced. Hence, differences in absorptive capacity appear as very important for productivity growth.

4.   CONCLUDING REMARKS

This paper has examined the impact of R&D and international technology diffusion on productivity growth. After a review of the available literature, we conclude that as far as diffusion is concerned, there are two main approaches in the field. One approach looks at international technology diffusion from a broad perspective, allowing for different channels and complementary factors. In this approach the potential for benefiting from international technology diffusion (catching up) is assumed to be (negatively) related to the level of initial labour productivity. The other approach takes a more narrow view and focuses on one channel of diffusion only, namely by R&D embodied in (imported) goods. Since both approaches

---

[13] The average growth rate of labour productivity is 2.6% per year.

[14] As argued previously, differences in absorptive capacity across countries are likely to be reflected in the estimated country dummies. Note that the choice of the US as the "reference" country implies that we set this country as the "standard" of absorptive capacity. The mean of the estimated country dummies is negative, indicating that on average absorptive capacity on average is below the US level. If we subtract this mean from "net catch up," we get a larger number, which reflect what the contribution might have been had absorptive capacity matched the level in the US ("potential catch up").

may have some merits, we have attempted to combine them in attempt to assess to the explanatory power of the two. Our conclusions are:

1. The conflicting evidence in the literature relates mainly to differences between cross-sectional and time-series tests. The former fail to reveal the full potential of technology diffusion for productivity growth, mainly due to the problems of taking into account differences in absorptive capacity across countries.

2. Both the scope for catch-up, own R&D, and R&D embodied in goods and services, whether of domestic origin or imported, are important for productivity, and appear as complementary rather than alternative sources of productivity growth. Overall, the impact of diffusion appears to be much larger than that of direct (own) R&D, consistent with previous findings in the literature (Coe and Helpman, 1995; Eaton and Kortum 1997). However, R&D embodied in purchase of goods and services appears to play a relatively minor role compared to other channels of diffusion.

3. Differences across countries in absorptive capacity appear to be very important growth, particularly for the ability to exploit disembodied technology flows, as emphasised by, among others, Gittleman and Wolff (1995) and Eaton and Kortum (1997).

4. Previous analyses on panel data (Coe and Helpman, 1995, Table 3; Verspagen, 1997b, Table 2) have found relatively high elasticities of embodied R&D flows (whether imported or domestic) compared to those of direct R&D. Our study, focusing more on the time-series aspects, finds smaller elasticities of embodied R&D flows than those reported previously, and definitely smaller than for direct R&D.

5. Investment in R&D and physical capital appear as complimentary, the one enhances the efficiency of the other. The productivity of R&D was also found to increase with labour productivity.

6. There are no signs of higher returns to R&D in larger economies, in contrast to some of the predictions of new growth theories.

In summary, the picture that emerges from this study is that there are several, complementary diffusion channels, of which R&D embodied in goods and services is only one (and not a major one), that differences in absorptive capacity matter a lot, and that own R&D is very important for productivity, both in its own right, and in interaction with other variables that take part in the growth process.

REFERENCES

Abramovitz, M.A. (1979), "Rapid Growth Potential and Its Realisation: The Experience of
    Capitalist Economies in the Postwar Period", in E. Malinvaud (ed.), *Economic Growth and
    Resources, vol. 1 The major Issues, Proceedings of the fifth World Congress of the
    International Economic Association*, London: Macmillan, pp. 1-51.

Coe, D.T. and E. Helpman (1995), "International R&D Spillovers," *European Economic
    Review* 39, pp. 859-887.

Coe, D.T., E. Helpman and A. Hoffmaister (1997), "North-South R&D Spillovers," *Economic
    Journal* 107, 134-149.

Eaton, J. and S. Kortum (1997), "Trade in Ideas - Patenting and Productivity in the OECD,"
    Journal of International Economics 40, pp. 251-278.

Fagerberg, J. (1987), "A Technology Gap Approach to Why Growth Rates Differ," *Research
    Policy* 16, pp. 87-99.

Fagerberg, J. (1994), "Technology and International Differences in Growth Rates," *Journal of
    Economic Literature* 32, pp. 1147-1175.

Gerschenkron, A. (1962), *Economic Backwardness in Historical Perspective*, Cambridge (USA):
    The Belknap Press.

Gittleman, M. and E. N. Wolff (1995), "R&D Activity and Cross-Country Growth Comparisons,"
    Cambridge Journal of Economics 19, pp. 189-207.

Grossman, G.M. and E. Helpman (1991), *Innovation and Growth in the Global Economy*,
    Cambridge(USA): The MIT Press.

Lichtenberg, F. and B. van Pottelsberghe (1996), "International R&D Spillovers: A Re-
    Examination," NBER Working Paper 5668, Cambridge MA.

Papaconstantinou, G., N. Sakurai, A. Wyckoff, J. Fagerberg and E. Ioannidis (1995), "
    Technology Diffusion and International Competitiveness, Report for DG 13, European
    Commission.

Van Meijl, H., (1995), *Endogenous Technological Change: The Case of Information Technology.
    Theoretical Considerations and Empirical Results*, PhD dissertation, Maastricht, Universitaire
    Pers.

Verspagen, B. (1991), "A New Empirical Approach to Catching up or Falling Behind," *Structural
    Change and Economic Dynamics* 2, pp. 359-380.

Verspagen, B. (1994), "Technology and Growth: The Complex Dynamics of Convergence and
    Divergence," in G. Silverberg and L. Soete (eds.), *The Economics of Growth and Technical
    Change. Technologies, Nations, Agents*, Aldershot: Edward Elgar Publishing Ltd., pp. 154-
    181.

Verspagen, B. (1997a), "Measuring Intersectoral Technology Spillovers: Estimates from the
    European and US Patent Office Databases," *Economic Systems Research* 9, pp. 47-65.

Verspagen, B. (1997b), "Estimating International Technology Spillovers Using Technology Flow
    Matrices," *Weltwirtschaftliches Archiv* 133, pp. 226- 248.

Chapter 13

Do Technology Spillovers Matter for Growth?

Marieke Rensman and Gerard H. Kuper
CCSO and Department of Economics, University of Groningen

Key words: R&D, Patenting, Technology, Productivity, Spillovers

Abstract: This chapter attempts to explain the growth of labour productivity by (inter)national spillovers from R&D and patenting. We develop a model that is tested for Germany, France, the United Kingdom and the United States of America using a new set of panel data for the period 1955 until 1991. The results indicate that domestic R&D has an indirect and, for Germany, a positive impact on productivity growth.

1.   INTRODUCTION

This chapter aims to explain differences in growth rates of labour productivity across countries and over time by changes in technological knowledge. Both formal economic theorists and empirical scholars have always been interested in explaining economic growth, because it affects the standards of living. On the empirical side, economic historians like David (1991), Mokyr (1990) and Abramovitz (1991) are convinced that technology plays a crucial role in explaining modern economic growth since the First Industrial Revolution around the turn of the 18th century. In their opinion, technological progress is a path-dependent process, as it involves a learning and feedback mechanism which depends on the specific characteristics of the economy (Abramovitz, 1991). Furthermore, they found that the diffusion of knowledge throughout the economy takes place only gradually (Salter, 1966) and that it varies across countries and over time (Gerschenkron, 1962). A second group of empirical scholars are the growth accountants like Denison (1967) and Maddison (1995a). They try to calculate the contribution of various economic factors, such as capital accumulation, on productivity growth using a Solovian type of growth model. The unexplained part in this model, the so-called Abramovitz Residual or Total Factor Productivity, is sometimes labelled as "technical change" (Solow, 1957). Growth accounts thus deal with technology as a purely exogenous variable. This does not help to assess the role of technology in growth (Aghion and Howitt, 1998, p.415-416). Therefore a part of the productivity growth differences cannot be explained within the growth accounting framework, and the residual remains a "measure of our ignorance" (Abramovitz, 1991).

In contrast, modern endogenous growth models attempt to endogenize technology. They explain international growth differences by differences in deliberate efforts to develop new products and technology. Dixit and Stiglitz (1977), Judd (1985), Romer (1990), Grossman and Helpman (1990, 1991), Aghion and Howitt (1998) and others contributed to the development of models in which imperfect competition with innovation-based growth combined with learning-by-doing results in spillovers from industrial research. These spillovers drive a wedge between private and social returns on Research and Development (R&D). This is an approach which according to Solow

"... has an air of promise and excitement about it..." (Solow, 1994, p.52),

since it models the interaction between technological change and labour productivity growth. Most of this research is based on Schumpeter's notion of creative destruction in which new technologies takes the place of existing technologies.

The contribution of this paper is twofold. First, it gives an explicit application and estimation of an endogenous growth model at an aggregate level. Second, it uses a new data set in which the time series of the variables are internationally comparable. This paper is organised as follows. Section 2 gives an overview of previous efforts to estimate the contribution of technological change to productivity growth. The subsequent Section is theoretical in nature and focuses on the importance of knowledge accumulation for long-run sustainable growth. In that Section we develop the benchmark model of growth and trade in which technology drives growth. Section 4 describes the construction of the data, while Section 5 presents and discusses the estimation results. Section 6 concludes.

2.   A REVIEW OF SPILLOVER STUDIES

Notwithstanding the encouraging development in formal theory, the empirical basis of the new growth models is still very thin. Various authors tried to estimate the contribution of R&D to productivity, either in levels or in growth rates and both at the micro and macro level. These studies use different methodologies and data, so that the outcomes are diverse and comparison is difficult. We will concentrate on the various results and focus on international spillovers between industrialized countries.

The subject of international spillovers is interesting as knowledge diffuses, but not necessarily evenly, across national borders by nature (Keely and Quah, 1998, p.24). However, much of the literature deals with intranational spillovers, *i.e,.* inter- and intra-industry spillovers within a country. Examples are micro- or meso-level studies like those by Wolff and Nadiri (1993). The interest in international spillovers revived after Grossman and Helpman (1991) emphasised the importance of openness and the distinction between international and intranational knowledge flows.

Recently, the idea of geographical localization as applied in, for instance, Jaffe *et al.* (1993) has come to the forefront again. However, evidence for international spillovers remains relatively weak. Some authors even argue that intranational spillovers exceed international spillovers significantly. Lichtenberg (1992), for instance, finds that there are no complete, or no instantaneous international R&D spillovers. Branstetter (1996) estimates intranational spillovers (which exceed international spillovers) using microlevel data. He shows that technological externalities can generate multiple equilibria and that growth differences persist. This he considers to support the assumptions of endogenous growth theory.

Despite the mixed results, the evidence tends to confirm the existence of international spillovers. Many studies conclude that the contribution of foreign R&D to domestic productivity is large. In a highly influential article, Coe and Helpman (1995) find that, in a sample of 22 countries, both domestic and foreign R&D contribute significantly to TFP growth. Moreover, foreign R&D is becoming increasingly important, especially for smaller countries. Finally, Coe and Helpman estimate large differences between world-wide and own rates of return of R&D for the G7-countries: about one quarter of the returns from R&D in these countries accrue to their trade partners. These results are not undisputed, however. According to Keller (1997a) the composition of imports, a measure that is used by Coe and Helpman, plays no particular role in estimating positive and large spillovers. He argues that this does not imply that diffusion of embodied technology is not trade-related. In another paper, Keller (1997b) models general spillovers versus trade-related spillovers from R&D. He calculates that 20 percent of productivity growth due to foreign R&D is channelled through international trade. He also finds that the contribution of foreign R&D varies across countries, and that a country's own R&D is more important than that of the average foreign economy. Finally, Keller tries to disentangle embodied and disembodied technology, but this appears to be difficult to do. Technology can be embodied in traded goods and intermediates, but can also flow disembodied as blueprints or ideas via investments, or via international communication networks. In his opinion, these alternative channels, such as Foreign Direct Investment (FDI), should be included in the analysis.

Lichtenberg and Van Pottelsberghe (1996) include both inward and outward FDI flows. The outward FDI flows are considered to proxy for technology sourcing, which is often done by multinationals. Using part of the sample of Coe and Helpman (1995) and employing an alternative weighting scheme for foreign R&D, Lichtenberg and Van Pottelsberghe (1996) find that domestic R&D is important, especially for the larger countries. This is similar to the result of Coe and Helpman, but the elasticities to output are lower. With respect to foreign R&D, imports and technology sourcing play a significant role while inward FDI does not. The latter result may be explained by the fact that multinationals are aiming for own benefits and not for international technology transfer per se. The rates of return on foreign R&D are very high. Finally, the impact of technology sourcing for many industrialised countries runs through the American R&D stock rather than via imports from the USA.

On the industry-level, Bernstein and Mohnen (1998) examine R&D intensive sectors in the USA and Japan and estimate their effects on each other's production structure and productivity. Over a short period of time, R&D appears to be complementary to international spillovers for both countries. However, over a longer period the results tend to differ between the USA and Japan, with Japan's R&D intensity decreasing. Furthermore, American R&D affects the productivity growth of Japanese industries more strongly than the other way around: 60 percent of the productivity growth in Japan is attributable to the American R&D, whereas it is 20 percent in the opposite case. Finally, private returns amount to about 17 percent in both countries and the social rates of return appear to be even 3.5 to 4 times higher. These private returns to R&D are not out of line as can be seen from Nadiri's (1993) overview of empirical studies on rates of return to R&D.

Similar to Lichtenberg in his 1992-article, Park (1995) distinguishes between government and private R&D. Park uses a panel data set (10 OECD countries over the period 1970-1991) instead of cross-country data. Furthermore, Park calculates the size of two kinds of spillovers, namely spillovers into production and spillovers into research. Foreign R&D appears to spill over via the domestic production function to productivity growth. This result is independent of whether the USA is included into the sample or not. However, the effect of foreign R&D on domestic R&D is only observed when American R&D is included. This is not surprising, as the USA carries out the bulk of world R&D. Like Lichtenberg (1992), Park (1995) concludes that once foreign private R&D is accounted for, foreign government-funded R&D is insignificant to productivity growth. However, foreign public R&D affects productivity growth indirectly via domestic private R&D, as public R&D is often basic research which does not have a direct impact on rates of growth.

Nadiri and Kim (1996) analyse the effect of R&D spillovers on TFP growth in the seven largest economies (G7) in the period 1965-1991. They criticise Coe and Helpman (1995) and Park (1995) in that they are not able to distinguish the productivity effect of R&D spillovers from the factor bias effect. The former occurs because R&D spillovers affects production costs, the latter accounts for the effect of R&D spillovers on the other factors of production. Furthermore, Nadiri and Kim account for country-specific effects. The results indicate that benefits from spillovers differ across countries, where domestic R&D is relatively important for the USA. International knowledge spillovers from the USA to other countries is sizeable, whereas less strong spillovers occur from those countries to the USA, with some exceptions (Canada and Japan). It seems that the USA acts as the technology leader. In narrowing the productivity gaps during the period under consideration, the international spillovers appear to have played a minor role. Furthermore, capital and R&D spillovers appear to substitute each other, while domestic R&D and international spillovers complement each other. Nadiri and Kim (1996) conclude that not only trade, but also the absorptive capacity of a country to utilize foreign knowledge is crucial.

Other studies do not focus on R&D, but on (international) patenting activity as a measure of knowledge accumulation and diffusion. Keely and Quah (1998) argue that intellectual property rights, as a patent system, can provide ex ante economic incentives although they generate ex post inefficiencies (p.16). However, the exact nature of the relationship between patents on the one hand and productivity and R&D on the other hand is not completely understood. An appropriate approach would be to consider patents as an output of the invention process generated by private R&D (Keely and Quah, 1998, p.21-22). An empirical study with patent data is that of Eaton and Kortum (1996). They argue that R&D expenditures are inputs in the innovation process while patents are an indirect measure of research output, and

"...where patent protection is sought reflects where inventors expect their ideas to be used" (Eaton and Kortum, 1996, p.252).

Eaton and Kortum (1996) use a cross-section of 19 OECD countries to estimate a simultaneous equations model. The data they use to estimate international diffusion are data of patent applications for the year 1988 in the

19 OECD countries. The patent applications are subdivided into the country of origin of the inventor. They conclude that the levels (instead of the growth rates) of productivity explain a country's ability to adopt or innovate. Furthermore, international diffusion rates are about half of the domestic diffusion rates on average. They also estimate that the contribution of the USA to productivity growth world-wide is sizeable, followed in size by Japan and Germany. Germany affects European economies relatively strongly, whereas Japan's influence is observable elsewhere. Notwithstanding the high rates of diffusion, barriers (*e.g.*, in the institutional area) are still large enough to let productivity differences persist. Finally, it appears that human capital (in the form of education and research scientists and engineers) is crucial for the ability to adopt, in addition to trade links and distance (or geographical localization). The importance of human capital and learning is thus confirmed again (see for instance, Benhabib and Spiegel, 1994). The results on trade supports the outcome of the study by Coe and Helpman (1995) mentioned earlier. In another study using cross-section data, Eaton and Kortum (1997) also include research (in particular, research employment) into a growth model in addition to patenting activity in order to explain productivity differences. This is a new step forward as the studies discussed above do not incorporate both variables. Their results indicate that foreign research is two-third as potent as domestic research. Furthermore, the USA and Japan together are again driving the bulk of growth in the sample (of five large industrialised countries).

To summarise, empirical studies on labour productivity growth and technology produce various outcomes. Some of them estimate reduced form equations or growth regressions in which technology is exogenous. Caballero and Jaffe (1993) explicitly apply an endogenous growth model using patent data. However, they do not consider international diffusion. The challenge is to develop and test models that are capable of explaining processes of growth and international spillovers. The mixed results of empirical studies on economic growth

> "...clearly underlines the need for growth economists to devote more time to the construction of data..." (Crafts, 1997, p.60),

because the results of these studies are sensitive to the data used. For the construction of proxies of the economic variables in the model, we constructed a new data set for the USA, UK, France and Germany, and present the resulting time series in Section 4. A detailed description of the construction and the sources of the data is provided in the appendix.

3.   MODEL

In this section, we formulate a model with international technology spillovers and catch-up. The empirical studies discussed in Section 2 give a handle on important research subjects. First, international technology spillovers do take place and flow through different channels such as trade and foreign direct investment. But these spillovers are, in general, not complete. So growth differences will persist (Keely and Quah, 1998, p.26). Nevertheless, spillovers from abroad seem to affect economic growth. Besides, technology flows within a country (intranational spillovers) also play a role in explaining productivity growth.

Second, both patenting activity as a proxy for knowledge flows and R&D expenditures should be incorporated into an empirical growth model. Cameron (1996) and Temple (1999) argue that in empirical applications the Aghion and Howitt model needs to be extended with knowledge spillovers from other countries. In this chapter we proxy these spillovers by patents. Some studies discussed above indicated that domestic R&D is crucial in order to be able to absorb new foreign technology. One of the results in our estimations in Section 5 is that domestic R&D works indirectly on productivity growth: a country needs a certain knowledge basis in order to be able to adopt and learn from new knowledge from abroad in the form of patents. Thus we may consider R&D expenditures as the input in the innovation process and patents as the output (see Griliches, 1990). Note that the R&D expenditures are privately-funded (business enterprise R&D). The differences in patenting activity in the various countries can indicate whether the national technological state of the art enables a country to catch up with the "technological leader," which in our case is the USA. Moreover, some studies indicate that R&D in the USA affect other economies' productivity growth significantly, but not evenly across countries. We thus also account for country-specific effects in our empirical research.

The model we use here draws heavily on Aghion and Howitt (1998, Ch.12) and it is driven by product differentiation, quality improvements and research spillovers. The underlying theory allows new intermediate products to open up, as in Romer's horizontal innovations model (Romer, 1990), which are then subject to quality improvements as in Young's vertical innovations model (Young, 1998). In order to test the model using aggregate data, it is shown that, with some convenient assumptions, the production function on the aggregate level can be written as a Cobb-Douglas production function. We discuss the underlying theoretical structure of the model in detail in the appendix and discuss technological progress and the role of spillovers in some more detail below.

3.1   Production and capital

On the aggregate level, there is a stock of capital K_t embodied in machines. New capital is produced at rate I_t. Gross investment I_t, consumption C_t and research N_t are produced by labour L_t and intermediate goods x_{it}:

$$Y_t = C_t + I_t + N_t = Q_t^{\alpha-1} \left[\int_0^{Q_t} A_{it} x_{it}^{\alpha} di \right] L_t^{1-\alpha} = A_t L_t k_t^{\alpha} .$$

Variable k_t is defined as the capital stock per efficiency unit of labour $K_t/(A_t L_t)$, where A_t indicates the average productivity of the economy, and Q_t is the number of intermediate goods that have been created in i industries.[1] The flow of intermediate products is such that the ratio of Q over L is constant. Capital-market equilibrium and the production function of final output produce the aggregate Cobb-Douglas production function. Finally, defining g_t as the growth rate of labour productivity $\Delta \ln Y_t - \Delta \ln L_t$, the basic equation in rates of growth is

$$g_t = g_{A,t} + \alpha \frac{dk_t / dt}{k_t} . \tag{1}$$

The second term on the right-hand side of Equation (1) is the rate of growth of output per efficiency unit of labour $f(k_t)$, where

$$\frac{dk_t / dt}{k_t} = \frac{dK_t / dt}{K_t} - \left(g_{A,t} + g_{L,t} \right).$$

Assuming a constant rate of depreciation of capital goods δ, and defining i_t as I_t/K_t. this can be written as:

$$\frac{dk_t / dt}{k_t} = i_t - \left(\delta + g_{A,t} + g_{L,t} \right). \tag{2}$$

---

[1] A sector in this model is defined as a certain kind of activity, such as doing R&D, producing intermediates or final goods, carried out by an agent. The term sector is sometimes used in a different sense, for instance in multi-sectoral models, in which each good or intermediate i is produced in sector i. Here we prefer the term industry. In empirical studies, a sector is part of the economy, such as the manufacturing sector, or at a lower level, industries.

3.2   Technological Progress

In the R&D sector of each industry, innovations of size σ occur at a rate ϕ_t with a probability as determined by a Poisson distribution. These innovations add to the stock of knowledge. The arrival rate reflects the probability of a researcher to innovate the next blueprint for intermediate good i which replaces the existing technology. The "leading-edge technology parameter," defined as the technology used by the "technological leader," grows at rate

$$g_{\hat{A},t} = \frac{d\hat{A}_t / dt}{\hat{A}_t} = \sigma\phi_t .$$

The technology of follower countries will evolve by own R&D efforts and by technology spillovers from the leading country to the followers. This may be interpreted as a limiting case of a more general model with mutual technology spillovers (see Aghion and Howitt, 1998, p.421). The arrival of new blueprints will gradually replace existing average technology A_t with the leading-edge technology. So the long-run change in productivity dA_t/dt equals the arrival rate of innovations times the average change of technology:

$$\frac{dA_t}{dt} = \phi_t \left(\hat{A}_t - A_t \right)$$

or

$$g_{A,t} = \frac{dA_t / dt}{A_t} = \phi_t \left(\frac{\hat{A}_t}{A_t} - 1 \right) = \phi_t \left(\Omega_t - 1 \right). \tag{3}$$

We may label Ω in Equation (3) as the technology gap of the follower with the leader country. We assume that Ω converges to a constant, say $1+\sigma$. This implies that in the long run[2]:

$$g_{\hat{A}} = g_A .$$

[2]   Note that in the long run when $g_\Omega=0$, $\Omega=1+\sigma$.

3.3   Empirical Specification

Above it was assumed that the flow of innovations depends on the arrival rate of innovations and the change of technology. In the remainder of this section, we take a somewhat different approach to arrive at a testable specification given the data available. In the process, inevitably, we have to make some *ad hoc* assumptions.

Suppose, there are m countries each with its own level of technolgy A^j. We define the leading-edge technology as:

$$\ln \hat{A}_t \equiv \sum_{j=1}^{m} \omega^j \ln A_t^j \, ,$$

where ω^j is the importance of country j as a source of new technological ideas for other countries, and $\Sigma_j \, \omega^j = 1$. Suppose that country k is the technological leader, then $\omega^k = 1$. The weighting scheme ω^j needs to be known *a priori*, and it is assumed that for the countries considered here, the USA is the technological leader.

As before, it is assumed that, in the long run, the technology gap converges to a constant, that is[3]

$$- \ln \Omega^j = \ln A_t^j - \ln \hat{A}_t = z^j \, .$$

This implies that, in the long run the growth rates of the technologies of the leader and the followers must be equal:

$$g_A^j = g_{\hat{A}} \, .$$

Now, suppose that the change in the level of technology in country j depends on the technological gap with the leader:

$$g_{A,t}^j = \Delta \ln A_t^j = -\lambda_t^j \left(\ln A_{t-1}^j - \ln \hat{A}_{t-1} - z^j \right) + \beta g_{\hat{A},t} \, , \tag{4}$$

where the term between brackets on the right-hand side of Equation (4) is the gap. The last term is the rate of growth of the technology of the leader country. Above we noted that in the longrun, when the gap is constant, we expect β to be equal to 1.

---

[3]   Note that for follower country j, $0<\Omega^j<1$, so that $z^j<0$.

Equation (4) is the empirical counterpart of Equation (3) above. Parameter λ^j measures the speed of convergence of country j's technology to the leading-edge technology. We loosely assume that the speed of convergence is influenced by own R&D:

$$\lambda_t^j = \lambda + \gamma \Delta \ln n_t^j, \tag{5}$$

where n^j reflects R&D productivity. This captures the notion of the theoretical arrival rates of innovation. The idea is that in order to adapt foreign technology, more R&D is needed to upgrade the skill-level of workers. It is likely that γ is positive, since doing R&D increases knowledge, either intentionally or by coincidence. Other factors than R&D that may attribute to the process of adjustment are simply captured by the constant term λ in Equation (5). One can think of organisational and managerial factors and knowledge not embodied in own R&D and in patents.

The composite term λ^j as determined in Equation (5) is assumed to be positive. If a country j lags behind in terms of technology, then a positive value for λ^j signals convergence to the leading-edge technology. For practical purposes we quantify technology A^j by the number of patents and the reciprocal of R&D productivity by the ratio of R&D expenses D^j over GDP Y^j (see Aghion and Howitt, 1998, p.418):

$$n_t^j \equiv \frac{D_t^j}{Y_t^j}.$$

3.4   The System

Above the model is presented. Summarising, the model consists of the following equations:

$$
\begin{aligned}
g_t^j &= g_{A,t}^j + \alpha g_{k,t}^j, \\
g_{A,t}^j &= -\lambda_t^j \left(\ln A_{t-1}^j - \ln \hat{A}_{t-1} - z^j \right) + \beta g_{\hat{A},t}, \\
\lambda_t^j &= \lambda + \gamma \Delta \ln n_t^j, \\
g_{n,t}^j &= g_{D,t}^j - g_{Y,t}^j, \\
g_{k,t}^j &= i_t^j - \left(\delta^j + g_{A,t}^j + g_{L,t}^j \right), \\
g_{Y,t}^j &= g_t^j + g_{L,t}^j.
\end{aligned}
$$

The symbols have the following meaning:

A_t^j the level of technology of country j

$\hat{A}_t^j$ the level of technology of the leading country, here the USA

g_t^j growth rate of labour productivity of country j at time t

$g_{A,t}^j$ growth rate of technology of country j at time t

$g_{k,t}^j$ growth rate of physical capital in efficiency units of country j at time t

$g_{\hat{A},t}^j$ growth rate of leading-edge technology at time t, here the USA

λ_t^j speed of convergence of technology of country j at time t

$g_{n,t}^j$ growth rate of the reciprocal of R&D productivity of country j at time t

$g_{D,t}^j$ growth rate of R&D expenses of country j at time t

$g_{Y,t}^j$ growth rate of GDP of country j at time t

i_t^j ratio of investment over capital of country j at time t

$g_{L,t}^j$ growth rate of employment of country j at time t

The first equation is the familiar log-linear Cobb-Douglas production function. The second equation describes the development of technological progress, which depends on the technological gap with the leader. The third equation describes the speed at which the technological gap is closed. These equations are the core of the model, the other equations are identities.

Substituting the identities and the convergence process in the first two equations we arrive at two equations, one for the growth rate of labour productivity and one for the growth rate of technology:

$$
\begin{aligned}
g_t^j &= g_{A,t}^j + \alpha g_{k,t}^j = g_{A,t}^j + \alpha\left(i_t^j - \left(\delta^j + g_{A,t}^j + g_{L,t}^j\right)\right) \\
&= (1-\alpha)g_{A,t}^j + \alpha\left(i_t^j - \delta^j - g_{L,t}^j\right)
\end{aligned}
\tag{6}
$$

$$
\begin{aligned}
g_{A,t}^j &= -\left(\lambda + \gamma g_{n,t}^j\right)\left(\ln A_{t-1}^j - \ln \hat{A}_{t-1}^j - z^j\right) + \beta g_{\hat{A},t}^j \\
&= -\left[\lambda + \gamma\left(g_{D,t}^j - g_t^j - g_{L,t}^j\right)\right]\left(\ln A_{t-1}^j - \ln \hat{A}_{t-1}^j - z^j\right) + \beta g_{\hat{A},t}^j.
\end{aligned}
\tag{7}
$$

Equations (6) and (7) will be estimated, but first we take a look at the data.

4. DATA

Testing formal models of the type presented in the previous section requires accurate data, on for instance physical capital and R&D, which are often not available on detailed level. Moreover, growth economists are interested in longrun development for a broad selection of countries in different phases of economic development, but internationally comparable and long time series are not always available. Measurement problems are huge (see for instance Griliches, 1994) so we want our model to be as simple as possible.

We constructed proxies for the variables in Equations (6) and (7) in order to estimate the effects of technological change on labour productivity growth.

The appendix shows a list of the variables, and the sources of the data used. In the current section, we show the development of the mentioned variables for the USA, UK, France and Germany in the period after the Second World War. Figure 1a on labour productivity in the total economy shows that France caught up with the USA during the period 1955 to 1991, while in 1955 it ranked lowest with Germany. The growth rate of labour productivity in France has always been positive in this period, whereas the other three countries experienced some repercussions (Figure 1b). German labour productivity has also increased fast, but it did not yet succeed in catching up with the USA (at least not until 1991). The Anglo-American gap remained relatively constant during the period under consideration.

Traditionally, physical capital accumulation has been assigned a crucial role in economic development. Growth accountants like Maddison (1995b) devote much time to the construction of data on capital stocks and investment in order to account for the share of capital accumulation in labour productivity growth. Figure 1c displays the growth of gross capital stocks. From Figures 1b and 1c, we can hardly draw unambiguous conclusions on the link between capital accumulation and labour productivity growth. Only the differences in growth rates of the gross capital stock between the countries are clear. Up to the early seventies, Germany experienced high growth rates, whereas in the subsequent decade, the rates of growth for France were larger. The British capital stock grew less rapidly, but in all three economies the growth rates declined over time. The growth rates for the USA are low on the average, but, given the size of the economy, the level of its capital stock is higher. Furthermore, the growth rates suggest that they go up and down with the business cycles, like the growth rates of labour productivity.

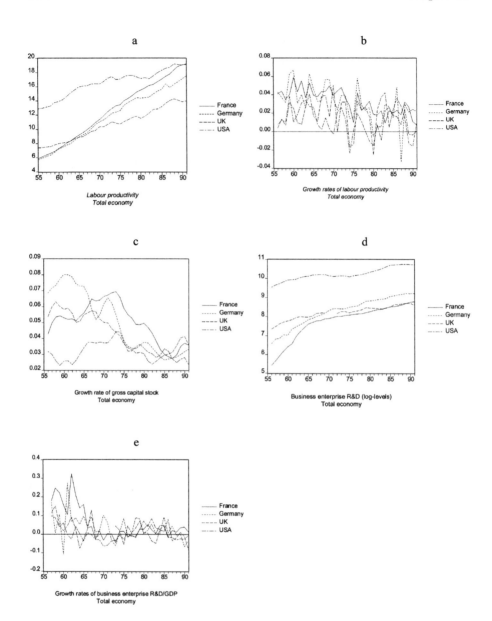

Figure 1. Total Economy, 1955-1991

According to endogenous growth models, technological development affects the national growth rates of labour productivity, and thus also differences between countries. Capital accumulation then plays only a supporting role. In our model in Section 3, technology is represented by cumulative experience in creating new knowledge (proxied by business enterprise R&D expenditures) and the speed of convergence towards the leading edge technology (proxied by patent activity). Figure 1e shows the growth rate of R&D expenditures-to-GDP ratio from 1956 to 1991 in total economy. Before 1965, the growth rates of the R&D-to-GDP ratio were high for France, with Germany a good second. Figure 1d shows that the American-British R&D ratio remained relatively constant, while Germany and France caught up to some extent. Especially French R&D grew fast before 1965. The explanation for the fact that the American R&D expenditures did not grow so fast may lie in its early development in this area. Already before the 1950s, the USA was the first western country to start with systematical R&D. Furthermore, the pattern of growth in R&D seems to be sensitive to the business cycle.

In Figure 2a, the yearly numbers of applications for patents (applications in short) in each country (both foreign and domestic applications) are presented. Applications for patents are made by inventors to the (inter-) national patent offices. The idea behind the use of data on patents is that they contain technological knowledge. Particularly, patents are the outcome of innovation processes, whether or not starting with formal R&D, and theoretically they should have an impact on labour productivity growth. Grants are those patents (or new knowledge) that will effectively come into use, but grant numbers are often sensitive to bureaucratic procedures at the patent offices. Applications are no patents yet (*i.e.*, grants), but they reflect the possibility in which a country is ready to gain or adopt new knowledge.

The total number of applications represents also an element of international knowledge spillovers. The countries under consideration are trading and communicating with each other, so that their national knowledge is spreading to other countries in some way. This diffusion takes place by trading goods and intermediates, investing abroad (capital flows) or by political and individual networks. Patents applied for by foreigners are also playing a role. In this way a general knowledge pool emerges, which may have a larger effect on the national growth rates of labour productivity than national expenditures on R&D alone.

a

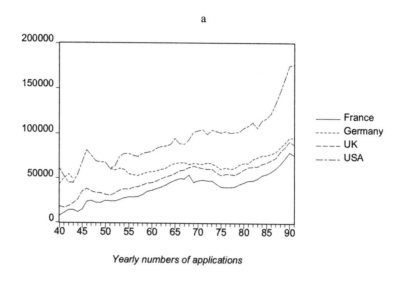

Yearly numbers of applications

b

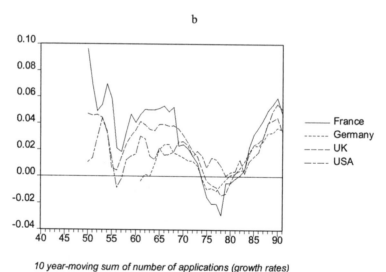

10 year-moving sum of number of applications (growth rates)

Figure 2. Applications, 1940-1991

Figure 2a shows that, as one may expect, the number of patents applied for in the USA by American and foreign inventors is clearly higher than those in the other three countries. The USA is attractive to patentees as it represents a large, more or less uniform market. It is a market in which most consumers show similar characteristics and demands, so that scale effects from production based on new technology can be exploited very well and one may expect certain profits. Furthermore, a nation's total number of applications can reflect its relative strength in technology. Particularly, it indicates a country's ability to turn new knowledge locked up in applications into economic growth. In the current chapter, the USA are considered as a "technological leader." The innovative effort of American firms and individuals is significant, although the share of foreigners has increasing during the period. The Anglo-American gap in applications is very large, but France and Germany do not perform much better. The American-German gap has even widened since the 1950s.

However, cumulation of patent numbers over a number of years is supposed to reflect the knowledge level of a country more effectively, as yearly numbers are very sensitive to the business cycle and some bureaucratic problems or measures, such as the change in the international patent law in the 1970s. Furthermore, we assume that patents from years ago will need time to come into use as the knowledge incorporated in the patent will have to be made concrete in products or production processes. So patents of, for instance, 10 years ago can still have impact on today's economic performance.

Figure 2b displays the time series on the growth rates of the 10-year moving sum of the number of applications in each country. All series show a clear trend, with a decline starting already in the 1960s. The lowest point is reached somewhere between 1975 and 1980. The French growth rates are fluctuating relatively strongly, whereas the American rates are on average lower than those of the other countries.

5. EMPIRICS

In Section 3 the model is presented and the equations are derived. Here we repeat the equations that are estimated. The first equation is the log-linear Cobb-Douglas production function:

$$g_t^j = (1 - \alpha)g_{A,t}^j + \alpha\left(i_{t-1}^j - \delta_{t-1}^j - g_{L,t-1}^j\right).$$

We lagged the investment term to obtain a statistically significant effect of investment on per capita income. Such a lag may be theoretically explained by a "time-to-build" argument: it takes some time for investment to become productive. This equation is estimated with iterative weighted least squares, where lagged productivity growth is added as an instrument. The second equation describes the development of technological progress, which depends on the technological gap with the leader:

$$g_{A,t}^j = -\left(\lambda + \gamma\left(g_{D,t}^j - g_t^j - g_{L,t}^j\right)\right)\left(\ln A_{t-1}^j - \ln \hat{A}_{t-1}^j - z^j\right) + \beta g_{A,t}^j.$$

This equation is estimated using iterative SUR.

Both equations are estimated on a panel of annual observations. The countries considered are France, Germany, the United Kingdom and the United States of America. The time period considered is 1957-1991. The interesting parameters are the capital share in output α and, more importantly, the parameters in the technological progress function: the R&D effect on adjustment λ, the non-R&D effect on adjustment γ and the long-run technology gap z.

5.1   Estimation Results

From the estimation results presented in Table 1 we can draw the following conclusions. First, the fit is not particularly good, especially not for the productivity equation. However, the capital share is 0.21 which seems reasonable. Second, most parameters are significant at a 5% significance level, and all parameters have the expected sign.

More important are the estimations for the technology function. Here, we present three versions: one equation with a common R&D effect λ and a common non-R&D effect γ for all countries considered (the first column in Table 1). The second equation (second column) allows the non-R&D effect to differ between countries, while the third equation (third column) allows both the R&D effect and the non-R&D effect to differ between countries. From the results we can conclude that own R&D significantly affects the speed at which countries adapt foreign technology for Germany only. For the UK and France own R&D seems to be less important. Other, non-R&D, factors seem to play a significant role in the adjustment process. These factors matter for all countries considered. For France and the UK these other factors are more important then own R&D.

Parameters z indicate the long-run technology level with respect to the USA. In the theoretical model these relative technology levels were supposed to be constant in the long run. From the estimation results we can conclude that, in the long run, France has a level of technology of about 51% (calculated from the first column as exp(-0.68)) of that in the USA. For Germany and the UK these numbers are 67% and 63%, respectively. These estimation results more or less are confirmed with the data as can be seen from Figure 3. Note that there are sharp differences in the data for the periods before and after 1970. Before the early 1970s relative technology levels seem to converge, whereas after 1970, relative technology levels more or less stayed constant or even dropped a little compared to the USA.

Table 1. Estimation Results, 1957-1991 (*t*-values between brackets)

	Productivity: g_t	Technology: $g_{A,t}$		
		1	2	3
α	0.21 (5.80)			
λ (common)		0.09 (6.63)	0.08 (5.95)	
λ France				0.09 (3.36)
λ Germany				0.12 (7.81)
λ UK				0.06 (3.38)
γ (common)		0.12 (1.56)		
γ France			0.04 (0.68)	-0.04 (-0.52)
γ Germany			0.53 (3.14)	0.47 (2.91)
γ UK			0.01 (0.09)	-0.01 (-0.20)
β		0.59 (5.66)	0.58 (6.34)	0.58 (5.50)
z France		-0.68 (-19.00)	-0.63 (-16.63)	-0.60 (10.11)
z Germany		-0.40 (-16.68)	-0.38 (-21.47)	-0.37 (-23.50)
z UK		-0.46 (-16.44)	-0.43 (-15.47)	-0.33 (-4.04)
Observations	136	98	98	98
Adj. R^2				
France	-[a]	0.32	0.31	0.25
Germany	-	0.39	0.34	0.17
UK	-	0.45	0.44	0.39
USA	-	N.A. [b]	N.A.	N.A.
Durbin-Watson Adj. R^2				
France	0.246	0.215	0.207	0.192
Germany	0.913	0.216	0.251	0.192
UK	0.719	0.132	0.119	0.105
USA	0.842	N.A.	N.A.	N.A.

[a] negative
[b] not applicable

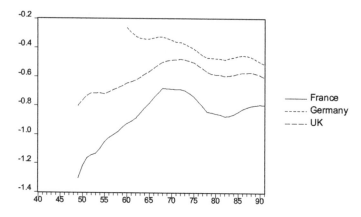

Technology gap with the USA
(difference in 10-year moving sums of number of applications, log-levels)

Figure 3. Technology Gap *vs.* USA, 1949-1991

6.   CONCLUSIONS

In this paper we try to explain growth differentials across countries by technological developments. It builds on recent endogenous growth models, which combine imperfect competition with innovation-based growth and learning-by-doing in innovation. These forces generate spillovers from industrial research and patenting activity. Our model is a multi-country model, with international technology spillovers and catch-up. The model is tested for the USA, UK, France and Germany using a new set of panel data for the total economy in the period 1956-1991.

From the estimation results we can draw a number of conclusions. First, most of the parameters of interest are significantly different from zero and have the expected sign. Second, technological development in the form of the growth rate of R&D expenditures and the growth rate of the gap with the technological leader USA appear to play a significant role in the explanation of the growth rate of labour productivity. Third, international spillovers do occur between the four countries under consideration, but they do not take place completely and not immediately, so that productivity growth rate differences continue to exist. Fourth, the growth in R&D expenditures has an indirect and positive effect via the adjustment of the gap with the USA only for Germany. Domestic efforts to gain knowledge thus are important to some countries as a learning mechanism for the adoption of foreign technology locked up in patents from abroad. Fifth, the diffusion of knowledge from the

USA to Germany, France and the UK differs. So, the technological gaps between these countries and the USA also differ, and so do the growth rates of productivity differ. The technology gaps converge over time, implying that knowledge diffuses only gradually and varies across countries, and that learning takes time. Finally, it may be expected (from estimations not included in this chapter) that the results also differ between time periods.

Despite these interesting and intuitively plausible results, one has to bear in mind that formal R&D expenditures and patenting activity do not capture all forms of knowledge. Think of tacit knowledge, which is important in some sectors of the economy. Furthermore, organisational and managerial knowledge are not accounted for explicitly. Human capital accumulation is only implicitly reflected in own R&D efforts, which appeared to be significant for the adjustment process. In order to catch up, a country thus needs a knowledge basis accumulated via learning-by-doing in the R&D process. This argument may be tested if the model is extended with (the effects of) skills. For reference on the complementarity between skills and R&D we refer to, for instance, Colecchia and Papaconstantinou (1996).

To conclude, the results vary across countries, sectors and over time. This is confirmed by other empirical studies (as discussed in Section 2) as well. Crafts argued that '

> "... success in 'technology transfer' varied and seems to have been affected by institutional and policy differences..." Crafts (1997, p.64).

This corresponds with the concept of "ultimate" causes of economic growth as defined by Maddison (1995a), and is also discussed by among others North (1990), on reducing transaction costs, Abramovitz (1991), on the residual as "our measure of ignorance," and Olson (1982) on the impact of political systems.

A   DATA[4]

We have constructed proxies for the variables in Equations (6) and (7) for the total economy. The original data used for construction of these proxies are discussed below. Note that total (gross) investment and capital are the sum of non-residential structures and machinery and equipment. Furthermore, the depreciation rate δ was assumed constant in the model discussed in Section 3. However, with help of the data on capital stocks and investments, we made time series on the depreciation rate, which we used in estimation. The proxies used in estimation are:
-   the growth rate of labour productivity:

---

[4]   With special thanks to Bart van Ark (updated production and employment data), Angus Maddison (standardised capital data), Bart Verspagen (updated R&D and patent data), and Jan Luiten van Zanden (national patent office data).

$$g_t^j = g_{Y,t}^j - g_{L,t}^j,$$

where g_Y and g_L is log-differenced GDP and employment, respectively,
- the growth rate of the reciprocal of R&D productivity:

$$g_{n,t}^j = g_{D,t}^j - g_{Y,t}^j$$

where g_D is log-differenced R&D expenditures,
- the growth rate of technology:

$$g_{A,t}^j$$

calculated as the log-difference of 10-year moving sum of the number of total applications for patents in country j,
- the growth rate of leading-edge technology:

$$g_{\hat{A},t}^j$$

calculated as the log-difference of 10-year moving sum of the number of total applications for patents in the USA,
- the level of technology

$$\ln A_{t-1}^j$$

calculated as the log of 10-year moving sum of number of total applications for patents in country j, lagged one year,
- the level of technology of leading country

$$\ln \hat{A}_{t-1}^j$$

calculated as the log of 10-year moving sum of number of total applications for patents in the USA, lagged one year,
- the growth rate of physical capital in efficiency units as defined in Equation (2)

$$g_{k,t}^j = i_t^j - \left(\delta^j + g_{A,t}^j + g_{L,t}^j\right),$$

where i_t is gross investment I divided by gross capital stock K and

$$\delta_t^j = \left(I_t - \Delta K_t\right)/K_t.$$

Output and employment
Data sources: van Ark (1996, updated), OECD (1997b).

The time series for GDP are updated (production census) series from Van Ark (1996, Appendix Tables 1.2,1.3,1.8,1.9). These series are in constant national prices, but not based on the same years. Table 3.4 from Van Ark (1996) gives the National Account equivalents for the census data in the year 1975 and are constructed in such a way that international comparison is meaningful (*e.g.*, GDP is at factor cost, while the national census series are sometimes at producer or market prices). Using Table 3.4, the census series can be re-based to the year 1975. As the data in Table 3.4 are in mln US$, the PPPs given in Table 3.3 can be used to convert them back into national currencies. The scale factor is the ratio in 1975 of the current value of GDP to the value at prices of the base year in the original series, both in national currencies. After re-basing, the series are converted into PPP in 1975 from OECD (1997b, Table 3, p. 162).

In Table 3.4 of Van Ark (1996), data are also given for the number of employees for total economy. These data are somewhat different from the census employment data in 1975 (updated series from Appendix Tables 2.2, 2.3, 2.8, 2.9), for the same reasons as above, namely that definitions of GDP and employment differ between National Accounts and national census series. Using the 1975 data on employment in both Table 3.4 and the census series, employment is re-scaled.

Capital stocks and investment
Data sources: Kravis *et al.* (1982), Maddison (1995b), OECD (1966, 1997b).

Time series for total economy on gross stock of fixed non-residential capital and gross investment in 1990 national currencies at midyear are from Maddison (1995), Tables 7 and 8 on Non-Residential Structures (NRS) and Machinery & Equipment (ME). Official data were standardised by Maddison with respect to asset lives and retirement patterns. All asset lives are as closely as possible to those in the USA, *i.e.*, 39 years for NRS and 14 years for ME, and all assets are scrapped when their expected life expires. The data were also corrected for war damage. With the 1990 price index for Gross Fixed Capital Formation (OECD, 1997b, Table 34, pp.146-147), the series were re-based to the year 1975. Data on prices before 1960 are indicated by the price index on GNP (OECD, 1966, table on price index of GNP, p. 6). The series were converted with 1975 PPPs calculated on the basis of data in Summary tables 6.1 and 6.3 in Kravis *et al.* (1982, p. 167 and p. 179). Following Maddison (1995), the PPPs for NRS are a weighted average of the PPPs for Non-Residential Buildings (lines 111-118) and Civil Engineering Works (lines 119-122), with the weights being their per capita expenditures in national currencies. PPPs for ME are from Table 6.3 (lines 123-144). The resulting 1975 PPPs are displayed in the table below.

Table 2. 1975 PPPs for Non-residential Structures (NRS) and Machinery & Equipment (ME)

	NRS	ME
UK	0.516	0.539
France	5.341	5.430
Germany	2.404	3.350

Technology indicators

Technology indicators are the most difficult part of the data construction. In the current chapter, R&D expenditure time series and data on patent numbers are applied to proxy the growth of knowledge in the economy.

Research and development

Data sources: OECD (1995b, 1997b), Verspagen (1996, updated).

The time series for Research and Development (R&D) in current national prices for total economy were from updated data of Verspagen (1996). Some gaps in the series of Verspagen (1996) were filled with ANBERD data from OECD (1995b). The OECD data and Verspagen's data namely do not differ when compared for other years, so that the data may not differ much for the years at which only OECD data are available. After filling the gaps as far as possible, only data for the UK in 1970 and 1971 could not be filled in.

The series are converted for each country into 1975 PPP$ using the 1990 price index for GDP (OECD, 1997b, Table 31, pp.144-145) and the GDP PPPs of 1975 in Table 3 on p. 162 in OECD (1997b). Special R&D price indices would be preferred, as "such special price indices indicate a higher rate of inflation for R&D than in the economy at large" (OECD, 1984, p. 309). So R&D growth rates calculated from time series converted with GDP indices may appear to be too optimistic. The use of GDP PPPs also reflect the relative purchasing power parities only broadly. Unfortunately, R&D indices or PPPs are not available for the present.

Applications for patents

Data sources: Deutsches Patentamt, I.N.P.I., OECD (1991, 1995a, 1997a), WIPO (1983).

The sources for data on the total number of applications for patents are:
- All countries from 1973 onwards: OECD (1991, Table 20) for 1973-1974, OECD (1995a, Table 20) for 1975-1987, OECD (1997a, Table 73) for 1988-1991.
- France before 1973: I.N.P.I. for 1962-1972; WIPO (1983) for 1940-1961.
- Germany before 1973: Deutsches Patentamt for 1949-1972; WIPO (1983) for 1940-1943.
- UK and USA before 1973: WIPO (1983) for 1940-1972.

B   MODEL

Consumers maximize utility over an infinite horizon given their budget constraint. They derive utility from a set of differentiated products. Basically the model is a multi-country model. In each country we have three sectors[5]:
1. An R&D sector producing blueprints (or patents) for new products i using primary resources and previous accumulated knowledge A, home and abroad.

---

[5]   In our model, multi-country spillovers only matter in the specification of technological progress, so we introduce the index denoting a specific country when we discuss technological progress.

2. An intermediate-goods sector with a total number of Q_t industries. In each industry a monopolist holds a patent to the latest generation of differentiated product x_{it}, and uses capital K_{it} as described in the simple production function for intermediate goods:

$$x_{it} = K_{it} / A_{it}$$

Here A_{it} is the productivity parameter of latest version of intermediate product i. We assume that successive vintages of the intermediate product are produced by increasingly capital intensive techniques. This implies that productivity A_{it} increases over time. Finally, profit maximizing behaviour implies that all producers of intermediates i supply a common amount of output (see below and Aghion and Howitt, 1998, p. 95).

3. A consumer-goods sector producing final output Y_t using technology, labour L_t and intermediate inputs measured by a Dixit-Stiglitz index of differentiated products:

$$Y_t = Q_t^{\alpha-1} \left[\int_0^{Q_t} A_{it} x_{it}^{\alpha} di \right] L_t^{1-\alpha}, \qquad 0 < \alpha < 1$$

where Q_t is the number of differentiated products. Brands x_{it} substitute well for each other: the elasticity of substitution between every pair of available brands $\varepsilon = 1/(1-\alpha) > 1$.

Resources devoted to R&D which improve the quality of existing products (vertical innovations) contribute over time to productivity in the production of final goods as well as to the stock of knowledge. Imitation of "old" products increases the number of differentiated products Q_t (horizontal innovations) but does not add to the social knowledge pool. Although in reality horizontal innovations do occur (increasing variety), the productivity effects of such innovations are not as clear as those of quality improvements. Despite increased possibilities to specialize and satisfying a variety of needs, more variety increases also complexity of production and thereby errors. Moreover, thin-market transaction costs will arise. To sum up, innovation generates growth and imitation spreads the research input over more sectors.

To avoid the scale effect of R&D (doubling the number of workers in research does not double growth rates, see Jones, 1995; and Aghion and Howitt, 1998, pp. 404-405), the number of sectors Q_t grows at the same rate as the number of workers L_t, that is L_t / Q_t is constant. Basically, it is assumed that imitation is a serendipitous process. This means that imitation just happens: no one spends resources attempting to imitate. The flow of imitation products can now be written as:

$$\frac{dQ_t}{dt} = \xi L_t, \qquad \xi > 0$$

The coefficient ξ is called the "imitation rate." The number of workers per product L_t / Q_t converges asymptotically to a constant $l \equiv L_t / Q_t$.[6] Each sector requires $K_{it} = A_{it} x_{it}$ units of

---

[6] If $dQ_t/dt = \xi L_t$ and $dL_t/dt = g_L L_t$, where g_L is the rate of growth of the number of workers, then $dQ_t/Q_t = dL_t/L_t$ implies that $\xi l = g_L$.

capital, and capital-market equilibrium requires equality between supply and demand of capital:

$$K_t = \int_0^{Q_t} K_{it}\, di = \int_0^{Q_t} A_{it} x_{it}\, di$$

Profit maximizing action implies that all sectors produce the same amount of output, *i.e.* $x_{it} = x_t$, for all *i*, so

$$K_t = \int_0^{Q_t} K_{it}\, di = \int_0^{Q_t} A_{it} x_{it}\, di = x_t \int_0^{Q_t} A_{it}\, di = x_t Q_t A_t$$

where A_t is the average productivity parameter:

$$A_t \equiv \frac{1}{Q_t} \int_0^{Q_t} A_{it}\, di$$

Define the capital stock per efficiency unit of labour as $k_t \equiv K_t /(A_t\, L_t)$. The common amount of output of each sector can now be calculated as

$$x_{it} = x_t = \frac{K_t}{A_t Q_t} = k_t l$$

This implies that the aggregate production function becomes

$$Y_t = Q_t^{\alpha-1} \left[\int_0^{Q_t} A_{it} x_{it}^{\alpha}\, di \right] L_t^{1-\alpha} = A_t L_t f(k_t)$$

where

$$f(k_t) = k_t^{\alpha} .$$

REFERENCES

Abramovitz, M. (1991), *Thinking About Growth*, Cambridge: Cambridge University Press.

Aghion, P. and P. Howitt (1998), *Endogenous Growth Theory*, Cambridge: MIT Press.

Ark, B. van (1996), "Sectoral Growth Accounting and Structural Change in Postwar Europe," in B. van Ark and N.F.R. Crafts (eds.), *Quantitative Aspects of Postwar European Economic Growth*, Paris: CEPR/Cambridge University Press, pp. 84-164.

Benhabib, J. and M.M. Spiegel (1994), "The Role of Human Capital in Economic Development: Evidence from Aggregate Cross-country Data," *Journal of Monetary Economics* 34, pp. 143-173.

Bernstein, J.I. and P. Mohnen (1998), "International R&D Spillovers between U.S. and Japanese R&D Intensive Sectors," *Journal of International Economics* 44, pp. 315-338.

Branstetter, L. (1996), "Are Knowledge Spillovers International or Intranational in Scope? Microeconometric Evidence from the U.S. and Japan," Working Paper 5800, National Bureau of Economic Research, Cambridge, MA.

Caballero, R.J. and A.B. Jaffe (1993), "How High are the Giants' Shoulders: An Empirical Assessment of Knowledge Spillovers and Creative Destruction in a Model of Economic Growth," in O.J. Blanchard and S. Fischer (eds.), *NBER Macroeconomics Annual 1993*, Cambridge: MIT Press, pp. 15-86.

Cameron, G. (1996), "Innovation and Economic Growth," Discussion Paper 277, Centre for Economic Performance, London.

Coe, D.T. and E. Helpman (1995), "International R&D Spillovers," *European Economic Review* 39, pp. 859-887.

Colecchia, A. and G. Papaconstantinou (1996), "The Evolution of Skills in OECD Countries and the Role of Technology," STI Working Paper 8, OECD, Paris.

Crafts, N.F.R. (1997), "Endogenous Growth: Lessons for and from Economic History," in D.M. Kreps and K.F. Wallis (eds.), *Advances in Economics and Econometrics*, Cambridge: Cambridge University Press, pp. 38-78.

David, P.A. (1991*), Computer and Dynamo. The Modern Productivity Paradox in a Not-Too-Distant Mirror*, OECD, Paris.

Denison, E.F. (1967), *Why Growth Rates Differ*, Washington, D.C.: The Brookings Institution.

Deutsches Patentamt (1951-1978), "Blatt für Patent, Muster- und Zeichenwesen," Technical report, Berlin.

Dixit, A.K. and J.E. Stiglitz (1977), "Monopolistic Competition and Optimum Product Diversity," *The American Economic Review* 67, pp. 297-308.

Eaton, J. and S. Kortum (1996), "Trade in Ideas: Patenting and Productivity in the OECD," *Journal of International Economics* 40, pp. 251-278.

Eaton, J. and S. Kortum (1997), "International Technology Diffusion: Theory and Measurement," unpublished manuscript, Boston University and NBER.

Gerschenkron, A. (1962*), Economic Backwardness in Historical Perspective: A Book of Essays*, Cambridge, Mass: Harvard University Press.

Griliches, Z. (1990), "Patent Statistics as Economic Indicators: A Survey," *Journal of Economic Literature* 28, pp. 1661-1707.

Griliches, Z. (1994), "Productivity, R&D, and the Data Constraint," *The American Economic Review* 84, pp. 1-23.

Grossman, G.M. and E. Helpman (1990), "Comparative Advantage and Long-run Growth," *The American Economic Review* 80, pp. 796-815.

Grossman, G.M. and E. Helpman (1991), *Innovation and Growth in the Global Economy*, Cambridge: MIT Press.

Institut National de la Propriété Industrielle (1958-1978*), Bulletin officiel de la propriété industrielle*, Paris.

Jaffe, A.B., M. Trajtenberg, and R. Henderson (1993), "Geographic Localization of Knowledge Spillovers as Evidenced by Patent Citations," *Quarterly Journal of Economics* 108, pp. 577-598.

Jones, C.I. (1995), "R&D-based Models of Economic Growth," *Journal of Political Economy*, 103, pp. 759-784.

Judd, K. (1985), "On the Performance of Patents," *Econometrica* 53, pp. 567-585.

Keely, L.C. and D. Quah (1998), "Technology and economic growth," unpublished manuscript, London School of Economics and CEP.

Keller, W. (1997a), "Are International R&D Spillovers Trade-related? Analyzing Spillovers among Randomly Matched Trade Partners," Working Paper 6065, National Bureau of Economic Research, Cambridge, MA.

Keller, W. (1997b), "How Trade Patterns and Technology Flows Affect Productivity Growth," Policy Research Working Paper 1831, World Bank, Washington, D.C.

Kravis, I.B., A. Heston, and R. Summers (1982*), World Product and Income. International Comparisons of Real Gross Product*, Baltimore: World Bank, Johns Hopkins UP.

Lichtenberg, F.R. (1992), "R&D Investment and International Productivity Differences," Working Paper 4161, National Bureau of Economic Research, Cambridge, MA.

Lichtenberg, F.R. and B. van Pottelsberghe de la Potterie (1996), "International R&D spillovers: A re-examination," Working Paper 5668, National Bureau of Economic Research, Inc., Cambridge, Massachusetts.

Maddison, A. (1995a), *Monitoring the World Economy, 1820-1992*, OECD Development Centre, Paris.

Maddison, A. (1995b), "Standardised Estimates of Fixed Capital Stock: A Six Country Comparison," in A. Maddison (ed.) *Explaining the Economic Performance of Nations: Essays in Time and Space*, Aldershot: Edward Elgar.

Mokyr, J. (1990), *The Lever of Riches: Technological Creativity and Economic Progress*, Oxford: Oxford University Press.

Nadiri, M.I. (1993), "Innovations and Technological Spillovers," Working Paper 4423, National Bureau of Economic Research, Inc., Cambridge, Massachusetts.

Nadiri, M.I. and S. Kim (1996), "International R&D Spillovers, Trade and Productivity in Major OECD Countries," Working Paper 5801, National Bureau of Economic Research, Cambridge, MA.

North, D.C. (1990), *Institutions, Institutional Change and Economic Performance*, Cambridge: Cambridge University Press.

OECD (1966), *National Accounts Statistics, 1955-1964*, OECD, Paris.

OECD (1991), *Basic Science and Technology Statistics*, OECD, Paris.

OECD (1995a), *Basic Science and Technology Statistics*, OECD, Paris.

OECD (1995b), *Research and Development Expenditure in Industry. 1973-92* (STAN/ANBERD Database, 1994), DSTI, Paris.

OECD (1997a), *Main Science and Technology Indicators, 1997-1*, OECD, Paris.

OECD (1997b), *National Accounts: Main Aggregates Volume I, 1960-1995*, OECD, Paris.

Olson, M. (1982*), The Rise and Decline of Nations. Economic Growth, Stagflation and Social Rigidities*, New Haven, Connecticut: Yale University Press.

Park, W.G. (1995), "International R&D Spillovers and OECD Economic Growth," *Economic Inquiry* 33, pp. 571-591.

Romer, P.M. (1990), "Endogenous Technological Change," *Journal of Political Economy* 98, pp. S71-S102.

Salter, W.E.G. (1966), *Productivity and Technical Change*, 2nd edition, Cambridge: Cambridge University Press.

Solow, R.M. (1957), "Technical Change and the Aggregate Production Function," *Review of Economic Studies* 39, pp. 312-330.

Solow, R.M. (1994), "Perspectives on Growth Theory," *Journal of Economic Perspectives* 8, pp. 45-54.

Temple, J. (1999), "The New Growth Evidence," *Journal of Economic Literature* 37, pp. 112-156.

Verspagen, B. (1996), "Technology Indicators and Economic Growth in the European Area: Some Empirical Evidence," in B. van Ark and N.F.R. Crafts (eds.), *Quantitative Aspects of Postwar European Economic Growth*, Paris: CEPR/Cambridge University Press, pp. 215-243.

WIPO (1983), *100 Years Protection of Industrial Property. Statistics. Synoptic Tables on Patents, Trademarks, Designs, Utility Models and Plant Varieties, 1883-1982*, WIPO, Geneva.

Wolff, E.N. and M.I. Nadiri (1993), "Spillover Effects, Linkage Structure, and Research and Development," *Structural Change and Economic Dynamics* 4, pp. 315-331.

Young, A. (1998), "Growth Without Scale Effects," *Journal of Political Economy* 106, pp. 41-63.

Author Index

Subject Index

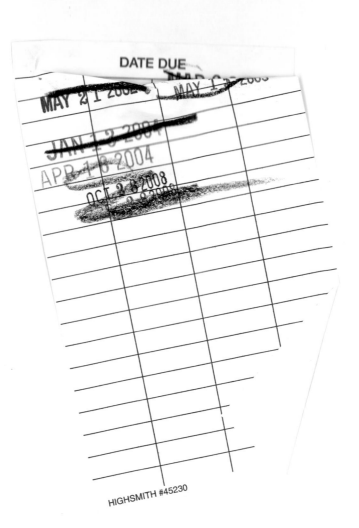

DATE DUE

MAY 2 1 2002   MAR 0 6 2003
MAY 1 2003

JAN 1 3 2004

APR 1 9 2004

OCT 2 8 2008